TRADING SYSTEMS AND MONEY MANAGEMENT

Other Books in The Irwin Trader's Edge Series

TRADING SYSTEMS AND MONEY MANAGEMENT

A Guide to Trading and Profiting in any Market

THOMAS STRIDSMAN

McGraw-Hill

New York   Chicago   San Francisco
Lisbon   London   Madrid   Mexico City
Milan   New Delhi   San Juan   Seoul
Singapore   Sydney   Toronto

The McGraw·Hill Companies

1 2 3 4 5 6 7 8 9 0 DOC/DOC 0 9 8 7 6 5 4 3

0-07-140019-2

This publication is designed to provide accurate and authoritative information in regard to the subject matter covered. It is sold with the understanding that neither the author nor the publisher is engaged in rendering legal, accounting, futures/securities trading, or other professional service. If legal advice or other expert assistance is required, the services of a competent professional person should be sought.

—From a Declaration of Principles jointly adopted
by a Committee of the American Bar Association
and a Committee of Publishers

McGraw-Hill books are available at special quantity discounts to use as premiums and sales promotions, or for use in corporate training programs. For more information, please write to the Director of Special Sales, Professional Publishing, McGraw-Hill, Two Penn Plaza, New York, NY 10121-2298. Or contact your local bookstore.

 This book is printed on recycled, acid-free paper containing a minimum of 50% recycled, de-inked fiber.

Library of Congress Cataloging-in-Publication Data

Stridsman, Thomas.
Trading systems and money management : a guide to trading and profiting in any market / by Thomas Stridsman.
　　　p. cm.
ISBN 0-07-140019-2
1. Stocks. 2. Stocks—Prices. 3. Finance. I. Title.
HG4661 .S875 2003
332.63'22—dc21
2002015461

This book is dedicated to my entire family in general, but to the little ones in particular. My niece Matilda and my nephews Erik and Albin, you make me laugh. One can only hope that you and your friends get to have a glass of beer...

Also, with the most sincere hopes for a full and speedy recovery for my mother after her severe traffic accident.

DISCLAIMER

The entire contents of this book, including the trading systems and all the analysis techniques to derive and evaluate them, is intended for educational purposes only, to provide a perspective on different market and trading concepts. The book is not meant to recommend or promote any trading system or approach. You are advised to do your own research to determine the validity of a trading idea and the way it is presented and evaluated. Past performance does not guarantee future results; historical testing may not reflect a system's behavior in real-time trading.

CONTENTS

Chapter 3

Probability and Percent of Profitable Trades   35

Chapter 4

Risk   47

Chapter 5

Drawdown and Losses   57

Chapter 6

Quality Data   67

PART TWO

TRADING SYSTEM DEVELOPMENT   79

Chapter 7

TradeStation Coding   83

Chapter 8

Hybrid System No. 1 97

Chapter 20

Adding Exits   219

Chapter 21

Systems as Filters   255

Chapter 22

Variables   271

Chapter 23

Evaluating Stops and Exits   281

Chapter 29

Consistent Strategies   379

INTRODUCTION

"This is Wall Street, no act of kindness will pass unpunished."
— Unknown

As an editor, writer, and technical analysis expert first for *Futures* magazine and later *Active Trader* magazine, I realized that although there are plenty of technical analysis books in general and on rule-based trading in particular, they were all saying the same thing and not bringing any new thinking into the subject. This is especially true when it comes to the intricate topic of how to build and evaluate a trading system so that it remains as robust and reliable when traded together with a professional money management regimen in the real world, as it seemed to be when tested on historical data.

In an effort to do something about this, I first wrote *Trading Systems That Work* (McGraw-Hill, 2000), which focused on longer-term systems on the futures markets, and now *Trading Systems and Money Management*, which focuses on short-term systems in the stock market. Both books combine featured systems with a fixed fractional money management regimen to maximize each system's profit potential, given the trader's tolerance for risk.

To combine a mechanical trading system (the rules for where and when to buy and sell a stock or commodity) with any money management strategy (the rules for how many to buy and sell, given the trader's risk–reward preferences and the behavior of the markets), is not as easy as taking any system, applying it to any market or group of markets, and deciding on not risking a larger amount per trade than what your wallet can tolerate.

Instead it's a complex web of intertwining relationships, where any change between two variables will alter the relationship between all the other variables. And, as if that's not enough, the strategy should be dynamic enough to mechanically self-adjust to the ever-changing market environment in such a way that the risk–reward potential remains approximately the same for all markets and time periods.

This book is for those traders who haven't been able to pinpoint what is missing to make the complete strategy larger than the sum of its parts. If you allow me to take a guess, I'd guess that what you feel is keeping you from succeeding as a trader is the overall understanding for how it all ties together and what really constitutes a more "sophisticated" strategy with a higher likelihood for success than the ones you're currently using. The way I see it, to simplify things, the development process could be divided into a few building blocks:

First, we need to learn what we need to measure to achieve robustness and reliability. Second, we need to learn to formulate and test the logic for the entry (and possibly also some sort of filtering technique). Third, we must understand and test different types of exits. The last point of actual research is to apply and test the money management according to our risk preferences.

The first part of the book will show you how to measure a system's performance to make it as forward-looking as possible. By forward-looking we mean that the likelihood for the future results resembling the historical results should be as high as possible. To do this, you will need to know the difference between a good working system and a profitable system and which evaluation parameters to use to distinguish between the two.

The emphasis will lie on making the system work, on average, equally as well on a large number of markets and time periods. We also will look at other common system-testing pitfalls, such as working with bad data and not normalizing the results. Another important consideration is to understand what constitutes realistic results and what types of results to strive for. A lot of the analysis work will be done in TradeStation and MS Excel.

In the second part, we will take a closer look at the systems we will work with throughout the rest of the book. All eight systems have previously been featured in *Active Trader* magazine's Systems Trading lab pages. The systems are selected only as good learning experiences, not for their profitability or trading results. We will look at the systems one at a time and determine how we can modify them to make them more robust and forward-looking.

All changes will be based on logic and reasoning, rather than optimization and curve fitting, and are aimed to improve the system's average performance over a large number of markets and time periods, rather than optimizing the profits for a few select markets. The working premise will be, the better we understand the logic behind the system and the less complex the system, the more we trust it will function as well in the future as it has in the past. For this, we will do most of the work in MS Excel, which means we need to learn how to export the data from our analysis software of choice.

Usually when I build a system, I don't count the stop-loss and exit rules to the core system logic. In Part 3 we therefore substitute all the old exit rules for all systems with a set of new rules, optimized to work on average equally as well on all markets at all times. To do this, we need to understand what types of exits are available, how to evaluate them, and how to avoid falling into any of the problems that adhere explicitly to the evaluation of exits. However, even though the larger part of Part 3 deals explicitly with stops and exits, the methods used (such as analyzing the results with a surface chart in MS Excel) also are applicable to other parts of the system-building process.

At the end of this part, we also will take a look at how to increase performance by adding a relative-strength or trend filter. Decreasing the number of trades might decrease the performance for any individual market, but by making room for more trades in more markets, we can increase performance thanks to a higher degree of diversification.

The last part of the book will tie it all together by applying a dynamic ratio money management (DRMM) regimen on top of all the trading rules. With DRMM, all markets traded will share the same account, so that the result for one market is dependent on the results from all other markets and how much we decide to risk in each trade. Also, the number of possible markets to be traded simultaneously and the amount risked per share in relation to the total amount risked of account equity will vary with the conditions of the markets.

Using DRMM, we also can tailor the amount risked per trade to fit our exact tolerance for risk given the system's statistical characteristics and expected market conditions. In this case, instead of optimizing the equity growth, we will optimize the smoothness of the equity curve. Even with this modest goal, we will achieve results far higher and better than comparable buy-and-hold strategies. But before we set out to test the systems using DRMM, in our custom-made Excel spreadsheet, we will learn exactly how DRMM works with all its mathematical formulas and why it is the supreme money management method.

However, when moving back and forth between the different steps in the development process we have to understand that any little change under any of these categories also will alter the characteristics produced by the others. Therefore, building a trading system is a never-ending task of complex intertwining dynamics that constantly alter the work process. This really creates a fifth element that runs through the entire process as a foundation for the other elements to rest on.

The fifth element is the philosophic understanding of how all the other parts fit together in the never-ending work process already mentioned. If anything, I hope that what makes this book unique is the overall understanding for the entire process and the way it will force you to think outside of the conventional box.

Developing a trading strategy is like creating a "process machine," in which each decision automatically and immediately leads to the next one, and next one, and next one … producing a long string of interacting decisions forming a process with no beginning or end. I further believe it is paramount to look at both the development and the execution of the strategy in the same way.

The purpose of this book is not to give you the best ready-made systems, but to show you how to go about developing your own systems—a development process that eventually and hopefully will allow you to put together a trading strategy that is a long-term work process as opposed to a series of single, isolated decisions.

The advantage of the concept of a work process, in comparison with decision, is that rule-based trading can be understood as a form of problem solving, using the four P's of speculation: philosophy, principles, procedures, and performance.

The emphasis in this book seems to be on the principles, procedures, and performance, but while reading we also need to at least try to understand the philosophy behind it all, because it is the philosophy that ties it all together and explains the value of the suggested principles and procedures in the rest of the book. That is what this book really is about. Good luck with your studying and trading.

ACKNOWLEDGMENTS

My most heartfelt gratitude to Dan and Maryanne Gramza.

Many thanks to Nelson Freeburg and his family.

My most sincere wishes for the future success of *Active Trader* magazine and its crew, Phil, Bob, Mark, Laura, Amy, and that other weird guy—you're the best.

There are no better friends than my dear friends Jill in Rockford, IL and Pär in Västerås, Sweden. Thanks for putting up with me.

To Robert, Brad, and the rest of the bunch at Rotella Capital: It's a true honor to work with and for you all. A special thanks to Rafael Molinero, for invaluable help with this book.

PART ONE

How to Evaluate a System

At the time of this writing, there's a TV commercial running on several of the business and news channels. The commercial is for an online direct-access brokerage company that claims to give you better fills than the brokerage company your cubicle-sharing colleague is using. The plot is as follows: Guy 1 proudly tells Guy 2 that he just bought 300 shares of XYZ for $25.10, only to hear that Guy 2 just bought 200 shares of the very same stock for $25.05. Of course, this 5-cent difference makes Guy 1 all upset, and Guy 2 takes advantage of it by smugly alerting everyone to "Tom's unfortunate stock purchase" over the company intercom system.

Obviously, the purpose of the commercial is to make us believe that the most important thing in trading isn't a long-term plan, involving such "mundane" factors as the underlying logic of your system and numbers of shares to trade, but only to get a 5-cent better fill than your cubicle buddy.

This is a good example of how many companies within the investment and trading industry don't know what they're talking about. Or if they do, they want to fool you into focusing on the wrong things, because if you were focusing on the right things, their services would be obsolete. I really don't know which is worse.

Basically, two types of companies try to feed on your trading. The brokerage companies try to make you believe that a 5-cent better fill makes all the difference in the world. The newsletter and market-guru companies claim that only their top-and-bottom-picking system will help you squeeze those extra 10 cents out of each trade, which will take your account equity to astronomical heights (or at least, finally make you profitable).

The truth is those few extra cents matter little in the end. To understand this, let's return to the guys in the cubicle and assume that XYZ indeed started to move in the anticipated direction. If that were the case, would you rather be Guy 1 or Guy 2? I don't know about you, but with the stock moving favorably, I'd rather own 300 shares bought at $25.10, than 200 shares bought at $25.05. Why? Because, if the stock moves in the anticipated direction, the profit from the 300 shares will soon—very soon—outweigh the profit made from the 200 shares. How soon? Only 10 cents later, at $25.20!

Now, because a TV commercial is a make-believe world in the first place, let's add another few make-believe assumptions to it. First, let's pretend that both guys had $25,000 on their trading accounts going into the trades, that XYZ continues to trend higher, and that both guys got out at 30. How much money did each guy make? Guy 1 made $1,470 [(30 − 25.10)*300], while Guy 2 made $990 [(30 − 25.05)*200].

Further, what if both guys were able to make 10 such trades in a row? How much money would each one of them have in his trading account after such a run? Guy 1 would have $39,700 (25,000 + [1,470*10]), while Guy 2 would have $34,900 (25,000 + [990*10]). Thus, over this 10-trade sequence, Guy 1 would have made $4,800 more than Guy 2.

As a final assumption in this make-believe world, let's back up to the first trade and assume that Guy 1, instead of always buying 300 shares, had continued to invest 30 percent [(25.10*300)/25,000] of his account balance in each trade, while Guy 2, the smug nickel-and-dimer that he is, continued to buy 200 shares per trade over the entire sequence of 10 trades. How much more would Guy 1 have on his account, compared to Guy 2? Guy 1 would have a total of $44,149, which would be $9,249 more than Guy 2.

So what have we learned from this? The answer is, while it is unrealistic to assume 10 such winning trades in a row (it happens every so often, but it's not a particularly realistic assumption), managing your trade size is way more important than chasing a nickel here and a dime there on your entry and exit levels. This is one of two important points I hope to get across in this book.

However, to be able to "optisize" the amount to risk and invest in each trade, you need to have a trading system you can trust and that allows you to do so. You can't do this without fully understanding the second most important point this book tries to convey. To illustrate the second point, let's change the topic completely:

Picture a cheetah on the African savannah. The cheetah is one of my favorite animals. It's a highly specialized, lean, mean, killing machine that can outrun just about anything and anyone. Its limber and muscular body and graceful moves ooze self-confidence. As a metaphor for a good trading system, however, the cheetah sucks. The reason is that it's simply too specialized in hunting and killing a certain sized prey in a certain natural habitat.

If the prey were slower but larger, the cheetah could outrun and catch it more easily, but waste time killing it and run a larger risk of being killed itself. If the prey were smaller but faster, the amount of energy gained from consuming it wouldn't make up for the amount of energy wasted hunting it down. The truth is that if the animals that make up the better part of a cheetah's diet disappeared, so would the cheetah. The same will happen if the environment changes and becomes more rocky, bumpy, or hilly, or if the forest takes over the savannah, so that the cheetah can't utilize its number-one hunting weapon—its speed. Thus, the cheetah is too dependent on its environment to survive in the long run.

Similarly, a trading system with the characteristics of a cheetah would cease to work properly if and when the environment it operates in changes ever so slightly (and in a myriad of ways), and the only way for you to find that out is when you're already in a drawdown you can't get out of. Therefore, it is paramount that your systems can work in as many market environments as possible, or to use the words of the analogy, find and catch its prey wherever possible, wasting as little energy as necessary.

Now, this doesn't have to mean that each system needs to work equally as well in all conditions. It means that a system needs to work well enough to keep you afloat, or at least out of disaster in less favorable conditions, while waiting for the good times to reappear. And the only way to achieve that is to familiarize the system with the less favorable market environments during the research and building process. More specifically, it means that you should let the system's final parameter settings be influenced by the best settings for less favorable conditions, no matter if those less favorable conditions actually produce a profit or not.

For example: Picture a moving average cross-over system, with a four-day short average and a 25-day long average, that produces great results in one market (or market condition), but terrible results in another. For a second market (condition), the best, but still negative, results might come from a 12-day short average and an 18-day long average. In that case, you might be better off, in the long run and on average, with a final setting of nine days for the short average and 20 days for the long average, which still might produce good results in the first market and a slight loss in the second market.

Whether you then decide to trade both markets or only the profitable one depends on other considerations and what you're trying to achieve with this particular system in the first place. Assuming you're only trading the profitable market, at least results won't be as bad as they could have been when the profitable market starts to behave as the unprofitable one, which you won't discover until it's too late.

If, on the other hand, you trade both markets, you might lower your profits initially because of the bad performance of the second market. But just as the first market might start to behave as the second market, the opposite is true as well, and when that happens, profits will increase. Trading more than one market most likely also will lower the fluctuations of the results and make the system less risky to trade over the long haul. Furthermore, a market that is losing money by itself can still add positively to your equity when traded together with other markets in a portfolio. It all depends on its correlation with the other markets. Or, to put it in less scientific terms: It all depends on how and when each market zigs and zags in relation to all the other markets.

When I build a system for the Trading Systems Lab pages in *Active Trader* magazine, I usually test it on 30 to 60 markets, not expecting it to be profitable on more than two-thirds of those. Preferably, I also want it to be only marginally profitable on the profitable markets, but, by the same token, only marginally unprofitable on the losing markets. Also, the fewer the markets that stick out (whether for good or bad), the better the system, as far as I'm concerned.

Hopefully, in the end, this will mean that all markets will go through both good and bad periods, but at each instance there will be, on average, more markets doing well than doing badly. Also, when one market moves from good to bad, which is easily done, most likely one or two markets will move the other way to pick up the slack.

So, which living creature do I want my trading systems to resemble? The cockroach, which can stay alive a week on the fat left behind by a fingerprint, with almost no concern for the environment or habitat.

PERFORMANCE MEASURES

Have you noticed that the financial press and television frequently report the daily price changes for a stock or an index in percentage terms, together with the dollar changes? Believe me, this has not always been the case. When I moved to Chicago from Sweden, back in 1997, hardly anyone presented the percentage changes, and I was just amazed at how the supposedly financially most sophisticated country in the world didn't know how to calculate percentages.

Everyone I tried to talk to about this just stared at me with blank eyes, and I found myself in constant arguments with both common men and distinguished system designers and money managers about why doing the analysis in percentage terms instead of dollars will result in better, more reliable, forward-looking trading systems. Most, however, seemed to be too blinded by the almighty dollar to understand what the hell I was talking about.

So, while writing for *Futures* magazine, I decided to start my own little percentage crusade by stressing the importance of measuring a price change in relation to the price level around which the change took place. After two years of doing that, I ended up writing a book on how measuring trading performance in percentages pertains to systematic trading using mechanical trading systems in the futures markets (*Trading Systems That Work*, McGraw-Hill, 2000).

As a senior editor for *Active Trader* magazine, I continued to stress the importance of using relative rather than absolute measurement techniques. At the time of this writing, things are getting better. People are beginning to understand what the hell I'm talking about, although so far the financial press and television haven't dared to stress the relative change as the more valid of the two figures.

To be sure, the academic community and the big boys of Wall Street have always known about this, although the academic community many times prefers to work with logarithmic changes instead (as for example, in the Black–Scholes options evaluation formula), which is essentially the same thing. Why they haven't stressed this to the average trader and investor is beyond me. Could it be that it provided them a good opportunity to make a buck at your expense?

CHAPTER 1

Percentages and Normalized Moves

You cannot evaluate a system properly—at least not during the research and building process—if you don't look at the right evaluation measures. And to look at the right evaluation measures, you need to know and do a few things before you can get started.

Basically, you can go about doing it correctly in two ways. Unfortunately, however, just buying the same amount of shares for all stocks you're looking at, not caring about the price of each stock at each instance, isn't one of them. Especially not if all you're interested in is dollars made during the testing period.

Weird, you say: Isn't that the sole purpose of my trading in the first place, making as much money as I can, while losing as little as I can? Yes it is, but we have to remember that there is a huge difference between testing a system on historical data and then trading it real-time on fresh, never before seen data.

When you're testing a system, you're doing just that. You're testing it—not trading it. It seems to me that many people believe that testing and trading is the same thing. This is not so! Therefore, when you're testing a system, you should concern yourself less with how much money you could have made in the past. Instead, you should concern yourself with how to make whatever testing results you've got as repeatable as possible in the future.

Not until that is achieved should you concern yourself with hypothetical profits. If the system also shows a profit, good: Now you can move on to the next step and eventually start trading it live and for real, but only for as long as you remember that the dollars made say nothing about the reliability of the system. As I said, there are two ways of doing it correctly. The first way is to make all hypothetical trades with one share, or one contract only, no matter which market you're testing, how much the price might fluctuate for a specific market, or how many markets you're testing the system on. But—and this is the important part—instead of measuring the results in dollars won or lost, the outcome of each trade should be measured in percentage terms in relation to the entry price of the trade.

The second way is to vary the number of shares or contracts traded in such a way that the number of shares increases as the price of the stock or the futures contract decreases. For example, if a stock is priced first at $100 and then $50, you should test the system with twice as many shares when the stock is priced at $50 as compared to when it was priced at $100. You should do this no matter if that's what you would have done in real life or not. Using this technique, the results can still be measured in dollars.

To illustrate why all this is important, let's look at two examples, both of them in the form of questions. (Hint: before you answer the questions, go back to the beginning of this part and re-read the story about the two cubicle buddies and "Tom's unfortunate stock purchase.")

Say that stock ABC currently is trading at $80, and a trading system that consistently buys and sells 100 stocks per trade shows a historical, back-tested profit of $250,000 over 500 trades, for an average profit per trade of $500 and an average profit per share of $5. These results are to be compared to those of stock XYZ, with a back-tested profit of $125,000, also over 500 trades, for an average profit per trade of $250 and an average profit per share of $2.50. Over the entire testing period, the price of XYZ has more or less constantly been half that of stock ABC. Now, everything else aside, do the above numbers indicate that stock ABC is a better stock to trade with this system than stock XYZ?

(This reasoning can also be translated over to a stock split. For example, say that stock QRS is trading at $90, and a trading system that consistently buys and sells 100 stocks per trade shows a historical, hypothetically back-tested profit of $150,000. Tomorrow, after the stock has been split 3:1 and the stock is trading at $30, the historical, hypothetically back-tested profit has decreased to $50,000. Does this mean that the system suddenly is three times as bad as the day before?)

No, it does not: A stock that is priced at twice the value of another stock also can be expected to have twice as large price swings, and therefore twice as high a profit per share traded. If you look at the above numbers, you will see that a profit per share of $2.50 relates to a stock price of $40 in the same way that a profit per share of $5 relates to a stock price of $80 (2.5 / 40 = 5 / 80 = 0.0625 = 6.25%). That is, in percentage terms, the profit per share is the same for both stocks. (As for the stock-split example, it is easy to see that after the split, we will need to trade the stock in lots of 300 shares per trade to make the new results comparable to the old presplit results.)

To make the same net profit trading stock XYZ as trading stock ABC, all you need to do is to trade twice as many XYZ stocks in each trade as you would stock

ABC. And why shouldn't you? If you can afford to buy 100 shares of a stock priced at $80, for a total value of $8,000, then you also can afford to buy 200 shares of stock priced at $40, also for a total value of $8,000. If you say you can only afford to buy 100 shares of a stock priced at $40, for a total value of $4,000, then you can still equalize the results by buying only 50 shares of the stock priced at $80, also for a total value of $4,000.

In the latter case, you won't make as much money in the end, but the point is that the dollars made are not a good indication of how good the system is or how likely it is that it will hold up in the future. In real-life trading, obviously, other considerations come into play when you decide how many shares to buy in each trade, but we will get to that later in the book.

For now, we have to remember that we're talking about how to build and evaluate a back-tested system, and during this process, we either need to adjust the number of shares traded to the price of the stock in question (so that we always buy and sell for the same amount), or buy and sell one share only (but measure the results in percentage terms). Otherwise, we won't place each trade in all markets on the same ground, or equal weighting, as all the other trades in all the other markets. And if we don't do that, we might come to a suboptimal conclusion, as this second example shows.

If you can choose between buying two different stocks, one currently priced at $12.50 and the other at $20, and you know for sure that the one priced at $12.50 will rise 1.75 points over the next couple of days, while the one priced at $20 will increase 2.60 points (almost a full point more) over the same period, which one would you buy? If you answer the one for $12.50, you probably have taken the story about the cubicle buddies to heart and understand what I am hinting at.

If, however, you answered the one for $20, you probably are a little too anxious to chase that elusive dollar. If you stop and think for a second, you will realize that there is a greater return for you if you just do the math. In this case, the price of the low-priced stock divided by the price of the higher-priced stock (12.5 / 20) equals 0.625, or 5/8. Thus, if you plan to invest $10,000, you can buy either 500 $20 shares, or 800 $12.50 shares. If you buy 500 $20 shares, you will make a profit of $1,300 (2.60 * 500), or 13 percent of the invested amount (1,300 / 10,000 = 0.13). If, on the other hand, you buy $10,000 worth of the $12.50 stock, your profit will be $1,400 (1.75 * 800), or 14 percent of the amount invested (1,400 / 10,000 = 0.14).

If you think this difference isn't that much to worry about, what if you could chose between 20 trades like this for the rest of the year, being able to use the profits from all trades going into the next one? Then your initial $10,000 would grow to $115,231 if you only bought the $20 stock, but to $137,435 if you only bought the $12.50 stock. And what if you could do this for three years straight? Then your initial $10,000 would grow to $15,300,534 if you only bought the $20 stock, but to $25,959,187 if you only bought the $12.50 stock. A difference of more than

$10,000,000 after only 60 trades. Although these are exaggerated numbers, they illustrate the point that it pays to take it easy and do the math before you jump into a trade. And it is exactly this type of math you also need to do while researching your systems. If for nothing else, wouldn't it be cool to know how much richer you are than your cubicle buddy, while five cents still is a significant amount of money to him?

The key point I'm trying to get across here is that there is a vast difference between a good system and a profitable system. The most profitable system doesn't have to be the best system or even a good system at all, with the best entry and exit points, and traded at the lowest commission. Those things help, but what is more important is that a good system is a system that works, on average and over time, equally as well on as many markets and market conditions as possible. The trades produced by a very good system don't deviate from their average trade as much as they do for a not-so-good system. A good system can always be turned into a more or less profitable system by being applied to the right markets and by altering the number of shares or contracts traded in each trade. A system that is only profitable on one or just a handful of markets can't be made more or less good by being applied to more (losing) markets, no matter how aggressively we're trading it.

The better the system, the more likely it is to hold up in the future, when traded on real-time, never before seen data, no matter in which market or under which market condition it is traded. The same does not hold true for a system that might show a profit here and now, but only in one or a handful of markets. To find out if a system is good or not, we need to measure its performance, either in percentage terms trading one share only, or in dollar terms always investing the same amount. Unfortunately, none of the market analysis and trading software packages of today allow you to do this right off the bat.

Because of this, I prefer to work with TradeStation, which is the only off-the-shelf program I know that allows you to write your own code to compensate for its shortcomings. When I am working with a system for the Trading System Lab pages in *Active Trader* magazine, I usually work in a two-step process.

For step 1, I attach the following code to the system that I'm working on, with the normalized variable set to true. In this way, the system will always buy as many shares as it can for $100,000, all in accordance with what we have learned about buying or selling more shares according to the price of the stock. With this piece of code in place, I can examine the results for each individual market using TradeStation's performance summary, which can look something like Figure 1.1. At this stage of the research process, I'm basically just interested in getting a feel for how many of the markets are profitable, and to get a feel for the profit factor, the value of the average trade, and the number of profitable trades.

Step 2, which incorporates exporting the percentage-based changes into a text file for further analysis in Excel, will be discussed more thoroughly later.

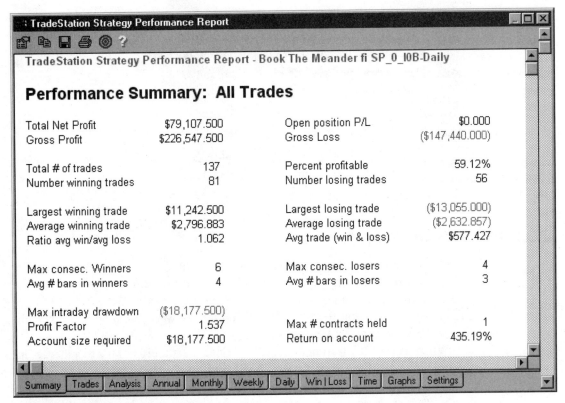

FIGURE 1.1

TradeStation performance summary.

Note: In the following code, the method for calculating the number of futures contracts differs from how to calculate the number of stock shares. This has to do with the limited life span of a futures contract and how you need to splice several futures contracts together to form a longer time series. If you're interested, a more thorough discussion surrounding these specific problems is found in *Trading Systems That Work*. For the purpose of this book, we will only touch on it briefly again in Chapter 6.

{For TradeStation reports. Set Normalize(False), when exporting for Money management.}

Variables:

{These variables can also be used as inputs for optimization purposes.}

Normalize(True), FuturesMarket(False), ContractLookback(20),

{Leave these variables alone.}

NumCont(1), NormEquity(100000), RecentVolatility(0);

```
If Normalize = True Then Begin
If FuturesMarket = True Then Begin
    RecentVolatility = AvgTrueRange(ContractLookback);
    NumCont = MaxList(IntPortion(NormEquity /
    (RecentVolatility * BigPointValue)), 1);
End
Else
    NumCont = MaxList(IntPortion(NormEquity /
    Average(AvgPrice, ContractLookback)), 1);
End;
```

ABOUT THE COSTS OF TRADING

Although there is no way around the costs of trading in real life, you should not concern yourself with slippage and commission in the initial stages of building and researching a trading system. To understand why this is, we once again have to remind ourselves that there is a big difference between building and research- ing a system and actually trading it.

When we're back testing on historical data, we should not try to squeeze out as many fantasy dollars or points as possible, but rather try to capture as many and as large favorable moves as possible, no matter what the cost of trading happens to be in each specific market. Even if a market turns out to be too costly to trade in the end, the results derived from researching that market still help us form an opinion on how robust the system is when traded on other markets.

For example, if a system that tries to pick small short-term profits seems to be working equally as well in two markets, but one of the markets is very expen- sive to trade when it comes to commission costs, the results from that market, when the system is tested without slippage and commission, still help us get a feel for how good the system is at finding the moves in any market. Had we performed the testing with slippage and commissions, the poor results from the too-expen- sive-to-trade market might have discouraged us from trading the profitable one. Further, considering commissions at this point will also result in suboptimal parameter settings for the variables in the system. Generally, considering these costs will favor systems with fewer or longer trades, the results are therefore skewed in those directions, and we might end up missing a bunch of good short- er-term trading opportunities.

For example, if you're building a short-term system for the stock market, it can be tricky to even come up with something that beats a simple buy-and-hold strategy. But with a buy-and-hold strategy, you are in the market 100 percent of the time, with the same amount of shares or contracts for the entire period. What if you could come up with a system that only kept you in the market 50 percent of the time, while the profit per share traded only decreased 40 percent? To assume the same effective risk as in the buy-and-hold system, you now can trade twice as many contracts per time units spent in the market. But with only a 40 percent drop in return per contract traded, the final net outcome measured in dollars will still be 20 percent higher than it would have been for the buy-and-hold strategy.

For example, say that investing in 100 shares in a buy-and-hold strategy resulted in a profit of $100. Then, trading 200 shares at the time, being in a trade only 50 percent of the time, would result in a profit of $120 [100 * 2 * (1 − 0.4)].

Hopefully, the final risk–reward relationship will be even better than that, because the whole point of a trading system, as compared to buy-and-hold, is that the system will keep you out of the market in bad and highly volatile times, when the result of the buy-and-hold strategy will fluctuate widely. Furthermore, with a trading system, you have the opportunity to reinvest previous winnings to speed up the equity growth even further, which you cannot do with a buy-and-hold strategy.

Remember that during the testing procedure, we're only interested in how well the system captures the moves we're interested in and how likely it is that it will continue to do so in the future. We are not interested in how much money it could have made us, whether we could have traded without any additional costs or not. Many times the value of these costs also will vary relative to the value of the market and the amount invested in the trade, which also is something most system-testing software cannot deal with.

For example, in a trending market, the commission settings will have a larger impact on your bottom line the lower the value of the market. We already touched on how the dollar value of the moves is likely to increase with the value of the market. Subtracting the same cost for slippage and commission across all trades in such a market will only lower the impact of the low-value trades even further. The same goes for comparing different-priced markets with each other.

To test a trade, first calculate the expected percentage move you are likely to catch, then transform that move into dollar terms in today's market by multiplying the percentage move by today's market value and the number of shares to trade. Then deduct the proper amount for slippage and commission. If this dollar value still looks good, you should take the trade.

CHAPTER 2

Calculating Profit

Although we haven't discussed it explicitly, by now it shouldn't be too hard to understand why net profit is not a good optimization measure to judge a system by. Remember, a profitable system doesn't necessarily have to be a good system, no matter how high its net profit. It's all a question of which market you apply the good system on and how aggressively you trade it.

But to clarify things a little further, let's start out with a little analogy. Imagine a downhill skier on his way down the slope to the finish line. About half-way down the slope, there's an interim time control. Let's say the skier passes that control after one minute, eight seconds. If the interim time control is one mile down the slope, then the skier has kept an average speed of 53 miles per hour. Now, although we need the interim time to calculate the average speed, it is not the interim time that gives the average speed; it is the average speed that gives the interim time.

Compare the above reasoning with the statistics of two trading systems that you have tested over the last 10 years. Halfway through the testing period, both systems show a net profit of $100,000. The only difference is that one system made that money in 250 trades, while the other one made it in 500 trades, for an average profit per trade of $400 and $200, respectively. Which one would you rather trade, knowing nothing else about these systems? I don't know about you, but I would go with the one that made the most money the fastest, with the speed in this case measured in trades instead of hours or days. That is, everything else aside, I would go with the system with the highest average profit per trade. At the very end of the testing period, the same reasoning applies, because even though you have reached the end of the testing period, it is still only an interim point in your life and career as a trader.

Thus, since it is the speed that is behind the final result, and not the other way around, why not aim for the source directly? Obviously, plenty of other factors influence which system to trade, but we will get to those in a little while. For one thing, the average profit per trade, looked at all by itself, says nothing about how reliable the system is and how likely it is that it will continue to perform well in the future.

Even so, a couple of other reasons exist for why the net profit should be avoided when evaluating a trading system, no matter how rigorous the testing has been and how robust the system seems to be. For example, the total net profit tells you nothing about when your profits occurred and how large they were in relation to each other. This is especially important if the markets you're comparing are prone to trending.

If you've tested the system with a fixed amount of shares for each trade, it is likely that the dollar value of each trade has increased with the increasing dollar value of the market. This, in turn, means that the profits are unevenly distributed through time, and the net profit is mostly influenced by the very latest market action. In a downtrend, the opposite holds true. Notice, however, that the trend of the market says nothing about whether the system has become more robust or not. In a market with several distinctive up and down trends, this matter becomes even more complex.

In a portfolio of markets, the total net profit tells you nothing about how well diversified your portfolio is. This is especially true if you stick to trading a fixed amount of shares for all stocks, because what is considered a huge dollar move in some stocks or markets is only considered a ripple on the surface in others.

AVERAGE PROFIT PER TRADE

Knowing nothing else about the different characteristics of three different systems, which one would you rather trade? One that shows an average profit per trade of $290 over 101 trades; one that shows an average profit of $276; or one with an average profit of $11. Assume all systems have been tested on the very same market, over the same time period, ending today, and with a fixed dollar amount invested in each trade. All profits are measured in dollars.

I take it most of you answered the first system, with an average profit of $290. But what if I told you that the first system also produced a distribution of trades like in Figure 2.1? Would this system still be your first choice after you've compared Figures 2.1 to 2.3? If not, which one would you have picked this time? Why?

If you said that System 1 (Figure 2.1) is not a good alternative because it's obvious that the trades these days are way below the value for the average trade over the entire period, you're on the right track—sort of. But if you also said that System 2 (Figure 2.2) is the best alternative because it's equally as obvious that the average trade for that system is way below what can be expected, as judged from the last few trades, you're still not right enough to justify real-life trading.

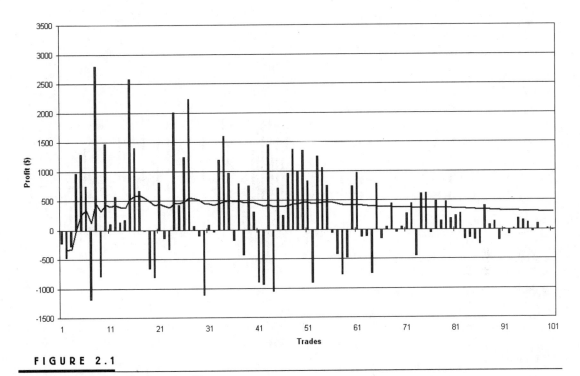

FIGURE 2.1

System 1 distribution of trades and profits.

Given the assumptions, there is only one reason why the distribution of trades can look as it does in Figure 2.2: System 2 has become more and more profitable over time, which could be a very dangerous situation, because the system might be optimized too hard to the most recent market conditions.

Personally, having seen Figures 2.2 to 2.3, and knowing nothing else about the systems, I would go with the last alternative (Figure 2.3), because the similarities of the trades over the entire time period indicate that it has worked equally as well all the time, which the other two obviously have not.

A system that has worked equally as well all the time will also have its parameters set in such a way that each trade influences the final parameter settings to an equal degree as all the other trades, no matter the underlying market conditions, such as the direction of the trend. A system in which performance has fluctuated over time (increased or decreased) will have its parameters set in such a way that the trades from the most profitable period have influenced the final parameter settings more than the trades from the less profitable period.

In the case of the three systems above, this means that Systems 1 and 2 are more likely to start to underperform (which might already be the case with System 1), and even cease to work completely, when market conditions change.

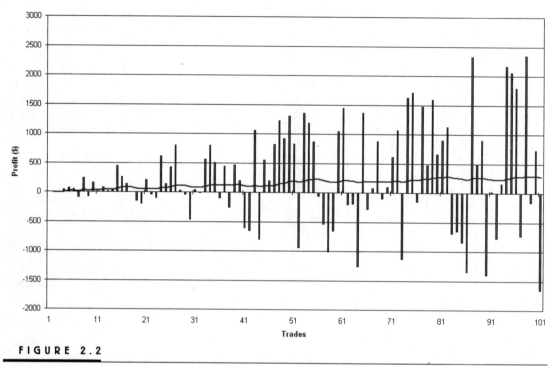

FIGURE 2.2

System 2 distribution of trades and profits.

Now, pretend the columns in Figures 2.1 to 2.3 represent percentage moves (never mind the scale on the y-axis) on a one-share (one-contract) basis. Which system version would you go with, assuming you know nothing else about the systems? Again, your answer should have been System 3 (Figure 2.3). Again, it's because it's the only system that works equally as well all the time, no matter the trend or the quality of the different market conditions. Because the outcomes from all the trades are very similar, it's the only system that gives all the trades the same weighting in deciding the parameter settings of the system.

The other systems will give more weight to the earliest trades (Figure 2.1) or the latest trades (Figure 2.2). This is especially dangerous in Figure 2.2, because if market conditions change back to what they were at the beginning of the test period, the system will start to produce significantly less profitable trades, and you won't know why until it's too late. A system like that represented by Figure 2.1 might, on the other hand, surprise you positively by starting to produce trades significantly more profitable than what you expected. But who in his right mind wants to trade a lousy system only on the assumption that it is more likely to surprise you in a positive way than a negative way? What if it doesn't surprise you at all and just continues to be plain lousy?

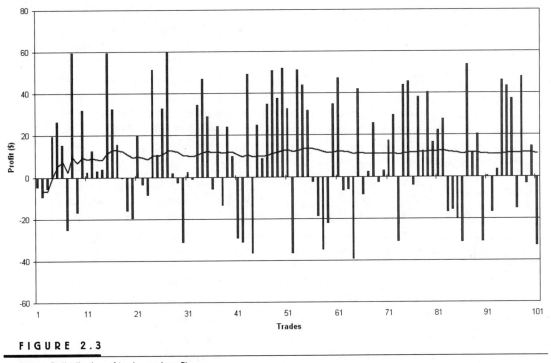

FIGURE 2.3

System 3 distribution of trades and profits.

Now, say you plan to trade System 3 (Figure 2.3). Using the equal-dollar position method, you might have decided to always tie up $100,000 in each trade to catch a 2-percent move (on average) in every stock you're interested in. If, for example, a stock is priced at $50, a 2-percent move on a one-share basis will be worth $1. Tying up $100,000 in a $50 stock means you can buy 2,000 shares, for a total estimated profit of $2,000 (50 * 0.02 * 2,000), which also is 2 percent of $100,000 (2,000 / 100,000).

Using the one-share percentage method, the average profit per trade in the future will equal the average percentage move the system is expected to catch, multiplied by the current stock price of each specific stock, multiplied by the number of shares invested in each specific trade. For example, if the average profit per trade is expected to be 2 percent per share, the price of the stock is $100, and you plan to buy 1,000 shares, the expected profit will come out to $2,000 per trade (100 * 0.02 *1,000). Buying 1,000 shares of a $100 stock also means that you will tie up $100,000, for a total percentage profit of 2 percent of the invested amount.

Note that in the first case, your plan is to tie up a certain dollar amount; in the second example, it is to buy a fixed amount of shares. In real trading, none of these methods are the preferred ways to go. Instead, you should always try to *risk* the same percentage amount of your equity, which will alter both the number of shares bought and the dollar amount invested with the changes in the equity. Only then will your profits per trade grow, as shown in Figure 2.2, no matter the current trend or market conditions. The discussion for why that is will have to wait until we get to Part 4. To get to this stage, you first need to test your system so that it trades equally as well, on average, at all times on a one-share basis, with the profits and losses measured in percentage terms, which is what we're discussing now.

We want to measure the system's performance in percentages, because as the dollar value of the market changes, so will the dollar values of its moves. Thus, the move in relation to the current market value will stay approximately the same. This means that a low-priced market is more likely to produce small dollar moves than a high-priced market, and vice versa. If you test a system on a low-priced market for an average profit of $1 per share, produced by an average move of 2 percent, the average profit in a higher-priced market will not be $1 per share, but 0.02 times whatever the market value of that market (everything else held equal and provided the system is considered robust and stable in the first place).

Had you not known that the average profit per share traded was higher than what your testing showed you, you might have discarded the system as not good enough. Worse yet, reverse the logic and you might have traded a system that you thought had a high average profit per trade when in fact it had not. Thus, the single most important thing to think about when building and examining a trading system is to do it in such a way that you can estimate what the profits and losses are likely to be at today's market value (or at any other point in the future), not what you could have made in the past. Only then can you make your results forward looking and, for example, calculate how many trades it should take you to make a certain amount of money or trade your way out of a drawdown, as this example will show you:

If you know that your average profit per trade, given the current market values of the markets you're trading and the number of shares you trade in each market, equals $500, and you currently are in a $7,200 drawdown, the estimated number of trades to get you out of the drawdown will be 15 [Integer(7,200 / 500) + 1].

AVERAGE WINNERS AND LOSERS

Note that a 2-percent move doesn't seem to be that much ($2 for a $100 stock and $1 for a $50 stock), but for now, we're talking on average over all trades, counting both winners and losers. The average winner might be larger, say 4 percent, but since we're bound to a have a few losers as well, the average profit for all trades might not be any larger than this.

Say you have a system with a stop loss of 1 percent and a profit target of 4 percent. This system is going into each trade with an estimated risk–reward relationship of 4:1. However, because not all trades will be winners and fewer still will be stopped out with a maximum profit of 4 percent, the actual risk–reward relationship over a few trades will be lower. To calculate the exact relationship we need to know exactly how many losers are likely for every winner; if those numbers are missing, we can estimate the number of winners and losers based on the system's characteristics and our experience.

Given the current volatility of the stock market, it's fair to assume that a 1-percent stop loss is quite tight, which should result in a rather large amount of losing trades. Assuming that only every third trade will be a winning trade, and that the average loser is equal to the stop-loss level of 1 percent, we can calculate the value of the average winner according to the following formula:

$$AW = (AT * NT + AL * NL) / NW$$

Where:

AW = Value of average winner
AT = Value of average trade
AL = Value of average loser
NT = Number of trades
NL = Number of losers
NW = Number of winners

In the above $7,200-drawdown example, we assumed the average trade to be worth $500 in today's market. Assume further that we are currently tying up $100,000 per trade, which then makes the average profit equal to 0.5 percent of both the tied-up capital and the expected move of the stock on a one-share basis. With three trades, of which one is a winner and two are losers, and the value of the average trade being 0.5 percent, the average winner comes out to 3.5 percent [(0.5 * 3 + 1 * 2) / 1]. The actual risk–reward relationship is then 3.5:1.

With this information at hand, we can calculate how many winners in a row we need to take us out of a drawdown. Continuing on the $7,200-drawdown example, it will take you three winning trades in a row to reach a new equity high if our average winning trade is worth $3,500 [Integer(7,200 / 3,500) + 1].

Now, three wining trades in a row doesn't seem to be too hard to produce, but because we know that only every third trade on average will be a winner, ask yourself how likely it is for this to happen. Provided it's highly unlikely that two or more winners will occur in a row, but very likely that the losers will come in pairs and that your average loser is for $1,000, then you know it can be expected to take at least 10 trades before you can see the sky again, provided you start out with a winning trade. If you instead start out with two losing trades, taking the drawdown down to $9,200, everything else held equal, the estimated number of trades would be 15.

Doing the same math, but on the assumption that as many as 50 percent of all trades will be winners, the average winner will be 2 percent [(0.5 * 2 + 1 * 1)

/ 1], for a risk–reward relationship of 2:1. If the average winning trade is worth $2,000, the number of winning trades needed to take you out of a drawdown will be four [Integer(7,200 / 2,000) + 1]. Now, how many trades will it take to get out of a $7,200 drawdown, assuming every other trade will be a winner and every other trade will be a loser? It will take 13 trades, provided the first trade is a winner, but 16 trades, provided the first trade is a loser.

Obviously, you should try to keep the number of winners as high as possible to feel comfortable with the system, but sometimes it could be a good thing to keep this number down in favor of a higher number of profitable months for the overall system or portfolio. Nonetheless, with these numbers at hand, we now can put together a more generic formula to calculate the estimated number of trades, N, to get out of a drawdown:

$$N = \text{Integer}[DDA / (X * AW - (1 - X) * AL)] + 1$$

Where:

DDA = Drawdown amount
X = Likelihood for winner, between zero and one
AW = Average winner
AL = Average loser, absolute value

For example, if the average winning trade is worth $3,500, the average losing trade $1,000, and the likelihood for a winner is 33 percent, then the estimated number of trades to take you out of a $7,200 drawdown is 15 [Integer(7,200 / (0.33 * 3,500 − 0.67 * 1,000)) + 1]. If the average winner is worth $2,000, and the likelihood for a winner is 50 percent, the estimated number of trades will also be 15 [Integer(7,200 / (0.5 * 2,000 − 0.5 * 1,000)) + 1]. (More about the likelihood for a certain amount of winners and losers is in Chapter 4: "Risk.")

STANDARD DEVIATION

Picture yourself as a quality controller standing at the end of an assembly line. Your pay (final estimated profit) for this job depends on how many units (number of trades) you and your machine (system) can produce, but also on the individual value of those units. However, because it takes the machine longer to produce a high-value unit, which also breaks much easier than a unit of lesser value does, it doesn't always pay to produce high-value units. In fact, the best payoff comes from producing nothing but average units; therefore, you're doing your best to get rid of

---

Although I actually took plenty of statistics courses during my university years, I would not have been able to write about all the statistics in this chapter without sneaking a peek at David M. Lanes' eminent statistics Web site at davidmlane.com/hyperstat/.

the defective units as quickly as possible, but also not letting the high-value units stay on the line for too long.

In short, you're trying hard to maximize your payoff by making all of the units deviate as little as possible from each other or from the average unit (to keep a low standard deviation). Obviously, you would like the assembly line to run as fast as possible, but only after you have examined one unit can the next unit be placed on the line. Thus, the longer the time spent examining a single unit, the lower your payoff will be.

Along comes an obviously defective unit that is bound to lower your results. Without wasting any time, you toss it in the garbage, freeing up the line for another unit. The next unit looks pretty average, but to be sure, you examine it for a while longer than you did the previous one before you take it off the line. In fact, without knowing it, with this average unit, you spent an average amount of time.

But the third unit that comes along is much trickier. This one shows all the right features for being a real money maker, and while you're watching it, these features grow even bigger, promising to make this unit at least three times as valuable as the average unit. What to do? Should you let it grow even bigger, or should you free up the line for more units? But then, all of a sudden it breaks. You freeze in panic, and more time passes before you come to your senses and throw it in the garbage. In the end, the time you spent processing this too-good-to-be-true unit could have been used processing three average units.

What happened here? By trying to increase your profits from an individual unit, you put yourself in unfamiliar territory, which made you act in panic, thus increasing the standard deviation of the outcome and lowering the number of units produced. In the end, this resulted in less overall profits.

But wait a minute, you say. What about the big winners? Doesn't the old adage say that I should let my profits run? Yes, it does, but there is a price to pay in doing so. The price is that you will lose track of what is average. The really big winners are usually few and far between; the rest are just a bunch of lookalikes that confuse you. By staying away from all of them, you are freeing both your time and money to produce several average units, which in the end should prove both more profitable and less risky. At the very least, you need to keep track of what is average and what is not.

This is where descriptive statistics and terms such as *standard deviation*, *kurtosis*, and *skew* come in. A system's standard deviation of returns tells you how much an individual trade is likely to deviate from the average trade, or rather, the likelihood that it will stay within certain boundaries, as indicated by the standard deviation interval.

For this to be true, we need to assume that all trades are normally distributed around their mean and that the outcome of one trade is independent of the outcome of the others. This isn't necessarily always the case, but we have to assume it is, because it will most likely cost us more to not do so, in the form of either larger than necessary losses or smaller than necessary profits. The formula to calculate the standard deviation follows:

$$s = Sqrt[(N * Sum(X_i^2) - Sum(X_i)^2) / N * (N - 1)]$$

Where:

N = Number of trades

X_i = Result of trade X_i, for i = 1 to N

If the return from a trading system is normally distributed, about 68 percent of the individual outcomes will be within one standard deviation of the mean, and about 95 percent will be within two standard deviations of the mean (1.96 standard deviations to be exact). For example, if the average profit for a trading system is $500, and the standard deviation is $700, then we can say that the profit for 68 percent of all trades falls somewhere in the interval of −$200 (500 − 700) to $1,200 (500 + 700), and that the profit for 95 percent of all trades falls somewhere in the interval of −$900 (500 − 2 * 700) to $1,900 (500 + 2 * 700). If, on the other hand, the one standard deviation boundary lies at $900, the outcome for 68 percent off all trades falls somewhere in the interval of −$400 (500 − 800) to $1,400 (500 + 900).

We can see that the wider the standard deviation boundaries, the more dispersed the trades; and the more dispersed the trades, the less sure we can be about the outcome of each individual trade. (Note that a large percentage of all trades falls into negative territory. It is virtually impossible to build a system that can keep its lower one standard deviation boundary in positive territory, with the results measured on a per-trade basis.)

If taking on risk means taking on uncertainty about an unknown future or the outcome of a specific event, then if we can be absolutely certain about the outcome of a specific trade, no matter if we know whether it will be a winner or a loser, we take no risk. (More about the distinction between risk and loss is in Chapter 5: "Drawdown and Losses.") Consequently, the less sure we are about the outcome, the more risk we're assuming, no matter if the outcome can be either negative and positive.

Note that, using the formula above, the standard deviation will be smaller the larger the denominator is in relation to the numerator, which happens with an increasing number of trades. This is also an important reason why a system should work on (or at least be tested on) as many markets as possible, because the more hypothetical trades we have, the more certain we can be about the outcome of each individual trade.

Finally, you probably have heard the old saying that the larger the profits you want to make, the larger the risks you need to assume. This is because the standard deviation most likely will increase with the value of the average trade. This doesn't always have to be the case, but most often it will. The trick, then, is to try to modify the system so that the standard deviation at least increases at a slower rate than the value of the average trade, or so that the ratio between the average trade and the standard deviation increases and becomes as large as possible. This is called the *risk-adjusted return*. The system with the highest risk-adjusted return is the safest one to trade, given its estimated and desired average profit per trade.

For example, a system with an average profit of $500 and a standard deviation of $700 has the same risk-adjusted return as a system with an average profit of $5,000 and a standard deviation of $7,000 (500 / 700 = 5,000 / 7,000 = 0.71). Consequently, both give you the same bang for your buck, and neither can be considered any better than the other, with only this information at hand. A system with an average profit of $300 and a standard deviation of $400, on the other hand, has a risk-adjusted return of 0.75 (300 / 400), which is higher than either of the other systems, and therefore makes it the safest one to trade. To increase the profits from a system with a low average profit but a high risk-adjusted return, simply utilize it on as many markets as possible to increase the number of trades and, in the end, the net profit.

DISTRIBUTION OF TRADES

So far, when we have used several of our statistical measurements, such as the average profit and the standard deviation of the outcomes, we have assumed that all our variables, such as the percentage profit per trade, have been normally distributed and statistically independent, continuous random variables. The beauty of these assumptions is that the familiar bell-shaped curve of the normal distribution is easy to understand, and it lends itself to approximate other close to normally distributed variables as well. Figure 2.4 shows what such a distribution can look like.

Note, however, that for a variable to be random, it does not have to be normally distributed, as Figure 2.5 shows. This chart is simply created with the help of the random function in Excel. Figure 2.4, in turn, is created by taking a 10-period average of the random variable in Figure 2.5. Many times, a random variable that is an average of another random variable is distributed approximately as a normal random variable, regardless of the distribution of the original variable. This is also called the *central limit theorem*. Therefore, it is likely that the average profit per trade from several individual markets will be normally distributed, no matter the distribution of trades within any of the individual markets, or that the profit over several similar time periods (say a month) will be normally distributed, although the distribution of the trades might not.

However, a normal distribution can very well be both higher and narrower, or lower and fatter, than that in Figure 2.4. The main thing is that it has a single mode (one value that appears more frequently than others) and is symmetrical, with equally as many observations on both sides of the mean. For a normally distributed variable the *mean*, *median* (the middle value, if all values are sorted from the smallest to the largest), and *mode* should be the same.

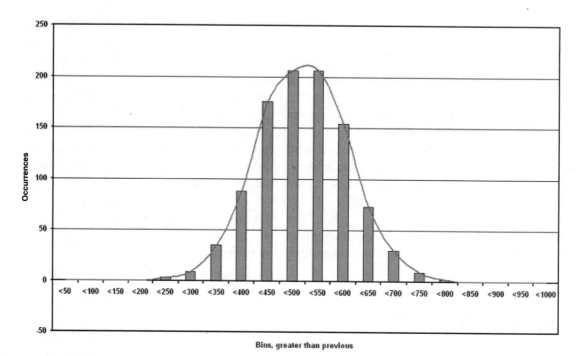

FIGURE 2.4

Normal distribution curve.

For the longest time, the normal distribution has been the statistical distribution most analysts used to calculate market returns, although it has long been evident that the market does not follow a normal distribution. This can be seen in Figure 2.6, which shows the daily percentage returns for the S&P 500 index over the period April 1982 to October 1999. As you can see, this curve is not entirely symmetrical, and it has much fatter tails than the normal distribution curve in Figure 2.4.

If a distribution has a relatively peaked and narrow body and fatter tails than a normal distribution, it is said to be *leptokurtic*. If the opposite holds true, it is said to be *platykurtic*. To calculate the kurtosis of a variable, you can use the *kurt* function in Excel. In the case of the daily distributions of returns for the S&P 500 index, the kurtosis equals 56. A positive value means that the distribution is leptokurtic, whereas a negative value means that it is platykurtic. When building a trading system, we prefer the distribution of returns be platykurtic, so that we make sure that the system does not stand or fall with any large outlier trades.

However, this is a double-edged sword: A positive value for the kurtosis (the distribution is leptokurtic with a narrow body) also might indicate that we are doing a good job in keeping most of our trades as similar as possible to the aver-

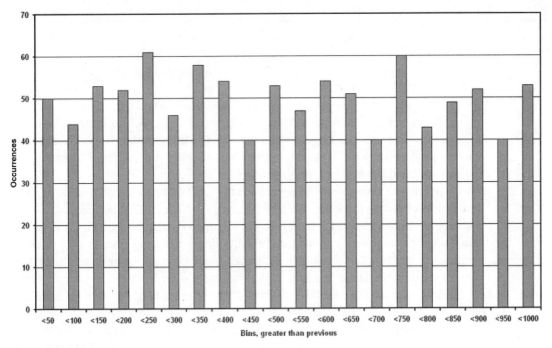

FIGURE 2.5

Random variables and distribution.

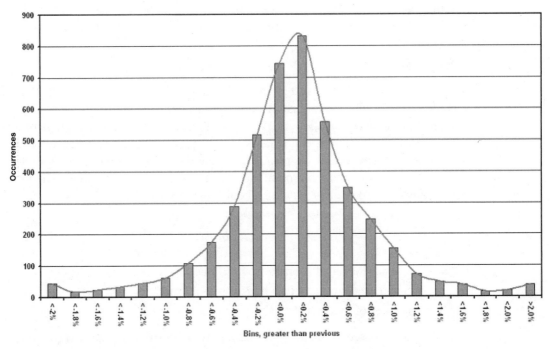

FIGURE 2.6

S&P 500–April 1982–October 1999.

age trade. If that is the case, the kurtosis should increase with the number of trades from which we can draw any statistical conclusions, while the dispersion of these trades stays the same. That is, the standard deviation should stay the same between alterations of the system. If both the standard deviation and the kurtosis increase, it could be because the new system is producing more outlier trades. (An outlier trade is an abnormally large winner or loser that we didn't expect to encounter, given the characteristics of the system.)

What probably cannot be seen from Figure 2.6 is that the distribution also is slightly skewed to the left (a negative skew), with the tail to the left of the body stretching out further than the tail to the right. Normally, a negative skew results in a mean smaller than the median. When building a trading system, we prefer the returns to be positively skewed, with the tail to the right stretching out further from the body than the tail to the left, so that we make sure that we're cutting our losses short and letting our profits run. In that case, the value of the average trade also will be larger than the median trade, which means that for most trades, we can expect to make a profit similar to the median value. Every so often, however, we will encounter a really profitable trade that increases the value of the average trade as well. This, too, is a double-edged sword in that the final outcome now is more dependent on a few large winners, which might or might not repeat themselves in the future. To calculate the skewness of the distribution, you can use the *skew* function in Excel. In this case, the skew equals -2.01, with the average return per day equal to 0.0296 percent and the median equal to 0.0311 percent, respectively.

STANDARD ERRORS AND TESTS

Many times, when testing a system on several markets, it is easier to work with the averages from each system/market combination (symac) and then calculate an average and standard deviation interval around this newly computed average of all other averages. This presents a small statistics problem, because when we work with averages from several samples to calculate an average of those averages and a standard deviation interval around the new average of averages (now called the *standard error*), we really should use the following formula:

$$s_M = \sqrt{\Sigma s_2^2} / \sqrt{N}$$

Where:

s_M = Standard error of average from all markets tested
Σs = Standard deviation of all trades from all markets
N = Number of markets tested

As you can see from the formula, s_M will be smaller than s (how much depends on N). Because both a single sample observation and a sample average are estimates of the same true average for the entire population, and because there is a higher likelihood for a sample average to come close to the true population average, the standard error for a set of sample averages will be smaller than the standard deviation for a set of individual observations.

The problem with this formula is that, if we first calculate an average profit per trade and market, we won't be able to find the standard deviation of all trades from all markets, and if we did, we wouldn't have a need for this formula in the first place. So, what to do, and why?

Let's start with the why. We're doing this because testing a system over several markets (I usually use 30 to 60 markets, tested over the last 10 years of market action) produces lot of trades, which makes things very cumbersome and results in very large Excel spreadsheets needed for the calculations. It is also valuable to know the standard error of the average for future reference, if and when we start to trade the system for real and would like to compare the averages it produces in real-life trading with those estimated from the testing.

Nonetheless, somehow we need to come up with a value for the standard deviation of all trades from all markets. To do this, assume that the variable we're investigating isn't the profit per trade, as in the original standard deviation formula, but the average profit per trade from several markets. Use the same formula to compute s. In that case, N in the original formula will represent number of markets tested, and X_i the average profit from a specific market, as indicated by i. (A more correct way would be to calculate all the averages and standard deviations for all the markets tested and then calculate a standard error of the averages as a function of the *mean square error*, which simply is the average of all standard deviations. But what the hell—this is not a book about statistics.)

It is important to remember that whatever variable we're investigating—such as the average profit per trade—will always be an estimate of the true average profit per trade. This is because no matter how many markets we're using and how far back in time we do the testing, the test will only contain a small sample of markets producing the price pattern the system is trying to catch. Think about it: There are various types of markets all over the place, and some of them are already several hundred years old. It would be impossible to collect all the data to test them to compute the true average profit per trade for a specific system, as of today. And even if we could do that, the true value, as of today, would be nothing but an estimate for what the true value will be at some point in the future, when all markets cease to exist.

Therefore, it would be interesting if we could calculate an estimate, or at least some sort of a confidence interval, for what the true average profit per trade might be. For example, what if we, using our 30 to 60 markets and 10 years of data, calculate the average profit per trade for a system to be $300, when in fact the true value is $100, and the system slowly but surely starts to move closer to that value over the next several years, when we're trading it live. In that case, the system has not broken down and the market conditions have not changed.

Unbeknown to us, it's just behaving as it always has and should. We just happened to do our research on a set of markets and a period that wasn't representative for the types of results this system really produced.

Remember that a one standard deviation interval around the mean should contain approximately 68 percent of all observations, and a two standard deviation interval around the mean should contain approximately 95 percent of all observations. Now we can twist that reasoning around a little bit and say that we can be 95 percent sure the true average value of the variable we're testing is between ± 2 standard errors around the just-computed average of averages. We do that using the following three-step process:

First, calculate the average profit per trade for each market tested (this is the variable we're investigating), an average for all those averages (this is the average to estimate the true average), and the standard deviation for those averages, using the standard deviation formula.

Second, use the standard deviation just calculated to calculate the standard error for all averages of averages. For example, for a standard deviation of $700 over thirty observations (markets tested), the standard error will be $128 [700 / Sqrt(30)].

Third, multiply the standard error by 2 (for two standard errors, to produce a 95 percent confidence interval), and add and deduct the product to and from the average profit per trade, calculated earlier as the average of several market averages. For example, with an average profit per trade of $300 and a standard error of $128, we now can say that we can be 95 percent sure that the true (always unknown) average profit per trade will fall somewhere in the interval $244 to $756.

Because the true standard deviation will always be unknown, the factor we're multiplying the standard error by actually should be slightly higher than the standard error interval for which we're creating the confidence interval, depending on the number of observations we're working with (30, in this case). You can look up the exact value in a so-called *t-table* in any statistics book. However, because 30 to 60 observations is considered to be a fairly high number of observations, this number will be very close to the standard error value anyway (2.0423 for 30 observations).

OTHER STATISTICAL MEASURES

Another way to make sure that a system is not too dependent on any outliers is to exclude them when you are calculating the average return. You can do this in Excel with the *trimmean* function, which excludes a certain percentage of observations from each end of the distribution. Ideally, when building a trading system, we prefer the trimmean to remain above zero, so that we make sure that the bulk of our trades behave as they should. If the trimmean is larger than the average return, it indicates that the positive outliers are larger than the negative outliers, and vice versa.

In this case, whatever you think is best depends on what you expect and how you would like the system to perform in the future. After a few bad trades, it could be comforting to know that the positive outliers historically have had a tendency to be larger than the negative ones; on the other hand, having to rely on a set of not-yet-seen outlier trades to find your way out of a drawdown seems awfully close to desperate gambling if you ask me.

If we don't know for sure whether the distribution is approximately normal or not, we cannot use our normal distribution measurements, which, for example, say that 68 percent of all observations will be within one standard deviation of the mean. Instead, we have to use *Chebychef's theorem*, which says that for a k greater than or equal to 1 ($k \geq 1$), at least $(1 - 1/k^2)$ observations will fall within k standard deviations of their mean value. Note that with this method, we cannot give an exact value.

For example, if we have a normal distribution, we know that 95 percent of all observations will fall within two standard deviations; but if we don't know what the distribution looks like, we can only say that at least 75 percent $(1 - 1/2^2)$ will fall within two standard deviations. Furthermore, without knowing the exact distribution, we cannot say if they will be equally distributed around the mean. We have to estimate this from our kurtosis and skew measurements. Similarly, to encapsulate at least 50 percent, 67 percent, and 90 percent of all observations, the standard deviations must be 1.41, 1.74, and 3.16, respectively.

When we're building a trading system, we do not want the distribution of trades to be normally distributed, but instead to fall into a few very distinctive bins or categories, such as a certain sized profit and a certain sized loss. Thus, we know exactly what we can expect from one trade to the next. Figure 2.7 shows one such distribution of trades. In fact, if you ask me, a normal distribution of trades within a specific market or time period indicates bad research and sloppy trading. Remember that the normal distribution is a function of a random variable, and we don't want the outcome of our trades to be entirely left to chance, do we?

TIME IN MARKET

Many traders and analysts pay very little or no attention to the number of trades a system is likely to generate. However, this is very important information that will give you a first clue to whether the system is suitable for you. The questions you need to ask yourself are, "Does this system trade often enough and does it keep me in the market enough to satisfy my need for action?" These are seemingly silly questions at first glance, but the truth is that a specific system will not suit everybody, no matter how profitable it is. If it doesn't fit your personality or style of trading, you will not feel comfortable trading it.

Even more important, however, is how much time the system is expected to stay in the market, because time spent in the market also equals risk assumed. Therefore, the less time you can spend in the market to reach a certain profit, the

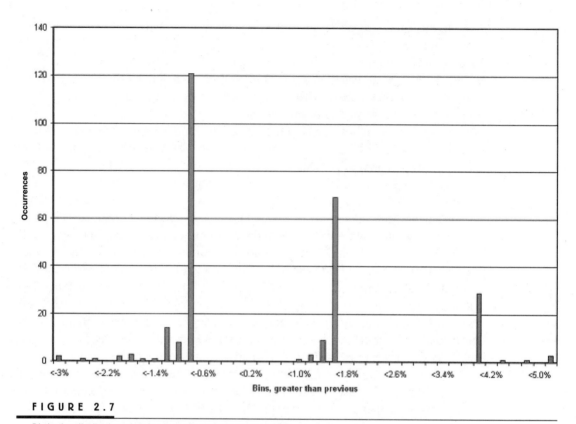

FIGURE   2.7

Distinctive distribution of trades from successful trading systems.

better off you are. (Recall the example in the section "Net Profit," which produced a higher return than a buy-and-hold strategy, even though it spent less time in the market and with a lower average profit per share traded.) To calculate the relative time spent in the market, multiply the number of winning trades by the average number of bars for the winners. Add this to the number of losing trades, multiplied by the average number of bars for the losers. Finally, divide by the total number of bars examined. Time spent in the market is a double-edged sword, because the less time spent in the market to reach a certain profit, the longer it also might take to get out of a drawdown.

Let's get back to the examples about trading your way out of a drawdown presented earlier. What if the system in question produces approximately two trades per month and market, and the average trade length is three days? If you only trade the system on one market, the number of days in a trade to get you out of a $7,200 drawdown is 45 (15 * 3). But because the system only spends about 30 percent of its time in a trade (6 / 20), the actual number of trading days to get back into the black is 150 (45 / 0.3). That is more than six months' worth of full-time trading to get out of a situation that at a first glance only looked like a situation that needed "just a few good trades."

This shows that trading is a very deceiving business, and that we'd better make sure that we know what we are doing. Obviously, one thing that could speed up things considerably is to trade the system on several markets. Using three markets, the system will spend approximately 90 percent of its time in the market (3 * 6 / 20) in one system or another, and the time to get out of the same drawdown will be 50 days (45 / 0.9). To get out of a $7,200 drawdown in only three days requires that the system is applied to a total of 50 markets [(45 / 3) * (20 / 6)]. Of course not all of them will be traded, but that's how many markets it takes, on average, to produce the 15 trades needed to get out of the drawdown in three days, considering how often and for how long the system is in a trade per market.

Obviously then, it becomes very important that the system works equally as well in all markets, on average, and at all times. And how do we assure that? By testing the system on as many markets as possible, covering as many different market conditions as possible, striving to make the system work equally as well, on average, at all times, no matter the trend or price of any individual market. The way to avoid fitting the system parameters to any specific market or market condition is to measure its performance in percentage terms on a one-contract basis. Have we stated this enough times now?

Note also that with 15 trades needed to get out of the drawdown in three days, and with the average time per trade also being three days, we need to be in all 15 trades simultaneously. Unfortunately, however, given the initial assumptions for this situation, being in 15 markets simultaneously is impossible for most of us. Remember that earlier we needed to tie up $100,000 in each trade, which means that, to be in 15 positions at one time, we need to have at least $1,500,000 on account.

But what if we only have, say $500,000, and never want to tie up more than 40 to 60 percent of that amount? Well, then we can only be in three trades at a time (500,000 * 0.6 = 300,000), which means we can only apply the system to 10 markets (20 * 3 / 6). If we apply it to more markets than that, we will have to start second-guessing the validity of the signals produced by the system and exclude some of the trades according to our own whims—something we most definitely do not want to do. Fortunately, there is a way to ease this dilemma, which we will get to in Parts 3 and 4. For now, however, we can only conclude that we also need to keep numbers and equations like this in the back of our minds so that we don't fool ourselves into trading a system that isn't suitable for us.

Note also that, in this example, we are working with fixed dollar amounts invested under the assumption that the market levels will stay approximately the same. In Part 4, where we start working with dynamic amounts, depending on both the market level and the account equity, an ever-changing number of shares will be traded on a wide variety of both markets and systems, which makes this matter even more complex.

CHAPTER 3

Probability and Percent of Profitable Trades

One of the most important factors to consider when researching a trading system is its percentage of profitable trades. Counterintuitive as it might seem, a higher percentage of profitable trades isn't necessarily better than a lower number. It all depends on what you're trying to achieve with the system, and how it relates to the average profit per trade, how often a trading opportunity presents itself, and how long a typical trade lasts.

Together with the profit factor, the percent profitable trades is the only performance measurement that has any value when it comes to estimating the system's future performance that can be derived immediately from the single-market performance summary produced by many off-the-shelf analysis programs. Again, this is assuming the underlying logic is sound and the system can be considered robust. Normalization should not matter. That is, for the number of profitable trades to be correct, you don't need to look at the results in terms of equal amounts invested or percentages.

It boils down to making sure that your system has a positive mathematical expectancy. Make sure that the relative amount of your winning trades (or percentage winners) multiplied by the average profit from those trades is sufficiently larger than the relative amount of the losing trades (or percentage losers) multiplied by the average loss from those trades. If this value is above zero, the system has a positive mathematical expectancy, which is a key criterion for any trading system.

CALCULATING PROFITABLE TRADES

To calculate the percentage of profitable trades, simply divide the number of winning trades by the total number of trades produced by the entry rule over the test period. For easier interpretation, you also can multiply by 100. For example, if a system has produced a total of 52 winners over 126 trades, the percentage profitable trades is 41.27 percent (52 * 100 / 126). From this, it follows that 58.73 percent [100 − 41.27, or (126 − 52) / 126] must be losers or break-even trades.

If the average winner and loser are worth $500 and $400, respectively, and the historical (or back-tested) track record shows that the system has produced 45 percent profitable trades (and consequently 55 percent losers), then the mathematical expectancy for the system equals $32.5 [(0.45 * 500) − (0.55 * 350)].

When looking at these numbers, it's important to remember that a historically high percentage of profitable trades doesn't necessarily mean an equally high likelihood for the very next trade, or each individual trade, to be a winner. The reason for this is somewhat abstract and philosophical: As soon as any series of words or numbers result in something that is not random, it contains information. And as soon as there is information in anything, we can distill it from the background noise and make it work in our favor.

In the case of a trading system, this is equal to refining the system to make better use of the nonrandom signals the market gives us. However, the consequence is that the closer we get to distilling all the information, the closer the system comes to acting in a random manner. When we have refined the system as much as we can, but still think we can detect some information, such as seemingly predictable runs of winners and losers, we are still better off assuming that information is not there. This is because even a very complex and seemingly nonrandom series of data still can be the product of randomness—as for example, this sentence (just kidding).

If we assume nonrandomness when none exists, we run the risk of trading too aggressively when we shouldn't, and not aggressively enough when we should, which over time will result in a less than optimal equity growth. The best way to avoid this dilemma is to assume randomness and to trade at an equally aggressive level all the time. Consequently, even if you have more than 50 percent profitable trades in your testing and historical trading, you are better off not assuming more than that in your real-life future trading.

In fact, considering that a random entry, at best, has a 50 percent chance of ending up with a profit (not considering slippage and commission), factoring in these costs of trading will take the likelihood below the 50 percent level. Exactly how much lower is hard to estimate and depends on how large these costs of trading are in relation to the profits and losses produced by the system. Therefore, if your back testing or historical trading results show a high percentage of winners, it could be because of two things: Either the system is good enough to overcome the negative biases stacked against you, or the results so far (whether actual or the product of back testing) are pure fluke.

Furthermore, assuming a 50 percent chance for the market to move a specific distance in either direction from the entry point, there still is a larger chance for a random trade to end up a loser, because of the mandatory risk–reward relationship of at least 2:1 that you should have in place when entering the trade. That is, because you should not enter into a trade if you don't believe that the profit potential is at least two times the value of the loss, a shorter distance between the entry point and the loss, than between the entry point and the estimated profit, still adds to the likelihood for the trade to become a loser.

Another reason why a high percentage of profitable trades isn't necessarily better than a low percentage is that a system with a low percentage of profitable trades is more likely to continue to produce that percentage, or better, in the future: The dollar value of the winners and losers aside, each trade only has two possible outcomes. It can end up either as a winner or as a loser. (Break-even trades don't count.) With each trade only having two outcomes, a sequence of two trades must look like any of the following four sequences: (Win, Win), (Win, Loss), (Loss, Win), or (Loss, Loss).

And a sequence of three trades must look like any of the following eight sequences: (Win, Win, Win), (Win, Win, Loss), (Win, Loss, Win), (Win, Loss, Loss), (Loss, Win, Win), (Loss, Win, Loss), (Loss, Loss, Win), or (Loss, Loss, Loss).

Thus, for every trade added to the total number of trades, the number of sequences doubles, so that with 10 trades, the number of possible sequences is 1,024 ($2 * 2 * 2 * 2 * 2 * 2 * 2 * 2 * 2 * 2 = 2^{10}$) and for 100 trades, the number of possible sequences is 1,267,650,600,228,229,401,496,703,205,376 (2^{100}, or approximately 12.7 billion * 10^{20}), ranging from 100 winners in a row to 100 losers in a row, covering every possible sequence in between, including the one produced by the system in question.

With that many possible outcomes, it's easy to see that the one sequence produced by any system is nothing but a freak occurrence that is very unlikely to repeat itself in the future, and that any system, in the future, is much more likely to produce any other sequence of trades but the one just produced. In fact, no matter the number of trades examined, the sequence just produced—no matter how many winners and losers it held—is no more likely to repeat itself the next time around than the one sequence containing only winning trades.

However, even if the likelihood for the exact same sequence to occur again is infinitesimal, a good chance still remains that the system in question will produce a sequence holding the same percentage of winners. How good depends on how many winners we're looking for. For example, in the three-trade sequence above, there is only a 12.5 percent chance (1 / 8) for each sequence to happen, but an 87.5 percent chance (7 / 8) that the sequence will hold at least one winner, and a 50 percent chance (4 / 8) that the sequence will hold at least two winners, placed somewhere within the sequence.

One interesting question to ask yourself when you're examining a trading system is how likely is it for the system to continue to produce the same percentage of winning trades? To answer that question, you need to apply the following piece of math to your trading statistics:

$$P(r) = [N! / (r! * (N - r)!] * p^r * (1-p)^{(N-r)}$$

Where:

P(r) = Probability for exactly r profitable trades
N = Total number of trades
r = Profitable trades
p = Probability for trade to be profitable

In Excel, the formula can look something like this:

=(FACT($G$2)/(FACT(ROUND($B5/100*$G$2,0))*FACT($G$2−ROUND($B5/100*$G$2,0)))*(C$4/100)^ROUND($B5/100*$G$2,0)*(1−C$4/100)^($G$2−ROUND($B5/100*$G$2,0)))*100

Where:

Cell G2 = Total number of trades
Cell B5 = Profitable trades
Cell C4 = Probability for trade to be profitable

Figure 3.1 shows how this formula can be used to create a matrix, with the data in the matrix indicating the likelihood for a specific amount of profitable trades, given the historical profitability and your estimate of how likely it is for each trade to be profitable in the future. Using the data in the matrix, you also can produce a chart like that in Figure 3.2, which shows the same thing in a graphic way. Looking at Figure 3.2 we can, for example, see that if the historical profitability is 60 percent, and you estimate the likelihood for a future trade to be a winner at 50 percent, there is only a 1 percent likelihood that the number of profitable trades will be 60 percent over a large number of trades.

Figure 3.3 shows the cumulative likelihoods for a certain percentage amount of trades to be profitable in the future. For example, with a 60 percent historical profitability, and the likelihood for a future trade to be profitable at 50 percent, an almost 100 percent likelihood exists that a longer series of future trades will hold 50 percent or less profitable trades.

The point is that no matter the percentage of profitable trades you had in the past, the likelihood to repeat that exact amount in the future is very small—not to mention the likelihood for producing a series of trades with the winners and losers in the same order as the historical or back-tested series.

The same goes for the number of winners and losers in a row. If for nothing else, you should try to keep these numbers as low as possible (especially the losers, if you like to feel comfortable with trading the system). However, for a cor-

Number of trades: 100

Percent likelihood of success for individual trade

Percent profitable trades	1	2	3	4	5	6	7	8	9
-	36.60	13.26	4.76	1.69	0.59	0.21	0.07	0.02	0.01
1	36.97	27.07	14.71	7.03	3.12	1.31	0.53	0.21	0.08
2	18.49	27.34	22.52	14.50	8.12	4.14	1.98	0.90	0.39
3	6.10	18.23	22.75	19.73	13.96	8.64	4.86	2.54	1.25
4	1.49	9.02	17.06	19.94	17.81	13.38	8.88	5.36	3.01
5	0.29	3.53	10.13	15.95	18.00	16.39	12.83	8.95	5.71
6	0.05	1.14	4.96	10.52	15.00	16.57	15.29	12.33	8.95
7	0.01	0.31	2.06	5.89	10.60	14.20	15.45	14.40	11.88
8	0.00	0.07	0.74	2.85	6.49	10.54	13.52	14.55	13.66
9	0.00	0.02	0.23	1.21	3.49	6.87	10.40	12.93	13.81
10	0.00	0.00	0.07	0.46	1.67	3.99	7.12	10.24	12.43
11	0.00	0.00	0.02	0.16	0.72	2.09	4.39	7.28	10.06
12	0.00	0.00	0.00	0.05	0.28	0.99	2.45	4.70	7.38
13	0.00	0.00	0.00	0.01	0.10	0.43	1.25	2.76	4.94
14	0.00	0.00	0.00	0.00	0.03	0.17	0.58	1.49	3.04

FIGURE 3.1

Matrix indicating likelihood of profitable trades.

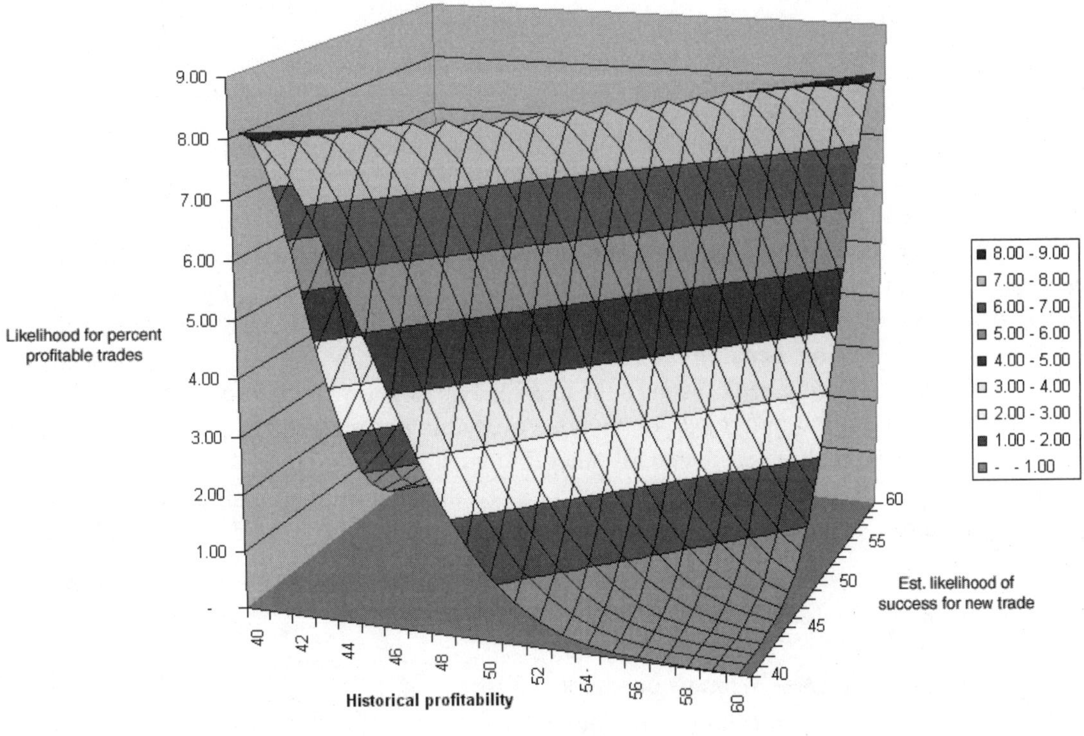

FIGURE 3.2

Chart indicating likelihood of profitable trades.

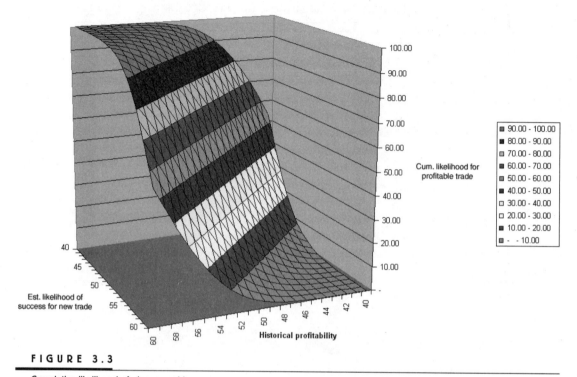

FIGURE 3.3

Cumulative likelihood of winners and losers.

rectly built system, with a relatively high amount of profitable trades, these numbers hold very little value and should be looked upon more as freak occurrences than anything else. Losing streaks will happen even for the most correctly built system, and sometimes it is good to have many losing trades in a row during the back testing, because the more losing trades in a row you've just experienced (for real or during back testing), the less likely it is you will go through the same experience again, provided you've done everything else correctly, the logic behind the system makes sense, and all other system statistics are reliable.

To calculate the likelihood for a certain amount of winning or losing trades in a row, given a certain amount of trades, you can use the following formula in Excel:

$$=MIN(MAX(0.5^{\wedge}(C\$3+2)*(\$B4-(C\$3+2)+1),0),1)$$

Where:

    Cell C3 = Winners or losers in a row
    Cell B4 = Total number of trades

Figure 3.4 shows how this formula can be used to create a matrix, with the data in the matrix indicating the likelihood for a specific amount of winners or los-

		Exact number of losers in a row								
		1	2	3	4	5	6	7	8	9
	1	0.00	0.00	0.00	0.00	0.00	0.00	0.00	0.00	0.00
	2	0.00	0.00	0.00	0.00	0.00	0.00	0.00	0.00	0.00
	3	12.50	0.00	0.00	0.00	0.00	0.00	0.00	0.00	0.00
	4	25.00	6.25	0.00	0.00	0.00	0.00	0.00	0.00	0.00
	5	37.50	12.50	3.13	0.00	0.00	0.00	0.00	0.00	0.00
Number of trades	6	50.00	18.75	6.25	1.56	0.00	0.00	0.00	0.00	0.00
	7	62.50	25.00	9.38	3.13	0.78	0.00	0.00	0.00	0.00
	8	75.00	31.25	12.50	4.69	1.56	0.39	0.00	0.00	0.00
	9	87.50	37.50	15.63	6.25	2.34	0.78	0.20	0.00	0.00
	10	100.00	43.75	18.75	7.81	3.13	1.17	0.39	0.10	0.00
	11	100.00	50.00	21.88	9.38	3.91	1.56	0.59	0.20	0.05
	12	100.00	56.25	25.00	10.94	4.69	1.95	0.78	0.29	0.10
	13	100.00	62.50	28.13	12.50	5.47	2.34	0.98	0.39	0.15
	14	100.00	68.75	31.25	14.06	6.25	2.73	1.17	0.49	0.20

FIGURE 3.4

Matrix indicating likelihood of winners and losers.

ers in a row, given a certain amount of trades. Note that we always need two trades or more for the total number of trades to be able to calculate an exact amount of winners and losers in a row.

For example, to calculate the likelihood to experience exactly two losers in a row, we need one winner to begin the sequence, then the two losers, and finally one more winner to put an end to the losing streak. This makes the trading sequence look like: (Win, Loss, Loss, Win). With a total of four trades, only one of the 16 possible sequences can look like this, which makes the likelihood for that particular sequence to happen equal to 6.25 percent (1 / 16). (See cell C7 in Figure 3.4.) With a total of five trades, four sequences are possible having two losers in a row, either (Win, Loss, Loss, Win, Win or Loss) or (Win or Loss, Win, Loss, Loss, Win), which makes the likelihood for any of them to come true equal to 12.5 percent (4 / 32). (See cell D8 in Figure 3.4.)

Using the data in the matrix, you also can produce a chart like that in Figure 3.5, which shows the same thing in a graphic way. Here, we can see that the likelihood of experiencing as many as 15 losing trades in a row is very small for a total number of trades ranging from 50 to 100. Now, that is not to say that it can't happen, but the likelihood for it is very small. If you already have experienced such a losing streak, either for real or during back testing, the likelihood for it to happen again within a 100-trade trading sequence is minuscule.

In fact, exactly how large the chance is, is depicted in Figure 3.6, which shows the likelihood for a few different trading scenarios, given a trading sequence of 100 trades. The line in the middle shows the likelihood to experience exactly a certain number of winners or losers in a row. The rightmost line shows the likeli-

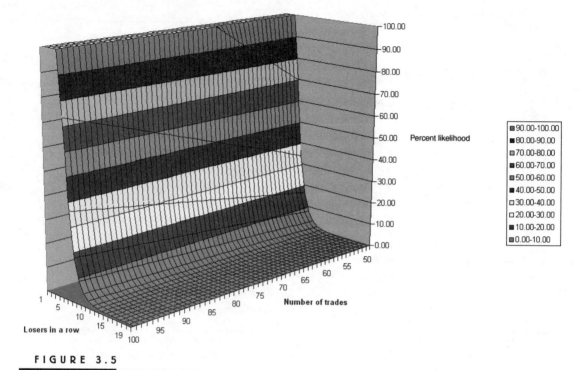

FIGURE 3.5

Chart indicating likelihood of winners and losers.

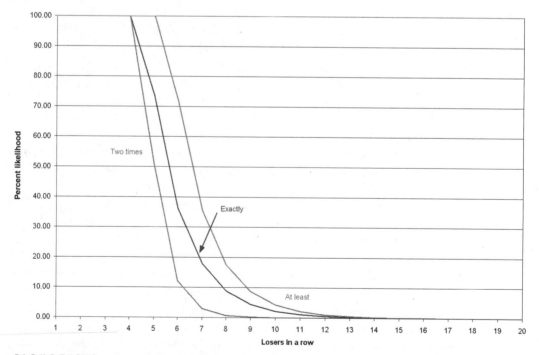

FIGURE 3.6

Relative likelihood of winners and losers.

hood to experience a streak of at least a certain number of winners or losers. For example, the likelihood to experience at least nine winners or losers in a row is just below 10 percent. The leftmost line shows the likelihood to experience two trading sequences of the same length within 100 trades. For example, for five winners or losers in a row, the likelihood to experience two such sequences is below 50 percent, and to experience two sequences of nine winners or losers in a row, the likelihood is almost 0 percent.

Note, however, that all this assumes that you've done everything correctly, the logic behind the system makes sense, and all other system statistics are reliable. Also, this statistic works both ways: If you just experienced a large number of winners in a row, it doesn't mean that the system has gotten much better and will continue to produce the same type of winning streaks in the future. Quite the contrary: Depending on the size of the winning streak, the more difficult it will be to repeat it. It's all a game of statistics. Nothing else.

THE DIFFERENCE BETWEEN TRADES AND SIGNALS

During the initial testing of a system, we really shouldn't concern ourselves with the performance of the system, but rather the reliability of the signals it generates. To do that, we really need to test all the signals generated, using standardized stops and exits—such as, always exit after a specific profit or loss or after a specific number of bars in trade.

Normal system testing usually only tests the first signal in a cluster of entry signals and assumes that the others can be ignored because you would have been in a trade already. However, whether you would have been in a trade or not depends on your stop-loss and profit-taking levels and how long the trade should last if none of these levels is hit. Plenty of other reasons could exist for why the first signal might have been ignored in real-life trading, such as already being fully invested because of previous trades, or simply because you missed trading that day.

Therefore, when researching a system, it's important to look at all the signals it generates, so that it can be trusted just as much on its second or third signals as it can on its first signal. For example, assume you missed a signal one day because of a doctor's appointment. The next day, you get a new signal in the same stock, despite the fact that you should have been in this stock already had you been able to trade the previous day. If you haven't done your research properly, you have no idea whether the second signal is likely to be as valid and reliable as the first one.

On a more hypothetical note, there also are plenty of days when the system just barely manages to produce a signal, or conversely, just barely misses producing a signal. (Should the near misses perhaps be as valid as the near hits? We won't answer that particular question here, but it's still worth asking.) Look at Figure 3.7, which shows a chart of all the signals that one of the systems featured in Part 2 generated in Microsoft during the fall of 2001. It shows that in early August 2001,

FIGURE 3.7

Microsoft performance signals—Fall 2001.

two signals went short only one day apart from each other. In late October and early November, two signals two days in a row went long. In the case of the short signals, clearly the second signal was better than the first signal. In the case of the long signals, the first signal was better. However, the point is that in either case, the second signal most likely would have gone unnoticed and unanalyzed, because you already would have been in a trade generated by the first signal.

Now, pretend that a few of the signals that came first in a row of two or more signals really didn't happen, or that you for one reason or another failed to act on them. Then you would have had to rely on the second signal. Transfer this reasoning to a real-life trading situation. How many days have you had when you saw a nice setup forming and readied yourself to place the trade if the stock in question only reached a certain level? Have they all resulted in a trade? Probably not. The next day, the stock takes off in the anticipated direction, leaving you behind until late in the day, when you actually get the signal you were looking for yesterday. With the market already having made a good move in the anticipated direction, do you trust your system enough to take the trade this time? Only a complete test of all signals will give you that confidence.

The same reasoning holds for the exit techniques as well. To make the most out of the chart pattern and the exit techniques that should go with it, you need to have done your homework before you set out to trade the pattern in question and analyze the exits in such a way so that they work, on average, equally as well for all signals, no matter whether each particular signal would have been traded or not. Therefore, the testing must be done in such a way that all signals will be tested at one time or another together with several different exit levels. To do this, trade the system at random several times.

To accomplish this, a random number generator that produces either a 0 or a 1 will be attached to the entry rules (see the TradeStation code in Chapter 7), so that the system only can enter when the random number is 1. For example, if the random number for the entry had been 0 for the late-October long-entry signal in Microsoft, that trade would not have been taken; this would have made it possible for the system to enter on the following day. Otherwise, this would not have happened, because we would have been in a trade already, which would have left the

FIGURE 3.8

Microsoft trading using RNG.

second signal unanalyzed. (To learn more about this system and its trailing stop version, see *Active Trader* magazine, February 2002 to June 2002.)

Once the system and all its signals is fully tested, the random number generator can be turned off, so that the system can be tested according to normal principles. Figure 3.8 shows a few sample trades in Microsoft, using the original model with the random number generator (RNG) set on. Compare these trades with the signals in Figure 3.7 and you will find that the RNG prevents you from taking all signals generated by the system, which means that the RNG version of the system will not always trade the first signal in a series of signals.

As discussed more thoroughly in Part 3, one way to alter the system's characteristics is to vary the stops and exits. Figure 3.9 also shows a few trades generated with the RNG set on, but also with a different set of exits than those used for Figure 3.8. In the case of Figure 3.9, the stops and exits are much tighter than those for Figure 3.8, which makes the system trade more frequently. Compare the trades with those in Figure 3.8 and the signals in Figure 3.7, and you will see that they are different. However, note also that another reason for the differences between Figures 3.8 and 3.9 is that the RNG is on in both cases; it therefore generates the trades in a random manner.

FIGURE 3.9

Microsoft trading RNG, but different exits.

CHAPTER 4

Risk

I once stumbled upon an Internet site dedicated to systems trading and design. The site presented a mailing list, with various postings from systems traders asking for and giving each other advice on various topics regarding this intricate subject. As I was sitting there skimming through the messages, a new message came in from a guy who asked all the other traders frequenting the site to join forces with him to build a truly professional system—a system unlike the ridiculous systems they all were trading right now, with back-tested profit factors (the gross profit divided by the gross loss) ranging from about two to four. Together, they should be clever enough, he reasoned, to come up with a system that had a profit factor of at least seven—just like the professionals.

I am sorry to say that this guy has it all wrong. There probably is no such thing as a trading system with a back-tested profit factor of seven that has continued to stay profitable at all in real-life trading, and there most definitely is no professional money manager trading such a system. A professional and successful money manager knows better than to fall into that trap, which unfortunately can't be said about many of the system vendors hawking their stuff to guys like the one who posted the message.

In fact, many system vendors and so-called trading experts don't want you to trade a system with a back-tested profit factor below three (the higher the better, they reason), because they know from experience with their own systems that the profit factor will decrease considerably when the system is traded live on unseen data. The only reason for this recommendation is that they do not understand how to build a robust trading strategy in the first place, which becomes painfully evident when they continue to use the total net profit and drawdowns as their most important performance evaluators.

The same goes for the message-posting guy. He probably has a bunch of trading systems with back-tested profit factors around four, none of which come anywhere close to showing the same profitability in real life—chances are he's even losing money. The solution, he believes, is to crank up the back-tested profit factor to around seven and hope that he will land somewhere around three or four in real life.

Two related objections against that type of reasoning need to be raised here. Number one is the robustness of a profit factor as high as seven, or even three. Number two is the absurdity of it in the first place. Let's start with the absurdity, which also will help us understand why such a high profit factor is more likely to ruin you than anything else.

Building a good and robust trading system is not a question of maximizing the profit factor, but simply making it as reliable as possible and just high enough to warrant trading at all. It should be high enough so that the return on the amount risked is higher than what you could have made elsewhere, plus an appropriate premium for assuming that risk. Think about it as any normal fairly long-term business endeavor. What is the most you expect to make on the amount risked when opening up a coffee shop, a dental practice, a small factory producing plastic thingies, on investing (not trading) in the stock market? Probably not more than 25 percent a year, and the stock market has an average long-term return of around 12 percent. Then what makes you think you can make so much more trading? Do you have any idea what type of returns on the amount risked that a profit factor of two, three, or seven represents? If not, I will tell you.

CALCULATING RISK

To calculate the profit factor, simply divide the gross profit by the gross loss. The answer will tell you how many dollars you are likely to win for every dollar you lose. For example, say that you have $2 and decide to take part in a game where you have a 50 percent chance to win and, every time you do so, you win twice the amount you risked. The first time you try, you risk $1. You lose, and your gross loss is therefore $1. With your last dollar, you take another chance and this time you win $2, ending up with a total of $3, and your gross profit is therefore $2. Two divided by one equals two, which is your profit factor.

Now assume that the game changes so that you only have a 33 percent chance to win, but when you win, you win three times the amount you risked. This time, you start out with two losing bets, and your gross loss, therefore, is $2. With your last dollar, you win $3 and end up with $4. In this case, the profit factor comes out to 1.5 (3 / 2). (If you look at all five trades, you lost three trades for a total of $3 and won two trades for a total of $5, for a total profit factor of 1.67 [5 / 3].)

The profit factor tells you how much money you made in relation to how much money you lost. How much money you lost and how much money you actually risked is not the same thing. The amount risked is equal to the total amount you are willing to lose in each and every trade, for the possibility of making a profit, just as you're willing to risk a certain amount to get a 25 percent yearly return on your dental practice.

Given the above numbers, it also is possible to calculate how much money you risked. In the first example, you made a total of two bets for $1 each, which means you risked $2 to increase your capital with $1. Consequently, your return on the amount risked was 50 percent (1 / 2). In the second example, your capital also increased with $1, but this time you had to risk $3, which resulted in a 33 percent (1 / 3) return on the amount risked. In total, you risked $5 to make $2 for a return of 40 percent on the amount risked.

Now, instead of talking about a few individual bets, let's compare each example with a year's worth of trading, risking $1,000 in each trade. For the first year 100 losers and 100 winners produce a profit factor of two [(100 * 2,000) / (100 * 1,000)], and the return on the amount risked is 50 percent [(100 * 2,000 − 100 * 1,000) / (200 * 1,000)]. For the second year, with 200 losers and 100 winners, the profit factor and the return on the risked amount will be 1.5 and 33 percent, respectively. (And for the two years combined, the profit factor and the return stay at 1.67 and 40 percent, respectively.)

Now, assuming a profit factor of seven for each year, let's try to calculate backwards to find out how large the winners need to be and what the return on the risked amounts will be, given that we have 50 percent profitable trades in year one and 33 percent profitable trades in year two. For year one, it's easy enough. The winners need to be worth $7,000, so that the calculation for the profit factor will look as follows: (100 * 7,000) / (100 * 1,000). If that is the case, the return on the amount risked will be 300 percent [(100 * 7,000 − 100 * 1,000) / (200 * 1,000) = 6 / 2]. For year two, to end up with a profit factor of seven, each profitable trade needs to be worth $14,000, so that a profit factor of seven can be calculated according to: 100 * 14,000 / 200 * 1,000. The return on the risked amount will then be 400 percent [(100 * 14,000 − 200 * 1,000) / (300 * 1,000) = 12 / 3].

Now, I'm asking you, when was the last time you saw a trader (professional or otherwise) produce a long-term sustainable return on total amount risked of 300 to 400 percent a year? Heck, when was the last time you saw any trader produce a long-term sustainable return of 40 percent (a profit factor of 1.67, with 40 percent profitable trades)? Never, I say. A return of 40 percent a year simply isn't sustainable in the long run, much less a return of 300 to 400 percent. Sure, every so often a lucky few manage to produce spectacular numbers over a year or two, but that is only because everything goes their way during that period, with a trading strategy or system using a long-term profit factor that could be as low as 1.25.

If it really was feasible for a professional money manager to trade long-term with a profit factor of seven, it would be a piece of cake for someone like me, who has dabbled around with this for ages, to come up with a system with a profit factor of at least four and more than double my money every year. But I still make the bulk of my money analyzing the markets, rather than trading them. And you, I assume, would not have bought this book if you already were doubling your money every year. Go figure.

Remember how earlier we calculated the risk–reward relationship for each individual trade to be 2:1 and 3.5:1, using a system with 50 percent and 33 percent profitable trades, respectively? Can we agree that those numbers are pretty much what any trader could ask for, professional or not? (The chart with its support and resistance levels doesn't look any different for you than for the professional money manager.) Well, in the above examples, with a profit factor of seven, these risk–reward relationships come out to 7:1 and 14:1, respectively. Where on Earth would those moves come from, when all we can agree to is that 3.5:1 is as good as it will ever get on a long-term, sustainable basis?

Nevertheless, say that you happen to have a system with a profit factor of seven, a risk–reward relationship of 7:1 and 50 percent profitable trades. What would happen if the market, unbeknown to you, changed its characteristics ever so slightly so that you would be better off with a $2,000 stop loss instead, and that it would be better with a profit target at $6,000, for a risk–reward relationship of 3:1 (6,000 / 2,000)? More trades would be stopped out with a $1,000 loss, and fewer would be stopped out with a $7,000 profit. Say that every other would-be $7,000 winner now turns into a $1,000 loser, and most of the remaining winners are stopped out for inactivity at $4,000. In that case, you're down to 25 percent profitable trades and a profit factor of 1.33 (4,000 / 3,000). Now, with such a high percentage of losing trades, you won't always experience one winner for every three losers. What if you have nine losing trades in a row? Then you need at least three winners to take you out of the drawdown, and with only a 25 percent likelihood of each trade being a winner, chances for that to happen aren't very high. All of a sudden your Holy Grail system has turned into something very nerve-racking to deal with, with drawdowns that most likely will force you out of business, even though it still has a profit factor as high as 1.33.

What I'm trying to say is that such a highly specialized machine as a trading system with a profit factor of seven will break apart very easily. And when one part goes, the real trouble starts. Even though it still might be profitable, the plunge in the profit factor will be deep, and it will be very nerve-racking to trade. And what if the relationship between that very complex pattern or indicator setup demanded for such a system, and the move that follows it, cease to exist completely? Compare such a system to the cheetah we talked about in the Introduction: You will have one dead trading system, or one that produces nothing but losers.

If you ask me, any system with a back-tested profit factor of more than two is suspect. To build a robust trading system that is likely to continue to perform well in the future, make sure that the underlying logic is sound and simple, that the trading rules are as simple and as few as possible, that it works just as well for a wide range of parameter settings, that it produces plenty of trades at all times, and that it works equally as well in all markets and market conditions. If you manage to do all this, you will be surprised at how much you can expect to produce from a system with a profit factor as low as 1.33 or even lower.

However, the system must be designed for such a profit factor from the very beginning, constantly taking a similar quantity of both small profits and small losses. The system above, which goes from a profit factor of 7 to 1.33, has to rely on one (still) relatively large winner to make up for a large number of losses. This is a not-so desirable feature in any system.

In fact, given approximately 50 percent profitable trades, to produce an annual long-term sustainable return of 25 percent, you don't need a system with a profit factor higher than 1.5, as the following math will show:

With 50 percent profitable trades, 200 trades, risking $1,000 per trade, a 25 percent return on the risked amount translates into a final profit of $50,000 (0.25 * 200 * 1,000). To make a $50,000 net profit while losing $100,000, the gross profit needs to be $150,000. A gross profit of $150,000 divided by a gross loss of $100,000 results in a profit factor of 1.5. With 33 percent profitable trades, 300 trades, risking $1,000 per trade, a 25 percent return on the risked amount translates into a final profit of $75,000 (0.25 * 300 * 1,000). To make a $75,000 net profit while losing $200,000, the gross profit needs to be $275,000. A gross profit of $275,000 divided by a gross loss of $200,000 results in a profit factor of 1.38.

Granted, such a system isn't particularly exciting or sexy to trade, but it isn't your trading that should be exciting and sexy. It's the lifestyle you can afford because of it that should be all that. Note also that the return numbers discussed so far in this chapter are based on constant-dollar risks and investments. But as we already know, we should not measure the results in dollars, but in percentages. In doing so, we start to compound the returns by making use of previous winnings in trades to come. We will talk more about this in Part 4, where we also will learn how working with compounded returns helps us tailor the risk–reward relationship to fit our precise needs and risk tolerances for expected returns.

A SAMPLE STRATEGY ANALYSIS

A very well known trader, system designer, and seminar speaker that I know of once held a short presentation for a group of traders and analysts, among whom I was one. Knowing about my work and my book *Trading Systems That Work*, and that all the other listeners did as well, she started out the seminar by looking in my direction while stating smugly, "Percentages, percentages, that is all fine and well, but the only thing I'm interested in are the dollars. Percentages won't put bread on my table; only dollars will."

She then went on telling the audience that her goal in trading was to make a net profit of $1,000,000 per year, or a net profit of approximately $4,000 per day. To achieve that, she started out the trading day by picking out a few stocks that she believed were poised for a four-point move and then bought 1,000 shares of any of those stocks when the move got started.

When someone asked what she did if she couldn't find any such stocks, she answered that she then picked the stocks that were poised for the largest moves and simply bought more of those stocks, so that the final estimated profit still reached $4,000. Then someone asked what happened if the stock in question only moved half the distance. The answer to that was to continue to look for other stocks that might be poised for a good move and buy enough of those to cover for the amount remaining, up to the $4,000.

Finally, someone asked what she did when she lost on the first trade, to which she responded that she now had to find several stocks to trade, or pick one that was poised for a large enough move to make up for the loss, as well as the $4,000 still missing in profits. When someone asked where she found these stocks, she admitted that they where easiest to find among those stocks already priced above $50. Too-cheap stocks weren't worth looking at because they never made moves large enough.

Okay, let's stop here and ask what's going on. She's working with percentages, and she doesn't even know it! Let's assume she actually manages to make $4,000 a day, in which case she's one hell of a trader. Can you imagine how much she could be making if she actually knew what she was doing? The sky is the limit.

Her mistake is to only look for moves of a certain point size, instead of moves of a certain size in relation to the estimated entry price, and then alter the number of shares bought to reach the estimated profit of $4,000. If she does that, she will always tie up the same amount of capital in each trade, no matter the price of the stock.

For example, if stock ABC, which is priced at $80, is poised for a four-point move, the amount of money she needs to tie up in the trade will be $80,000. If, on the other hand, stock XYZ, currently priced at $40, is poised for a four-point move, the amount of money tied up in the trade will only be $40,000. But as we all know by now, and as the speaker admitted, the lower priced the stock, in general, the smaller the moves. A $40 stock only needs to move half as much in dollar terms as an $80 stock, to move the same distance in relation to their respective entry prices.

That is, if you want to give yourself the same chance to make $4,000 out of a $40 stock as out of a four-point move in an $80 stock, you only have to look for a two-point move and buy twice as many stocks, so that the amount invested will be $80,000 for the $40 stock as well. But all this about the price of the stocks and the number of shares to buy we have talked about already. Given what we have just learned about the profit and risk factors, let's instead look to see if this $4,000-a-day (or trade) strategy could be something for you.

Let's assume we have $100,000 to play with. To make $4,000 a day, with 50 percent profitable trades, we need to have a fairly tight stop loss; otherwise, the winners needed to make up for the losses as well as the desired profits will be placed too far away from the entry price to be reached within a day. Let's say we use a 2 percent stop, also equal to a 2-point move for a stock trading at $100 (1 point for a $50 stock, 1.5 points for a $75 stock, and 0.5 points for a $25 stock, but because this trader didn't believe in percentages these numbers don't apply). Buying $100,000 worth of a $100 stock means we can buy 1,000 shares. Therefore, if the trade goes against us, we lose $2,000 every other trade. To make $4,000 on average over two trades, the winning trade must generate a profit of $10,000 (4,000 * 2 + 2,000), or $10 per share, which also equals a 10 percent move and a 10 percent return on account.

(Note that if the trading ended at that value for the day, the profit would have been $8,000 for that day. But because both winning days and losing days occur, we still need to assume that we must make $4,000 on average, per trade. For example, if the next day were to end in a loss of $2,000, the average profit per day would now be down to $3,000 [(8,000 − 2,000) / 2], and we would have to make $6,000 to compensate for that the following day [(8,000 − 2,000 + 6,000) / 3]).

First, how often do you see a $100 stock make a 10-point move over a day, not to mention an even lower priced stock? And how often have you identified it beforehand, so that you actually had a chance to ride the move? Once or twice maybe, but not often enough to come even close to make any $4,000 a day. Second, with the winning trade having to be worth $10,000 to compensate for the $2,000 loss, to make an average profit per trade of $4,000, the profit factor has to be five (10,000 / 2,000). Third, making $8,000 while risking $4,000 (2 * 2,000), the risk factor comes out to two, or a 200 percent return on the risked amount. Knowing what we now know about the profit and risk factors, how likely is it, do you think, that we will be able to sustain these numbers, day in and day out, over the next several days and months? Not likely at all, I say.

Obviously then, we need to adjust our strategy somehow. Let's say we adjust our stop loss to only one point per share, but because of this, the percent of profitable trades decreases to 33 percent, or only every third trade will be a winner. Now, to make $4,000 on average per trade over three trades, the winner needs to be $14,000 (4,000 * 3 + 1,000 * 2). Now the winning trade needs to be even larger, so obviously this is not the way to go, even though we don't need to find as many winners as before.

What happens if we go the other way around? Let's say we set the stop four points away, so that the percentage of profitable trades increases to 67 percent. In that case, two winning trades will have to make up for one $4,000 loss, plus an additional $12,000 profit to make the profit per trade equal to $4,000 (4000 * 3 + 4000), which means that the profit per trade for the profitable trades needs to be for $8,000 each. OK, with a total profit of $16,000 and a total loss of $4,000, we're down to a profit factor of four and a risk factor of one (12,000 / 12,000).

Obviously, even these numbers are too high to be sustainable, but the only way to lower them further would be to increase the percentage of profitable trades by placing the stop loss even further away from the entry point. However, no matter how good our system is, it is not likely that we will increase the percentage of profitable trades that much more. As things are right now, the risk–reward relationship going into the trade is already down to 2:1, the minimum required by most system builders and traders. So, is there yet another way to make this strategy more tradable?

Yes, there is, actually: Place both the profit target and the stop loss closer to the entry price and simply put on larger positions, so that the decreased profit per share is counteracted by more shares, for a constant average profit per trade of $4,000. So, what makes sense for a day-trading strategy? Placing the target four points away from the entry price? Nah, that still feels a little much to be able to keep up on a long-term sustainable basis. One point? Perhaps a little too tight, considering the stop loss then needs to be only 50 cents away from the entry. Let's say that a profit target of two points makes sense. Thus, we're back where we started, so to speak, and the stop loss needs to be at one point away from the entry.

To make $8,000 with a two-point target applied on a $100 stock, we therefore need to buy 4,000 shares, for a total of $400,000. Now it all makes sense. We have counted backwards to come up with the characteristics our strategy needs to make $4,000 a day and per trade on average, and how much money we need to tie up in one trade. Now we only need to come up with an actual strategy with a profit factor of 4, a risk factor of 1, and 67 percent profitable trades. How many of us have ever come up with such a strategy, which also remained robust when traded for real on unseen data? Well, I don't know about you, and I most certainly don't want to argue against the system designer who apparently has such a strategy, but I for one have never and will never come up with such a strategy. If that is the type of strategy you'd like to find in this book, you might just as well stop reading right now.

Note also that we now need to tie up $400,000 in each trade (not $100,000 as originally stipulated). How many of us have that kind of money to place in one trade only? And what if we would like to diversify a little? Then we need another multiple of $400,000 for each stock we'd like to trade. Say you'd like to be in at least three trades at a time and also have the money available for one additional trade, just in case. Then you'd need $1,600,000.

What if $100,000 is all we have (which is still a lot of money for many of my readers), and we would like to be in three to four positions at the same time? Given that we do have a long-term sustainable strategy with a profit factor of 4, a risk factor of 1, and 67 percent profitable trades (yeah, right), then how much can we expect to make per trade and day, on average? The answer is $500 (25,000 / 100 * 2), or approximately $125,000 per year (500 * 250).

The point I'm trying to make with all this is that with only $100,000 at hand, you need a fantasy system (at least for most of us) to even make what you are making already—especially if you don't understand how to calculate percentages, the magic of proper money management (which we address more thoroughly in Chapter 4), and the power of trading several seemingly less tantalizing systems on several markets. That is what this book is about.

Before we close this chapter, let me once again draw your attention to *Active Trader* magazine, which during the fall of 2001, featured a series of articles by the renowned systems developer Dennis Meyers, Ph.D. In these articles, Mr. Meyers showed that the larger the profit factor (above two) during initial testing, the less likely a system is to hold up in the future, when the system is traded for real or tested on previously unseen data. In these articles, the system was an intraday breakout system tested and traded on IBM with five-minute bars.

CHAPTER 5

Drawdown and Losses

The only thing true about trading is that we will all go broke if we just stay at it long enough. The longer we stay in the game, the closer we get to that one freakish trading day, week, month, or year when everything goes against us. For some, it might happen tomorrow; for others, it won't happen in their lifetime but would have happened had they been able to trade for another 1,000 years. The trick is to make this freakish occurrence as freakish as possible. But no matter how freakish we make it, the chance of it happening at any time (however minuscule) will always be there, no matter how rigorous we've been at putting together our systems.

Most people don't understand what I mean by this, and meet me with arguments such as, "but I always have my stops in place," or "I alter my systems with the market conditions." But it doesn't matter what you do: the chance is always there that at one time everything can and will go against you—whether the situation of bad luck lasts for two seconds or several years doesn't matter. At some point, it can and will happen, if you just stay in the game long enough.

One way to look at it is to compare yourself to one of the Highlanders in the old *Highlander* movie. These supernatural beings could only die by having their heads chopped off. Well, there are people getting their heads chopped off all around the world, all the time, be it by accident or by intent, and if that is the only way to go for a Highlander, sooner or later it will happen to him as well.

Another way to look at it over a longer period is to compare it to a monkey in front of a typewriter, typing out Shakespeare's *Hamlet* by pure chance. Chances are slim, but they're there, and it won't happen overnight.

By the same token, the old trading adage, "your worst drawdown is still to come" is equally as true. But it doesn't have to happen first thing tomorrow, provided you've done your homework correctly. Unfortunately, however, very few systems designers (professionals and amateurs alike) know how to evaluate a system's drawdown, as the following little story will show you:

As an editor first for *Futures* magazine and later for *Active Trader* magazine, one of my duties was to visit many of the various trading seminars and conferences, held annually around the country. During one of these conferences, I attended a seminar where a very popular and famous system designer talked about system design and evaluation, and especially about how to limit a system's maximum drawdown.

One of the most important aspects of system design and evaluation, he explained, was to keep the drawdown to a minimum. To illustrate his point for the large and sacredly quiet audience, he first showed a performance summary for a system with a certain maximum drawdown amount, measured in dollars. Then he went on explaining how he modified the system to lower this amount, which he then showcased with yet another performance summary.

Now, this would have been all fine and well had he moved on to talk about the many aspects of exactly why the second, lower drawdown was better than the first one. But this never happened. Instead, he went on with example after example for about two hours straight, with most systems altered with a trend filter of some sort or a fixed dollar–based stop loss. Needless to say, at the end of his seminar, the audience was awestruck by his system-design capabilities and analytical mind. To me, it was painfully clear that not only the audience didn't have a clue, but worse still—neither did the speaker!

DRAWDOWN COMPARED TO EQUITY

To compare two drawdown figures to each other, you simply cannot only look at these two numbers and say that the lower one is better than the higher one—not even for two similar systems, traded on the same market, over the same period. Instead, you must put the numbers in relation to where and when the drawdowns took place, in regards to both your latest equity peak and the level at which the market traded.

For example, by altering a system ever so slightly by adding a trend filter, a drawdown that was caused by a series of long trades when the market was in a downtrend can be washed away completely. This means that the second, improved drawdown must have taken place at a completely different time and place, in regard to both the account equity going into the drawdown and the level at which the market traded.

Say, for example, that the drawdown for the first, unimproved system was for $60,000, at the end of a couple of years of good trading that had taken the equity from an initial $100,000 to $300,000. In that case, the drawdown depleted the trading capital by 20 percent (60,000 / 300,000), leaving you with $240,000. For the "improved" system, a maximum drawdown of $30,000 might have taken place right off the bat, depleting the capital by 30 percent (30,000 / 100,000), leaving you with $70,000.

Now, I don't know about you, but I would rather have a 20 percent drawdown leaving me with $240,000, than a 30 percent drawdown leaving me with $70,000. Hence, everything else aside, the first unimproved system is better than the second improved one, no matter if the end result for the second system was higher than $240,000. To measure the drawdown in relation to the equity, it might be a good idea to put together a so-called *underwater equity chart* like that in Figure 5.1, which shows that the maximum historical drawdown for this particular system is approximately 5 percent.

DRAWDOWN COMPARED TO THE MARKET

Comparing the drawdown to the equity leading into it only addresses a small part of the problem. Another important aspect to consider is the level at which the market traded at the time. It should come as no surprise by now that the higher the dollar value of the market, the wider its price swings will be, also measured in dollars.

In that case, a low drawdown, taking place when the market is at a high level, is preferred over a high drawdown with the market trading at a low level. However,

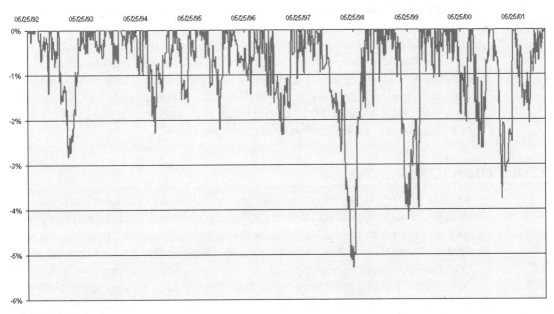

FIGURE 5.1

Underwater equity chart.

provided you go long or short the same number of shares throughout both trading sequences, a high drawdown still can be better than a low drawdown, if the market also is sufficiently higher in the case of the high drawdown compared to where it is during the low drawdown.

This is easier to understand if you isolate your drawdown to one single trade. For example, if a stock is priced at $60, and you buy 1,000 shares and lose $5 per share, you have lost a total of $5,000 (1,000 * 5), or 8.3 percent (60 * 1,000 / 5,000) of your investment. If, on the other hand, the stock is priced at 30, and you buy 1,000 shares and lose $3 per share, you have lost a total of $3,000 (1,000 * 3), or 10 percent (30 * 1,000 / 3,000) of your investment. Thus, even though the higher priced market (and its inherent larger price swings) forced you to invest and lose more dollars, the fewer dollars lost in the lower-priced market resulted in a relatively larger loss of equity.

Thus, if you apply a trading system that buys or sells a constant amount of shares on a trending market, the value of the losing (and winning) trades should be sufficiently lower in a low-priced market, compared to a high-priced market. That is, the wider the price swings, measured in dollars, the larger the drawdown, also measured in dollars, should be. If that is not the case, there is something wrong with the logic behind the system.

One such logical blunder people make all the time is to apply a fixed dollar–based stop that will have you stopped out after a trade has moved against you a specified amount. However, the effect of such a stop is that it will have you stopped out repeatedly on a high-priced market, but hardly ever on a low-priced market: It will be too tight for the high-priced market, but too wide for the low-priced market, in relation to the respective markets' normal price swings.

Furthermore, this system-design blunder can be very hard to detect via the drawdown because, in the case of the low-priced market, a larger than necessary drawdown can be a result of a few but larger than necessary losers, while in the case of the high-priced market, a larger than necessary drawdown can be a result of a large amount of unnecessarily small losers.

MEAN–MEDIAN COMPARISONS

Another oft-forgotten attribute of the maximum drawdown is how it relates to the average drawdown. Ask yourself the following questions, "Would I rather experience plenty of tiny drawdowns than a few really large ones?" I think most of us agree that we prefer even an infinite amount of smaller drawdowns to one large one.

However, when designing and examining a trading system, one large drawdown doesn't necessarily have to be that bad, as long as you understand what might have caused it and trust all the other aspects of the system. The trick is to get a feel for what created this drawdown and how it relates to all the other drawdowns created by the system.

Basically, there are two ways to get a better feel for the maximum drawdown. One is to calculate the average drawdown and the standard deviations of all drawdowns, and then see where the maximum drawdown fits within this spectrum. The further away from the average drawdown the standard deviation boundaries are located, the more dispersed the drawdowns and the less sure you can be about what to expect in the future. Remember also that all drawdowns will be represented by either a negative or a positive number (depending on how you measure them), with zero drawdown being a definitive boundary in either case. Thus, the distribution of the drawdowns won't take the familiar bell-shaped curve associated with a normal distribution. (What you really should do in this case is measure the value of all runs, both positive and negative, from equity lows to equity peaks, and vice versa.)

Another way to get a feel for the maximum drawdown is to compare it to both the average value and the median value of all drawdowns. For example, in the number series 2, 1, 14, 6, 12, the mean is equal to 7 [(2, 1, 14, 6, 12) / 5], whereas the median is represented by the number 6: 2, 1, 14, 6, 12 (sorted: 1, 2, 6, 12, 14). The higher the maximum drawdown is in relation to the median drawdown, the more of a freak occurrence the maximum drawdown has been, especially if the average drawdown is closer to the maximum drawdown than to the median drawdown. For the example above, the maximum value being 14, the average value is much closer to the median value, which indicates that a drawdown of 14 isn't as much of a freak occurrence as we would like it to be.

A bad situation occurs when the median drawdown is larger than the average drawdown. Then the smaller drawdowns are in minority, representing the freak occurrences, all the more so, the closer the average drawdown is to the smallest drawdown. To express this mathematically, divide the average drawdown, by the median drawdown. The higher this value is above one, the more freakish the large drawdowns behind the large average drawdown. Similarly, dividing the maximum drawdown by the average drawdown, gives an indication of how large the maximum drawdown is in relation to the average drawdown, with a value of two indicating that the maximum drawdown is twice as large as the average drawdown. An alternative is to divide half the maximum drawdown by the average drawdown, so that the 2:1 relationship will be represented by the value one.

Multiplying these formulas with each other gives us a combined value for how freakish the average drawdown is in relation to the median drawdown, and how freakish the maximum drawdown is in relation to the average drawdown:

$$DFI = (AD / MeD) * [(MaD / 2) / AD] = (MaD / 2) / MeD$$

Where:

DFI = Drawdown freak index
AD = Average drawdown

MeD = Median drawdown

MaD = Maximum drawdown

Note, however, that this analysis says nothing about whether any or all of the different drawdown values fall within tolerable limits in the first place. All this analysis does is help you decide if the relatively large or relatively small drawdowns are in minority and considered to be the least expected in the future.

Nonetheless, sometimes you could be better off trading a system with a very large maximum historical drawdown, as compared to a system with a seemingly more reasonable maximum drawdown, because you know that the very large historical drawdown was due to a freak occurrence that you expect won't happen again anytime soon, which is not the case with the seemingly more tolerable drawdown.

As should be clear by now, the largest drawdown, especially if it's measured in dollars, says very little about what you can expect from your system in the future. In fact, because the drawdown is a function of other system characteristics, rather than a core characteristic in itself, the best way to come to grips with it is to analyze and modify these characteristics, instead of trying to modify the drawdown directly.

More specifically, the drawdown is a function of the mathematical expectancy (i.e., the average profit per trade) and the percentage of profitable trades. Table 5.1 shows how it all ties together.

Using the information from Table 5.1 and the DFI, you can analyze the maximum drawdown for a system in relation to the core system characteristics before you set out to trade your way into any unpleasant surprises, or perhaps even start to trade a system that you otherwise would have discarded because of the high historical drawdown.

For example, if the system characteristics indicate that the system you're examining (whether the results are for real or back tested) has a high average prof-

TABLE 5.1

Mathematical Expectancy and Percent Profitable Trades

		Average profit per trade	
		Low	**High**
Percent profitable trades	**Low**	Many and steep made up of many trades Can take time to get out of	Many and shallow made up of many trades Usually needs only one or a few trades to get out of
	High	Few but explosive and deep Can take time to get out of	Few and shallow, with few trades Easy to get out of with one or a few trades

it per trade and a high number of profitable trades, but also a very high DFI, you can conclude that the maximum drawdown most likely was a freak occurrence that will not repeat itself in the near future. On the other hand, if both the average profit per trade and the number of profitable trades are low, and are also combined with a low DFI, you can conclude that no matter the actual size of the drawdowns experienced so far, you're lucky to still be in the game and should not trade this system for another day. Note also, that in the first example I use the words "most likely." This is because, no matter how rigorous your testing has been, there are no guarantees. As already stated, every drawdown will be surpassed at one time or another. All we can do is to make the likelihood of that happening tomorrow as small as possible.

TYPES OF DRAWDOWN

The drawdown should by no means be neglected completely, but in researching, you need to know what it is you are doing and what it is you are investigating. For one thing, the estimated largest drawdown holds valuable information about how large your account size must be and can give you an indication of whether you have the psychologic profile to trade the system in question. The several different types of drawdowns all need to be dealt with in a different manner. I have discussed these in detail in *Trading Systems That Work*, so I will only touch on this subject briefly here.

Aside from not putting the drawdown in relation to the market situation at the time, another major error most system designers make when they are building and evaluating systems is to look only at the overall *total equity drawdown* (TED), which is calculated using both the open trade profits and losses, and the already closed out equity on your account. However, to fully investigate the drawdown, we also need to divide the TED into several subcategories, namely the *start trade drawdown* (STD), the *end trade drawdown* (ETD), and the *closed trade drawdown* (CTD). To understand why, look at Figure 5.2 and follow along in the following example:

Let's say that you currently don't have any positions on and that your last trade was a $3,000 winner that also took your account to a new total equity high of $10,000. But before you managed to exit the position, it gave back $1,000 of its open equity, so that your equity currently stands at $9,000 (day 0 in Figure 5.2). According to most analysis packages, this means that, even though you managed to add $3,000 to your closed-out equity, you now are $1,000 in the hole when compared to your latest total equity high. Furthermore, if your next trade turns out to be a loser, that immediately stopped out with a $4,500 loss, your closed-out equity now is $4,500, and your drawdown is $5,500 (day 1). If you then have a $5,000 winner which, before it took off started out going the wrong way with an additional $1,000 loss (day 2)—at which point you would have been $6,500 in the

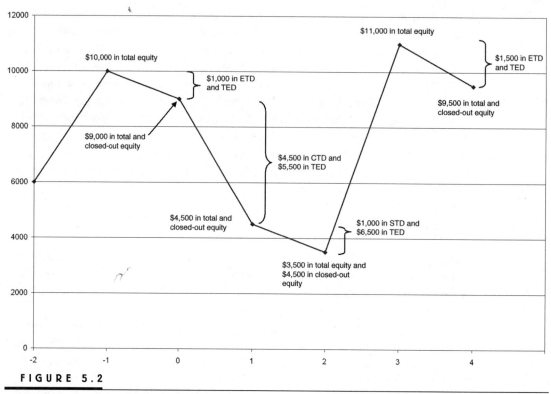

FIGURE 5.2

Total equity drawdown (TED) and subcategories.

hole—and then gave back $1,500 of the open profit, your total equity drawdown would now be $1,500 (day 4).

If you look closely at these numbers, they consist of three different types of drawdowns. At day 0, we are dealing with the ETD, that tells us how much of the open profit we had to give back before we were allowed to exit a specific trade. At day 1, we are looking at the CTD that measures the distance between the entry and exit points without taking into consideration what is going on within the trade. At day 2, we are dealing with the STD, that measures how much the trade went against us after the entry and before it started to go our way. And at day 4, we again have the ETD.

Of course, we would like to keep all these drawdown numbers as small as possible, but when only examining the overall drawdown number (the TED) and blindly trying to do something about it, there is no way of knowing what it is we're really doing and what is actually changing within the system when we're making any changes to the input parameters.

To be sure, in recent years a few system developers and market analysts have addressed this issue in various ways, but as far as I know, nobody has really nailed it down when it comes to how one must go about examining the markets and the systems in an appropriate and scientific fashion. One of these analysts is John Sweeney, who, in his two books *Campaign Trading* (Wiley Finance Editions, 1996) and *Maximum Adverse Excursion* (Wiley Trader's Advantage Series, 1997) came up with the concepts of *maximum adverse excursion* (MAE) and *maximum favorable excursion* (MFE). More recently, RINA systems has taken this further and developed a method to calculate the efficiency of a trade. I, too, have written several articles on closely related topics for both *Futures* magazine and *Active Trader* magazine.

Depending on what type of entry technique you use, many of your trades will experience an STD before they start going your way. This is especially true for short-term top and bottom picking systems, where you enter with a limit order. In this case, the only way to avoid an STD is to enter at the absolute low or absolute high—and how often will that happen?

Longer-term breakout systems also many times experience both an STD and an ETD when they enter and exit with a stop order on the highest high or lowest low over the lookback period. Usually, the entry level coincides with a pivotal resistance or support level in the market. After this level has been tested and you've entered the trade, the market usually makes yet another correction before the final penetration, and follow-through takes us away in a major trending move. At the exit, most long-term systems give back a substantial part of the open profit before the exit is triggered by a breakout in the opposite direction.

(To learn more about the different types of drawdowns and the maximum excursion analysis for stop placements, see *Trading Systems That Work*. We will talk more about stops and exits in Part 3 of this book, but will focus on techniques and analysis methods different from those in *Trading Systems That Work*.)

CHAPTER 6

Quality Data

All that we have talked about so far matters very little, however, if we don't have the right and appropriate data to work with. The truth of the matter is that several of the largest data suppliers have it all wrong. Look at Figure 6.1, which shows the closing price of Microsoft as it actually was reported back in 1986, Microsoft's first year as a listed company. Note how it wiggles and squiggles, with hardly any two adjacent closing prices being the same. (I downloaded this data myself from Microsoft's Web site.)

Now, look at Figures 6.2 and 6.3, which are taken from two different and very popular data providers. These charts show their respective versions of how the Microsoft stock moved during its first year traded. The charts differ from the one in Figure 6.1 because of the added high and low prices, but two important things must be noted here: First, because the Microsoft stock has been split several times, the price of the stock in these charts is much lower. This is all fine and well and can be dealt with, using proper system testing and design.

More alarming, however, is the fact that most of the wiggles and squiggles are gone: Instead, the closing price seems to jump between a few very distinct price levels. For each split, these data vendors also adjusted the new and lower split-adjusted price to match the nearest tradable fraction. For example, if the historical stock price came out to $4.76, it was adjusted down to $4.75, because $4.76 was not a tradable price. Over time and many stock splits, this smoothed out the data. Note also that even these charts differ—one of the data providers hasn't even done the smoothing correctly. Figure 6.4 shows the data from yet another data provider. Although this is not as bad as the other two, it still doesn't look perfect.

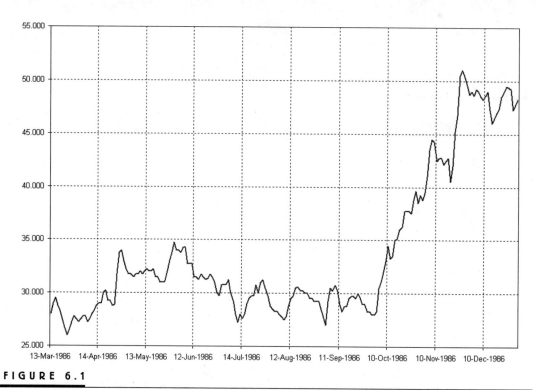

FIGURE 6.1

Microsoft trading data—1986. Actual performance.

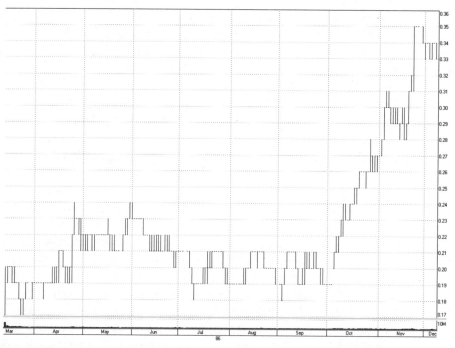

FIGURE 6.2

Microsoft trading data—1986. Version 1.

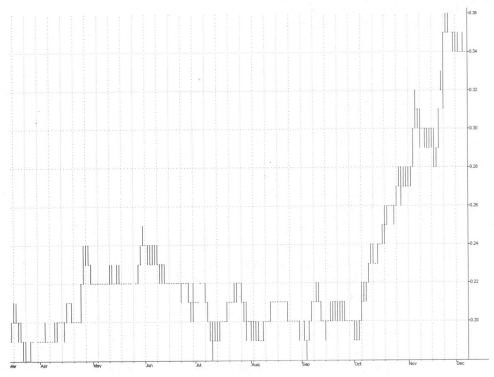

FIGURE 6.3

Microsoft trading data—1986. Version 2.

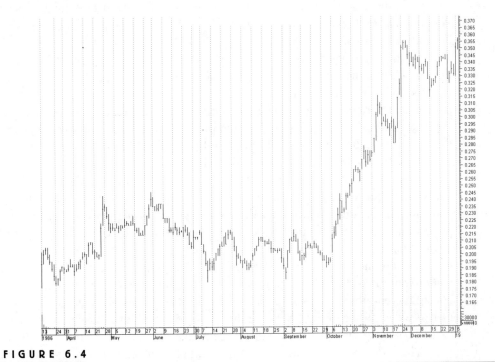

FIGURE 6.4

Microsoft trading data—1986. Version 3.

Obviously, the data providers behind the data in Figures 6.2 and 6.3 thought that they were doing me a favor by not letting me believe that Microsoft traded at the impossible price of $4.76, so that I wouldn't go and build myself a strategy that tried to trade Microsoft at that price. Therefore, in an effort to make things as realistic as possible, they adjusted the price to the closest tradable fraction. But this is all wrong and backwards thinking. Because no matter at what level Microsoft actually traded several years back, or no matter what the true split-adjusted price is (or the split-adjusted price that these data providers provide me with), I can't turn back time and go trade Microsoft at any of these prices anyway. What interests me is to see if I can come up with a way to catch the wiggles that the Microsoft stock created at that time and that it continues to produce today.

All I am interested in, as an analyst, is examining if my system in fact manages to catch the wiggles and squiggles as they actually took place. For this, it doesn't matter what the actual price of the stock is pre- and post-splits. What is important is that the relationship between price points stays the same. Clearly, they do not in Figures 6.2 and 6.3. Therefore, these data are useless for historical testing.

We are not interested in "realistic" back testing in dollar terms, because we can't trade at those dollar values anyway, no matter how much we want to, because they represent foregone opportunities. The best we can do is use data in such a way so that we make our back-tested results as robust and forward-looking as possible. And the way to do that, as we already know, is to work with percentage moves and normalized results.

With percentage moves, the distance between point A and point B relates to point A exactly the same, no matter the price of point A. Look at the two charts of Microsoft, by Microsoft (Figures 6.1 and 6.5). They are identical, except for the difference in price. The price differences are because of stock splits, but no matter the price before and after the split, each price level relates to all the other levels the same way in both charts. Thus, in the split-adjusted chart, the price might seem to have been low, but it behaves as it did when it was higher.

That last sentence is very important to understand completely and fully, because in Part 3, we talk about the various methods for placing stops and exits. For now, let's just mention briefly that many system builders think that the lower-priced the stock, one should work with wider stops, relative to the entry price. They believe that lower-priced stocks are more volatile than higher-priced stocks, and therefore they need a little extra leeway. There might be something to that reasoning, but for system testing purposes, it is no good, because, as we have just discovered, even though a stock seems to be priced as low as 20 cents, it still can act as if it were trading at $80, because this was the actual level at which the trading took place in the first place, with the 20-cent level implemented long after the fact.

Therefore, no matter the price of the market, each stop must relate to its entry price exactly the same way as all the other stops, no matter which entry price each

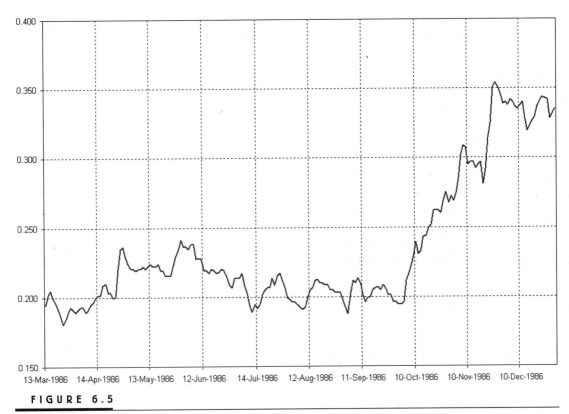

FIGURE 6.5

Microsoft trading data—1986. Microsoft's performance data.

stop relates to. And the only way to achieve that is to work with percentage-based (normalized) calculations.

A SCARY FUTURES-MARKET EXAMPLE

If you are a commodity futures trader, one of the main obstacles when testing trading strategies on historical data is the limited life span of a futures contract. To overcome this, various methods on how to splice several contracts together to form a longer time series have been invented. This is especially important when it comes to making your system reports as forward-looking as possible, and if you would like to use the percentage-based calculations described earlier.

Basically, three different methods can be used to splice contracts together: the *nonadjustment method*, the *back-adjustment method*, and the *perpetual adjustment method*. The back-adjustment method can further be subdivided into *point-based adjusted* and *ratio adjusted*. (All these methods are described in greater detail in *Trading Systems That Work*.)

Using the nonadjustment method, you simply stop charting one contract when it expires, or when you otherwise deem it justifiable to do so, and continue to chart the next contract in line. This contract is the new front contract. Usually, this coincides with when the market as a whole moves from one contract to the next, resulting in an increase in the open interest for the new front contract surpassing the open interest for the old contract.

The main advantage with the nonadjusted time series is that it shows you exactly how the front contract was traded at that particular time, with all trading levels and price relationships intact and exactly as they once appeared in real life. Figure 6.6 illustrates what this looked like for the December contract on the S&P 500 index during the crash of 1987. From a high of 333 on October 2, the market fell a total of 152 points, or $38,000 (152 * 250), to a low of 181 on October 20. In percentage terms, this equals a drop of 45.6 percent (152 / 333) of the total market value.

The main disadvantage of the nonadjustment method is the differences in price that frequently appear on the day for the roll; these distort your back-testing

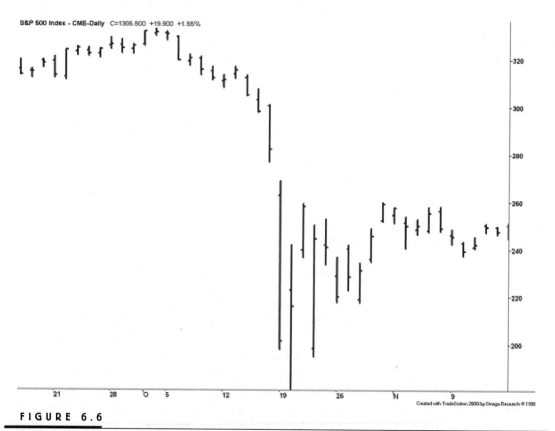

FIGURE 6.6

S&P 500 December contracts—crash of 1987.

results. Therefore, nonadjusted data are best for day traders with very short trading horizons, who more often than not close out all their trades at the end of the day. To overcome the distortions on the historical system's testing results induced by the nonadjustment method, the point-based back-adjusted contract was invented.

If the new front contract is trading at a premium compared to the old contract, the entire historical time series leading up to the roll will be adjusted upward with that distance. A similar but opposite adjustment takes place each time the new contract is trading at a discount. Figure 6.7 shows what the October 1987 market action looks like using a point-based back-adjusted contract, with the latest roll made in September 1999. In this chart, the high on October 2 is at 567.35, and the low on October 20 is at 415.35, for a total difference of 152 points. However, because of the transition upward, the original percentage difference of 45.6 percent now has decreased to 26.8 percent (152 / 567.35). For each roll, all these values continue to change slightly, presumably upward, resulting in an ever-decreasing percentage difference.

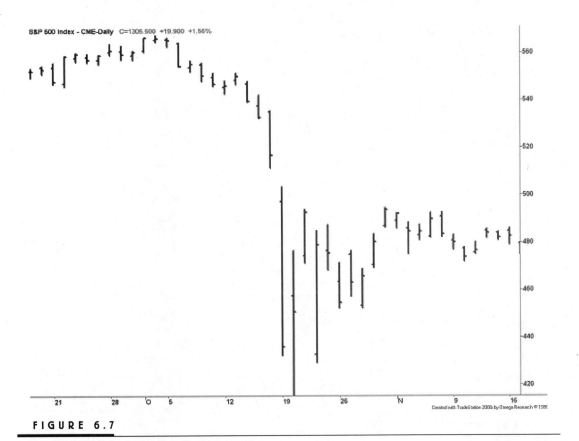

FIGURE 6.7

October 1987 using point-based back-adjusted contracts.

   This continuing decrease (increase) of the relative importance of historical moves in an up trend (down trend) and markets that are traded at a premium (discount) is the main disadvantage of the point-based back-adjusted contract. For instance, if the 26.8 percent drop—as implied by the back-adjusted contract—were to be used to calculate the dollar value of the drop from the actual top of 333, we would come up with $22,311 (0.268 * 333 * 250) instead of $38,000 (0.456 * 333 * 250). Therefore, to keep the relative importance of all historical moves constant, these moves must be viewed in percentage terms.

   In an article for *Futures* magazine ("Data pros and cons," *Futures*, June 1998) and later in a second article ("Truth be told," *Futures*, January 1999), I suggested that a better way to adjust a spliced-together time series would be to use ratio adjustments rather than points or dollars. In doing so, this new time series will also vary in levels when compared to where the true contract was traded, but instead of keeping the point- or dollar-based relationship between two points in time intact, the percentage relationship will stay the same.

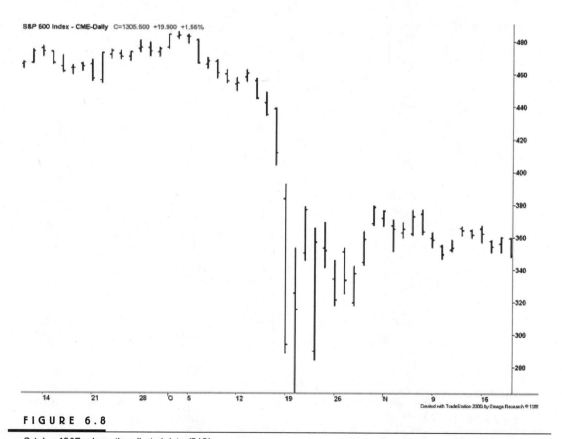

FIGURE 6.8

October 1987 using ratio adjusted data (RAD).

Figure 6.8 shows what the October 1987 crash looks like through the perspective of the ratio adjusted data (RAD) contract, with the latest roll made in September 1999. This time, the high of October 2 is at 486, and the low of October 20 is at 264.15, for a point difference of 221.85 points, but with a percentage difference once again equal to 45.6 percent [(486 − 264.15) * 100 / 486]. This increase in magnitude measured in points is due to the upward transition because of the many rolls. The important thing is, however, that the percentage-based move stays intact at 45.6 percent.

To get a better feel for the benefits of the RAD contract, let's compare it to the drop during the fall of 1998, which became the new dollar-based record drop. During October 1987, the market fell 152 points, or $38,000, or 45.6 percent—this we know. During the fall of 1998, the market fell from a July high of 1199.4 to an October low of 929, for a total drop of 270.4 points (as measured on the nonadjusted contract). In dollar terms, this equaled a drop of $67,600 (270.4 * 250). That is, almost twice as much as the October 1987 drop. In percentage terms, however, the drop of 98 only equaled 22.5 percent of total market value. That is, the drop in 1998 was not even half as bad as the crash of 1987. In fact, to equal the crash of 1987 in relative terms, the 1998 drop would have had to continue all the way down to the 652.5 level, for a total drop of 546.9 points, or $136,725.

Thus, the crash of 1987 is still the largest relative drop in equity in modern times (aside from the latest bear market in NASDAQ). And, if you, in your system building and analysis work, would like to treat it as such to make your systems more robust and give them a better chance to hold up in the future, the only way to do that is to use the RAD contract in combination with the percentage-based performance measurements described earlier.

Another major advantage of the RAD contract is that it can never go negative, which can happen with the point-based contract. The major disadvantage of the RAD contract is that it's not supported by any major analysis software packages, although it is supported by a couple of data providers, such as CSI data (www.csidata.com) and Genesis data (www.gfds.com). To calculate the values for the RAD contract yourself, using the nonadjusted contracts as a base, you can use the following formula:

$$NPOC = OPOC * [(PNC - OPOC) / PNC + 1]$$

Where:

NPOC = New price of old contract

OPOC = Old price of old contract

PNC = Price of new contract

UNDERSTANDING PROFITABILITY

In this first part of the book, we have learned that, to build good and profitable trading systems, there are a lot of things to think about. One thing we need to understand is the huge difference between a good trading system and a profitable one. Any good trading system can be made into a profitable trading system when traded on the right market or portfolio of markets, or together with other good trading systems. The paradox is, however, that not all profitable trading systems have to be good systems. Most systems will and can be profitable at one time or another and just because a system is profitable here and now doesn't mean that it is a good system.

To understand this, we must understand the difference between the terms "good" and "profitable" when it comes to system testing and design. A good system is a system that works, on average, equally as well on several different markets. It isn't always profitable on all of them, but being so on average over time ensures it is robust and will generate a steady profit over time, when applied to the right markets. Some markets should not be traded with certain types of systems: The moves the system aims to catch aren't profitable enough to make trading worthwhile on that particular market. A good system that is worthwhile trading on a market to generate a profit from that market also is a profitable system on that very market.

To build a good system, we must make sure that the system catches the types of moves it is intended to catch, no matter where and when those moves took place, in relation both to time and the current price of the market. To do that, we must normalize the system's results in such a way that all back-tested trades get an equal weighting. This can either be done by always trading one contract only and measuring the results in percentage terms, or by always trading a fixed dollar amount so that the number of shares will vary with the market price (higher price, fewer shares, and vice versa). Only by doing this will a profitable trade in a low-priced market influence the final parameter setting to the same degree as a profitable trade in a high-priced market.

Also, during this initial research, we should not consider the cost of trading, such as slippage and commissions. We're only interested in finding out if the system is efficient enough to catch the types of moves on the chart that we want it to catch. The efficiency is measured in the average profit per trade, which should be high enough to warrant trading with the costs of trading taken into account. Taking the costs of trading into account at this initial stage of the testing procedure will only favor more long-term systems, using few trades that seem to be particularly profitable on high-priced markets.

However, to do our research correctly, we also must be careful about the data we use. Many data providers have rounded the data to the nearest tradable fraction of price after a stock has made a split. After several splits, this error compounds over time, resulting in a data series that is far from being representative of the way the stock actually traded at the time, before the splits took place.

The efficiency of a system is mainly measured via the average profit per trade in normalized terms. It is better to look at the average profit per trade, rather than the final net profit, because it is the final net profit that is a function of the outcomes of the many trades, instead of the other way around. The average profit per trade is also called the mathematical expectancy of the system. From this, it follows that for a system to be profitable, the mathematical expectancy must be positive.

However, because the outcome of any individual trade most likely will not be the same as for the average trade, it also is important to know how much all trades are likely to deviate from the average trade. This measure is called the standard deviation and is a measure of the risk involved in trading the system. The higher the standard deviation, the less sure we can be of the outcome of any individual trade, and the riskier the system. Dividing the average profit per trade by the standard deviation of all trades gives us the risk-adjusted return. The higher the risk-adjusted return, the higher the average profit in relation to the risk of trading the system.

It also is good to know the normalized values of a system's average winner and loser. In the best of worlds, the losers only have one size—that of the stop loss—which makes the average loser equal to the largest loser. Knowing this, we can calculate a system's true risk–reward relationship and experiment with different types of profit-taking techniques, such as profit targets and trailing stops, to create a trade profile that suits our needs.

Managing your trades this way also means that most trades should fall within a few very distinct categories, the two most obvious being the maximum winner and the maximum loser. The distribution of your trades should not follow the regular normal distribution, which implies that the outcomes are random. The monthly results, however, could follow a normal distribution around a positive mean.

Knowing the size of the average winners and losers also makes it possible to calculate a realistic number of trades to get out of a drawdown. Adding the average time spent in a trade to this equation also makes it possible to calculate a realistic time horizon for the same dilemma.

Talking about drawdown, it is a sad but true fact that your worst drawdown is always still to come. No matter how severe your worst historical drawdown is today, if you only stay in the game long enough, another drawdown will occur that will surpass it, both in time and in magnitude. From this, it also follows that if you only stay in the game long enough, you will encounter a drawdown that will be deep or long enough to take you out of the game completely.

The only thing we can do about this is to make the likelihood for these drawdowns as small as possible, so that, statistically speaking, it shouldn't happen anytime within, say, the next 1,000 years or so. But even so, and no matter the precautions, for some it can and will happen tomorrow, simply because of bad luck.

To come to grips with drawdowns, we need to put them in relation to both the equity peaks preceding them and the value of the market at the approximate time of the drawdown.

But even more important, we need to understand that the drawdown is not a main system characteristic, but rather a function of the average profit per trade and the percentage of profitable trades. By focusing on these numbers and making them as high and as robust as possible, we're also minimizing the risk for any devastating drawdowns. It is, therefore, important to get a feel for the number of winning and losing trades in a row that a system is likely to encounter and how likely it is for a similar sequence of trades to happen again.

However, boosting these and other performance measures to sky-high levels isn't necessarily a good thing either. Instead, we need to work with numbers that are reasonable, when compared to other investment or trading opportunities and the way the market actually behaves. For example, a system with a profit factor of two and 50 percent profitable trades also has a return of 50 percent on the total capital risked, whereas a system with a profit factor of 1.5 and 33 percent profitable trades has a return of 33 percent on the total capital risked. For two systems to produce results like this, they need to have initial risk–reward relationships, going into their trades, of 2:1 and 3.5:1, respectively.

If we compare these return numbers with other investment opportunities and the way the market behaves, we realize that this is as good as it will get, and that looking for systems with higher profit factors results in impossible initial risk–reward relationships. If the initial risk–reward relationships aren't sustainable in the long run, the future performance of the system will plummet. This might result in a system that still produces a decent profit factor, but has other system characteristics making it untradable, such as an unreasonably high percentage of losers and a high standard deviation to the outcome of the trades.

Tying all the above together and making an analogy with the animal kingdom, it probably is fair to say that most of us would like to trade a system behaving like a cheetah—a mean, lean, killing machine. However, because the cheetah is too dependent on its environment for its survival, trading a system that behaves like a cheetah is not a good idea, because even small changes in its environment will lead to its extinction. Instead, a trading system should behave like a cockroach that can live and eat almost without concern for the rest of the world.

In trading system terms, the system should function equally as well on average over as many markets as possible, grinding out small profits wherever possible and staying afloat during tougher times. Granted, there is little sex appeal to such a system. But it isn't your trading that should be sexy, but rather the lifestyle you can afford because of it.

PART TWO

Trading System Development

In my opinion, coming up with a smart system idea to trade the markets is a little like composing a new piece of music. To the untrained ear, it seems as if there are only so many notes, tones, and octaves to go around, so that all their possible combinations should be exhausted by now. Similarly, to the untrained eye, there seem only so many different short-term bar combinations on a chart and indicators to combine them with. But even so, a lot of people are coming up with new music all the time, just as a few market technicians have the ability to come up with new short-term trading patterns.

Although most of the patterns and systems in this part are of my own creation, the ideas behind them are not. In my former positions as a writer for *Active Trader* magazine, and before that *Futures* magazine, I often found myself in a situation where I had tons of good ideas presented to me, ready to run, with very little or no additional effort on my part. Many of the systems here are the fruits of such ideas.

One of those who seems to come up with one great idea after another is Michael Harris, who, in a couple of articles for *Active Trader* magazine, presented the Harris 3L-R pattern variation, featured in Chapter 14. Another never-ending source for inspiration is Tom DeMark, who gave me the idea for the expert exit system, featured in Chapter 15. The system presented there isn't Tom's, but the idea for it came to me after having read his material and discussed a few concepts with him.

Yet another great source for inspiration is my friend Mark Etzkorn, the editor-in-chief of *Active Trader* magazine. Mark is a swing-trading guy who came up with the concepts and ideas behind the hybrid system in Chapter 8. And behind Mark lurks Linda Bradford-Raschke, who most certainly has proved herself, both as a great developer of swing-trading strategies and good friend and inspirational source for both of us.

For the relative-strength type systems, no inspirational source is greater than Nelson Freeburg. Nelson's systems usually follow a more long-term investor-like philosophy, which makes it more natural for him to think in terms of the rotation of assets based on relative strength and momentum.

Finally, no cooler trader exists than Dan Gramza. Without my discussions with Dan, I would not have been able to develop my own philosophies surrounding where, how, and when to look for an exit, no matter which system I'm working on. This is especially true when it comes to the time-based stops for trades that go nowhere. Dan knows how to not get married to his trades.

All systems presented in this book can be divided into four different system categories, with a few of the systems belonging to several of these categories. In the retracement and swing trading category, I count hybrid system No. 1, meander system V. 1.0, the volume-weighted average system, the expert exits system, and the Harris 3L-R pattern variation system.

Of these systems, the *meander system* is the only one using limit orders for the entry. In fact, it's one of the few systems I have ever seen that produces consistent results using limit orders. This system is based on my favorite indicator, which I developed during my time with *Futures* magazine and while writing my first book, *Trading Systems That Work*. I like that meander is both scientifically correct and at the same time well suited for short-term trading. The logic and reasoning behind meander is not based on any homemade technical analysis mumbo jumbo. Because I like this indicator so much, I also have tinkered around with it quite a bit. Therefore, the code presented here is not the code presented with the system in *Active Trader* magazine. The function and the logic are the very same, but this version runs much smoother and faster, and also holds the possibility for altering the lookback period for the calculations, which the first version did not. This is one of the best limit-order systems I've ever seen.

Another system that had a very scientific approach to its development is the *expert exits* system. This system is interesting because I developed the exit rules using the same type of surface charts I discuss in greater detail in Part 3. Using this technique, there is no way you can optimize the system to any specific market, type of market, or market condition. Instead, you're bound to end up with a system that will work, on average, equally as well over all types of markets and market conditions. Whether it is profitable enough for you to trade is a different story, but no other system will beat a system developed in this way when it comes to robustness and stability.

Another cool concept among these systems is the *volume-weighted average* system, which basically first calculates a stochastic indicator for the volume, multiplies that stochastic value by today's price, and adds it to a running total, very much in the same way as a regular exponential moving average is constructed.

The *volume-weighted average* system also belongs to the volume-related systems, together with *RS system No. 1*, which really doesn't care that much about the price of the market that is about to get traded, other than how the momentum of the price compares to a comparable index. This system also is a so-called *relative-strength system* and also belongs to that group of systems, together with the *relative-strength bands system* and the *rotation system*; as such, it stands out among these three systems as the only one where the market to be traded is compared to an index (which otherwise is the most common way to do it) instead of a group of other markets, as the other two systems do.

The relative-strength bands and rotation systems are a little different from most relative-strength systems in that they compare the stock in question with several other stocks, rather than a comparable index. For this book, I picked all stocks completely at random, but for your own research, I suggest you group them according to sectors and industry groups. It also is possible to trade various indexes against each other and thereby set up market-neutral positions, or positions that are more or less biased according to your current beliefs about the market. In this part of the book, I look at all the relative-strength systems individually, but in Parts 3 and 4 we primarily use them as filters together with the other systems.

For the relative-strength bands system, an error appeared in the original text in *Active Trader* magazine. Instead of computing the Bollinger bands for the RSL lines, as originally stated, the bands should be computed on the product of all RSV lines (PRSV). The original code did it correctly, but the original system logic explained it incorrectly.

Among the breakout systems, the *hybrid system No. 1* seems to have withstood the test of time very well. This was one of the first systems featured in *Active Trader* magazine. When I put it together, no one knew how severe the subsequent bear market would be and, being busy with other things, I did not look at it again until it was time to write this book.

By the way, none of these systems is picked because of their extraordinary profits or anything like that, but rather only because they represent different concepts and learning experiences. As a matter of fact, as I re-do the research, it's apparent that most of them have not coped all that well with the most recent bear market. As such, they also represent additional challenges for getting back in shape (more about this in a little while).

One of the systems that I had to tweak most was the *Harris 3L-R pattern variation*; although not because it hadn't held up over time. Rather, the original logic for the system called for a profit target too far away from the entry price, which made it too long-term in nature. This, however, had nothing to do with the original and clever entry idea by Michael Harris.

Over the next several pages, I indulge in a lot of tweaking and modifications to the original systems, which some of you might call curve fitting after the fact. I do not call it that, however, and my arguments for that are several. First, I am not optimizing the systems, but rather trying to find the most robust solution that should work on average equally as well on as many markets as possible, without really taking the actual profitability into question until the very last moment. Second, the little "optimizing" I do (if you still call it that), is very coarse and based more on my own reasoning and understanding of the systems' underlying logic than on actually stepping through each and every input combination. Finally, the systems are tested on as many as 65 different markets, and I don't care which markets the systems are profitable on or not, or on which markets the systems will be traded in the future.

There are ways to decide that as well, among which one major way is to study the correlation between all systems and markets and the portfolio as a whole. We will talk more about this in Part 4, so for now I will only say that sometimes it is a good thing to trade a losing market. More specifically, when the losing market still behaves in a way that it performs well when the portfolio as a whole performs badly, it will decrease the risk for the overall portfolio and sometimes even add positively to the bottom line. In this case, the risk is measured in standard deviations away from the average equity growth, both for the portfolio as a whole and for the individual market.

In all the research done in this part of the book, I have not deducted any money for commissions. As already discussed in Part 1, the most important thing for now is to see how well the improved or altered systems capture the moves they are intended to catch, no matter the values of the moves in dollars. Our focus is to make sure that the average profit per trade is large enough to make trading worthwhile, knowing that the commissions need to be considered at a later stage. We will, however, deal with this in more detail in Part 4, so in the end, all results will be burdened with the cost of trading.

Another parameter that will be of importance during this stage of the testing is the time spent in the market. The more time each individual stock spends in a trade, either the fewer stocks we can be in simultaneously or the smaller each position has to be. But the fewer the shares in each position, the greater the risk per share must be for the entire position to reach the desired risk level as a specified percentage of the overall equity. Consequently, if the risk per share is too large, it won't make sense for a short-term trading strategy. Therefore, the trade length and the amount of time spent in a trade need to be in proportion to the amount risked per share. We have already touched on this subject in Chapter 1 and will work with it extensively again throughout Parts 3 and 4.

Before we move on, I would like to point out that the TradeStation code following each system modification is the code for the modified version of the system that I decided to take with me to Parts 3 and 4.

CHAPTER 7

TradeStation Coding

As most of you who have followed my work over the years know, I prefer to work with TradeStation. Currently, I use the 2000i version, which is the second to last version of the program. I prefer TradeStation because, although the program certainly has its fair share of idiosyncrasies and annoying "features," it is the only off-the-shelf analysis platform I know of that allows you to, at least partially, work around these shortcomings by adding your own code.

For example, no program allows me to do the type of portfolio-based money management I would like to do. Therefore, I need to do all my portfolio management and analysis in Excel or with the help of Visual Basic, and TradeStation is the only program I know of that allows me to export the data I need into a text file for further analysis the way I like to do it.

I know of a few new programs out there that have started to allow portfolio testing and analysis, but so far, I haven't found one that completely satisfies my needs or allows me to develop my techniques further. There might be such a program available, but I only have 24 hours to spend per day, and I simply haven't had the time to shop around, much less figure out how it works. Therefore, we're stuck with TradeStation this time around as well.

I almost feel the need to apologize for that, but on the other hand, TradeStation's EasyLanguage code isn't all that hard to understand if you give it a serious effort. More often than not the code is in plain English, with the addition of a set of regular mathematical expressions and signs. I truly believe you're doing yourself a great favor if you try to decipher the code, whether you're a TradeStation user or not. Once you get used to it (which shouldn't take long), I'm sure you will find that many times it's even easier to understand how a system works by looking through the code instead of reading through the spelled-out logic and rules.

To assure robustness and reliable results, with only a couple of exceptions, I did all the research on 63 different markets. The entire testing portfolio consists of the 30 stocks making up the Dow Jones Industrial Average, the 30 highest capitalized stocks on the NASDAQ 100 index, and five major market indexes. Because Intel and Microsoft belong to both the Dow and the NASDAQ groups, they have been used twice, for a total of 65 test runs per system (see below).

Because of the latest bear market, many of the NASDAQ stocks might no longer belong to the group of the highest capitalized stocks. But this was the group I started out with, this is the group I will continue to use. The two systems that haven't been tested on the complete portfolio are the relative-strength bands and rotation systems, which have been tested on 25 markets each.

The 30 Dow stocks are: Alcoa (AA), American Express (AXP), Boeing (BA), Citigroup (C), Caterpillar (CAT), Dupont (DD), Disney (DIS), Eastman Kodak (EK), General Electric (GE), General Motors (GM), Home Depot (HD), Honeywell (HON), Hewlett-Packard (HWP), IBM (IBM), Intel (INTC), International Paper (IP), Johnson & Johnson (JNJ), JP Morgan (JP), Coca-Cola (KO), McDonalds (MCD), 3M (MMM), Philip Morris (MO), Merck (MRK), Microsoft (MSFT), Procter & Gamble (PG), SBC Communications (SBC), AT&T (T), United Technologies (UTX), Wal-Mart Stores (WMT), and Exxon Mobil (XOM).

The 30 NASDAQ stocks are: Altera (ALTR), Applied Material (AMAT), Amgen (AMGN), Bed, Bath & Beyond (BBBY), Concord Computing (CEFT), Chiron (CHIR), Comcast (CMCSK), Cisco Systems (CSCO), Dell (DELL), eBay (EBAY), Flextronics (FLEX), Genzyme (GENZ), Gemstar (GMST), Immunex (IMNX), Intel (INTC), JDS Uniphase (JDSU), K L A Tencor (KLAC), Linear Technologies (LLTC), Microsoft (MSFT), Maxim Integrated (MXIM), Nextel Communications (NXTL), Oracle Systems (ORCL), Paychex (PAYX), People Soft (PSFT), Qualcomm (QCOM), Siebel Systems (SEBL), Sun Microsystems (SUNW), Veritas Software (VRTS), WorldCom (WCOM), and Xilinx (XLNX).

The five stock indexes are the S&P 500, S&P 400 Midcap, NASDAQ 100, Dow Jones Industrial Average, and Russell 2000.

I used no futures markets for this research, for two reasons. First, up to this point I have only worked with stocks when building the systems for *Active Trader* magazine. Second, when I wrote *Trading Systems That Work*, I worked exclusively with futures contracts, which made the book a little hard to grasp at times for those who only trade stocks. However, most, if not all, of these ideas should be applicable on all types of markets, so if you're a futures trader, you should have little problem transferring these ideas to the futures markets of your interest. Whether the system will be profitable on any particular market is, however, a completely different story. As already mentioned, I don't care so much if the system is profitable on all markets tested as long as it works, on average, well on a majority of them.

Note that because Intel and Microsoft belong to both the NASDAQ and Dow groups they have been used twice throughout the research, which means that the results from these markets carry twice the weight compared to all other markets when it comes to the final influence of the system variables. Of course, it would have been a little better had I substituted for both these stocks other stocks in the NASDAQ group, but because I am using so many stocks and indexes in the first place, it doesn't matter that much.

For example, with 65 markets, each market influences the end result by 1.54 percent (100 / 65), which means that Intel and Microsoft influence the end result by 3.08 percent each, or 6.16 percent in total. In turn, this is only one-sixteenth of the total weight. It turned out this way simply because this was the way my workgroups were set up for testing my systems in *Active Trader* magazine, where I only test one group at a time.

It doesn't take a rocket scientist to recognize that there are significant differences in the characteristics for the stocks of the Dow Jones Industrial Average compared to the stocks of the NASDAQ 100 index. For one thing, for each system lab, I also show the latest development for the major market indexes as a comparison to the system's results. For one of the latest systems I did (September 2002 issue, using data through April 2002), the Dow had increased by 206 percent since September 1992, but was currently in a 31.5 percent drawdown that had lasted for 28 months. The same numbers for the NASDAQ 100 were a 302 percent increase and a 77.5 percent drawdown that had lasted for 25 months.

We really don't need to know why there are such differences in the behavior between the different stocks making up the indexes. It doesn't take much, however, to understand that the calmer behavior of the Dow is because it's made up of older, larger, old-economy companies that are not as sensitive to the psychologic twists and turns of the general market as are the younger, new-technology, and high interest rate–sensitive companies of the NASDAQ 100. Be that as it may, all we need to acknowledge is that differences are present and we should come up with a system that works, on average, equally as well on all markets.

As the systems were featured in *Active Trader* magazine, they included the results from using dynamic ratio money management (DRMM), which basically means that all markets will benefit from the results from all other markets, resulting in a faster equity growth, a smoother equity curve, and more often than not, lower drawdowns. The new results from the initial research do not depend on DRMM. Instead, they include only the normalized results from investing $100,000 per trade.

Looking at the buy-and-hold performance numbers for the Dow and NASDAQ 100, we can calculate the average annual return for the two indexes to 7.5 percent per year $[((206 / 100)^{\wedge}(1/10) - 1) * 100]$ and 11.7 percent per year $[((302$

/100)^(1/10) − 1) * 100], respectively. Now, knowing that both markets currently are in rather severe drawdowns, we understand that the good years normally are much better than that, but this is what we can expect the long-term growth of a well-diversified buy-and-hold type portfolio to be, given the last 10 years of market data.

As systems traders, naturally we would like to beat that. But beating the actual return numbers isn't the only thing we like to do. We also would like to do it while spending less time in the market, avoiding any 77 percent drawdowns and generally increasing our wealth at a calmer and steadier pace than the buy-and-hold strategy. That is, we would like to keep the volatility down to a minimum, given our desired return on the capital. But sometimes we also need to go the other way around, and lower our expectations regarding the final return in favor of the steady but slower equity growth. All this will make sense in Part 4. But to get there, we first need to come up with a set of systems that work, on average, well on as many types of markets as possible.

EXPORT CODE

```
{1}{Individual market export, with Normalize(True). Set ExportSwitch(True).}
Variable: ExportSwitch(True);
If ExportSwitch = True Then Begin
    Variables:
    StartPeriod(0), EndPeriod(0), PeriodLength(0), TradeType(""),
    NameLength(0), FileString(""), TestString(""), NoTrades(0),
    SetExportArray(0), TradeCounter(0), SumProfit(0), MaxProfit(0),
    DrawDown(0), MaxDrawDown(0), DDPercent(0), MaxDDPercent(0),
    WinningTrades(0), SumTrLen(0), ExportArrayPos(0), PercentInTrade(0),
    AverageProfit(0), AverageTrLen(0), SumSquareProfit(0),
    StDevProfit(0), RiskRatio(0), PercentWinners(0), ProfitFactor(0),
    LosingTrades(0), RiskFactor(0);
{2} Arrays:
    TradeProfit[1000](0), TradeLength[1000](0);
{3} If BarNumber = 1 Then Begin
        StartPeriod = DateToJulian(Date);
        If AllowLong = True Then
            TradeType = "Long";
        If AllowShort = True Then
            TradeType = "Short";
        If AllowLong = True and AllowShort = True Then
            TradeType = "Both";
```

```
            NameLength = StrLen(GetStrategyName) - 6;
            FileString = "D:\BookFiles\InitTest-" +
            RightStr(GetStrategyName, NameLength) + "-" +
            RightStr(NumToStr(CurrentDate, 0), 4) + ".csv";
            TestString = "Market" + "," + "Direction" + "," + "Trades" + "," +
            "PercWin" + "," + "NetProfit" + "," + "AvgProfit" + "," +
            "StDevProfit" + "," + "RiskRatio" + "," + "ProfitFactor" + "," +
            "RiskFactor" + "," + "MaxDD" + "," + "PercDD" + "," +
            "PercTime" + "," + "AvgLength" + NewLine;
            FileAppend(FileString, TestString);
        End;
{4}  NoTrades = TotalTrades;
     If NoTrades > NoTrades[1] Then Begin
         TradeProfit[SetExportArray] = PositionProfit(1);
     TradeLength[SetExportArray] = DateToJulian(ExitDate(1)) -
     DateToJulian(EntryDate(1)) + 1;
     SetExportArray = SetExportArray + 1;
     End;
{5}  If LastBarOnChart Then Begin
     {Alt: If LastCalcDate = Date + 1 Then Begin}
         EndPeriod = DateToJulian(Date);
         PeriodLength = EndPeriod - StartPeriod;
         For ExportArrayPos = 0 To (NoTrades - 1) Begin
             SumProfit = SumProfit + TradeProfit[ExportArrayPos];
             If SumProfit > MaxProfit Then
                 MaxProfit = SumProfit;
             DrawDown = MaxProfit - SumProfit;
             If MaxProfit > 0 Then
                 DDPercent = DrawDown * 100 / (100000 + MaxProfit)
             Else
                 DDPercent = DrawDown * 100 / 100000;
             If DrawDown > MaxDrawDown Then
                 MaxDrawDown = DrawDown;
             If DDPercent > MaxDDPercent Then
                 MaxDDPercent = DDPercent;
             If TradeProfit[ExportArrayPos] > 0 Then
                 WinningTrades = WinningTrades + 1;
```

    SumTrLen = SumTrLen + TradeLength[ExportArrayPos];

  End;

{6} If PeriodLength <> 0 Then

   PercentInTrade = SumTrLen * 100 / PeriodLength

  Else

   PercentInTrade = 0;

  If NoTrades <> 0 Then Begin

   AverageProfit = SumProfit / NoTrades;

   AverageTrLen = SumTrLen / NoTrades;

   PercentWinners = WinningTrades * 100 / NoTrades;

  End

  Else Begin

   AverageProfit = 0;

   AverageTrLen = 0;

   PercentWinners = 0;

  End;

{7} For ExportArrayPos = 0 To (NoTrades - 1) Begin

   SumSquareProfit = SumSquareProfit +

   Square(TradeProfit[ExportArrayPos]);

  End;

{8} If NoTrades <> 0 Then

   StDevProfit = SquareRoot((NoTrades * SumSquareProfit -

   Square(NetProfit)) / (NoTrades * (NoTrades - 1)))

  Else

   StDevProfit = 0;

  If StDevProfit <> 0 Then

   RiskRatio = AverageProfit / StDevProfit

  Else

   RiskRatio = 0;

{9} If GrossLoss <> 0 Then Begin

   ProfitFactor = GrossProfit / -GrossLoss;

   LosingTrades = NoTrades - WinningTrades;

   If LosingTrades <> 0 and NoTrades <> 0 Then

    RiskFactor = NetProfit / ((-GrossLoss / LosingTrades) * NoTrades)

   Else

    RiskFactor = 0;

```
                End
                    Else Begin
                        ProfitFactor = 0;
                        RiskFactor = 0;
                    End;
                TestString = LeftStr(GetSymbolName, 5) + "," + TradeType + "," +
                NumToStr(NoTrades, 0) + "," + NumToStr(PercentWinners, 2) + "," +
                NumToStr(NetProfit, 2) + "," + NumToStr(AverageProfit, 2) + "," +
                NumToStr(StDevProfit, 2) + "," + NumToStr(RiskRatio, 2) + "," +
                NumToStr(ProfitFactor, 2) + "," + NumToStr(RiskFactor, 2) + "," +
                NumToStr(MaxDrawDown, 2) + "," +
                NumToStr(MaxDDPercent, 2) + "," +
                NumToStr(PercentInTrade, 2) + "," +
                NumToStr(AverageTrLen, 2) + NewLine;
    {10}    FileAppend(FileString, TestString);
                End;
    End;
```

COMMENTS ON THE CODE

Let's go through the code step-by-step to see how it works:

1. The variable ExportSwitch(True) must be placed on top of the code or even as an Input. The other variables only become active when ExportSwitch is set to True. To speed up the computing time, the program will not run through the rest of the code, when ExportSwitch is set to False.

2. We need to create two arrays to contain the data for our calculations. We could have done without the arrays and instead run through all the calculations for each bar, but to speed up the computing time, we will do most of the calculations only once, on the very last bar on the chart. The arrays are now set to hold 1,000 trades each. The larger the arrays, the slower the calculations, so you might want to change this number to what makes the most sense for the system you currently are working on.

3. These calculations and exports only need to be done once, on the very first bar on the chart. By altering the state of the variables AllowLong and AllowShort at the very top of the code (see the code for any of the individual systems), we can test all long and short trades, either separately or together. Then we create the file that we will import into Excel (variable FileString), and the column headers for the data we need to export later (variable TestString).

4. These calculations are done on every bar on the chart. We are now filling the array TradeProfit with the result of each trade. An array is a series of values stored in a specific order. In this case, the first position in the array will hold the result of the first trade, and so on. The second array, TradeLength, is filled with data regarding the length of the trade. Each array can store 1,000 trades, as specified under step two.

5. All remaining calculations will only be executed on the very last bar on the chart. Note: If you plan to use this code and use the criteria Open Next Bar (or Open Tomorrow) for your entries and exits, you need to use the alternative function. The first thing we need to do is to run a loop (that starts with the word "For") to calculate the total profit (variable SumProfit) by adding all the values contained in the array TradeProfit. Take note of all new equity highs (variable MaxProfit): From these, we can calculate the maximum drawdown (variables DrawDown, MaxDrawDown, DDRatio, and MaxDDRatio). We also count the number of winning trades (variable WinningTrades) and sum up the length of all trades in the variable SumTrLen, using the data from the array TradeLength.

6. Moving out of the first loop, we now can calculate the variables PercentInTrade, AverageProfit, AverageTrLen, and PercentWinners, which all should be self-explanatory.

7. The second loop (also starting with the word "For") sums up the squared profits from all trades in the SumSquareProfit variable.

8. Moving out of the second loop, we can go on and calculate the standard deviation of all trades (variable StDevProfit), and the ratio between the average trade and the standard deviation of all trades (variable RiskRatio). The variable RiskRatio measures the risk of the system by comparing the average trade with the dispersion of all trades (the standard deviation). The higher the value of the average trade and the less dispersed all the individual trades, the more sure you can be regarding the outcome of each individual trade, and, consequently, the less risky the system.

9. The calculation for the variable LosingTrades should be self-explanatory. The variable ProfitFactor stores the relation between every dollar earned and every dollar lost, calculated as the gross profit, divided by the gross loss. Obviously, if the gross profit from all winning trades is larger than the gross loss from all losing trades, the variable ProfitFactor will be greater than 1, which is a must for a profitable system. The variable RiskFactor calculates the relationship between the final (net) profit and every dollar risked, which is not the same as every dollar lost. To calculate the dollars risked, the system must have a stop-loss level. To calculate the dollars risked for all trades, first divide the gross loss by the number of losing trades, to get a value for the average losing trade. Second, assuming the dollars lost in the average losing trade also represent the value we were willing to risk and lose in each and every trade (this is not always the case and depends on a few assumptions, but will do as a good approximation), multiply the dollars lost in the average losing trade by the total number of trades to arrive at the total value the system risked throughout all trades over the entire test period. Third, divide the net profit by this value to arrive at the RiskFactor.

10. The file export takes place in the command FileAppend. The name of the file is specified by the variable FileString, created in step three.

THE EXPORTED DATA

Once you've exported all the necessary data for all markets to be analyzed together, you can open the newly created file in Excel for further analysis. Figure 7.1 shows what this may look like after the data have been sorted on the ticker symbol for each market.

If you compare all column headers in Figure 7.1 with the lowest part of the TradeStation *export* function, you will see that each variable is exported to its own column in the same way for all markets tested. For example, the value in cell G3 tells us that the average profit per trade for Altera (ALTR) is $1,847.63, whereas cell L9 tells us that the worst drawdown, measured in percentage terms, for Citicorp is 9.91 percent. Arranging the statistics in this way makes it is easy to rank and compare all the markets with each other by simply using the sort buttons on the Excel toolbar. Note that the percent drawdown is allowed to surpass 100 percent in this table.

However, to find out how reliable and robust a system is when traded on several markets and during various market conditions, we also need to summarize the results from all markets in one easy to understand table. Figure 7.2 shows what such a table may look like when placed directly under the exported data for all the markets.

Because we will work extensively with this table over the next several pages, let's take the time to step through it, to make sure we understand how to calculate all the values and how to interpret their meanings.

Cell H68 shows how many markets were profitable. The value 81.54 is calculated using the formula =COUNTIF(E$2:E66,">0")*100/COUNT(E$2:E66),

	A	B	C	D	E	F	G	H	I	J	K	L	M	N
1	Market	Direction	Trades	PercWin	NetProfit	AvgProfit	StDevProfit	RiskRatio	ProfitFactor	RiskFactor	MaxDD	PercDD	PercTime	AvgLength
2	AA	Long	58	24.14	-24999.8	-431.03	7418.89	-0.06	0.88	-0.09	53119.8	49.66	31.4	23.57
3	ALTR	Long	73	38.36	134877	1847.63	9218.63	0.2	1.58	0.36	43261.8	21.06	14.58	8.7
4	AMAT	Long	75	21.33	-79193	-1055.91	6951.51	-0.15	0.71	-0.23	123250	118.03	11.69	6.79
5	AMGN	Long	51	31.37	39197.3	768.58	8489.31	0.09	1.23	0.16	54709.2	32.88	23.59	20.14
6	AXP	Long	51	23.53	-19176.6	-376.01	7206.56	-0.05	0.89	-0.09	52886.1	39.55	19.38	16.55
7	BA	Long	59	37.29	110287	1869.27	8201.48	0.23	1.68	0.43	35149.6	30.72	33.49	24.71
8	BBBY	Long	42	33.33	26463	630.07	9135.17	0.07	1.17	0.11	67478.1	67.48	13.33	11
9	C	Long	48	50	198665	4138.86	8885.95	0.47	2.79	0.9	32862.9	9.91	25.06	22.73
10	CAT	Long	63	23.81	-20415.8	-324.06	7049.44	-0.05	0.9	-0.08	74087.2	48.21	30.13	20.83

FIGURE 7.1

Excel file showing sorted data.

	A	B	C	D	E	F	G	H	
1	**Market**	**Direction**	**Trades**	**PercWin**	**NetProfit**	**AvgProfit**	**StDevProfit**	**RiskRatio**	**P**
65	XLNX	Long	67	29.85	24359.9	363.58	8715.69	0.04	
66	XOM	Long	28	35.71	45869.5	1638.2	8157.63	0.2	
67									
68							**PercProf:**	81.54	
69			**Trades**	**PercWin**	**NetProfit**	**AvgProfit**	**ProfitStD**	**RiskRatio**	
70		Average:	50.20	34.10	62,126.82	1,295.04	**Market**		
71		St. Dev:	11.73	7.70	64,447.90	1,344.95	8,337.05	0.15	
72		High:	61.93	41.80	126,574.73	2,639.99	9,632.09	**Portfolio**	
73		Low:	38.47	26.40	(2,321.08)	(49.90)	(7,042.01)	0.96	
74			**ProfitFactor**	**RiskFactor**	**MaxDD**	**PercDD**	**PercTime**	**AvgLength**	
75		Average:	1.48	0.28	42,058.76	31.15	25.77	23.55	
76		St. Dev:	0.52	0.29	18,687.90	18.84	14.41	19.33	
77		High:	2.00	0.57	60,746.66	49.99	40.18	42.88	
78		Low:	0.96	(0.01)	23,370.87	12.31	11.37	4.22	
79									

FIGURE 7.2

Summary table showing market results.

where column E refers to the net profit for all markets. The dollar mark inside the cell reference E$2 makes the formula adjust automatically to the number of markets tested. This makes it easy to copy and paste tables between spreadsheets, instead of having to create a new table for every new spreadsheet.

Cell C70 shows the average number of trades for each market. The value 50.20 is calculated using the formula =AVERAGE(C$2:C66), in which column C refers to the number of trades produced by each market.

Cell C71 shows the standard deviation of the number of trades produced. The value 11.73 is calculated using the formula =STDEV(C$2:C66). It indicates that 68 percent of all trading sequences will produce somewhere between 38.47 (50.20 − 11.73) to 61.93 (50.20 + 11.73) trades, which is further indicated by cells C72 (=C70 + C71) and C73 (=C70´− C71).

The formulas for cells D70 to F73 are the same as those used in cells C70 to C73, except that the calculations are based on the data in columns D to F.

If you ask me, I think a high number of profitable markets (cell H68) is way more important than a high number of profitable trades (cell D70). You shouldn't care so much about the outcome of the very next trade, as long as you know you will end up on top if you do what you should over a longer sequence of trades. A psychiatrist specializing in "treating" traders once told me that he wished all traders could learn to focus on the trading procedure over a specified time period instead of the event (trade) at hand. Then, all traders would have a much easier time cutting their losses, because letting a losing or slow trade run only makes it more difficult to reach the true goal—to produce a profit at month's end instead of with every single trade. From this it also follows that a high number of profitable months is more important than a high number of profitable trades, and sometimes it might be a good idea to take a higher number of losing trades to increase the number of profitable months. This is especially true when we need to free up capital from trades that are going nowhere.

Sometimes, when testing the same system on several markets, or the same market with several systems, the average net profit from all trading sequences (cell E70) can be negative despite a positive average profit per trade (cell F70), or vice versa. Because the number of trades can vary within each trading sequence, a trading sequence with a high number of relatively small losses will weigh down the average net profit relatively more than the average profit per trade. A trading sequence with a low number of relatively large winners, on the other hand, will increase the value of the average profit per trade relatively more than the average net profit.

However, because we don't know if a market that produced relatively few or many trades over the testing period will continue to do so in the future, we cannot place any significance on the net profit produced by that market. All we can do is use the average profit per trade, regardless of how many trades it is based on, as one of many estimates for the average profit per trade for all markets. We use the average of all averages from all markets as an estimate for the true, but always unknown, average profit per trade.

Another way to look at it is to assume that each market is producing approximately the same number of trades, no matter how many trades there are behind a certain average profit per trade for a certain market. In that case, a positive (negative) average profit per trade will also produce a positive (negative) average net profit per market. This is also more in line with what we can expect in real-life trading. One error we deliberately make during this stage of the testing is to equalize one trading sequence with trading one market over a longer period of time (say 10 years). In real life, one trading sequence is instead equal to trading several markets (10, for example) over a shorter period of time (say one year). In this case, different markets will produce a varying number of trades over different periods, but the number of trades over all trading sequences (in this case defined by units of time, rather than specific markets) is more likely to stay approximately the same.

Cell G71 shows the average standard deviation for the profit per trade produced by each market. The value, 8,337.05, is calculated using the formula =AVERAGE(G$2:G66), where column G refers to the standard deviation of profits produced by each market. It indicates that 68 percent of all trades within one trading sequence will result in a profit ranging from −$7,042.01 (1,295.04 − 8,337.05) to $9,632.09 (1,295.04 + 8,337.05), which is further indicated by cells G72 (= F70 + G71) and G73 (= F70 − G71).

Note that the values in cells G71 to G73 are much larger (positive or negative) that those in cells F71 to F73. This is because the values in cells G71 to G73 give an indication of how much the results per trade can vary within one market, or one trading sequence, whereas cells F71 to F73 indicate how much the average profit per trade is likely to vary over several markets or several trading sequences. It only makes sense that the average profit per trade is likely to vary less than the actual profit per trade, just as, for example, a moving average of prices fluctuates less than the price itself. Normally, the values in cells F71 to F73 are of greater interest than those in cells G71 to G73.

Cell H71 shows the average risk-adjusted return for one market or trading sequence. The value 0.15 is calculated using the formula =AVERAGE(H$2:H66), where column H refers to the risk ratio as calculated with the TradeStation export function. The value in column H also could have been calculated using the values from columns F and G, so that the value in cell H_n would equal F_n / G_n.

Cell H73 shows the risk-adjusted return over several markets or trading sequences. The value 0.96 is calculated using the formula =F70/F71. Note that the value in cell H73 is much higher than that in cell H71. This is because in cell H73, we're using the standard deviation of the average profit per trade from several markets, as opposed to the standard deviation of the profit per trade from individual markets, as in cell H71. Because the standard deviation of the average profit per trade is less than the standard deviation of the outcome of all individual trades, the risk-adjusted return will be greater over several markets or trading sequences than over one single market or sequence given that the returns are similar from all markets. The value in cell H73 is of greatest interest to us.

The calculations and values in cells C75 to H78 should be pretty much self-explanatory. The most important cells or values to consider in the bottom half of the table are the average profit and risk factors and their respective standard deviations. An average profit factor above one means that the system tested profitably enough on the profitable markets to make up for the losses made in the losing markets. The same goes for a risk factor above zero. One way to get a dollars-and-cents feel for the risk factor is to equal its value to dollars made per dollar risked. In the case of Figure 7.2, a value of 0.28 indicates that the system is likely to make 28 cents per dollar risked. Note, however, that if the standard deviation for the risk factor is higher than the risk factor itself, a number of trading sequences will lose money. In this case, a value of 0.29 in cell D76 indicates that 68 percent of all trading sequences will produce a profit per dollar risked ranging from -1 cent to 57 cents.

As already mentioned in the beginning of this section, the trade length and time spent in the market variables are important in that we need to balance these numbers against the number of markets we would like to trade and the nature of the trading strategy. Aside from that, because this is a book about relatively short-term trading strategies, we will try to keep the average trade length down to approximately five to ten days. Finally, at this point of the analysis work, we won't care so much about the drawdown values. As mentioned in Chapter 5, the drawdown is not a core system characteristic and is more efficiently dealt with via mathematical expectancy and the probability for a winning trade.

INITIAL DESCRIPTION OF THE SYSTEMS

Before we look at the individual systems, I would like to point out that all original systems are completely unoptimized, and the little optimization or tweaking I indulged in doesn't take us too far away from the type of reasoning I used when I put the systems together in the first place.

When it comes to finding an entry technique, I am not all that interested in finding the most optimal parameter settings. What is more important is to find settings that make sense to me and that I can live with because I understand why they are as they are. In fact, the better you know and understand the system, the less optimizing you need to do, at least when it comes to the entry techniques.

However, I do like to optimize the stops and the exits, but that will wait until Part 3. For now, we will keep most of the exits in the systems as they were presented originally. If you read through this part and still are interested in finding the most optimal parameters for the entry, you can use the techniques given in Part 3 to optimize the exits.

The original results also are presented as they were in *ATM*, which means that sometimes the terminology is different from that used in the rest of the book. For example, for the hybrid system No. 1 and the RS system No. 1, I use the term *risk–reward ratio* as a ratio between the final net profit and the maximum historical drawdown. This is not a correct use of this term, and in the rest of the book, the risk–reward ratio refers to the average profit per trade divided by the standard deviation of all trades.

For the Harris 3L-R pattern variation system, I also use the term *profit–loss ratio*. Throughout the rest of the book, this term is replaced by the (initial) risk–reward relationship, which refers to the distances between the entry price, the stop loss, and profit target (or final profit) when entering into a trade. The risk–reward relationship is expressed as the profit target in relation to the stop loss, as in "2:1," which means that the profit target is placed twice as far from the entry point as the stop loss. OK, let's get to it.

CHAPTER 8

Hybrid System No. 1

Originally presented in September 2000, this is a short-term hybrid system that falls somewhere between a bottom-picking strategy and a trend-following breakout strategy. The system waits for a retracement to occur, then enters when the market reverses by an amount equal to half the retracement. For example, if a stock rallied to a new high at 80, then retraced to 70, the system would go long when the stock moved back above 75 (halfway between the high and the retracement low).

As a bottom-picking strategy, it requires that the bottom be confirmed by a move retracing half the previous decline. As a breakout system, it tries to anticipate the breakout by going long at the halfway point between the most recent highs and lows.

SUGGESTED MARKETS

Stocks, stock index futures, and index shares (SPDRs, DIAs, QQQs).

ORIGINAL RULES

Enter long with a stop order after the market has made a nine-day low and then retraced half the move from that low to the highest high of the last nine days.

Risk 0.5 percent of the available equity per trade. At the time of entry, calculate the number of stocks per trade as 0.005 multiplied by available equity, divided by the dollar value of the distance between the entry price and the lowest low of the last nine days.

Exit with a trailing stop if the market falls below the lowest low of the last nine days.

Exit with a loss if the market is below the entry price after nine days.

TEST PERIOD

January 1, 1990 to July 12, 2000.

TEST DATA

Daily stock prices for the 25 most-traded stocks on the NASDAQ 100 list, excluding those stocks that also can be found in other indexes, such as Microsoft and Intel in the Dow Jones Industrial Average and S&P 500 index.

STARTING EQUITY

$100,000 (nominal).

SYSTEM PROS AND CONS

The long-only trend-following nature of the system makes it vulnerable to market corrections, which explains the rather extensive drawdowns over the last few months (not shown). This system would probably benefit from the addition of a trend filter (such as a long-term moving average) that would only allow trades in the direction of the prevailing trend.

Other enhancements include only trading those stocks that show the highest relative strength compared to the market as a whole (i.e., the underlying index), or including some sort of volume confirmation, such as an increasing on balance volume (OBV) value.

Although this system does better than buy-and-hold for both the Dow and S&P 500, it doesn't manage to keep up with the NASDAQ 100. Note, however, that the system only risks 0.5 percent of available equity per trade, which translates into a risk–reward ratio of 21.8 (in this case, calculated as total return divided by max drawdown). For a buy-and-hold strategy for the NASDAQ 100, the same ratio is 40.9. However, a buy-and-hold strategy is in the market all the time, which also adds to the risk, albeit on a more subjective level.

Risking 1 percent per trade produced a return and drawdown of 1,514 percent and 52.89 percent, respectively, for a risk–reward ratio of 28.6 (1,514 / 52.89). (Note that in some of the original system texts, I defined the risk–reward ratio as the net profit divided by the largest drawdown. This is not the best or correct definition, but only an easy and commonly used way to get a first feel for the system compared to other systems.) This is still not as good as a buy-and-hold, but some of the 25 stocks in the test portfolio were not listed until very recently (such as Amazon.com, which didn't start contributing to the portfolio equity until August 1997). During the first year of trading, only 14 of our 25 stocks were tradable.

REVISING THE RESEARCH AND MODIFYING THE SYSTEM

Because the original testing showed some very good results, I had high hopes that so would this second run of testing on more markets and fresher data. Table 8.1 shows that I had no reason to be disappointed, with as many as 91 percent of all tested markets delivering a profit. The average profit per trade came out to $1,048 and the profit and risk factors to 1.39 and 0.24, respectively. The most important standard deviation numbers also are very low, which among other things, results in a very good risk–reward ratio of 0.91 (1,049 / 1,149—the average profit per trade divided by its standard deviation, a more correct definition of the risk–reward ratio). The only negative is the average trade length at 20 days and the average time spent in the market, which both are a little too high for the system to be considered short term. Therefore, I tried to modify the rules a bit to make it more short term, hopefully, without losing any or as little performance as possible.

The first thing I did was to shorten the slow-trade stop to four days, but that did not change the performance or the system characteristics all that much, which gave a first indication that the slow-trade stop might not be needed at all. With the slow-trade stop at its original nine-day setting, I changed the retrace period between the most recent high and low prices to six days, expecting a larger num-

TABLE 8.1

Retesting the Original Hybrid System I

		Original system, long only				PercProf: 90.77
	Trades	**PercWin**	**NetProfit**	**AvgProfit**	**ProfitStD**	**RiskRatio**
Average:	140.83	34.38	122,904.33	1,048.92		**Market**
St. Dev:	34.87	4.35	105,868.56	1,149.15	10,311.97	0.09
High:	175.70	38.73	228,772.90	2,198.07	11,360.89	**Portfolio**
Low:	105.96	30.04	17,035.77	(100.22)	(9,263.04)	0.91
	ProfitFactor	**RiskFactor**	**MaxDD**	**PercDD**	**PercTime**	**AvgLength**
Average:	1.39	0.24	82,151.19	39.37	69.44	20.47
St. Dev:	0.41	0.24	42,524.99	20.80	6.35	2.62
High:	1.80	0.49	124,676.17	60.17	75.80	23.09
Low:	0.98	0.00	39,626.20	18.57	63.09	17.86

ber of shorter trades, but also an increasing number of losing trades, which would deteriorate performance somewhat.

As it turned out, Table 8.2 shows that the average trade length did decrease from 20 days to 15 days, but surprisingly, the percentage of winning trades also increased to 36 percent, increasing the average net profit to $141,896, despite a slightly lowered average profit per trade. The profit and risk factors also increased a little, but what is more important is that all the important standard deviation numbers decreased, indicating that the system actually became more reliable.

Of course, these surprisingly positive results prompted a test with an even shorter retrace period of three days. However, this did not better the results enough to warrant an even shorter retrace period. Note that I did not test any other retrace periods than those mentioned. It might be that other retrace periods, surrounding those tested, might work better.

With the retrace period back at six days, the next step was to once again test various values for the slow-trade stop. But with the slow-trade stop set to six days, results did not improve enough, if at all, as Table 8.3 shows. In fact, with a shorter slow-trade stop only decreasing performance, it is clear that it can be removed completely, as it has in Table 8.4, which shows that the aggressive level for the entry also has been increased to a factor of three, meaning the entry will now take place after only a third of the distance between the lowest low and highest high has been taken back.

Table 8.4 shows the results for a system based on a six-day retrace period, no slow-trade stop, and a one-third retracement of the highest-high to lowest-low distance to trigger an entry. It shows that the results continued to improve the more

TABLE 8.2

Revised Performance Results, with Six-day Retrace Period

		Long only: six-day retrace period			PercProf: 90.77	
	Trades	**PercWin**	**NetProfit**	**AvgProfit**	**ProfitStD**	**RiskRatio**
Average:	187.55	36.08	141,896.16	915.26		**Market**
St. Dev:	49.77	5.33	119,300.04	958.46	8,510.40	0.10
High:	237.32	41.41	261,196.20	1,873.72	9,425.66	**Portfolio**
Low:	137.78	30.74	22,596.12	(43.20)	(7,595.14)	0.95
	ProfitFactor	**RiskFactor**	**MaxDD**	**PercDD**	**PercTime**	**AvgLength**
Average:	1.42	0.25	77,839.56	36.55	68.97	15.35
St. Dev:	0.49	0.25	42,152.75	23.87	6.06	2.10
High:	1.91	0.50	119,992.31	60.42	75.02	17.45
Low:	0.93	(0.00)	35,686.81	12.68	62.91	13.25

TABLE 8.3

Slow-trade Stop at Six Days

	Long only: six-day retrace period, six-day slow-trade stop PercProf: 89.06					
	Trades	**PercWin**	**NetProfit**	**AvgProfit**	**ProfitStD**	**RiskRatio**
Average:	195.73	34.76	139,303.16	857.00		**Market**
St. Dev:	50.16	5.60	117,466.37	923.85	8,300.17	0.10
High:	245.90	40.36	256,769.53	1,780.85	9,157.17	**Portfolio**
Low:	145.57	29.16	21,836.79	(66.85)	(7,443.17)	0.93
	ProfitFactor	**RiskFactor**	**MaxDD**	**PercDD**	**PercTime**	**AvgLength**
Average:	1.41	0.25	78,570.71	36.12	67.56	14.35
St. Dev:	0.50	0.25	42,015.00	21.56	5.96	1.90
High:	1.91	0.50	120,585.70	57.69	73.52	16.26
Low:	0.92	(0.00)	36,555.71	14.56	61.59	12.45

aggressive the system. The most important thing to notice is a risk–reward ratio for the entire portfolio above one, which means that at least 84 percent (68 + 32 / 2) of all trading sequences now have or should have a positive average profit per trade. This is further confirmed by a positive value for the lower one standard deviation boundary for the risk factor. The profit factor is also at its highest so far at 1.44. I settled for this version of the system before I decided to test both the long and the short side simultaneously.

TABLE 8.4

Removing Slow-trade Stops

	Long only: six-day retrace period, no slow-trade stop, aggressive level three				PercProf: 96.88	
	Trades	**PercWin**	**NetProfit**	**AvgProfit**	**ProfitStD**	**RiskRatio**
Average:	212.14	33.42	162,892.09	923.64		**Market**
St. Dev:	59.42	4.82	109,794.45	872.67	8,423.52	0.10
High:	271.56	38.24	272,686.55	1,796.31	9,347.16	**Portfolio**
Low:	152.72	28.60	53,097.64	50.97	(7,499.88)	1.06
	ProfitFactor	**RiskFactor**	**MaxDD**	**PercDD**	**PercTime**	**AvgLength**
Average:	1.44	0.28	77,309.40	34.52	71.87	14.30
St. Dev:	0.48	0.25	40,877.93	19.05	5.04	2.62
High:	1.93	0.53	118,187.32	53.56	76.91	16.92
Low:	0.96	0.02	36,431.47	15.47	66.83	11.68

FIGURE 8.1

NASDAQ 100 index traded using Hybrid System I.

Unfortunately, the short side did not produce good enough results to warrant trading without any other types of adjustments, such as the addition of a trend filter or relative-strength filter. Nonetheless, we will take this version of the system with us to Part 3 where we will try to substitute the stops and make the system more short term. We will also look at how the system will operate with a trend or relative-strength filter, in an effort to decrease the percentage of time spent in the market. Figure 8.1 shows a few sample trades in the NASDAQ 100 index, generated with this latest version of the system.

TRADESTATION CODE

Variables:

{These variables can also be used as inputs for optimization purposes.}

AllowLong(True), AllowShort(False), RetracePeriod(6), Aggressiveness(3),

{Leave these variables alone.}

RetraceDistance(0), LongEntryLevel(0), ShortEntryLevel(0);

{Code for normalizing the number of contracts traded goes here.}

RetraceDistance = (Highest(High, RetracePeriod) - Lowest(Low, RetracePeriod)) / Aggressiveness;

LongEntryLevel = Lowest(Low, RetracePeriod) + RetraceDistance;

ShortEntryLevel = Highest(High, RetracePeriod) - RetraceDistance;

If MarketPosition = 0 Then Begin

    If AllowLong = True and Close < LongEntryLevel Then

       Buy ("L-Sep 00") NumCont Contracts Next Bar on LongEntryLevel Stop;

    If AllowShort = True and Close > ShortEntryLevel Then

       Sell ("S-Sep 00") NumCont Contracts Next Bar on ShortEntryLevel Stop;

End;

If EntryPrice > 0 Then Begin

    ExitLong ("L-Stop") Next Bar at Lowest(Low, RetracePeriod) Stop;

    ExitShort ("S-Stop") Next Bar at Highest(High, RetracePeriod) Stop;

End;

{Code for testing stops in Excel goes here (see Part 3 of book), with Normalize(False). Set SurfaceChartTest(True). Disable original stops in system.}

{Code for initial market export goes here, with Normalize(True). Set ExportSwitch(True).}

{Code for testing robustness goes here (see Part 3 of book), with Normalize(True). Set RobustnessSwitch(True).}

{Code for exporting results for money management analysis goes here (see Part 4 of book), with Normalize(False). Set MoneyExport(True).}

CHAPTER 9

RS System No. 1

Originally presented in October 2000, this is a short-term relative strength (RS) system that compares the stock price with its underlying market index, but also looks for confirmation from volume. The first step is to calculate the relative strength of the stock compared to the market as a whole, then take the percentage difference between the relative strength curve and its five-day moving average. A value above one (the higher the better) indicates the stock has moved stronger than the market as a whole.

The second step is to calculate the percentage difference between the on-balance-volume indicator and its five-day moving average. A value above one (the higher the better) indicates the volume fueling the move is above its five-day moving average and that the market has a short-term interest in the stock.

The final step is to multiply both the percentage differences to create a volume-weighted relative-strength curve. A value above one (the higher the better) indicates that the market has a short-term interest in the stock, but also that it is doing better than average in terms of the overall market. (Or, if the interest is low, the stock is still moving strongly enough to warrant a trade, and vice versa.)

SUGGESTED MARKETS

Stocks, stock index futures, and index shares (SPDRs, DIAs, QQQs).

ORIGINAL RULES

Enter long at the close when the volume-weighted relative-strength curve crosses above one.

Risk 0.5 percent of available equity per trade. At the time of entry, calculate the number of shares to buy as 0.005 multiplied by available equity, divided by the dollar value of the distance between the entry price and the stop loss.

Exit at the close when the volume-weighted relative-strength curve crosses below one.

Exit with a loss if the market falls below the entry price minus 4 percent.

TEST PERIOD

December 11, 1985 to July 12, 2000.

TEST DATA

Daily stock prices for the 30 most actively traded NASDAQ 100 stocks, excluding those stocks that also can be found in other indexes, such as Microsoft and Intel in the Dow Jones Industrial Average and S&P 500 index. The amount of $20 per trade has been deducted for slippage and commission.

STARTING EQUITY

$100,000 (nominal).

SYSTEM PROS AND CONS

This is a long-only system, which makes it vulnerable to market conditions. The system probably would benefit from the addition of a trend filter (such as a long-term moving average) that would only allow trades in the direction of the prevailing trend. Developing a similar strategy for the short side would make it possible to make money no matter what direction the market is heading.

Although this system does better than buy-and-hold for both the Dow and S&P 500, at first glance it doesn't quite seem to keep up with the NASDAQ 100. However, looking closer at the numbers reveals that the risk–reward ratio (in this case, total return divided by maximum drawdown) for a buy-and-hold strategy for the NASDAQ 100 comes out to 68.6. For this system, only risking 0.5 percent of available equity per trade, the same number comes out to 80.8, which is a clear indication that it allows you to make more money while risking less.

Another favorable aspect of the system is that a buy-and-hold strategy is always in the market, risking 100 percent of available equity. While being in the market all the time might not add to the risk, it sure adds to the agony. Finally, some of the 30 stocks in the test portfolio were not listed until very recently (such as Amazon.com, which didn't start contributing to the portfolio equity until August 1997).

REVISING THE RESEARCH AND MODIFYING THE SYSTEM

Table 9.1 shows the results produced by the original system. This is a pretty good start, showing a high percentage of profitable trading sequences and a decent profit factor. The average profit per trade is, however, a little too low. If we can increase the average profit per trade, we also should be able to increase the profit and risk factors. Hopefully, this can be done while also increasing the risk–return ratio, currently at 0.60.

Because this is a relative-strength system that we later will try to use as a filter for the other short-term systems, we will start by trying to increase the average trade length by getting rid of the stop loss. If the results change for the better or remain relatively stable, the stop loss fulfilled little purpose anyway, and the fewer rules we can get by with, the better off we are. Table 9.2 shows that this actually improved results quite a bit. The average profit increased to $229.77, while the profit and risk factors increased to 1.14 and 0.08, respectively. The risk–reward ratio also increased, which indicates the system produces more homogeneous and similar-looking trades. However, for a trend filter, the trading horizon is still a little short at 6.18 days, on average.

Let's keep testing the system without the stop loss, but try to come up with a way to lengthen the number of days in a trade, while decreasing the time spent in the market. To do this, the number of trades must be decreased; you could work with a longer lookback period for the relative strength calculation. Table 9.3 shows the result for a version of the system with a 20-day relative strength lookback. It contains both good and bad news. The good news is that the average profit per trade increased together with the profit and risk factors. The average trade length

TABLE 9.1

Retesting of RS System No. 1

	Original system, long only					PercProf: 70.00
	Trades	**PercWin**	**NetProfit**	**AvgProfit**	**ProfitStD**	**RiskRatio**
Average:	405.60	38.64	53,487.76	155.09		**Market**
St. Dev:	74.91	3.86	90,677.39	257.41	4,865.10	0.03
High:	480.51	42.50	144,165.15	412.50	5,020.19	**Portfolio**
Low:	330.69	34.78	(37,189.63)	(102.31)	(4,710.00)	0.60
	ProfitFactor	**RiskFactor**	**MaxDD**	**PercDD**	**PercTime**	**AvgLength**
Average:	1.09	0.06	98,225.82	53.55	56.61	5.68
St. Dev:	0.15	0.09	49,403.31	30.82	3.43	0.38
High:	1.25	0.15	147,629.13	84.37	60.04	6.06
Low:	0.94	(0.04)	48,822.50	22.73	53.19	5.31

T A B L E   9 . 2

Removing the Stop Loss

	Long only: No stop loss				PercProf: 80.00	
	Trades	**PercWin**	**NetProfit**	**AvgProfit**	**ProfitStD**	**RiskRatio**
Average:	405.55	40.39	82,811.65	229.77		**Market**
St. Dev:	74.96	3.55	98,064.36	278.19	5,130.55	0.04
High:	480.51	43.95	180,876.01	507.96	5,360.32	**Portfolio**
Low:	330.59	36.84	(15,252.70)	(48.42)	(4,900.78)	0.83
	ProfitFactor	**RiskFactor**	**MaxDD**	**PercDD**	**PercTime**	**AvgLength**
Average:	1.14	0.08	94,117.39	48.08	61.53	6.18
St. Dev:	0.16	0.10	50,003.95	26.36	1.65	0.37
High:	1.30	0.18	144,121.34	74.44	63.18	6.55
Low:	0.98	(0.01)	44,113.43	21.73	59.89	5.81

also increased to about 13 days. The bad news is that risk–return ratio decreased a little, as did the number of profitable markets.

Increasing the lookback even further, to 50 days, continued to increase the average profit and the profit and risk factors. The risk–return ratio also increased somewhat, but not enough to take us back to what we had in Table 9.2. This tells us that increasing the lookback period is not the best way to go. Another way to make the average trade length longer is to make it easier for an individual stock to

T A B L E   9 . 3

Twenty-day Relative Strength Lookback

	Long only: No stop loss, 20-day lookback				PercProf: 75.00	
	Trades	**PercWin**	**NetProfit**	**AvgProfit**	**ProfitStD**	**RiskRatio**
Average:	184.30	36.86	114,309.41	761.90		**Market**
St. Dev:	40.05	5.01	144,384.69	1,048.93	8,696.44	0.07
High:	224.35	41.87	258,694.10	1,810.84	9,458.34	**Portfolio**
Low:	144.25	31.86	(30,075.27)	(287.03)	(7,934.53)	0.73
	ProfitFactor	**RiskFactor**	**MaxDD**	**PercDD**	**PercTime**	**AvgLength**
Average:	1.33	0.20	80,636.09	44.10	58.36	13.07
St. Dev:	0.40	0.24	38,344.13	28.01	3.53	1.73
High:	1.73	0.44	118,980.21	72.11	61.89	14.80
Low:	0.93	(0.04)	42,291.96	16.09	54.82	11.34

enter into a trade. Unfortunately, however, most likely this will also increase the time spent in the market and the number of markets being in a trade at once.

Table 9.4 shows what happened when the required strength was lowered to 0.95 (as opposed to the original strength of one), meaning the relative-strength and volume conditions for entering have been relaxed quite a bit. Thus, either one of the original conditions doesn't have to be completely fulfilled. This did improve performance quite a bit. The average profit per trade came out to $1,300, with the risk–reward ratio at 0.93, which is very good. These good numbers also found confirmation from high profit and risk factors, which both have their lower standard deviation boundaries above one and zero, respectively. The average trade length came out close to 20 days, which is what we're looking for. The only negative is the high percentage of time spent in the market. Over 70 percent is a little too much, but because this system will primarily be used as a filter for other systems, we will live with this number.

It seems that decreasing the required strength for the entry even further would continue to improve on the results. However, decreasing the required strength too much soon will result in a system that keeps us in a trade in all markets all the time, and the purpose behind the system will be lost. Therefore, I will not experiment with this number any further, but only conclude that a system with a 20-day lookback period and a required strength of 0.95 produces the types of trades we're interested in, and I'll settle for this version.

Repeating the research, trading both the short and the long side of the market, did not produce good results at all. Therefore, for now, this system will remain long only. Perhaps the short side still can work as a filter for other systems trading

TABLE 9.4

Lowered Relative Strength

	Long only: No stop loss, 20-day lookback, strength minus five					PercProf: 88.33
	Trades	**PercWin**	**NetProfit**	**AvgProfit**	**ProfitStD**	**RiskRatio**
Average:	148.95	36.53	165,028.79	1,300.99		**Market**
St. Dev:	34.42	4.83	147,743.71	1,395.89	11,312.66	0.10
High:	183.37	41.36	312,772.50	2,696.88	12,613.65	**Portfolio**
Low:	114.53	31.70	17,285.07	(94.89)	(10,011.66)	0.93
	ProfitFactor	**RiskFactor**	**MaxDD**	**PercDD**	**PercTime**	**AvgLength**
Average:	1.51	0.32	85,968.44	39.60	70.99	19.89
St. Dev:	0.46	0.28	39,057.74	22.04	5.19	4.20
High:	1.97	0.60	125,026.18	61.64	76.18	24.09
Low:	1.05	0.03	46,910.70	17.56	65.80	15.69

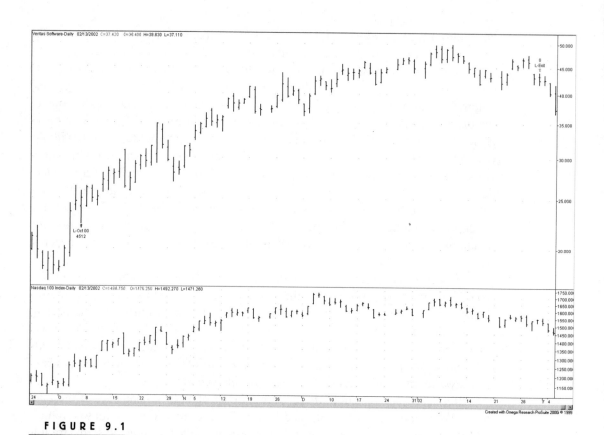

FIGURE 9.1

Veritas trading using revised RS System No. 1.

the short side. Figure 9.1 shows a sample trade in Veritas, using this version of the system.

Before we move on, it's also worth noticing that just because an individual market has a low relative strength, it doesn't have to mean it's in a downtrend (or vice versa). It still could be in an uptrend, but in the midst of a retracement, which creates the low relative strength as compared to the market as a whole. Because many of the short-term systems in this book look for retracements before they enter on a breakout or other type of short-term chart formation, this system or filter also could work in a contrarian fashion, meaning that we should only look to enter into stocks with a low relative strength.

TRADESTATION CODE

Variables:

{These variables can also be used as inputs for optimization purposes.}

AllowLong(True), AllowShort(False), StrengthLookback(20), StrengthModifier(-5),
{Leave these variables alone.}
RelStrength(1), AvgRelStrength(1), LongPercRelStrength(1),
ShortPercRelStrength(1), VolStrength(1), AvgVolStrength(1),
LongPercVolStrength(1), ShortPercVolStrength(1),
LongPercStrength(1), ShortPercStrength(1), EntryStrength(1);
{Code for normalizing the number of contracts traded goes here.}
If BarNumber = 1 Then
    EntryStrength = 1 + StrengthModifier * 0.01;
If Close Data2 <> 0 Then
    RelStrength = Close / Close Data2
Else
    RelStrength = RelStrength[1];
AvgRelStrength = Average(RelStrength, StrengthLookBack);
If AvgRelStrength <> 0 Then
    LongPercRelStrength = RelStrength / AvgRelStrength
Else
    LongPercRelStrength = LongPercRelStrength[1];
VolStrength = OBV;
AvgVolStrength = Average(VolStrength, StrengthLookBack);
If AvgVolStrength <> 0 Then
    LongPercVolStrength = VolStrength / AvgVolStrength
Else
    LongPercVolStrength = LongPercVolStrength[1];
LongPercStrength = LongPercRelStrength * LongPercVolStrength;
If LongPercStrength <> 0 Then
    ShortPercStrength = 1 / LongPercStrength
Else
    ShortPercStrength = ShortPercStrength[1];
If MarketPosition = 0 Then Begin
    If AllowLong = True and LongPercStrength crosses above EntryStrength Then
        Buy ("L-Oct 00") NumCont Contracts Next Bar at Market;
    If AllowShort = True and ShortPercStrength crosses above EntryStrength Then
        Sell ("S-Oct 00") NumCont Contracts Next Bar at Market;
End;
If EntryPrice > 0 and ShortPercStrength Crosses above EntryStrength Then
    ExitLong ("L-Exit") Next Bar at Market;

If EntryPrice > 0 and LongPercStrength Crosses above EntryStrength Then
   ExitShort ("S-Exit") Next Bar at Market;

{Code for initial market export goes here, with Normalize(True). Set ExportSwitch(True).}

{Code for testing robustness goes here (see Part 3 of book), with Normalize(True). Set RobustnessSwitch(True).}

{Code for exporting results for money management analysis goes here (see Part 4 of book), with Normalize(False). Set MoneyExport(True).}

CHAPTER 10

Meander System V.1.0

Originally presented in January/February 2001, this system is based on the meander indicator, which is a price-band indicator that takes all data points within a bar into consideration when calculating moving-average and standard-deviation levels. Or, more precisely, it calculates the percentage difference between the previous bar's closing price (or average price) and the next bar's different price levels (open, high, low, and close) before it adds to the latest bar's closing price (or average price). For a detailed description of this indicator and for programming code, refer to "Moving beyond the closing price" (*Active Trader*, October 2000, p. 60) and www.activetradermag.com/code.htm.

The combination of using all price points and their relative distance from the previous bar's close (average price) results in an indicator that hugs price more closely than other kinds of price bands, making it especially useful for the short-term trader.

If today's market action takes us below the lower band (the bands are two standard deviations away), the system will signal to go long on a limit order, on the assumption that the market has overextended itself to the short side and in the short run.

SUGGESTED MARKETS

Stocks, stock index futures, and index shares (SPDRs, DIAs, QQQs).

ORIGINAL RULES

Enter long with a limit order if the market trades below the lower two standard deviation meander boundary.

Risk 4 percent of available equity per trade.

Exit with a loss if the market drops below the entry price, minus the difference between the forecasted average price and the lower meander boundary.

Exit with a trailing stop (win or loss) if the trade is more than one day old and the market once again falls below the forecasted lower meander boundary.

Exit with a profit if the market trades above the forecasted upper meander boundary.

TEST PERIOD

March 1, 1990 to November 11, 2000.

TEST DATA

Daily stock prices for the 30 stocks included in the Dow Jones Industrial Average (DJIA). A total of $20 per trade has been deducted for slippage and commission.

STARTING EQUITY

$100,000 (nominal).

SYSTEM PROS AND CONS

Because this is a long-only system, it can stall during prolonged market corrections. However, because the system has no trend filter to keep it out of the market during the early and late stages of a trend, it should react very quickly to favorable market conditions.

This system clearly illustrates the importance of having a stable profit factor and average profit per trade over a large number of markets and market conditions, rather than a few higher but less robust values. In this case, only 15 out of 30 markets had a profit factor above 1.10 when analyzed individually; no market was above 1.4. Bottom line: A strategy that incorporates good money management and constantly grinds out even marginal profits can make good money over time.

The total portfolio profit factor of only 1.2 isn't eye grabbing. But that's not the point. The point is that despite this low profit factor, the system manages to produce a risk–reward ratio well in line with the closest comparable market index (DJIA) and a buy-and-hold strategy, while only spending a fraction of the time in the market—24 percent on average per stock, compared to 100 percent per stock for a buy-and-hold strategy.

Note also that both the worst drawdown and the longest flat time happened very early on, during the October 1990 scare. Unfortunately, it took a little longer for the system to recover from this debacle than it did for the market itself. However, since then, results have been very stable, with very few drawdowns extending further than 10 percent, and since 1992, no drawdown below 15 percent.

REVISING THE RESEARCH AND MODIFYING THE SYSTEM

For the original presentation of this system, I wrote that it was just marginally profitable for no more than 50 percent of the market tested. That was one year ago (at the time of this writing) and, because this is a long-only system, performance has continued to deteriorate since then. Table 10.1 shows that of all 65 markets tested this time, 61 percent were profitable, which resulted in an average profit factor of 1.05. What is strange with these results is that, despite the low number of profitable markets and not-so-good performance numbers, the system still produces a relatively high number of profitable trades.

Obviously, it still does a good job identifying good trading opportunities, but somehow a relatively large number of winners still won't make up for the losses. The reason may be that the risk–reward relationship between the forecasted profit target and the expected stop-loss level isn't what it should be. To explore that, I started out by moving the profit target one standard deviation further away from the entry price so that the initial risk–reward relationship, going into the trade, would be 3:1 instead of only 2:1.

TABLE 10.1

Average Profitability Using Meander System V.1.0

	Trades	PercWin	NetProfit	AvgProfit	ProfitStD	RiskRatio
			Original system, long only			PercProf: 61.54
Average:	546.52	50.90	24,671.08	48.99		Market
St. Dev:	144.60	4.19	125,491.47	221.95	3,772.27	0.01
High:	691.12	55.09	150,162.54	270.94	3,821.25	Portfolio
Low:	401.93	46.71	(100,820.39)	(172.96)	(3,723.28)	0.22
	ProfitFactor	RiskFactor	MaxDD	PercDD	PercTime	AvgLength
Average:	1.05	0.02	99,648.87	66.84	51.12	3.90
St. Dev:	0.31	0.11	47,720.10	49.37	4.62	0.55
High:	1.36	0.12	147,368.97	116.22	55.74	4.46
Low:	0.74	(0.09)	51,928.76	17.47	46.49	3.35

TABLE 10.2

Adjusting Risk–Reward Relationship

		Long only: Higher target			PercProf:	87.69
	Trades	**PercWin**	**NetProfit**	**AvgProfit**	**ProfitStD**	**RiskRatio**
Average:	465.95	48.22	95,316.78	239.85		**Market**
St. Dev:	122.09	3.00	96,837.43	257.05	4,720.86	0.05
High:	588.04	51.22	192,154.21	496.90	4,960.71	**Portfolio**
Low:	343.87	45.23	(1,520.65)	(17.20)	(4,481.01)	0.93
	ProfitFactor	**RiskFactor**	**MaxDD**	**PercDD**	**PercTime**	**AvgLength**
Average:	1.14	0.07	83,423.90	45.99	59.26	5.32
St. Dev:	0.14	0.07	42,437.97	34.13	4.38	0.76
High:	1.28	0.14	125,861.87	80.12	63.64	6.08
Low:	0.99	(0.00)	40,985.93	11.86	54.88	4.56

As Table 10.2 shows, this made a huge difference in the results. All of a sudden the average profit factor increased to 1.14 and the average profit to $239.85, making the system quite tradable already. The standard deviations for the average profit and the profit and risk factors also are very low, which indicates that the results are very robust.

Concluding that it is better for the trade to run a little longer, the next step was to get rid of the initial slack period after which the stop was tightened. Table 10.3 shows that this too increased performance a little, but the bad news is that it did so by sacrificing some robustness and reliability, most clearly indicated by a lower risk–reward ratio (0.90 compared to 0.93 in Table 10.2). Usually, we would go with that version of the system that had the highest risk–reward ratio, but because this time we're getting rid of a variable completely, it's worth doing the opposite. The price we pay for a system that is slightly less curve fitted is a slightly decreased certainty of the outcome. (Not that the system was curve fitted from the beginning.)

Another performance number that could be improved a little is the percentage of time spent in a trade. As you can see, Table 10.3 indicates that it is close to 70 percent, which is a little too much if we would like to trade the system together with several other systems, on a good sized portfolio of markets. However, because we don't have that many variables or criteria to work with, we have to add a new one. In the final decision to keep a new criteria, that criterion needs to improve results considerably. The criterion I decided to go with was to require that the day before the entry should be a down day.

Table 10.4 shows the result of this version of the system. And as you can, see this is a big improvement compared to the version in Table 10.3. The average profit per trade now is $559.05, and the profit factor has now increased to 1.30. But

TABLE 10.3

Removing Slack Period

		Long only: Higher target, no slack period			PercProf: 80.00	
	Trades	**PercWin**	**NetProfit**	**AvgProfit**	**ProfitStD**	**RiskRatio**
Average:	357.23	50.52	108,822.59	354.08		**Market**
St. Dev:	92.41	3.12	117,386.63	392.64	5,846.09	0.06
High:	449.64	53.64	226,209.22	746.72	6,200.17	**Portfolio**
Low:	264.82	47.40	(8,564.04)	(38.56)	(5,492.01)	0.90
	ProfitFactor	**RiskFactor**	**MaxDD**	**PercDD**	**PercTime**	**AvgLength**
Average:	1.17	0.08	89,412.68	46.11	68.12	8.02
St. Dev:	0.20	0.09	43,735.98	32.16	4.01	1.43
High:	1.38	0.18	133,148.65	78.27	72.12	9.45
Low:	0.97	(0.01)	45,676.70	13.95	64.11	6.58

the really good stuff is that this improvement also increased the robustness and reliability of the system. The risk–reward relationship is now at 1.11, which means that more than 84 percent of all trading sequences now can be expected to produce a profit. This is further indicated by the lower one standard deviation levels for the profit and risk factors, which are above one and zero, respectively.

As a final step in this research process, I decided to review the lookback period for the meander calculations, by increasing it to 10 days. Table 10.5 shows that this too improved the results quite considerably. Again, this is most notable when

TABLE 10.4

New Criteria Added

		Long only: Higher target, no slack period, one down day			PercProf: 86.15	
	Trades	**PercWin**	**NetProfit**	**AvgProfit**	**ProfitStD**	**RiskRatio**
Average:	224.11	53.70	108,022.77	559.05		**Market**
St. Dev:	60.62	3.74	97,584.38	504.25	5,541.34	0.09
High:	284.72	57.44	205,607.15	1,063.30	6,100.39	**Portfolio**
Low:	163.49	49.97	10,438.40	54.80	(4,982.29)	1.11
	ProfitFactor	**RiskFactor**	**MaxDD**	**PercDD**	**PercTime**	**AvgLength**
Average:	1.30	0.13	61,157.25	33.37	39.46	7.36
St. Dev:	0.27	0.12	31,606.34	23.46	4.58	1.17
High:	1.56	0.25	92,763.59	56.83	44.03	8.53
Low:	1.03	0.01	29,550.90	9.90	34.88	6.19

TABLE 10.5

Increasing lookback Period

	Long only: Higher target, no slack period, one down day, 10-day lookback period				PercProf: 90.77
	Trades	**PercWin**	**NetProfit**	**AvgProfit**	**ProfitStD**	**RiskRatio**
Average:	200.98	52.68	138,385.04	788.35		**Market**
St. Dev:	55.04	4.23	102,071.61	652.01	6,378.93	0.12
High:	256.02	56.90	240,456.66	1,440.36	7,167.28	**Portfolio**
Low:	145.95	48.45	36,313.43	136.33	(5,590.59)	1.21
	ProfitFactor	**RiskFactor**	**MaxDD**	**PercDD**	**PercTime**	**AvgLength**
Average:	1.38	0.17	60,164.33	31.99	44.81	9.37
St. Dev:	0.30	0.13	30,118.05	19.17	4.76	1.70
High:	1.68	0.30	90,282.38	51.16	49.57	11.07
Low:	1.09	0.04	30,046.28	12.83	40.05	7.67

looking at the standard deviation numbers for the profit and risk factors, and the risk–reward ratio based on the average profit per trade. All these numbers now indicate that a majority of all trading sequences should produce a profit. And with the average expected profit per trading sequence at $788.35, this system could now help us make a good living.

Unfortunately, trading the system from the short side as well did not produce good enough results to warrant trading from both sides. However, with a little tinkering, tweaking, and experimenting, you should be able to come up with something good. I dare to say that because, even though the short side seems to lower the overall results quite a bit, the number of profitable trades still is very high, which means the system is doing a good job identifying good setups for a trade on the short side as well. It doesn't work this way probably because the risk–reward ratio going into the trade needs to be different between the two sides. Alternatively, the short side should not be traded with limit orders, considering the inherent upside bias in the stock market. Table 10.6 shows how the latest version of the system behaved when traded from both sides simultaneously.

Figure 10.1 shows what the meander indicator can look like with the lines adjusted for the long side only. Note in the series of trades that this version of the system is still quite dangerous in that it can move considerably against the trade as long as the volatility stays low and it avoids touching the lowest meander line. We will try to come to grips with this later, when we will try to substitute all current stops with a set of new ones.

If you compare Tables 10.1 and 10.5 you can see that a disadvantage stemming from all the changes we made is that the average trade length increased by

TABLE 10.6

Trading Both Long and Short Sides

			Both sides: Higher target, no slack period, one day against, 10-day lookback period			PercProf: 69.23
	Trades	**PercWin**	**NetProfit**	**AvgProfit**	**ProfitStD**	**RiskRatio**
Average:	281.95	50.64	60,737.50	227.86		**Market**
St. Dev:	76.61	3.82	131,776.44	577.92	6,743.58	0.04
High:	358.57	54.46	192,513.94	805.78	6,971.45	**Portfolio**
Low:	205.34	46.82	(71,038.94)	(350.05)	(6,515.72)	0.39
	ProfitFactor	**RiskFactor**	**MaxDD**	**PercDD**	**PercTime**	**AvgLength**
Average:	1.12	0.05	104,425.04	69.56	67.78	10.14
St. Dev:	0.25	0.12	65,068.06	47.83	4.67	1.93
High:	1.37	0.17	169,493.09	117.39	72.45	12.08
Low:	0.87	(0.07)	39,356.98	21.73	63.10	8.21

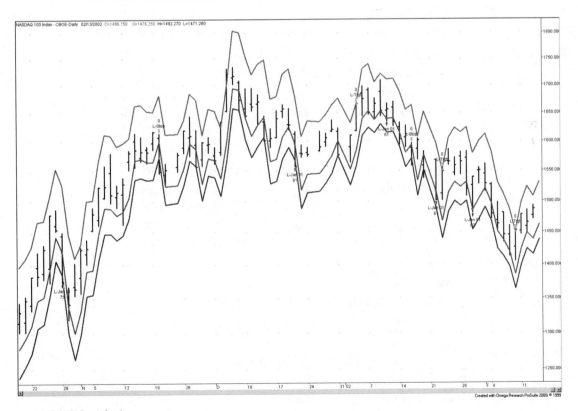

FIGURE 10.1

Long side trading using meander system V.1.0.

about 200 percent. But because the time spent in a trade remained approximately the same, while the number of trades decreased by more than 50 percent, we can conclude that the changes only made the system make the most of the most favorable market situations. In Part 3, we will try to decrease the time spent in a trade further, to make room for more diversification possibilities.

TRADESTATION CODE

```
Variables:
{These variables can also be used as inputs for optimization purposes.}
AllowLong(True), AllowShort(False), MeanderLookback(10) {Max: 25},
{Leave these variables alone.}
LookbackPoints(0), SetMeanderArray(0), MeanderArrayPos(0), SumDiff(0),
AverageDiff(0), SumSquareError(0), SumError(0), SquareSumError(0),
MeanderStDev(0), Meander(0), MeanderHigh(0), MeanderHighest(0),
MeanderLow(0), MeanderLowest(0);
Array: PriceDiff[100](0);
{Code for normalizing the number of contracts traded goes here.}
If BarNumber = 1 Then
    LookbackPoints = MeanderLookback * 4;
For SetMeanderArray = 0 To (MeanderLookback - 1) Begin
    PriceDiff[SetMeanderArray * 4 + 0] = (Open[SetMeanderArray] -
    Close[SetMeanderArray + 1]) / Close[SetMeanderArray + 1];
    PriceDiff[SetMeanderArray * 4 + 1] = (High[SetMeanderArray] -
    Close[SetMeanderArray + 1]) / Close[SetMeanderArray + 1];
    PriceDiff[SetMeanderArray * 4 + 2] = (Low[SetMeanderArray] -
    Close[SetMeanderArray + 1]) / Close[SetMeanderArray + 1];
    PriceDiff[SetMeanderArray * 4 + 3] = (Close[SetMeanderArray] -
    Close[SetMeanderArray + 1]) / Close[SetMeanderArray + 1];
End;
SumDiff = 0;
For MeanderArrayPos = 0 To (LookbackPoints - 1) Begin
    SumDiff = SumDiff + PriceDiff[MeanderArrayPos];
End;
AverageDiff = SumDiff / (LookbackPoints);
SumSquareError = 0;
SumError = 0;
For MeanderArrayPos = 0 To (LookbackPoints - 1) Begin
```

```
      SumSquareError = SumSquareError +
      Square(PriceDiff[MeanderArrayPos] - AverageDiff);
      SumError = SumError + (PriceDiff[MeanderArrayPos] - AverageDiff);
   End;
   SquareSumError = Square(SumError);
   MeanderStDev = SquareRoot((LookbackPoints * SumSquareError -
   SquareSumError) / (LookbackPoints * (LookbackPoints - 1)));
   Meander = Close * (1 + AverageDiff);
   MeanderHighest = Close * (1 + AverageDiff + 2 * MeanderStDev);
   MeanderHigh = Close * (1 + AverageDiff + MeanderStDev);
   MeanderLow = Close * (1 + AverageDiff - MeanderStDev);
   MeanderLowest = Close * (1 + AverageDiff - 2 * MeanderStDev);
   If MarketPosition = 0 Then Begin
      If AllowLong = True and Close < Close[1] and Close < Open Then
         Buy ("L-Jan 01") NumCont Contracts Next Bar at MeanderLow Limit;
      If AllowShort = True and Close > Close[1] and Close > Open Then
         Sell ("S-Jan 01") NumCont Contracts Next Bar at MeanderHigh Limit;
   End;
   If EntryPrice > 0 Then Begin
      ExitLong ("L-Stop") Next Bar at MeanderLowest Stop;
      ExitLong ("L-Trgt") Next Bar at MeanderHighest Limit;
      ExitShort ("S-Stop") Next Bar at MeanderHighest Stop;
      ExitShort ("S-Trgt") Next Bar at MeanderLowest Limit;
   End;
   {Code for testing stops in Excel goes here (see Part 3 of book), with
   Normalize(False). Set SurfaceChartTest(True). Disable original stops in system.}
   {Code for initial market export goes here, with Normalize(True). Set
   ExportSwitch(True).}
   {Code for testing robustness goes here (see Part 3 of book), with Normalize(True).
   Set RobustnessSwitch(True).}
   {Code for exporting results for money management analysis goes here (see Part 4
   of book), with Normalize(False). Set MoneyExport(True).}
```

CHAPTER 11

Relative Strength Bands

Originally presented in March 2001, this system had an error in the original text in *Active Trader* magazine. Instead of computing the Bollinger bands for the relative strength line (RSL), as originally stated, the bands should be computed on the product of all RSV lines (PRSV). The original code did it correctly, but the original system logic explained it all wrong.

This system uses a mix of relative strength (not RSI) analysis and Bollinger bands to identify markets that are about to break out of congestion areas. In this case, relative strength is calculated by taking the closing price of market No. 1 and dividing it by market No. 2. Doing this for every bar creates an RSL.

Market No. 1 is stronger than market No. 2 when the RSL is above its n-bar (in this case 21-day) moving average, and vice versa when the RSL is below its relative moving average (RMA). Calculating the percentage difference between the RSL and RMA creates the relative strength value (RSV = RSL / RMA). The higher the value above 1.00, the stronger market No. 1 is in comparison to market No. 2 and vice versa.

To measure the relative strength among several markets, first divide the price of market No. 1 by the price of each of the other markets, creating several RSLs. Then calculate a moving average for each RSL. Then calculate the RSV for each RSL, as described above. Multiply all the RSVs together to create a product RSV for each market (PRSV). If the end result is above 1.00, market No. 1 is relatively stronger than the majority of the other markets.

Bollinger bands of each PRSV are used to determine whether a particular market is stronger relative to a large majority of the other markets. If the PRSV for a specific market is above its one-standard-deviation (SD) Bollinger band, it is relatively stronger than approximately 84 percent (100 − 16) of all other markets. (A one-SD interval should hold approximately 68 percent of all the data, leaving approximately 16 percent of the data on either side of the SD boundaries. A two-SD interval should hold approximately 95 percent of all the data, leaving approximately 2.5 percent of the data on either side of the SD boundaries.)

Long signals are generated when the PRSV moves above its one-SD boundary; short signals are created when the PRSV moves below its two-SD boundary. (The asymmetrical SD boundaries are used because of the natural upward drift of the market and to limit short-side trades for "catastrophe protection.")

SUGGESTED MARKETS

Index tracking stocks (SPYs, DIAs, QQQs) and stock index futures.

ORIGINAL RULES

Look for long signals only when the PRSV is above its 21-day, one-SD Bollinger band.

Look for short signals only when the PRSV is below its 21-day, two-SD Bollinger band.

Enter long at the close when the PRSV is above its value of two days ago, but never on the same bar as a previously exited trade.

Enter short at the close when the PRSV is below its value of two days ago, but never on the same bar as a previously exited trade.

Risk 2 percent of available equity per trade.

Exit long trades with a trailing stop (profit or loss) if the market drops below the lowest low of the last two bars, or if the PRSV drops below its value of four days ago.

Exit short trades with a trailing stop (profit or loss) if the market trades above the highest high of the last two bars, or if the PRSV rises above its value of four days ago.

Exit all trades on the close if they're not profitable after eight bars.

TEST PERIOD

March 22, 1990 to December 14, 2000.

TEST DATA

Daily prices for the NASDAQ 100 (NDX), S&P 500 (SPX), and Dow Jones Industrial Average (DJIA) indices.

STARTING EQUITY

$100,000 (nominal).

SYSTEM PROS AND CONS

This test revealed some interesting system characteristics—and there is no way we could have found out about them using any of the publicly available system testing programs.

Running this system on any of the three individual markets in the portfolio resulted in less-than-desirable results. The NASDAQ 100 index, for instance, performed fairly well up until the last several months, at which point it gave back all its previous profits and more.

The DJIA, however, didn't trade well at all until the last year or so, at which point it started to post terrific results. The S&P 500 had a steady upward-sloping equity curve over the test period, but the result was a mere doubling of the initial equity over more than 10 years of trading. Simply summing the results of the three markets traded individually would have resulted in the portfolio just breaking even.

But when we combine all markets into one portfolio and use a fixed-fractional money management strategy (risking 2 percent of equity per trade), as we did in this test, things start to happen. The interaction between the markets creates much better results. First, the steady upward slope of the S&P 500 equity creates stability. Second, the combined positive returns of the S&P 500 and NASDAQ over the first several years results in much faster equity growth than that of any individual markets.

Naturally, the fixed-fractional money management strategy also adds to this growth in a way other money management techniques do not, because you're risking more when your equity is increasing and risking less when your equity is decreasing.

Third, because this system looks at the relative strength among several markets and allows both long and short signals, there are plenty of situations where one market acts as catastrophe protection for another, which is exactly what happened over the last few months when the NASDAQ underperformed and the DJIA performed better than ever.

Finally, if two markets signal entry on two consecutive days, it may or may not be possible to enter into the second market, depending on how much capital is tied up in the first market. This often prevents entry into bad trades in the weaker of the markets. Both these factors also work together to produce very low drawdown numbers.

REVISING THE RESEARCH AND MODIFYING THE SYSTEM

For the original system, I only looked at three indexes: S&P 500, NASDAQ 100, and DJIA. As it turned out, the result produced by these three markets has not held up since the system was published. We'll discuss the reasons for this while we make a new attempt to come up with a better, more robust system, given the initial logic.

One major reason for why the results haven't held up is because the original system was only tested on three markets, which is far too few to produce results that can be trusted in the long run. To come to grips with that, I expanded the research for this book by adding two more indexes to the equation, so that the relative strength of one market was calculated in relation to four other markets, instead of only two. The code below is set to calculate the relative strength between the market to be traded and the four markets it's compared to.

Adding only two more indexes would give us a total of just five trading sequences, which still isn't enough. Therefore, I also picked 10 markets each from the NASDAQ 100 index and the DJIA, respectively, to be compared to eight other markets each, from their respective indexes. All markets were selected at random. For example, from the DJIA group, I randomly picked American Express (AXP) to be compared against Citigroup (C), Eastman Kodak (EK), General Electric (GE), Home Depot (HD), IBM, United Technologies (UTX), 3M (MMM), and Merck (MRK). Only AXP would be traded. The other markets are only there to construct a randomly created RSI for American Express to generate trading signals. In total, this gives us 25 different trading sequences to analyze. Because the original model was asymmetric in nature, with different rules for long and short trades, each side will be analyzed individually.

Table 11.1 shows the results of the original model, tested on our 25 different markets. With an average profit of $-\$52.69$, a profit factor just above one, and a risk factor just below zero, the results are not satisfactory, and the conclu-

TABLE 11.1

Trading Original Relative Strength Bands

		Original system, long only			PercProf: 48.00	
	Trades	**PercWin**	**NetProfit**	**AvgProfit**	**ProfitStD**	**RiskRatio**
Average:	150.24	36.94	(5,312.70)	(52.69)		**Market**
St. Dev:	60.55	5.36	50,710.57	402.95	4,294.81	(0.01)
High:	210.79	42.30	45,397.88	350.27	4,242.13	**Portfolio**
Low:	89.69	31.58	(56,023.27)	(455.64)	(4,347.50)	(0.13)
	ProfitFactor	**RiskFactor**	**MaxDD**	**PercDD**	**PercTime**	**AvgLength**
Average:	1.01	(0.00)	55,162.30	42.18	25.43	5.22
St. Dev:	0.29	0.18	27,778.81	24.46	2.57	0.58
High:	1.30	0.18	82,941.11	66.65	28.00	5.80
Low:	0.72	(0.18)	27,383.48	17.72	22.86	4.64

sion is that something needs to be done. There are several things we could do, such as altering the lookback period for the standard-deviation calculations, otherwise making it more or less difficult for the system to generate a signal, or altering the stop-loss and trailing-stop levels.

Let's start by making the lookback period for the standard-deviation calculations longer. Table 11.2 shows that using a 200-day lookback period, the average profit is above zero, and the positive result is further confirmed by a profit factor of 1.08 and a risk factor of 0.02. The results in Table 11.2 are confirmed by additional tests with other lookback periods, which are not shown. Apparently, a 21-day lookback period is not enough for this system to produce good results on the long side.

Going with a longer lookback period than the original 21 days, I arbitrarily set it to 100 days and continued the research by looking into other parameters to examine. Table 11.3 shows what happened with the result when I altered the standard-deviation interval for the entry to zero. With the standard deviation set to one, as it was originally, the market we're looking to trade needs to be relatively stronger than 84 percent of all the markets it's compared to. With the standard deviation set to zero, the market we're looking to trade only needs to be relatively stronger than 50 percent of all the markets it's compared against.

Making it easier to enter into the trade by requiring that the market we want to trade only needs to be relatively stronger than 50 percent of the markets it's compared against improved the results considerably. The average profit is now well above zero at $110.85, and a profit factor above 1.10 indicates the system will remain profitable when the cost of trading is added as well. The number of prof-

TABLE 11.2

Altering Lookback Period

		Long only: 200-day lookback period				PercProf: 52.00
	Trades	**PercWin**	**NetProfit**	**AvgProfit**	**ProfitStD**	**RiskRatio**
Average:	85.40	35.27	13,998.08	6.14		**Market**
St. Dev:	51.10	9.82	46,357.47	1,109.99	4,338.73	(0.06)
High:	136.50	45.09	60,355.55	1,116.13	4,344.87	**Portfolio**
Low:	34.30	25.45	(32,359.39)	(1,103.84)	(4,332.58)	0.01
	ProfitFactor	**RiskFactor**	**MaxDD**	**PercDD**	**PercTime**	**AvgLength**
Average:	1.08	0.02	31,546.25	26.76	15.54	5.71
St. Dev:	0.48	0.34	16,273.03	16.35	6.25	0.74
High:	1.55	0.36	47,819.28	43.12	21.78	6.44
Low:	0.60	(0.33)	15,273.22	10.41	9.29	4.97

TABLE 11.3

Setting the Standard Deviations to Zero

	Long only: 100-day lookback period, zero st. devs.				PercProf: 64.00	
	Trades	**PercWin**	**NetProfit**	**AvgProfit**	**ProfitStD**	**RiskRatio**
Average:	171.04	36.75	22,036.35	110.85		**Market**
St. Dev:	72.35	4.50	61,617.06	397.01	4,633.09	0.02
High:	243.39	41.24	83,653.41	507.85	4,743.94	**Portfolio**
Low:	98.69	32.25	(39,580.71)	(286.16)	(4,522.24)	0.28
	ProfitFactor	**RiskFactor**	**MaxDD**	**PercDD**	**PercTime**	**AvgLength**
Average:	1.11	0.06	51,937.08	40.43	36.46	6.16
St. Dev:	0.29	0.18	21,924.01	24.04	6.57	0.74
High:	1.39	0.24	73,861.08	64.46	43.03	6.90
Low:	0.82	(0.12)	30,013.07	16.39	29.88	5.42

itable markets now increased to 64 percent. The number of profitable trades is, however, still relatively low at 36.75 percent.

Satisfied with these results, I finally decided to test how the system would fare without the stops applied directly on the market traded. My thinking was that this would increase the number of profitable trades somewhat, making the system less nerve-racking to trade. This turned out to be exactly right, but not only that: As indicated by Table 11.4, all other evaluation parameters soared as well. The

TABLE 11.4

Revised Relative Strength Bands

	Long only: 100-day lookback period, zero st. devs, no stops				PercProf: 76.00	
	Trades	**PercWin**	**NetProfit**	**AvgProfit**	**ProfitStD**	**RiskRatio**
Average:	49.60	42.16	115,503.24	3,577.65		**Market**
St. Dev:	26.91	12.35	188,866.63	6,094.46	20,217.42	0.15
High:	76.51	54.50	304,369.87	9,672.11	23,795.07	**Portfolio**
Low:	22.69	29.81	(73,363.40)	(2,516.82)	(16,639.78)	0.59
	ProfitFactor	**RiskFactor**	**MaxDD**	**PercDD**	**PercTime**	**AvgLength**
Average:	2.23	0.72	44,369.24	28.10	54.36	35.21
St. Dev:	1.41	0.89	26,314.45	21.07	9.32	8.71
High:	3.64	1.60	70,683.70	49.16	63.68	43.92
Low:	0.81	(0.17)	18,054.79	7.03	45.04	26.50

number of profitable markets continued higher to 76 percent, the average profit per trade increased to $3,577, the profit factor to 2.23, and according to the risk factor, we're now making a whopping 72 cents for every dollar risked.

At first glance, this looks very good indeed, but as already pointed out earlier, when a system produces results this good, they might be too good to be true, and these results are no exception to that rule. Let's start by comparing the average profit per trade with the standard deviation for all average profits. Note that the standard deviation, at $6,094, is almost twice as large as the average profit of $3,577, which results in a one-standard-deviation interval stretching from −$2,516 to $9,672. Thus, this system still produces a lot of trading sequences with an average profit per trade below zero, and the chances for the true, always unknown, average profit to actually be negative are quite high. This annoying fact is also confirmed by the profit factor that has its lower one-standard-deviation boundary at 0.81 and the risk factor with its lower one-standard-deviation boundary indicating a loss of 17 cents per dollar risked. Another unwanted feature of this system is that the average trade length increased from around six days to 35 days, which no longer can be considered short-term and may be too long when using the system as a filter for other systems.

The high standard deviations probably ruined the original version of this system. Testing it on only three markets, unknowingly and unwillingly, I managed to produce a system with a decent hypothetical average profit per trade, but also a very high standard deviation, thus making it very likely that the system would lose plenty of money over long periods, which was exactly what happened during the period following the original testing period.

Granted, the upper one-standard-deviation boundary for the average profit indicates also a high likelihood that the system will perform better than indicated by the original research, but good periods are easy to deal with. Of the really bad periods, we only need one to end our careers as traders (and find a cheaper place to live). The trick is to keep the likelihood of this happening as small as possible; for that we also need to sacrifice some upside potential.

Before we move on to the short side, I would like to make one more adjustment, and that is to equalize the lookback periods for the entry and exit formations that now are set to two and four days, respectively. I would like to do this because otherwise this system simply has too many adjustable and optimizable variables, and as we will see later, when we talk about stops and exits, finding robust solutions for more than three variables is very difficult. It also is important that we keep the entry as simple and logical as possible, with as few rules as possible. Therefore, if it turns out we're better off without these variables, or if the results are inconclusive, the variables will be scratched. If not, they will both be set to the same value.

As it turned out, the results were rather inconclusive, so both variables will be scratched. The results of this version of the system can be seen in Table 11.5.

TABLE 11.5

More Variables Altered

		Long only: 100-day lookback period, zero st. devs, no stops, no trailing strength test			PercProf: 80.00	
	Trades	**PercWin**	**NetProfit**	**AvgProfit**	**ProfitStD**	**RiskRatio**
Average:	57.72	39.47	113,784.90	2,746.38		**Market**
St. Dev:	30.85	13.47	186,768.28	4,494.59	18,421.02	0.13
High:	88.57	52.95	300,553.18	7,240.97	21,167.40	**Portfolio**
Low:	26.87	26.00	(72,983.38)	(1,748.20)	(15,674.64)	0.61
	ProfitFactor	**RiskFactor**	**MaxDD**	**PercDD**	**PercTime**	**AvgLength**
Average:	2.19	0.73	43,547.04	28.29	54.09	29.72
St. Dev:	1.45	0.93	26,720.15	20.88	9.54	7.18
High:	3.64	1.65	70,267.19	49.17	63.63	36.90
Low:	0.74	(0.20)	16,826.89	7.41	44.55	22.54

The two variables we've left are RelStrengthLookback and LongStDevs, set to 100 days and zero standard deviations, respectively (see code below).

Despite the rather high likelihood for this version to move into negative territory, this is the version I will take with me to Part 3, where we will try to use it as a filter for the other more short-term systems featured in this book. To be sure, at this point the next step could have been to look closer into the results produced by various combinations of the two remaining optimizable variables. The same techniques used to find the best and most reliable stops and exit levels, (which we look at more closely later), also can be used to fine-tune and optimize the entry variables for robustness and likelihood for future success. I will not do this here, but you are free to do so if you wish. Note also that if you do, and altering the LongStDevs variable doesn't produce significantly improved results while maintaining robustness, it too could be scratched, and you'd be down to one optimizable variable.

Now, let's follow the same line of reasoning for the short side and see what we can come up with. Table 11.6 shows the results for the original model, tested on our 25 different markets. With an average profit of −$281.39, a profit factor below 0.9, and a risk factor of −10 cents, the original results for the short side are a long way from being satisfactory.

Altering the lookback period, first to 50 days and then to 100 days, indicated that sticking to a shorter lookback period in the neighborhood of 20 to 60 days is the way to go. In this case, a 50-day lookback period produced a small profit, whereas the 100-day lookback period dragged the results back into negative territory again. The deteriorating performance from using a too long lookback period

TABLE 11.6

Short Side Trading Using Original Relative Strength Bands

	Original system, short only				PercProf: 40.00	
	Trades	**PercWin**	**NetProfit**	**AvgProfit**	**ProfitStD**	**RiskRatio**
Average:	56.32	32.23	(13,229.68)	(281.39)		**Market**
St. Dev:	33.20	10.23	29,241.64	1,022.98	4,477.42	(0.11)
High:	89.52	42.46	16,011.96	741.59	4,196.03	**Portfolio**
Low:	23.12	22.01	(42,471.31)	(1,304.38)	(4,758.81)	(0.28)
	ProfitFactor	**RiskFactor**	**MaxDD**	**PercDD**	**PercTime**	**AvgLength**
Average:	0.88	(0.10)	34,525.10	32.43	8.82	5.09
St. Dev:	0.42	0.31	19,478.50	19.33	2.47	1.05
High:	1.30	0.21	54,003.60	51.75	11.29	6.14
Low:	0.46	(0.42)	15,046.60	13.10	6.35	4.05

also is confirmed by a test of a 200-day lookback. Therefore, it seems best to stay with a shorter lookback period for the short side. This also makes sense when remembering that the original logic for the system said that the short side was only going to work as catastrophe protection. Using a shorter lookback period, the system will react faster to those swift moves against the general upward drift of the markets.

With such a short lookback period of 20 to 60 days, to make sure the system doesn't trade too often or stop out the more long-term trades on the long side, keep the standard deviation-based trigger level as far away from the average relative strength as possible so that only the very weakest markets will be traded. Table 11.7 shows what happened when the standard deviation setting was altered from two to three standard deviations. Note that the lookback period also is altered to 21 days. Other tests (not shown) with altering lookback periods confirmed that this was the best combination.

What we would like to happen happens: The profitability of the system increases considerably using a higher standard deviation setting. Table 11.7 shows that for a lookback period of 21 days, combined with a three-standard-deviation trigger level, the average profit per trade has increased to $323.92, the profit factor is now at a decent 1.52, and the risk factor indicates that we could make as much as 16 cents per dollar risked, on average.

Having decided that we're better off with a three-standard-deviation entry level, it's time to examine the stops applied directly to the market in question. Table 11.8 shows that a system without stops has a higher average profit per trade ($449.59), but also lower profit and risk factors at 1.30 and 0.08, respectively. The risk–reward ratio also is slightly lower at 0.17. However, although this version of

TABLE 11.7

Altering Standard Deviation (2)

	Short only: 21-day lookback period, three st. devs.				PercProf: 44.00	
	Trades	**PercWin**	**NetProfit**	**AvgProfit**	**ProfitStD**	**RiskRatio**
Average:	21.32	38.67	(2,714.99)	323.92		**Market**
St. Dev:	13.48	13.19	18,602.76	1,618.80	4,876.61	(0.04)
High:	34.80	51.86	15,887.78	1,942.72	5,200.54	**Portfolio**
Low:	7.84	25.48	(21,317.75)	(1,294.87)	(4,552.69)	0.20
	ProfitFactor	**RiskFactor**	**MaxDD**	**PercDD**	**PercTime**	**AvgLength**
Average:	1.52	0.16	17,915.29	17.03	3.47	5.21
St. Dev:	1.92	0.74	13,635.08	13.32	1.65	1.91
High:	3.44	0.89	31,550.37	30.35	5.12	7.12
Low:	(0.40)	(0.58)	4,280.21	3.70	1.82	3.30

the system is trading less (approximately 17 trades per market tested), the higher average profit at $449 produces a higher expected net profit than for the system with the stops (17 * 449 = 7633, compared to 21 * 324 = 6804). (Never mind that the average net profit is negative in both tables.) Another positive is that this version of the system produces a higher percentage of profitable trades.

If it was up to me, I would go with the system with the highest risk–reward ratio and lowest standard deviations and trade it on as many markets as possible,

TABLE 11.8

Removing Stops

	Short only: 21-day lookback period, three st. devs, no stops				PercProf: 44.00	
	Trades	**PercWin**	**NetProfit**	**AvgProfit**	**ProfitStD**	**RiskRatio**
Average:	17.24	41.83	(4,177.05)	449.59		**Market**
St. Dev:	10.25	12.82	22,461.44	2,723.90	6,248.83	(0.06)
High:	27.49	54.65	18,284.40	3,173.48	6,698.41	**Portfolio**
Low:	6.99	29.00	(26,638.49)	(2,274.31)	(5,799.24)	0.17
	ProfitFactor	**RiskFactor**	**MaxDD**	**PercDD**	**PercTime**	**AvgLength**
Average:	1.30	0.08	20,753.24	20.12	4.58	8.37
St. Dev:	1.31	0.66	14,816.11	14.65	2.28	4.27
High:	2.61	0.75	35,569.34	34.77	6.86	12.65
Low:	(0.00)	(0.58)	5,937.13	5.48	2.30	4.10

but because the results from the two latest versions of the system are somewhat contradictory, we will do the rest of the testing on both versions (with and without the stops).

As was the case for the long side, the final step will be to try to equalize the lookback periods for the entry and exit formations, which now are set to two and four days, respectively. Testing these variables, both with and without the stops, continued to produce contradictory results. Keeping the stops produced the best results with both variables set to two days, but without the stops, the best results came from scratching both variables completely. When the results are contradictory like this, the rule is that we should strive towards using as few variables as possible. Therefore, I will scratch both the stops and the trailing-strength test on the short side as well.

As was the case for the long side, despite the rather high likelihood for this version of the system to move into negative territory, this is the version I will take with me to Part 3, where we will try to use it as a trend filter for other systems. To be sure, at this point the next step could have been to look closer into the results produced by various combinations of the two variables RelStrengthLookback and ShortStDevs, which now are set to 21 days and three standard deviations, respectively. The same techniques used to find the best and most reliable stops and exit levels (which we explore later), also can be used to fine-tune and optimize the entry variables for robustness and likelihood for future success. I won't do this here, but you are free to do so if you wish. Figure 11.1 shows a few long trades in the Russell 2000 index.

TRADESTATION CODE

This code is for the index version of the system discussed above. For the stocks version, more stocks (nine) have been used to calculate the total relative strength for the market to be traded (variable TotRelStrength). To add markets to the calculations, first add the necessary variables (RelStrength.1n, AvgRelStrength.1n, and PercRelStrength.1n), then add the necessary calculations in accordance with the logic in the code. For example, the variable AvgRelStrength.1n would be calculated as Average(RelStrength.1n, RelStrengthLookback), the variable PercRelStrength.1n would be calculated as RelStrength.1n / AvgRelStrength.1n, and the TotRelStrength variable as PercRelStrength.12 * PercRelStrength.13 * … * PercRelStrength.1N.

```
Variables:
{These variables can also be used as inputs for optimization purposes.}
AllowLong(True), AllowShort(True), LongRelStrengthLB(100),
ShortRelStrengthLB(21), LongStDevs(0), ShortStDevs(3),
{Leave these variables alone.}
```

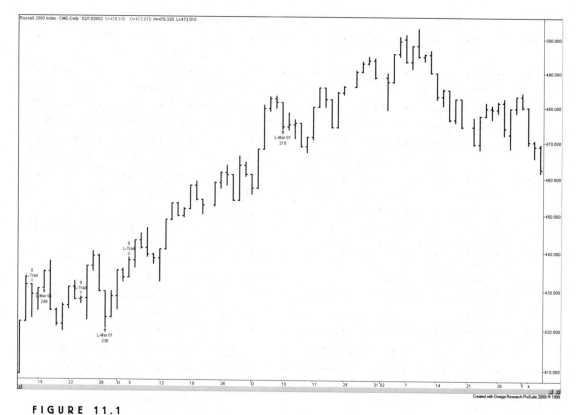

FIGURE 11.1

Long trading in the Russell 2000 Index.

RelStrength.12(0), LongAvgRelStre.12(0), ShortAvgRelStre.12(0), LongPercRelStre.12(0), ShortPercRelStre.12(0),

RelStrength.13(0), LongAvgRelStre.13(0), ShortAvgRelStre.13(0), LongPercRelStre.13(0), ShortPercRelStre.13(0),

RelStrength.14(0), LongAvgRelStre.14(0), ShortAvgRelStre.14(0), LongPercRelStre.14(0), ShortPercRelStre.14(0),

RelStrength.15(0), LongAvgRelStre.15(0), ShortAvgRelStre.15(0), LongPercRelStre.15(0), ShortPercRelStre.15(0),

LongTotRelStre(0), ShortTotRelStre(0), LongBaseTriggerCalc(0), ShortBaseTriggerCalc(0), LongTriggerStrength(0), ShortTriggerStrength(0);

{Code for normalizing the number of contracts traded goes here.}

RelStrength.12 = Close / Close Data2;

RelStrength.13 = Close / Close Data3;

RelStrength.14 = Close / Close Data4;

```
RelStrength.15 = Close / Close Data5;
If AllowLong = True Then Begin
    LongAvgRelStre.12 = Average(RelStrength.12, LongRelStrengthLB);
    LongAvgRelStre.13 = Average(RelStrength.13, LongRelStrengthLB);
    LongAvgRelStre.14 = Average(RelStrength.14, LongRelStrengthLB);
    LongAvgRelStre.15 = Average(RelStrength.15, LongRelStrengthLB);
    LongPercRelStre.12 = RelStrength.12 / LongAvgRelStre.12;
    LongPercRelStre.13 = RelStrength.13 / LongAvgRelStre.13;
    LongPercRelStre.14 = RelStrength.14 / LongAvgRelStre.14;
    LongPercRelStre.15 = RelStrength.15 / LongAvgRelStre.15;
    LongTotRelStre = LongPercRelStre.12 * LongPercRelStre.13 *
LongPercRelStre.14 * LongPercRelStre.15;
    LongBaseTriggerCalc = StdDev(LongTotRelStre, LongRelStrengthLB);
    LongTriggerStrength = 1 + LongBaseTriggerCalc * LongStDevs;
    If MarketPosition = 0 and LongTotRelStre > LongTriggerStrength Then
        Buy ("L-Mar 01") NumCont Contracts Next Bar at Market;
End;
If AllowShort = True Then Begin
    ShortAvgRelStre.12 = Average(RelStrength.12, ShortRelStrengthLB);
    ShortAvgRelStre.13 = Average(RelStrength.13, ShortRelStrengthLB);
    ShortAvgRelStre.14 = Average(RelStrength.14, ShortRelStrengthLB);
    ShortAvgRelStre.15 = Average(RelStrength.15, ShortRelStrengthLB);
    ShortPercRelStre.12 = RelStrength.12 / ShortAvgRelStre.12;
    ShortPercRelStre.13 = RelStrength.13 / ShortAvgRelStre.13;
    ShortPercRelStre.14 = RelStrength.14 / ShortAvgRelStre.14;
    ShortPercRelStre.15 = RelStrength.15 / ShortAvgRelStre.15;
    ShortTotRelStre = ShortPercRelStre.12 * ShortPercRelStre.13 *
ShortPercRelStre.14 * ShortPercRelStre.15;
    ShortBaseTriggerCalc = StdDev(ShortTotRelStre, ShortRelStrengthLB);
    ShortTriggerStrength = 1 - ShortBaseTriggerCalc * ShortStDevs;
    If MarketPosition = 0 and TotRelStrength < ShortTriggerStrength Then
        Sell ("S-Mar 01") NumCont Contracts Next Bar at Market;
End;
If EntryPrice > 0 and LongTotRelStre < LongTriggerStrength Then
    ExitLong ("L-Trail") Next Bar at Market;
If EntryPrice > 0 and TotRelStrength > ShortTriggerStrength Then
    ExitShort ("S-Trail") Next Bar at Market;
```

{Code for initial market export goes here, with Normalize(True). Set ExportSwitch(True).}

{Code for testing robustness goes here (see Part 3 of book), with Normalize(True). Set RobustnessSwitch(True).}

{Code for exporting results for money management analysis goes here (see Part 4 of book), with Normalize(False). Set MoneyExport(True).}

CHAPTER 12

Rotation

Originally presented in May 2001, this is a longer-term position trading system designed to trade (from the long side) the two strongest indexes of the Dow Jones Industrial Average (DJIA), NASDAQ 100, and the S&P 500. As a partial hedge, the system goes short in the weakest market. The logic behind this system rests on three assumptions:

The stock market has a long-term upward bias. Always having a long position in two out of three markets should capture this bias.

When a market proves itself to be stronger or weaker than other markets, this relationship is likely to continue for some time.

If a large, adverse move occurs, it will likely affect all markets simultaneously, but will be particularly devastating for the weakest market; therefore, this market will be reserved for short trades only.

The indicator used to calculate the relative strength of the three markets is similar to the 80-day moving average slope (MAS) indicator described in "Building a Better Trend Indicator" (*Active Trader*, May 2001, p. 80). However, instead of analyzing each market directly, the MAS indicator is applied to the ratio between two markets (i.e., market one divided by market two).

When one market is gaining or losing strength relative to another market, the 80-day MAS indicator's 20-day slope (today's MAS—the MAS 20 days ago) will change direction. Trades are signaled when the short-term volatility is less than the long-term volatility, as described in the rules.

SUGGESTED MARKETS

Index tracking stocks (SPDRs, DIAs, QQQs), futures, and currencies.

ORIGINAL RULES

Prepare to go long when the MAS indicator signals the trend strength in a market. (Long positions are established in the two strongest markets.)

Prepare to go short in the market that the MAS indicator identifies as the weakest of all three markets.

Enter tomorrow (long and short) at the open if the average trading range for the past three days is less than the average trading range for the last 30 days.

Exit long trades: with a stop loss equal to two times the average trading range of the three days preceding the entry;

With a trailing stop if the market goes against the trade two times the average trading range of the past three days, deducted from the previous day's close;

With a profit target if the market moves in the direction of the trade six times the average trading range of the past three days.

Exit short trades: with a stop loss equal to three times the average trading range of the day preceding the entry;

With a trailing stop if the market goes against the trade three times the average trading range of the past three days, added to the previous day's close;

With a profit target if the market moves in the direction of the trade three times the average trading range of the past three days.

TEST PERIOD

March 1991 to February 2001 (2,500 days of data per market).

TEST DATA

Daily index notations for DJIA, NASDAQ 100, and S&P 500. A total of $20 has been deducted for slippage and commission per trade.

STARTING EQUITY

$100,000 (nominal).

SYSTEM ANALYSIS

The settings for the MAS indicator in this system are totally unoptimized. It should be possible to improve the system's performance by finding a better setting for this indicator.

The system doesn't take into consideration the direction of the trend, only whether one market is stronger or weaker relative to the others. Thus, plenty of situations occur where all three indexes are declining, but the system still trades the two strongest of them from the long side. By adding a trend filter to each market, results should improve considerably.

The asymmetrical stops are designed to distinguish between different market characteristics that depend on the long-term trend. For example, because markets generally are more volatile when they fall than when they rally, the trailing stop is placed further away for the weakest of the markets than it is for the two strongest ones (to avoid getting stopped out too often).

The trailing stop will only stop out the quickest and most adverse moves against the trade. If the market moves slowly against the trade for a prolonged period, the trade won't be exited until the price reaches the stop-loss level.

REVISING THE RESEARCH AND MODIFYING THE SYSTEM

The reasoning for this system is pretty much the same as for the relative-strength bands, discussed previously. For the original system, I only looked at the three indexes: S&P 500, NASDAQ 100, and DJIA. Therefore, I once again had to expand the research for this book by adding two more indexes and 20 stocks to achieve statistically reliable results. The code below is set to calculate the relative strength between one of the indexes and the four indexes it's compared to.

All stocks were once again picked at random from a population of 30 stocks in each subgroup. Each stock that was to be traded was compared to eight other stocks from the same group. For example, from the NASDAQ 100 group, I randomly picked QUALCOMM (QCOM) to be compared against Altera (ALTR), Bed Bath & Beyond (BBBY), Chiron (CHIR), Dell (Dell), Flextronics (FLEX), Immunex (IMNX), KLA Tencor (KLAC), and Nextel (NXTL). Only QCOM would be traded. The other markets are only there to construct a randomly created relative-strength indication for QCOM to generate trading signals. In total, this will give us 25 different trading sequences to analyze. Because the original model was asymmetrical in nature, with different rules for long and short trades, each side will be analyzed individually.

Table 12.1 shows the results of the original model, traded from the long side only. As you can see, this is a good start, with very high profit and risk factors. The major negative is that most standard deviation measures are a little too high.

For the original testing of this system, I decided to always go long, the two strongest indexes out of the three making up the portfolio. During this research process, I decided to go long two out of five indexes and long a stock if it belonged to the four strongest in its group of nine stocks. I settled for these numbers, and decided to keep them constant, because during the many years of bull market, the system most likely will seem to perform better the more markets traded, and if that's the case, we might just as well trash this relative-strength system completely. However, during this stage of the research process, what seems to be best isn't always what will work best in the end. By limiting the number of markets traded

TABLE 12.1

Trading Original Rotation System

	Trades	PercWin	NetProfit	AvgProfit	ProfitStD	RiskRatio
			Original system, long only			PercProf: 68.00
Average:	47.08	37.44	57,123.57	1,197.99		Market
St. Dev:	23.77	9.40	82,533.95	2,684.63	10,348.07	0.11
High:	70.85	46.84	139,657.53	3,882.63	11,546.07	Portfolio
Low:	23.31	28.04	(25,410.38)	(1,486.64)	(9,150.08)	0.45

	ProfitFactor	RiskFactor	MaxDD	PercDD	PercTime	AvgLength
Average:	1.49	0.25	44,060.96	31.05	43.96	29.20
St. Dev:	0.71	0.40	20,939.63	18.61	11.49	13.82
High:	2.20	0.65	65,000.59	49.66	55.44	43.02
Low:	0.77	(0.15)	23,121.33	12.44	32.47	15.39

at each instance in time, we can risk more and make more on a few well-selected stocks, than we could trading all stocks at all times. This will become clearer to you in Part 4, where we discuss various money management issues and how to always risk the most optimal amount according to your own scientifically determined preferences.

Given that the average trade length is rather high, the most obvious alteration would be to shorten the lookback periods for the relative strength calculations. However, doing so would most likely also result in more losing trades, and because we don't have that many winners to begin with, I decided to leave the testing of different lookback periods until last. The first thing then, is to see if we can get rid of any other variables or criteria. In this case, the most obvious one is the trailing stop. Doing without it resulted in a slight deterioration of most performance measures (as can be seen in Table 12.2), but because the changes were rather small, it is still wise to get rid of this criterion to keep the complexity of the system to a minimum.

Because we started by looking at the stops, the next logical step would be to look at alternative settings for the stop-loss and profit-target levels. However, as it turned out, the original settings worked best. Having settled for the exit levels, it is time to move on to the true range variables, which monitor the volatility of the market. Altering the lookback period for the long-term true range between 10 and 60 days indicated that the model would work better, the shorter the lookback period. Table 12.3 shows that what we lost in reliability by taking away the trailing stop, we gained back by making the system more sensitive to the changes in volatility. The average profit per trade is now at $1,577.59 and the profit factor at 1.46. The risk–reward ratio is its highest so far, at 0.49.

TABLE 12.2

Removing Trailing Stop

		Long only, no trailing stop			PercProf: 68.00
	Trades	**PercWin**	**NetProfit**	**AvgProfit**	**ProfitStD**	**RiskRatio**
Average:	42.84	35.34	55,604.80	1,351.85		**Market**
St. Dev:	21.99	11.54	82,839.09	3,119.58	11,379.08	0.10
High:	64.83	46.88	138,443.90	4,471.43	12,730.94	**Portfolio**
Low:	20.85	23.81	(27,234.29)	(1,767.72)	(10,027.23)	0.43
	ProfitFactor	**RiskFactor**	**MaxDD**	**PercDD**	**PercTime**	**AvgLength**
Average:	1.43	0.20	46,035.35	32.08	45.39	33.62
St. Dev:	0.71	0.36	20,680.92	18.18	10.91	14.61
High:	2.14	0.56	66,716.27	50.25	56.30	48.23
Low:	0.73	(0.16)	25,354.43	13.90	34.47	19.01

The original setting for the lookback period for the short-term true range was three days. If it turns out that the system is getting better, or at least not significantly worse, if we shorten it to one or two days, we should be able to get rid of this variable as well. As it turned out, however, the best result came from setting this variable to five days, as Table 12.4 reveals.

With no other variables to change and with the percentage profitable trades and the average trade length even longer than when we started, it's finally time to examine the lookback periods for the relative strength calculations. Altering the lookback period for the moving average to between 40 and 120 days, and the

TABLE 12.3

Increasing Sensitivity to Volatility

		Long only, no trailing stop, 10-day long true range			PercProf: 76.00
	Trades	**PercWin**	**NetProfit**	**AvgProfit**	**ProfitStD**	**RiskRatio**
Average:	52.56	36.15	72,058.83	1,577.59		**Market**
St. Dev:	35.83	11.03	88,306.76	3,220.31	11,580.11	0.11
High:	88.39	47.18	160,365.60	4,797.91	13,157.70	**Portfolio**
Low:	16.73	25.12	(16,247.93)	(1,642.72)	(10,002.52)	0.49
	ProfitFactor	**RiskFactor**	**MaxDD**	**PercDD**	**PercTime**	**AvgLength**
Average:	1.46	0.23	48,207.20	30.16	53.07	34.84
St. Dev:	0.63	0.36	26,902.27	17.89	15.53	18.90
High:	2.09	0.59	75,109.47	48.05	68.60	53.74
Low:	0.82	(0.13)	21,304.93	12.27	37.55	15.94

TABLE 12.4

Altering Lookback Period (1)

	Trades	PercWin	NetProfit	AvgProfit	ProfitStD	RiskRatio
Long only, no trailing stop, ten-day long true range, five-day true range						**PercProf: 76.00**
Average:	46.40	34.72	68,107.46	1,397.73		**Market**
St. Dev:	30.87	9.50	83,157.63	2,696.36	12,298.44	0.12
High:	77.27	44.22	151,265.10	4,094.10	13,696.17	**Portfolio**
Low:	15.53	25.22	(15,050.17)	(1,298.63)	(10,900.70)	0.52
	ProfitFactor	**RiskFactor**	**MaxDD**	**PercDD**	**PercTime**	**AvgLength**
Average:	1.45	0.24	47,787.58	29.29	53.65	38.82
St. Dev:	0.61	0.32	28,645.41	16.95	15.37	21.53
High:	2.06	0.57	76,433.00	46.24	69.02	60.35
Low:	0.85	(0.08)	19,142.17	12.33	38.28	17.29

lookback for the slope of the average between 10 and 60 days, only resulted in one change, and that was to shorten the lookback period for the slope to 10 days. Table 12.5 shows that with this change incorporated into the system, the average profit came out to $1,407, and the profit and risk factors to 1.44 and 0.25, respectively (although we didn't manage to shorten the trade length).

Although we will take this version of the system with us to the upcoming parts of the book, it still has several shortcomings that need to be pointed out

TABLE 12.5

Altering Lookback Period (2)

	Trades	PercWin	NetProfit	AvgProfit	ProfitStD	RiskRatio
Long only, no trailing stop, ten-day long true range, five-day short true range, ten-day slope						**PercProf: 76.00**
Average:	48.12	34.64	70,693.68	1,407.35		**Market**
St. Dev:	30.98	8.33	84,219.20	2,194.06	12,502.29	0.13
High:	79.10	42.97	154,912.88	3,601.42	13,909.64	**Portfolio**
Low:	17.14	26.31	(13,525.52)	(786.71)	(11,094.94)	0.64
	ProfitFactor	**RiskFactor**	**MaxDD**	**PercDD**	**PercTime**	**AvgLength**
Average:	1.44	0.25	50,858.30	28.59	54.74	38.03
St. Dev:	0.55	0.29	37,473.66	16.23	14.64	18.25
High:	1.99	0.54	88,331.96	44.82	69.38	56.28
Low:	0.89	(0.04)	13,384.65	12.36	40.10	19.78

before we move on to the short side. The major shortcoming is that the risk–reward ratio, at 0.64, isn't much to brag about. With such a low number, there still is a high likelihood that the system will lose money over an extended period of time, and perhaps even over several such periods. Another major negative is the low percentage of profitable trades, which can make the system tough to trade for those traders who demand a high percentage of winners to feel safe with the system. Combine this with the low number of trades and the conclusion is that it can take a long time to get out of one of those losing periods. Finally, the average trade length is about three times too long for the system to be considered short-term, according to the definition used in this book. However, in Part 3 the average trade length still can do us some good, when we try to use this system as a filter for the other short-term systems.

Moving on to the short side, Table 12.6, which shows the results from the original system tested on our new markets, indicates this can be a tough cookie to play with. An average profit of −$845 and only 20 percent profitable trading sequences signal we have a long way to go with this baby.

As with the long side, I started out testing the system without the trailing stop. Again, a slight loss in performance occurred, but not enough to justify keeping the stop (see Table 12.7). One good thing, compared to the long side, however, is that the short side has a rather high percentage of profitable trades (44.11 percent). When this is the case and the system is still losing money, the best place to start is with the initial risk–reward relationship when entering the trade. In this case, both the profit target and the stop loss are placed three average true ranges away from the entry point.

TABLE 12.6

Short-side Trading Using Original Rotation System

		Original system, short only				PercProf: 20.00
	Trades	**PercWin**	**NetProfit**	**AvgProfit**	**ProfitStD**	**RiskRatio**
Average:	37.84	43.68	(30,953.23)	(845.08)		**Market**
St. Dev:	31.27	11.08	44,520.70	2,556.92	10,769.67	(0.11)
High:	69.11	54.76	13,567.47	1,711.85	9,924.60	**Portfolio**
Low:	6.57	32.60	(75,473.93)	(3,402.00)	(11,614.75)	(0.33)
	ProfitFactor	**RiskFactor**	**MaxDD**	**PercDD**	**PercTime**	**AvgLength**
Average:	0.86	(0.12)	66,079.31	59.15	25.25	23.43
St. Dev:	0.47	0.22	29,751.43	29.15	9.73	12.13
High:	1.33	0.10	95,830.74	88.30	34.99	35.56
Low:	0.40	(0.34)	36,327.89	30.00	15.52	11.30

T A B L E   1 2 . 7

Removing Trailing Stop for Short-side Trading

	Short only, no trailing stop				PercProf: 16.00
	Trades	**PercWin**	**NetProfit**	**AvgProfit**	**ProfitStD**	**RiskRatio**
Average:	37.64	44.11	(32,843.74)	(932.72)		**Market**
St. Dev:	31.11	11.15	46,210.94	2,628.95	10,911.51	(0.12)
High:	68.75	55.26	13,367.20	1,696.23	9,978.79	**Portfolio**
Low:	6.53	32.96	(79,054.68)	(3,561.68)	(11,844.24)	(0.35)
	ProfitFactor	**RiskFactor**	**MaxDD**	**PercDD**	**PercTime**	**AvgLength**
Average:	0.86	(0.12)	66,756.83	59.82	25.48	23.67
St. Dev:	0.47	0.22	31,145.23	30.73	9.83	12.08
High:	1.33	0.10	97,902.06	90.55	35.30	35.74
Low:	0.39	(0.35)	35,611.60	29.09	15.65	11.59

Of course, a 1:1 risk–reward relationship can only be profitable if the percentage of profitable trades is at least 50 percent. With a better risk–reward relationship we might, however, get by with considerably fewer winning trades than that. Basically, we can address this in two ways: We could either place the stop loss closer to the entry or place the profit target further from the entry. In this case, it turned out the system did best with a 1 percent stop loss and a 3 percent profit target. The results of this version can be seen in Table 12.8. The average profit is now

T A B L E   1 2 . 8

Changing Risk–Reward Relationships

	Short only, no trailing stop, 1 percent stop, 3 percent target				PercProf: 28.00
	Trades	**PercWin**	**NetProfit**	**AvgProfit**	**ProfitStD**	**RiskRatio**
Average:	71.36	25.03	(20,038.60)	(133.77)		**Market**
St. Dev:	58.74	6.42	32,195.33	1,117.11	6,578.99	(0.06)
High:	130.10	31.45	12,156.73	983.35	6,445.22	**Portfolio**
Low:	12.62	18.61	(52,233.93)	(1,250.88)	(6,712.75)	(0.12)
	ProfitFactor	**RiskFactor**	**MaxDD**	**PercDD**	**PercTime**	**AvgLength**
Average:	0.91	(0.09)	49,783.28	44.82	19.46	9.30
St. Dev:	0.35	0.25	23,790.41	22.75	7.75	2.83
High:	1.26	0.16	73,573.68	67.57	27.21	12.13
Low:	0.56	(0.33)	25,992.87	22.07	11.72	6.47

up to −$133. There is still some way to go, but a considerable improvement, despite the fact that the tighter stop lowered the percentage profitable trades to just above 25 percent.

When the time came to alter the long-term and short-term true range calculations, it hit me that down markets more often than not are accompanied by an increase in volatility, while the original model was looking for the opposite. Therefore, I decided to reverse the criteria for the volatility, demanding higher short-term volatility to enter a trade on the short side. This continued to improve the results (not shown), so for the remainder of the research, this was the logic I decided to go with.

Experimenting with various true range settings resulted in a long-term true range of 10 days and a short-term true range of five days, which is the same as for the long side, but with the logic and ruling reversed. This is good news, as it indicates some sort of observable way of distinguishing between uptrends and downtrends. That is, when the five-day volatility is lower than the 10-day volatility, the trend is up and vice versa—perhaps something for you to look into on your own? Table 12.9 shows that the system now is very close to breaking even and that the number of profitable trading sequences has increased to 36 percent. We're getting there.

Experimenting with the lookback periods for the relative strength calculations, the same as for the long side, once again resulted in a 10-day lookback for the slope, but also in a slightly shorter lookback period for the moving average calculation. In this case, it turned out that a lookback period of 60 days produced the

TABLE 12.9

Reversed the TR Criteria

		Short only, no trailing stop, 1 percent stop, 3 percent target, 10-day long TR, five-day short TR, reverse TR criteria				PercProf: 36.00
	Trades	**PercWin**	**NetProfit**	**AvgProfit**	**ProfitStD**	**RiskRatio**
Average:	64.32	26.55	(13,380.47)	(19.58)		**Market**
St. Dev:	49.41	7.00	38,338.45	1,478.71	7,444.69	(0.05)
High:	113.73	33.54	24,957.98	1,459.13	7,425.11	**Portfolio**
Low:	14.91	19.55	(51,718.92)	(1,498.29)	(7,464.27)	(0.01)
	ProfitFactor	**RiskFactor**	**MaxDD**	**PercDD**	**PercTime**	**AvgLength**
Average:	0.96	(0.05)	54,450.76	49.27	21.38	11.07
St. Dev:	0.36	0.25	26,916.56	25.83	7.30	3.01
High:	1.32	0.20	81,367.31	75.09	28.68	14.08
Low:	0.60	(0.30)	27,534.20	23.44	14.08	8.05

TABLE 12.10

Short-side Trading Using Revised Rotation System

		Short only, no trailing stop, 1 percent stop, 3 percent target, 10-day long TR, five-day short TR, reverse TR criteria, 60-day average, 10-day slope				PercProf: 36.00
	Trades	**PercWin**	**NetProfit**	**AvgProfit**	**ProfitStD**	**RiskRatio**
Average:	66.00	27.24	(7,415.45)	586.65		**Market**
St. Dev:	46.50	9.98	65,572.19	2,139.61	7,468.95	(0.02)
High:	112.50	37.22	58,156.74	2,726.27	8,055.60	**Portfolio**
Low:	19.50	17.26	(72,987.65)	(1,552.96)	(6,882.30)	0.27
	ProfitFactor	**RiskFactor**	**MaxDD**	**PercDD**	**PercTime**	**AvgLength**
Average:	1.12	0.03	55,184.50	48.95	22.32	11.20
St. Dev:	0.67	0.42	30,346.12	29.72	6.93	3.23
High:	1.79	0.45	85,530.61	78.66	29.25	14.42
Low:	0.46	(0.39)	24,838.38	19.23	15.39	7.97

best results. Just as was the case with relative strength band system, the short side needs to operate a little more quickly to be at its best. In all honesty though, I was surprised that this period wasn't even shorter. Table 12.10 shows that the short side also is profitable, with an average profit per trade of $586.65. Never mind that the risk factor indicates that we're only likely to make three cents for every dollar risked.

Looked at all by itself, this seems hardly worth bothering with, but the key question is *when* this small profit takes place in relation to the profits and losses on the long side, and for any other system you're trading. If it turns out that the short side essentially broke even until Spring 2000, and only made money over the last few years, wouldn't it still be worthwhile to trade the short side during the next bull market as well, since you never know when the next bear market will start after that? Figure 12.1 shows a few sample trades for both the long and the short side on the S&P 500 index during and after the September 11 tragedy. Note how well the system coped with this situation in this market.

TRADESTATION CODE

Variables:

{These variables can also be used as inputs for optimization purposes.}

AllowLong(True), AllowShort(True), LongRelStrenLookb(80),

ShortRelStrenLookb(60), SlopeLookback(10), NoLongMarkets(4),

FIGURE 12.1

S&P 500 Index trading—September 2001.

NoShortMarkets(2), LongTermTRLookback(10), ShortTermTRLookback(5),
LongStopMulti(2), ShortStopMulti(1), LongTargetMulti(6), ShortTargetMulti(3),
{Leave these variables alone.}
RelStrength.12(1), RelStrength.13(1), RelStrength.14(1), RelStrength.15(1),
LongAvgRelStren.12(1), LongAvgRelStren.13(1),LongAvgRelStren.14(1),
LongAvgRelStren.15(1), ShortAvgRelStren.12(1), ShortAvgRelStren.13(1),
ShortAvgRelStren.14(1), ShortAvgRelStren.15(1), LongAvgSlope.12(0),
LongAvgSlope.13(0), LongAvgSlope.14(0), LongAvgSlope.15(0),
LongTotStrength.1(0), ShortAvgSlope.12(0), ShortAvgSlope.13(0),
ShortAvgSlope.14(0), ShortAvgSlope.15(0), ShortTotStrength.1(0),
RelStrength.21(1), RelStrength.23(1), RelStrength.24(1), RelStrength.25(1),
LongAvgRelStren.21(1), LongAvgRelStren.23(1),LongAvgRelStren.24(1),
LongAvgRelStren.25(1), ShortAvgRelStren.21(1),
ShortAvgRelStren.23(1),ShortAvgRelStren.24(1), ShortAvgRelStren.25(1),

LongAvgSlope.21(0), LongAvgSlope.23(0), LongAvgSlope.24(0), LongAvgSlope.25(0), LongTotStrength.2(0), ShortAvgSlope.21(0), ShortAvgSlope.23(0), ShortAvgSlope.24(0), ShortAvgSlope.25(0), ShortTotStrength.2(0), RelStrength.31(1), RelStrength.32(1), RelStrength.34(1), RelStrength.35(1), LongAvgRelStren.31(1), LongAvgRelStren.32(1), LongAvgRelStren.34(1), LongAvgRelStren.35(1),

ShortAvgRelStren.31(1), ShortAvgRelStren.32(1), ShortAvgRelStren.34(1), ShortAvgRelStren.35(1), LongAvgSlope.31(0), LongAvgSlope.32(0), LongAvgSlope.34(0), LongAvgSlope.35(0), LongTotStrength.3(0),

ShortAvgSlope.31(0), ShortAvgSlope.32(0), ShortAvgSlope.34(0), ShortAvgSlope.35(0), ShortTotStrength.3(0), RelStrength.41(1), RelStrength.42(1), RelStrength.43(1), RelStrength.45(1), LongAvgRelStren.41(1), LongAvgRelStren.42(1), LongAvgRelStren.43(1), LongAvgRelStren.45(1),

ShortAvgRelStren.41(1), ShortAvgRelStren.42(1), ShortAvgRelStren.43(1), ShortAvgRelStren.45(1), LongAvgSlope.41(0), LongAvgSlope.42(0), LongAvgSlope.43(0), LongAvgSlope.45(0), LongTotStrength.4(0),

ShortAvgSlope.41(0), ShortAvgSlope.42(0), ShortAvgSlope.43(0), ShortAvgSlope.45(0), ShortTotStrength.4(0), RelStrength.51(1), RelStrength.52(1), RelStrength.53(1), RelStrength.54(1), LongAvgRelStren.51(1), LongAvgRelStren.52(1),LongAvgRelStren.53(1), LongAvgRelStren.54(1),

ShortAvgRelStren.51(1), ShortAvgRelStren.52(1),ShortAvgRelStren.53(1), ShortAvgRelStren.54(1), LongAvgSlope.51(0), LongAvgSlope.52(0), LongAvgSlope.53(0), LongAvgSlope.54(0), LongTotStrength.5(0),

ShortAvgSlope.51(0), ShortAvgSlope.52(0), ShortAvgSlope.53(0), ShortAvgSlope.54(0), ShortTotStrength.5(0), MinLongStrength(0), MaxShortStrength(0), LongTermTrueRange(0), ShortTermTrueRange(0);

{Code for normalizing the number of contracts traded goes here.}

RelStrength.12 = Close / Close Data2;

RelStrength.13 = Close / Close Data3;

RelStrength.14 = Close / Close Data4;

RelStrength.15 = Close / Close Data5;

LongAvgRelStren.12 = Average(RelStrength.12, LongRelStrenLookb);

LongAvgSlope.12 = LongAvgRelStren.12 / LongAvgRelStren.12[SlopeLookback];

LongAvgRelStren.13 = Average(RelStrength.13, LongRelStrenLookb);

LongAvgSlope.13 = LongAvgRelStren.13 / LongAvgRelStren.13[SlopeLookback];

LongAvgRelStren.14 = Average(RelStrength.14, LongRelStrenLookb);

LongAvgSlope.14 = LongAvgRelStren.14 / LongAvgRelStren.14[SlopeLookback];

LongAvgRelStren.15 = Average(RelStrength.15, LongRelStrenLookb);

LongAvgSlope.15 = LongAvgRelStren.15 / LongAvgRelStren.15[SlopeLookback];

ShortAvgRelStren.12 = Average(RelStrength.12, ShortRelStrenLookb);

ShortAvgSlope.12 = ShortAvgRelStren.12 / ShortAvgRelStren.12[SlopeLookback];

ShortAvgRelStren.13 = Average(RelStrength.13, ShortRelStrenLookb);

ShortAvgSlope.13 = ShortAvgRelStren.13 / ShortAvgRelStren.13[SlopeLookback];

ShortAvgRelStren.14 = Average(RelStrength.14, ShortRelStrenLookb);

ShortAvgSlope.14 = ShortAvgRelStren.14 / ShortAvgRelStren.14[SlopeLookback];

ShortAvgRelStren.15 = Average(RelStrength.15, ShortRelStrenLookb);

ShortAvgSlope.15 = ShortAvgRelStren.15 / ShortAvgRelStren.15[SlopeLookback];

LongTotStrength.1 = LongAvgSlope.12 * LongAvgSlope.13 * LongAvgSlope.14 * LongAvgSlope.15;

ShortTotStrength.1 = ShortAvgSlope.12 * ShortAvgSlope.13 * ShortAvgSlope.14 * ShortAvgSlope.15;

RelStrength.21 = Close Data2 / Close;

RelStrength.23 = Close Data2/ Close Data3;

RelStrength.24 = Close Data2/ Close Data4;

RelStrength.25 = Close Data2/ Close Data5;

LongAvgRelStren.21 = Average(RelStrength.21, LongRelStrenLookb);

LongAvgSlope.21 = LongAvgRelStren.21 / LongAvgRelStren.21[SlopeLookback];

LongAvgRelStren.23 = Average(RelStrength.23, LongRelStrenLookb);

LongAvgSlope.23 = LongAvgRelStren.23 / LongAvgRelStren.23[SlopeLookback];

LongAvgRelStren.24 = Average(RelStrength.24, LongRelStrenLookb);

LongAvgSlope.24 = LongAvgRelStren.24 / LongAvgRelStren.24[SlopeLookback];

LongAvgRelStren.25 = Average(RelStrength.25, LongRelStrenLookb);

LongAvgSlope.25 = LongAvgRelStren.25 / LongAvgRelStren.25[SlopeLookback];

ShortAvgRelStren.21 = Average(RelStrength.21, ShortRelStrenLookb);

ShortAvgSlope.21 = ShortAvgRelStren.21 / ShortAvgRelStren.21[SlopeLookback];

ShortAvgRelStren.23 = Average(RelStrength.23, ShortRelStrenLookb);

ShortAvgSlope.23 = ShortAvgRelStren.23 / ShortAvgRelStren.23[SlopeLookback];

ShortAvgRelStren.24 = Average(RelStrength.24, ShortRelStrenLookb);

ShortAvgSlope.24 = ShortAvgRelStren.24 / ShortAvgRelStren.24[SlopeLookback];

ShortAvgRelStren.25 = Average(RelStrength.25, ShortRelStrenLookb);

ShortAvgSlope.25 = ShortAvgRelStren.25 / ShortAvgRelStren.25[SlopeLookback];

LongTotStrength.2 = LongAvgSlope.21 * LongAvgSlope.23 * LongAvgSlope.24 * LongAvgSlope.25;

ShortTotStrength.2 = ShortAvgSlope.21 * ShortAvgSlope.23 * ShortAvgSlope.24 * ShortAvgSlope.25;

RelStrength.31 = Close Data3 / Close;

RelStrength.32 = Close Data3/ Close Data2;

RelStrength.34 = Close Data3/ Close Data4;

RelStrength.35 = Close Data3/ Close Data5;

LongAvgRelStren.31 = Average(RelStrength.31, LongRelStrenLookb);

LongAvgSlope.31 = LongAvgRelStren.31 / LongAvgRelStren.31[SlopeLookback];

LongAvgRelStren.32 = Average(RelStrength.32, LongRelStrenLookb);

LongAvgSlope.32 = LongAvgRelStren.32 / LongAvgRelStren.32[SlopeLookback];

LongAvgRelStren.34 = Average(RelStrength.34, LongRelStrenLookb);

LongAvgSlope.34 = LongAvgRelStren.34 / LongAvgRelStren.34[SlopeLookback];

LongAvgRelStren.35 = Average(RelStrength.35, LongRelStrenLookb);

LongAvgSlope.35 = LongAvgRelStren.35 / LongAvgRelStren.35[SlopeLookback];

ShortAvgRelStren.31 = Average(RelStrength.31, ShortRelStrenLookb);

ShortAvgSlope.31 = ShortAvgRelStren.31 / ShortAvgRelStren.31[SlopeLookback];

ShortAvgRelStren.32 = Average(RelStrength.32, ShortRelStrenLookb);

ShortAvgSlope.32 = ShortAvgRelStren.32 / ShortAvgRelStren.32[SlopeLookback];

ShortAvgRelStren.34 = Average(RelStrength.34, ShortRelStrenLookb);

ShortAvgSlope.34 = ShortAvgRelStren.34 / ShortAvgRelStren.34[SlopeLookback];

ShortAvgRelStren.35 = Average(RelStrength.35, ShortRelStrenLookb);

ShortAvgSlope.35 = ShortAvgRelStren.35 / ShortAvgRelStren.35[SlopeLookback];

LongTotStrength.3 = LongAvgSlope.31 * LongAvgSlope.32 * LongAvgSlope.34 *
LongAvgSlope.35;

ShortTotStrength.3 = ShortAvgSlope.31 * ShortAvgSlope.32 * ShortAvgSlope.34
* ShortAvgSlope.35;

RelStrength.41 = Close Data4 / Close;

RelStrength.42 = Close Data4/ Close Data2;

RelStrength.43 = Close Data4/ Close Data3;

RelStrength.45 = Close Data4/ Close Data5;

LongAvgRelStren.41 = Average(RelStrength.41, LongRelStrenLookb);

LongAvgSlope.41 = LongAvgRelStren.41 / LongAvgRelStren.41[SlopeLookback];

LongAvgRelStren.42 = Average(RelStrength.42, LongRelStrenLookb);

LongAvgSlope.42 = LongAvgRelStren.42 / LongAvgRelStren.42[SlopeLookback];

LongAvgRelStren.43 = Average(RelStrength.43, LongRelStrenLookb);

LongAvgSlope.43 = LongAvgRelStren.43 / LongAvgRelStren.43[SlopeLookback];

LongAvgRelStren.45 = Average(RelStrength.45, LongRelStrenLookb);

LongAvgSlope.45 = LongAvgRelStren.45 / LongAvgRelStren.45[SlopeLookback];

ShortAvgRelStren.41 = Average(RelStrength.41, ShortRelStrenLookb);

ShortAvgSlope.41 = ShortAvgRelStren.41 / ShortAvgRelStren.41[SlopeLookback];

ShortAvgRelStren.42 = Average(RelStrength.42, ShortRelStrenLookb);

ShortAvgSlope.42 = ShortAvgRelStren.42 / ShortAvgRelStren.42[SlopeLookback];

ShortAvgRelStren.43 = Average(RelStrength.43, ShortRelStrenLookb);

ShortAvgSlope.43 = ShortAvgRelStren.43 / ShortAvgRelStren.43[SlopeLookback];

ShortAvgRelStren.45 = Average(RelStrength.45, ShortRelStrenLookb);

ShortAvgSlope.45 = ShortAvgRelStren.45 / ShortAvgRelStren.45[SlopeLookback];

LongTotStrength.4 = LongAvgSlope.41 * LongAvgSlope.42 * LongAvgSlope.43 * LongAvgSlope.45;

ShortTotStrength.4 = ShortAvgSlope.41 * ShortAvgSlope.42 * ShortAvgSlope.43 * ShortAvgSlope.45;

RelStrength.51 = Close Data5 / Close;

RelStrength.52 = Close Data5/ Close Data2;

RelStrength.53 = Close Data5/ Close Data3;

RelStrength.54 = Close Data5/ Close Data4;

LongAvgRelStren.51 = Average(RelStrength.51, LongRelStrenLookb);

LongAvgSlope.51 = LongAvgRelStren.51 / LongAvgRelStren.51[SlopeLookback];

LongAvgRelStren.52 = Average(RelStrength.52, LongRelStrenLookb);

LongAvgSlope.52 = LongAvgRelStren.52 / LongAvgRelStren.52[SlopeLookback];

LongAvgRelStren.53 = Average(RelStrength.53, LongRelStrenLookb);

LongAvgSlope.53 = LongAvgRelStren.53 / LongAvgRelStren.53[SlopeLookback];

LongAvgRelStren.54 = Average(RelStrength.54, LongRelStrenLookb);

LongAvgSlope.54 = LongAvgRelStren.54 / LongAvgRelStren.54[SlopeLookback];

ShortAvgRelStren.51 = Average(RelStrength.51, ShortRelStrenLookb);

ShortAvgSlope.51 = ShortAvgRelStren.51 / ShortAvgRelStren.51[SlopeLookback];

ShortAvgRelStren.52 = Average(RelStrength.52, ShortRelStrenLookb);

ShortAvgSlope.52 = ShortAvgRelStren.52 / ShortAvgRelStren.52[SlopeLookback];

ShortAvgRelStren.53 = Average(RelStrength.53, ShortRelStrenLookb);

ShortAvgSlope.53 = ShortAvgRelStren.53 / ShortAvgRelStren.53[SlopeLookback];

ShortAvgRelStren.54 = Average(RelStrength.54, ShortRelStrenLookb);

ShortAvgSlope.54 = ShortAvgRelStren.54 / ShortAvgRelStren.54[SlopeLookback];

LongTotStrength.5 = LongAvgSlope.51 * LongAvgSlope.52 * LongAvgSlope.53 * LongAvgSlope.54;

ShortTotStrength.5 = ShortAvgSlope.51 * ShortAvgSlope.52 * ShortAvgSlope.53 * ShortAvgSlope.54;

MinLongStrength = NthMaxList(NoLongMarkets, LongTotStrength.1, LongTotStrength.2, LongTotStrength.3, LongTotStrength.4, LongTotStrength.5);

MaxShortStrength = NthMinList(NoShortMarkets, ShortTotStrength.1,

```
ShortTotStrength.2, ShortTotStrength.3, ShortTotStrength.4, ShortTotStrength.5);
LongTermTrueRange = AvgTrueRange(LongTermTRLookback);
ShortTermTrueRange = AvgTrueRange(ShortTermTRLookback);
If MarketPosition = 0 Then Begin
    If AllowLong = True and LongTotStrength.1 >= MinLongStrength and
    LongTermTrueRange > ShortTermTrueRange Then
        Buy ("L-May 01") NumCont Contracts Next Bar at Market;
    If AllowShort = True and ShortTotStrength.1 <= MaxShortStrength and
    LongTermTrueRange < ShortTermTrueRange Then
        Sell ("S-May 01") NumCont Contracts Next Bar at Market;
End;
If EntryPrice > 0 Then Begin
    ExitLong ("L-Stop") Next Bar at EntryPrice –
    (ShortTermTrueRange * LongStopMulti) Stop;
    ExitLong ("L-Trgt") Next Bar at EntryPrice +
    (ShortTermTrueRange * LongTargetMulti) Limit;
    ExitShort ("S-Stop") Next Bar at EntryPrice +
    (ShortTermTrueRange * ShortStopMulti) Stop;
    ExitShort ("S-Trgt") Next Bar at EntryPrice –
    (ShortTermTrueRange * ShortTargetMulti) Limit;
End;
{Code for initial market export goes here, with Normalize(True). Set
ExportSwitch(True).}
{Code for testing robustness goes here (see Part 3 of book), with Normalize(True).
Set RobustnessSwitch(True).}
{Code for exporting results for money management analysis goes here (see Part 4
of book), with Normalize(False). Set MoneyExport(True).}
```

CHAPTER 13

Volume-weighted Average

Originally presented in July 2001, this system tries to identify short-term corrections that have exhausted themselves by ending with a final move in the direction of the correction accompanied by an increase in volume. When this happens, the system enters in the opposite direction if the market turns and takes out the highest high or lowest low for the previous two days. The direction of the correction is indicated by the latest closing price in relation to a short-term volume-weighted average (VWA), which is similar to a regular exponential moving average. Calculating the VWA is a two-step process:

Calculate the current average volume (AV) in relation to the highest average volume (HAV) and lowest average volume (LAV) of the lookback period. For example, if the lookback period is set to nine days, as it is for this particular system, calculate AV for the last nine days together with HAV and LAV for the same nine days. Then, take the difference between AV and LAV and divide it by the difference between HAV and LAV. The result will be a value between zero and one. If this relative value (RV) is increasing from one bar to the next, the average volume is not only increasing, it is also moving closer to a short-term extreme level. Reverse the reasoning if RV is decreasing. The formula for calculating RV looks like this:

$$RV = (AV - LAV) / (HAV - LAV)$$

Multiply the closing price (C) for each bar by RV, and multiply the previous bar's VMA (PVMA) by one minus RV. Then add the two totals together to reach the VWA for the current bar. The VWA for the first bar in the sequence will be its closing price multiplied by RV. The higher the average volume, the higher the RV, and the more weight given to the latest closing price. A simplified formula for calculating VWA looks something like this:

$$VWA = RV * C + (1 - RV) * PVWA$$

SUGGESTED MARKETS

Stocks and index shares (SPDRs, DIAs, QQQs).

ORIGINAL RULES

Prepare to go long if today's closing price is below VWA and if VWA is lower today than yesterday.

Prepare to go short if today's closing price is above VWA and if VWA is greater today than yesterday.

Enter long tomorrow if the market trades above the highest high of the previous two days. Risk 1 percent of available equity per trade.

Enter short tomorrow if the market trades below the lowest low of the previous two days. Risk 1 percent of available equity per trade.

Exit all trades: On the close, if the market does not follow through on its move that triggered the trade, by also closing above (below for short trades) the VWA;

If the market moves against you more than 4 percent.

TEST PERIOD

September 1991 to April 2001 (2,500 days of data per market).

TEST DATA

Daily notations for the 30 stocks making up the Dow Jones Industrial Average (DJIA). A total of $20 per trade was deducted for slippage and commission.

STARTING EQUITY

$100,000 (nominal).

SYSTEM PROS AND CONS

For this particular system, we took the liberty of defining the trend using hindsight, allowing only long trades until April 1990 and only short trades thereafter (basically just to provide an example of how this can be done). While this type of hindsight analysis is not the way to go during the final stages of your system design and testing process, it is a valid approach in the initial stages, when you want to know how the system would have operated in "the best of both worlds." This will give you an indication if the idea is worth pursuing any further.

Other than that, this system provides no other type of technical indicator to measure the direction or strength of the longer-term trend. Therefore, it should be possible to still achieve good results by substituting for the hindsight trend indicator a good trend filter, such as a long-term moving average.

The nine-day lookback period for the VWA is totally unoptimized. Experimenting with this number should make it possible to increase performance. It also is possible to reverse the reasoning for the second equation in the composition of VWA and give the latest closing price less weight, the higher the volume. The new formula would look like this: $VWA = (1 - RV) * C + RV * PVWA$. In this way, the distance between the VWA and the closing price widens during high-volume breakouts, which gives the market more wiggle room when trending.

REVISING THE RESEARCH AND MODIFYING THE SYSTEM

From Tables 13.1 and 13.2, it seems that this system has held up well since it was put together, and that it's also doing exceptionally well on previously untested markets. Granted, the system is losing money on the short side, but that doesn't have to be a bad thing as long as the profits on the short side come when the long side is doing bad.

For the original article in *Active Trader* magazine, this system was fitted with a trend filter that operated with the benefit of hindsight. As mentioned, this is a

TABLE 13.1

Retesting Original Volume-weighted Average System

		Original system, long only			PercProf: 87.30	
	Trades	**PercWin**	**NetProfit**	**AvgProfit**	**ProfitStD**	**RiskRatio**
Average:	78.94	44.73	52,768.38	758.85		**Market**
St. Dev:	27.48	7.82	46,759.75	870.70	4,889.35	0.14
High:	106.41	52.55	99,528.13	1,629.56	5,648.20	**Portfolio**
Low:	51.46	36.91	6,008.64	(111.85)	(4,130.50)	0.87
	ProfitFactor	**RiskFactor**	**MaxDD**	**PercDD**	**PercTime**	**AvgLength**
Average:	1.70	0.34	25,968.61	20.06	10.13	5.42
St. Dev:	0.77	0.33	14,556.43	12.64	2.74	0.65
High:	2.46	0.67	40,525.04	32.69	12.87	6.07
Low:	0.93	0.01	11,412.18	7.42	7.39	4.77

TABLE 13.2

Less Tantalizing Results for the Short Side

	Trades	PercWin	NetProfit	AvgProfit	ProfitStD	RiskRatio
			Original system, short only		**PercProf: 39.68**	
Average:	19.40	36.87	(2,394.46)	(28.61)		**Market**
St. Dev:	4.24	13.04	26,927.83	1,654.87	4,875.63	(0.08)
High:	23.64	49.91	24,533.37	1,626.26	4,847.02	**Portfolio**
Low:	15.15	23.83	(29,322.29)	(1,683.47)	(4,904.24)	(0.02)
	ProfitFactor	**RiskFactor**	**MaxDD**	**PercDD**	**PercTime**	**AvgLength**
Average:	1.21	0.00	21,910.62	20.05	1.93	3.90
St. Dev:	1.49	0.54	14,267.27	13.32	0.99	1.10
High:	2.70	0.54	36,177.89	33.36	2.92	5.00
Low:	(0.28)	(0.54)	7,643.35	6.73	0.94	2.80

valid approach when you want to see how the system would have performed given ideal conditions that could only be observed with the help of hindsight. It is not, however, recommended that you trade a system with such a filter built into it. The first thing to do in this round of renewed research is to get rid of the trend filter.

Originally, the system was also fitted with a 4 percent stop loss. As it turned out, this stop loss made absolutely no difference whatsoever. It was only there for money management purposes, but because we will address the money management issue later, we can get rid of the stop loss for now and save ourselves an optimizable variable. Table 13.3 shows that the system continues to perform well on the long side without the stop loss and the trend filter. The average profit did decrease by close to $200, but the risk–return ratio is still at a healthy 0.86 and, because of a few more trades, the average net profit still came out to close to $50,000. Unfortunately, however, the short side (Table 13.4) did not do as well as the long side, primarily because of an increasing number of bad trades during the long bull market in the 1990s. A profit factor of 0.92 and an average profit per trade of −$119 indicates that we are losing money at a slow but steady rate.

Just to make sure that the logic behind the system was correct, I decided to test the entry rules. Instead of demanding the close to be lower than the volume-weighted average for a long trend, I wanted it to be higher than the average, more in line with a normal technical-analysis trend interpretation (reverse the reasoning for the short side). But this did not better the results for either side. The same was true for altering the way to calculate the average, as suggested at the end of the original system presentation, by giving the latest closing price less weight the higher the volume for the moving-average calculation. (No use in showing the results for either one of these alterations.)

TABLE 13.3

Removing Stop Loss and Trend Filter, Long-side Trades

	Long only: No trend filter, no stop loss				PercProf: 84.13
	Trades	**PercWin**	**NetProfit**	**AvgProfit**	**ProfitStD**	**RiskRatio**
Average:	98.24	43.57	49,535.85	560.13		**Market**
St. Dev:	28.02	6.76	55,195.62	651.52	4,984.54	0.10
High:	126.26	50.34	104,731.47	1,211.65	5,544.67	**Portfolio**
Low:	70.21	36.81	(5,659.77)	(91.39)	(4,424.41)	0.86
	ProfitFactor	**RiskFactor**	**MaxDD**	**PercDD**	**PercTime**	**AvgLength**
Average:	1.45	0.23	37,398.52	25.83	12.58	5.31
St. Dev:	0.51	0.25	21,925.40	15.65	2.55	0.57
High:	1.97	0.47	59,323.92	41.48	15.13	5.88
Low:	0.94	(0.02)	15,473.12	10.18	10.02	4.73

Keeping the original rules and calculations, let's look at another strange feature of this system: Namely, the condition for staying in a trade, which doesn't have to be fulfilled at the entry. Because the close needs to be above (below for a short trade) the volume-weighted average to stay in the trade, it also would make sense to ask the price to cross the volume-weighted average instead of the highest high of the last two days (lowest low for a short trade) to trigger a trade. As it turns out, however, this actually lowers the results somewhat—probably because the sys-

TABLE 13.4

Short-side Trades without Stop Loss and Trend Filter

	Short only: No trend filter, no stop loss				PercProf: 34.92
	Trades	**PercWin**	**NetProfit**	**AvgProfit**	**ProfitStD**	**RiskRatio**
Average:	96.75	33.24	(19,619.26)	(119.43)		**Market**
St. Dev:	31.42	6.51	48,768.85	687.87	4,098.89	(0.06)
High:	128.17	39.75	29,149.59	568.44	3,979.45	**Portfolio**
Low:	65.33	26.73	(68,388.10)	(807.31)	(4,218.32)	(0.17)
	ProfitFactor	**RiskFactor**	**MaxDD**	**PercDD**	**PercTime**	**AvgLength**
Average:	0.92	(0.07)	53,285.06	47.99	9.16	3.97
St. Dev:	0.41	0.24	28,905.17	28.57	2.12	0.57
High:	1.33	0.17	82,190.23	76.56	11.29	4.53
Low:	0.52	(0.32)	24,379.89	19.42	7.04	3.40

tem does a good job in catching the anticipated move early with its original rules, instead of waiting for the move to get started.

Having tested the logic behind the system (which was obviously there for some reason I had forgotten about), it is time to test the lookback periods for the volume-weighted average and its highest high and lowest low values. As it turned out, there was no rhyme or reason to how the results changed with individual changes in the lookback periods. Therefore, I set both lookback periods to the same value and thereby got rid of another optimizable variable before I tested for lookback periods longer and shorter than the original nine days.

The testing indicated that the long side worked best, with a slightly longer lookback period of 21 days, which also equals one month. Good results for surrounding lookback periods, such as 18 to 25 days confirmed that this also is a robust solution. For the short side, the best and most robust results came with a lookback period of 10 days, or two weeks. By the way, I like it when the lookback periods align themselves with calendar periods: It helps me make sense of and put trust in the logic behind the system, even though I shouldn't have a problem with that, since I built it myself in the first place.

Table 13.5 shows that the average profit for the long side now is $661, with a risk–reward ratio of 0.95. These very good numbers indicate that the system has a large likelihood to be profitable in the future as well as in the past. This is further confirmed by the lower standard deviation boundaries for the profit and risk factors, which both are safely above one and zero, respectively. The risk factor tells us that we can expect to make 26 cents for every dollar risked, which is very good indeed.

TABLE 13.5

Altering Lookback Period for Long-side Trading

	Long only: No trend filter, no stop loss, 21-day lookback				PercProf: 87.30	
	Trades	**PercWin**	**NetProfit**	**AvgProfit**	**ProfitStD**	**RiskRatio**
Average:	110.92	42.80	64,023.40	661.56		**Market**
St. Dev:	30.86	6.58	56,981.64	695.88	5,423.76	0.11
High:	141.78	49.39	121,005.04	1,357.45	6,085.32	**Portfolio**
Low:	80.06	36.22	7,041.77	(34.32)	(4,762.20)	0.95
	ProfitFactor	**RiskFactor**	**MaxDD**	**PercDD**	**PercTime**	**AvgLength**
Average:	1.49	0.26	37,481.14	24.85	15.08	5.64
St. Dev:	0.47	0.23	18,477.53	14.51	3.00	0.75
High:	1.96	0.49	55,958.67	39.36	18.08	6.40
Low:	1.02	0.03	19,003.61	10.34	12.07	4.89

TABLE 13.6

Altering Lookback Period for Short-side Trading

		Short only: No trend filter, no stop loss, 10-day lookback				PercProf: 33.33
	Trades	**PercWin**	**NetProfit**	**AvgProfit**	**ProfitStD**	**RiskRatio**
Average:	99.98	32.95	(22,515.10)	(126.88)		**Market**
St. Dev:	31.31	7.14	48,348.58	871.36	4,023.59	(0.06)
High:	131.29	40.08	25,833.48	744.48	3,896.71	**Portfolio**
Low:	68.68	25.81	(70,863.68)	(998.24)	(4,150.47)	(0.15)
	ProfitFactor	**RiskFactor**	**MaxDD**	**PercDD**	**PercTime**	**AvgLength**
Average:	0.97	(0.06)	53,793.11	48.74	9.37	3.92
St. Dev:	0.74	0.30	31,310.98	30.96	2.16	0.53
High:	1.71	0.24	85,104.09	79.71	11.53	4.45
Low:	0.23	(0.36)	22,482.12	17.78	7.20	3.39

The short side is still not as good as it was in the original model, using a trend filter based on hindsight. But, as Table 13.6 indicates, a profit factor of 0.97 and a risk factor of −0.06 (meaning we're losing six cents for every dollar risked) still isn't too bad, considering the long up trend this side of the system had to battle. These versions of the system will go with us to the next section, where we will try to improve on the results further by adding a few stops and exits. Hopefully this will make the short side profitable as well. Figure 13.1 shows one good short trade in Merck, followed by a series of whipsaw trades, some winners, and some losers.

TRADESTATION CODE

Variables:

{These variables can also be used as inputs for optimization purposes.}

AllowLong(True), AllowShort(True), AverageUpLength(21), AverageDownLength(10), TriggerLength(2),

{Leave these variables alone.}

AverageUpVolume(0), HighAvgUpVolume(0), LowAvgUpVolume(0), RelAvgUpVolume(0), InvRelAvgUpVolume(0), AvgVolumeUpWeight(0), VolWeightedUpAvg(0), AverageDownVolume(0), HighAvgDownVolume(0), LowAvgDownVolume(0), RelAvgDownVolume(0), InvRelAvgDownVolume(0), AvgVolumeDownWeight(0), VolWeightedDownAvg(0);

{Code for normalizing the number of contracts traded goes here.}

If AllowLong = True Then Begin

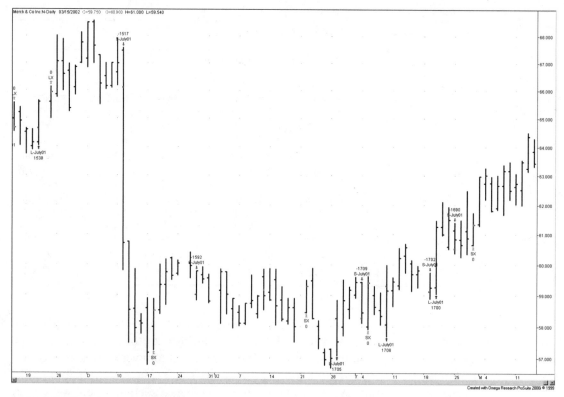

FIGURE 13.1

Merck trading using revised volume-weighted average system.

AverageUpVolume = Average(Volume, AverageUpLength);

HighAvgUpVolume = Highest(AverageUpVolume, AverageUpLength);

LowAvgUpVolume = Lowest(AverageUpVolume, AverageUpLength);

RelAvgUpVolume = (AverageUpVolume - LowAvgUpVolume) /
(HighAvgUpVolume - LowAvgUpVolume);

InvRelAvgUpVolume = 1 - RelAvgUpVolume;

VolWeightedUpAvg = RelAvgUpVolume * AvgPrice +

InvRelAvgUpVolume * VolWeightedUpAvg;

    If MarketPosition = 0 and Close < VolWeightedUpAvg and

    VolWeightedUpAvg < VolWeightedUpAvg[1] Then

        Buy ("L-July01") Next Bar NumCont Contracts at Highest(High,
        TriggerLength) Stop;

End;

If AllowShort = True Then Begin

AverageDownVolume = Average(Volume, AverageDownLength);

HighAvgDownVolume = Highest(AverageDownVolume, AverageDownLength);

LowAvgDownVolume = Lowest(AverageDownVolume, AverageDownLength);

RelAvgDownVolume = (AverageDownVolume - LowAvgDownVolume) /
(HighAvgDownVolume - LowAvgDownVolume);

InvRelAvgDownVolume = 1 - RelAvgDownVolume;

VolWeightedDownAvg = RelAvgDownVolume * AvgPrice +
InvRelAvgDownVolume * VolWeightedDownAvg;

If MarketPosition = 0 and Close > VolWeightedDownAvg and
VolWeightedDownAvg > VolWeightedDownAvg[1] Then

    Sell ("S-July01") Next Bar NumCont Contracts at Lowest(Low,
    TriggerLength) Stop;

End;

If MarketPosition = 1 and Close < VolWeightedUpAvg Then

    ExitLong on Close;

If MarketPosition = -1 and Close > VolWeightedDownAvg Then

    ExitShort on Close;

{Code for testing stops in Excel goes here (see Part 3 of book), with
Normalize(False). Set SurfaceChartTest(True). Disable original stops in system.}

{Code for initial market export goes here, with Normalize(True). Set
ExportSwitch(True).}

{Code for testing robustness goes here (see Part 3 of book), with Normalize(True).
Set RobustnessSwitch(True).}

{Code for exporting results for money management analysis goes here (see Part 4
of book), with Normalize(False). Set MoneyExport(True).}

CHAPTER 14

Harris 3L-R Pattern Variation

Originally presented in November 2001, this system shows that you don't have to be a rocket scientist to come up with a profitable trading strategy. It is based on a simple pattern developed by Michael Harris (www.TradingPatterns.com) and previously featured in *Active Trader* ("Keeping It Simple," September 2001, p. 82). It consists of two simple principles that are likely to remain true, no matter how much the general market conditions change.

The first principle is that no market is likely to continue in the same direction more than a few days in a row before it reverses. That doesn't necessarily mean the longer-term trend has to change or that the move in the opposite direction will be large enough to produce a profitable trade. For example, if the market were truly random (they almost are, but not quite), the likelihood for three up or down days in a row would be a mere 12.5 percent (0.5 * 0.5 * 0.5 = 0.125).

The second principle states that you are better off trading with the momentum of the market and, more often than not, using breakout trades. In this case, the breakout is signaled on a higher high than the high of three days ago.

When both of the prerequisites have been met, enter a long position on the next open and stay in the trade for either a 12 percent profit or a 4 percent loss. This system is changed slightly from the one featured in the September 2001 issue, because the profit–loss ratio is changed from 1:1 to 3:1 (throughout the rest of the book, I use the term risk–reward relationship to describe this).

SUGGESTED MARKETS

Stocks, stock index futures, index shares (SPYs, DIAs, QQQs), commodity futures, and currencies.

ORIGINAL RULES (LONG TRADES ONLY)

Go long on the next open if today's high is higher than the high three days ago, yesterday's low is lower than the low two days ago, and the low two days ago is lower than the low three days ago.

Risk 1 percent of available equity per trade for all trades.

Exit all trades with a loss if the market moves against the position by 4 percent or more.

Exit all trades with a profit if the market moves in favor of the position by 12 percent or more.

TEST PERIOD

January 1992 to August 2001 (2,500 days of data per security).

TEST DATA

Daily stock prices for the 30 highest capitalized stocks in the NASDAQ 100, excluding Intel and Microsoft (which also are in the Dow Jones Industrial Index). A sum of $20 per trade has been deducted for slippage and commission.

STARTING EQUITY

$100,000 (nominal).

SYSTEM PROS AND CONS

This version of the system does not take into account the opening price before the trade is entered. One way to filter out a few likely losers is to enter a trade only on those days the open confirms the previous day's breakout, by either opening higher than the previous day's close or at least not so low that the breakout is completely negated. Along the same lines, it also could be a good idea to make sure the market doesn't open too high above the breakout, lest the better part of the move is over before you get a chance to enter.

The original 1:1 profit–loss relationship did not work very well. I therefore arbitrarily changed it to a 4 percent stop loss and a 12 percent profit target. Both stops are, however, completely unoptimized, which means a little fine-tuning could help. It also could be a good idea to add a trailing stop that, for example, never lets you lose more than half your profits, or that tightens as your profits increase. To avoid tying up valuable resources in trades that go nowhere, a time-based stop could be added that exits all trades after a certain number of days, no matter what.

As usual, it also would be a good idea to add a trend filter, such as a long-term moving average, and allow the system to trade short by reversing the logic. It has been proven that a trend filter—allowing only those trades that go with the direction of the underlying trend—improves performance in most systems.

Finally, note that many of the stocks traded in this example weren't tradable until a few years ago, which explains the exceptionally long flat period halfway through the testing period (not shown). Had we been able to test the same 30 stocks throughout the entire period, it's highly likely that it would have increased performance considerably. This is indicated by the latest drawdown, which comes nowhere near the current drawdown in the NASDAQ, and which would probably have been smaller still had we traded the market from the short side as well.

REVISING THE RESEARCH AND MODIFYING THE SYSTEM

Testing this system anew over the period January 1990 to February 2002, on the 30 stocks making up Dow Jones index, the 30 stocks with the highest market capitalization in NASDAQ 100, and five different stock indexes (Dow Industrial, S&P 500, NASDAQ 100, S&P MidCap, and Russell 2000) show that the results on the long side hold up well. An average profit factor of 1.48 and an average risk factor of 0.28 are not bad. A risk–reward ratio of 0.96 means that we can be pretty sure that the average profit will not turn negative when the system is traded for real. Also, of all the markets tested, more than 80 percent were profitable, which is very good indeed. Table 14.1 shows the combined results from all markets tested.

As Table 14.2 shows, adding the short side to the equation seems not to have been such a good idea. The number of profitable markets sank to 61.5 percent, the profit factor is just barely high enough to compensate for slippage and commission, and the risk factor is a mere 6 cents per dollar risked. The risk–reward ratio for the entire portfolio, which measures the risk-adjusted return by dividing the average profit per trade by the standard deviation of the average profit per trade, also is too low, at 0.04, thus indicating that the trades produced by this system are all over the place.

One big negative with this system is its average trade lengths of 23 and 12 days, respectively. This is way too long, considering that the trade is based on a three-day pattern and the fact that it should be a short-term strategy. Looking through the charts, it is easy to find trades that last for as long as six months and longer. We will talk more about this in Part 3, where we discuss various types of

TABLE 14.1

Retesting Results of Harris 3L-R Pattern System

	Original system, long only					PercProf: 81.54
	Trades	**PercWin**	**NetProfit**	**AvgProfit**	**ProfitStD**	**RiskRatio**
Average:	50.20	34.10	62,126.82	1,295.04		**Market**
St. Dev:	11.73	7.70	64,447.90	1,344.95	8,337.05	0.15
High:	61.93	41.80	126,574.73	2,639.99	9,632.09	**Portfolio**
Low:	38.47	26.40	(2,321.08)	(49.90)	(7,042.01)	0.96
	ProfitFactor	**RiskFactor**	**MaxDD**	**PercDD**	**PercTime**	**AvgLength**
Average:	1.48	0.28	42,058.76	31.15	25.77	23.55
St. Dev:	0.52	0.29	18,687.90	18.84	14.41	19.33
High:	2.00	0.57	60,746.66	49.99	40.18	42.88
Low:	0.96	(0.01)	23,370.87	12.31	11.37	4.22

stops and exit techniques. For now, let's just state that we should not stay in a trade for any longer than what can be validated by the entry signal and the underlying fundamental reason why this signal came about. Obviously, it does not make sense to enter into a six-month trade based on a three-day pattern.

The reason why this currently is the case can be found in the rudimentary stop-loss and profit-target exits. The stop was set in such a way that it would be sufficiently far from the entry so that we wouldn't be stopped out immediately

TABLE 14.2

Short-side Trading

	Original system, both sides					PercProf: 61.54
	Trades	**PercWin**	**NetProfit**	**AvgProfit**	**ProfitStD**	**RiskRatio**
Average:	105.51	26.71	21,948.35	30.20		**Market**
St. Dev:	20.61	5.53	75,765.43	822.11	6,720.68	(0.02)
High:	126.11	32.24	97,713.78	852.31	6,750.87	**Portfolio**
Low:	84.90	21.18	(53,817.09)	(791.91)	(6,690.48)	0.04
	ProfitFactor	**RiskFactor**	**MaxDD**	**PercDD**	**PercTime**	**AvgLength**
Average:	1.10	0.06	76,602.44	63.90	32.56	12.80
St. Dev:	0.29	0.20	31,358.80	31.53	13.19	5.49
High:	1.39	0.26	107,961.24	95.43	45.75	18.29
Low:	0.81	(0.14)	45,243.64	32.38	19.37	7.30

after the entry in case of a high-volatility day, which hasn't been all that uncommon recently. To achieve a desired 3:1 risk–reward relationship, the profit target then needed to be as far as 12 percent away from the entry, which, as indicated by the trade length, is too far for a short-term system.

To see if we can make the system a little more short-term, let's see how it will function with a stop loss of 1 percent together with a profit target of 3 percent (for a 3:1 risk–reward relationship). Table 14.3 shows that the average profit per trade for all long trades diminished considerably compared to the original system, as did the risk–reward ratio for all markets, as indicated by a risk ratio of 0.58. The profit and risk factors also decreased a great deal, but at least the profit factor is within a tolerable limit at this stage of the research. One worrying thing is that the number of trades didn't increase that much at all, despite a shortening of the average trade length. Apparently, this is a very rare pattern, and perhaps it should be treated as such, letting it continue to catch those longer-term moves on the long side. Let's stick to the short-term strategy for now, however, and see if we can improve it further.

My main criticism when I tested this system for *Active Trader* was that no criteria existed for the opening price on the day for the entry. Entering blindly on the open might result in an entry so far away from the break through the trigger level that the reason for the trade might have not only been negated, but also even reversed. Making the system more short term makes it even more important to do something about this.

To check if the results could be improved by adding some sort of volatility criteria for the open, I altered the entry rule to require an opening price not more than one average true range (measured over the last 20 days) from the trigger level,

TABLE 14.3

Changed Risk–reward Relationship

		Long only, 3:1 risk–reward relationship			PercProf: 73.85
	Trades	**PercWin**	**NetProfit**	**AvgProfit**	**ProfitStD**	**RiskRatio**
Average:	64.55	37.41	15,271.85	267.46		**Market**
St. Dev:	15.70	7.17	24,347.84	459.34	3,483.27	0.06
High:	80.25	44.58	39,619.68	726.80	3,750.73	**Portfolio**
Low:	48.85	30.24	(9,075.99)	(191.88)	(3,215.81)	0.58
	ProfitFactor	**RiskFactor**	**MaxDD**	**PercDD**	**PercTime**	**AvgLength**
Average:	1.21	0.11	23,308.50	20.15	6.33	4.01
St. Dev:	0.31	0.18	10,809.47	9.93	2.84	1.65
High:	1.51	0.29	34,117.97	30.08	9.17	5.66
Low:	0.90	(0.07)	12,499.03	10.22	3.50	2.36

which is the high from four days prior. The test was done on the system with the 1 percent stop and the 3 percent profit target. But because this did little to better the results, I decided to stay with the original logic.

However, because it didn't seem to matter where the opening and the entry price were in relation to the trigger level, which was the high four days before the open, it is questionable if the opening price is needed at all. What if we just enter one day earlier with a stop order, immediately when the trigger level is hit? Tables 14.4 and 14.5 show the result from this test for the short-term risk–reward relationship version of the system.

And what do you know! As Tables 14.4 and 14.5 show, we're definitely on the right track here. Waiting to enter until the open following the move that actually triggered the trade did little good. After a little experimenting, the profit and risk factors are back to relatively high levels, at least for the long-only version. The results for the both-sides version are still a little so-so, but the way it's improving gives plenty of hope.

Now, there's only one more thing to address in regards to the entry and that is the relatively small amount of trades generated. So far, the system has required two lower lows in a row to enter on the long side. But what would happen if we altered that rule a bit, to only require two lows lower than a third preceding low. Will that increase the number of trades without ruining the results? Let's try it.

Tables 14.6 and 14.7 show that not only did this modification more than double the number of trades, it even improved the results quite a bit—so much so, that the risk–reward ratio for the portfolio traded on both sides now is above 1 (1.11), which is very good indeed. Granted, this number is contradicted somewhat by the

TABLE 14.4

Testing Short-term Risk–reward Relationship (1)

	Long only, 3:1 risk–reward relationship, open excluded			PercProf: 81.54		
	Trades	**PercWin**	**NetProfit**	**AvgProfit**	**ProfitStD**	**RiskRatio**
Average:	60.85	38.91	21,953.83	377.95		**Market**
St. Dev:	18.89	9.21	30,078.20	510.36	3,226.06	0.11
High:	79.74	48.12	52,032.03	888.30	3,604.01	**Portfolio**
Low:	41.96	29.71	(8,124.37)	(132.41)	(2,848.12)	0.74
	ProfitFactor	**RiskFactor**	**MaxDD**	**PercDD**	**PercTime**	**AvgLength**
Average:	1.39	0.20	19,873.20	16.87	5.77	3.88
St. Dev:	0.51	0.27	12,016.79	11.29	3.13	1.75
High:	1.90	0.47	31,889.99	28.15	8.90	5.63
Low:	0.88	(0.07)	7,856.41	5.58	2.65	2.13

TABLE 14.5

Testing Short-term Risk–reward Relationship (2)

	Both sides, 3:1 risk–reward relationship, open excluded PercProf: 64.62					
	Trades	**PercWin**	**NetProfit**	**AvgProfit**	**ProfitStD**	**RiskRatio**
Average:	115.15	35.31	14,542.14	254.39		**Market**
St. Dev:	34.97	7.09	39,415.20	356.10	3,022.69	0.08
High:	150.12	42.40	53,957.34	610.49	3,277.08	**Portfolio**
Low:	80.18	28.22	(24,873.06)	(101.71)	(2,768.30)	0.71
	ProfitFactor	**RiskFactor**	**MaxDD**	**PercDD**	**PercTime**	**AvgLength**
Average:	1.15	0.08	26,899.76	22.43	10.06	3.58
St. Dev:	0.33	0.21	16,040.17	15.27	4.94	1.54
High:	1.49	0.29	42,939.92	37.70	15.00	5.12
Low:	0.82	(0.13)	10,859.59	7.16	5.12	2.04

low values for the lower one-standard-deviation boundaries for both the profit factor and the risk factor. But both the profit and risk factors are still good enough.

For now, however, we won't care so much about the negatives, but instead rejoice in the high risk–reward ratios for both the latest portfolios, and an ever-increasing number of profitable markets. Another cool thing is that this latest version of the system, despite a much lower average profit per trade and shorter trade length, actually nets more money than the original system. This can be estimated

TABLE 14.6

Increasing Number of Trades Generated (1)

	Long only, 3:1 risk–reward relationship, slightly altered PercProf: 89.23					
	Trades	**PercWin**	**NetProfit**	**AvgProfit**	**ProfitStD**	**RiskRatio**
Average:	147.09	38.94	49,746.53	357.54		**Market**
St. Dev:	38.29	6.78	48,002.37	381.51	3,305.81	0.10
High:	185.39	45.72	97,748.91	739.04	3,663.35	**Portfolio**
Low:	108.80	32.16	1,744.16	(23.97)	(2,948.27)	0.94
	ProfitFactor	**RiskFactor**	**MaxDD**	**PercDD**	**PercTime**	**AvgLength**
Average:	1.31	0.17	31,047.12	22.31	14.33	4.10
St. Dev:	0.30	0.17	15,214.45	13.82	5.02	1.65
High:	1.61	0.35	46,261.58	36.14	19.36	5.75
Low:	1.01	0.00	15,832.67	8.49	9.31	2.45

TABLE 14.7

Increasing Number of Trades Generated (2)

	Trades	PercWin	NetProfit	AvgProfit	ProfitStD	RiskRatio
Both sides, 3:1 risk–reward relationship, slightly altered PercProf: 73.85						
Average:	279.43	35.30	37,765.83	308.13		**Market**
St. Dev:	74.17	5.55	67,417.87	277.14	2,991.74	0.10
High:	353.60	40.86	105,183.70	585.27	3,299.87	**Portfolio**
Low:	205.27	29.75	(29,652.04)	31.00	(2,683.60)	1.11
	ProfitFactor	**RiskFactor**	**MaxDD**	**PercDD**	**PercTime**	**AvgLength**
Average:	1.15	0.09	37,529.46	28.07	23.08	3.46
St. Dev:	0.26	0.17	23,935.55	22.85	6.70	1.10
High:	1.40	0.26	61,465.01	50.92	29.78	4.56
Low:	0.89	(0.08)	13,593.91	5.22	16.38	2.36

FIGURE 14.1

Citigroup traded using revised Harris 3L-R pattern–Winter 2001–2002.

by multiplying the average number of trades per market by the average profit per trade and market. For the original system, this value comes out to $64,750 (1,295 * 50), but with the latest version of the system, traded from both sides, the average net profit per market comes out to $85,932 (308 * 279). We will carry this version with us for further testing in Parts 3 and 4. Figure 14.1 shows a few sample trades in Citigroup during the winter of 2001–2002.

TRADESTATION CODE

```
Variables:
{These variables can also be used as inputs for optimization purposes.}
AllowLong(True), AllowShort(True), PercentTarget(3), PercentLoss(1),
{Leave these variables alone.}
ProfitTarget(0), StopLoss(0), LongProfit(0), LongStop(0), ShortProfit(0),
ShortStop(0);
{Code for normalizing the number of contracts traded goes here.}
If BarNumber = 1 Then Begin
    ProfitTarget = PercentTarget * 0.01;
    StopLoss = PercentLoss * 0.01;
End;
If MarketPosition = 0 Then Begin
    If AllowLong = True and Low < Low[2] and Low[1] < Low[2] Then
        Buy ("L-Nov 01") NumCont Contracts Next Bar on High[2] Stop;
    If AllowShort = True and High > High[2] and High[1] > High[2] Then
        Sell ("S-Nov 01") NumCont Contracts Next Bar on Low[2] Stop;
End;
If EntryPrice > 0 Then Begin
    LongProfit = EntryPrice * (1 + ProfitTarget);
    LongStop = EntryPrice * (1 - StopLoss);
    ShortProfit = EntryPrice * (1 - ProfitTarget);
    ShortStop = EntryPrice * (1 + StopLoss);
    If MarketPosition = 1 Then Begin
        ExitLong ("L-Stop") Next Bar at LongStop Stop;
        ExitLong ("L-Trgt") Next Bar at LongProfit Limit;
    End;
    If MarketPosition = -1 Then Begin
        ExitShort ("S-Stop") Next Bar at ShortStop Stop;
        ExitShort ("S-Trgt") Next Bar at ShortProfit Limit;
```

    End;

End;

{Code for testing stops in Excel goes here (see Part 3 of book), with Normalize(False). Set SurfaceChartTest(True). Disable original stops in system.}

{Code for initial market export goes here, with Normalize(True). Set ExportSwitch(True).}

{Code for testing robustness goes here (see Part 3 of book), with Normalize(True). Set RobustnessSwitch(True).}

{Code for exporting results for money management analysis goes here (see Part 4 of book), with Normalize(False). Set MoneyExport(True).}

CHAPTER 15

Expert Exits

Originally presented in June 2002, the idea behind this simple swing trading system is to maintain profitability while keeping losses as small as possible. The basic system is the same as that used in the risk control and money management articles about finding the best exit level (*Active Trader*, March through June 2002).

When a market makes a lower high than the previous day's high and closes below the open (reverse the reasoning for short trades), the system identifies this as a correction against the anticipated direction of the trade. Any market that has fulfilled these two criteria at the open of the next day's trading is a potential trading candidate.

On the day of the anticipated trade, the stock also needs to open below the previous day's high (above the previous day's low, for a short trade). With the final criteria in place, an order can be placed to buy a break above yesterday's high (below yesterday's low).

The logic can easily be altered. For example, you could require the stock to take out the high from two days ago, or the close to be less than the previous day's close rather than the same day's open.

The entry strategy is accompanied by a 1 percent stop loss and a 4.5 percent profit target. To avoid tying up money in trades that go nowhere, any open trades are exited after eight days.

A trade-sizing model was added to the entry rule. The system trades fewer shares or contracts when the market is more volatile. In such conditions, the trade size is based on four times the average true range over the last 10 days, with a maximum risk per trade of no more than 2.5 percent of available equity.

SUGGESTED MARKETS

Stocks, stock index futures, index tracking stocks (SPDRs, DIAs, QQQs), futures, and currencies.

ORIGINAL RULES (REVERSE THE LOGIC FOR SHORT TRADES)

Yesterday's high should be lower than the previous day's high; yesterday's close should be lower than yesterday's open; and today's open should be lower than yesterday's high.

Go long on a break above yesterday's high.

Risk 2.5 percent of available capital per trade.

Exit with a loss if the market moves against you more than 1 percent.

Take profits if the market moves in your favor by more than 4.5 percent.

Liquidate any remaining trades after eight days.

TEST PERIOD

July 1992 to February 2002 (2,500 days of data per security).

TEST DATA

Daily stock prices for the 30 highest capitalized stocks in the NASDAQ 100. A sum of $20 per trade has been deducted for slippage and commission.

STARTING EQUITY

$100,000 (nominal).

SYSTEM PROS AND CONS

Unlike many other systems, this one trades the short side as well as the long—a necessary criterion to keep the drawdown to a minimum during prolonged downtrends, such as the one we're currently experiencing. The system, in fact, is in the midst of its worst drawdown since the start of the testing period, but so is the NASDAQ 100 index; so far the system's drawdown doesn't come anywhere near that of the NASDAQ 100. Other than the recent drawdown, the system's history has been very good indeed, as indicated by the drawdown chart (not shown).

Note that the average time spent in a trade—1.6 days—is very short. This, in turn, results in a low average profit per trade of $70. This may not seem much, but remember that it is the average profit for all trades, including losers. The average winner is larger, but because there's only one winner for two losers, the average profit per trade is affected.

Another important thing to remember is that this number also is highly influenced by many trades made at the beginning of the testing period, when the markets were trading at considerably lower levels. The average profit per trade in today's markets (in dollar terms) is considerably higher.

Nonetheless, this system is a good example of how a steady stream of small-dollar gains can accumulate significantly over time. Systems that profit in this way can be considerably more profitable than a buy-and-hold strategy, or a trade approach that shoots for the big bucks on every trade.

REVISING THE RESEARCH AND MODIFYING THE SYSTEM

This system really doesn't have any optimizable variables to work with, except for the exit levels (which we will leave for Part 3) and the option to work with a trailing stop instead of a fixed stop loss. However, I decided to feature it here as an example of a different testing methodology. The logic for researching the signals in this system has already been discussed in Chapter 1. Therefore, I will only run through it again very briefly.

During the initial testing of a system, we really shouldn't concern ourselves with the performance of the system, but rather the reliability of the signals it generates. To do that, you need to test all the signals generated, using standardized stops and exits. Normal system testing usually only tests the first signal in a cluster of entry signals, assuming the others can be ignored because you would have been in a trade already. However, whether you would have been in a trade or not depends on your stop-loss and profit-taking levels and how long the trade should last if none of these levels is hit.

Therefore, when researching a system, it's important to look at all signals it generates, so that it can be trusted just as much on its second or third signals as it can on its first signal. For example, assume that you, for some reason, missed a signal one day. The next day you get a new signal in the same stock, despite the fact that you should have been in this stock already had you been able to trade. If you haven't done your research properly, you have no idea whether the second signal is likely to be as valid and reliable as the first one.

Look at Figure 15.1, which shows a chart of all signals this particular system generated in Microsoft during the fall of 2001. It shows that in early August 2001, two signals indicated to go short only one day apart from each other. In late October and early November, two signals two days in a row indicated to go long. The point is that, in either case, the second signal most likely would have gone unanalyzed, because you already would have been in a trade generated by the first signal.

The same reasoning holds for the exit techniques as well. To make the most out of the chart pattern and its exit techniques, you need to have done your

FIGURE 15.1

Microsoft traded using original expert exits system–Fall 2001.

homework before you set out to trade the pattern in question and analyzed the exits in such a way that they would work on average equally as well for all signals, no matter whether each specific signal would have been traded or not. Therefore, the testing must be done in such a way that all signals will be tested at one time or another, together with several different exit levels. To do that, trade the system at random several times. (To learn more about this system and how to test other systems the same way, see *Active Trader* magazine, February 2002 to June 2002.)

Once the system and all its signals are fully tested, using a random number generator, the system can be tested according to normal principles. Table 15.1 shows the results for the system, as featured in the original article, when tested on 65 different markets. As you can see, it's doing really well, with an average profit per trade of $348, and profit and risk factors of 1.49 and 0.30, respectively. The risk–reward ratio of 1.06 also is very good, and indicates that at least 84 percent of all trading sequences will end in a profit.

TABLE 15.1

Retesting the Original Expert Exits System

			Original system, both sides		PercProf: 89.23	
	Trades	**PercWin**	**NetProfit**	**AvgProfit**	**ProfitStD**	**RiskRatio**
Average:	297.22	32.52	92,316.40	348.56		**Market**
St. Dev:	83.60	6.34	90,092.46	328.64	3,485.34	0.09
High:	380.82	38.86	182,408.86	677.21	3,833.91	**Portfolio**
Low:	213.61	26.18	2,223.93	19.92	(3,136.78)	1.06
	ProfitFactor	**RiskFactor**	**MaxDD**	**PercDD**	**PercTime**	**AvgLength**
Average:	1.28	0.18	47,367.80	34.00	30.96	4.32
St. Dev:	0.28	0.18	38,828.29	39.93	9.87	1.32
High:	1.57	0.36	86,196.09	73.93	40.83	5.64
Low:	1.00	(0.00)	8,539.51	(5.93)	21.08	3.00

Tables 15.2 and 15.3 show how the original system performed on the long and the short side, respectively. As you can see, the system is doing very well on the long side: 93.85 percent profitable markets mean that 61 out of the 65 markets tested profitably, which is very good indeed. That the lower one-standard-deviation boundaries for the risk and profit factors are well above one and zero, respectively, confirms that this is a very robust system on the long side.

For the short side, however, the results are less tantalizing. It's true the system is profitable overall, with a healthy 69 percent of the markets producing prof-

TABLE 15.2

Long-side Trading Using Original Expert Exits System

			Original system, long only		PercProf: 93.85	
	Trades	**PercWin**	**NetProfit**	**AvgProfit**	**ProfitStD**	**RiskRatio**
Average:	179.46	35.29	87,812.22	563.07		**Market**
St. Dev:	53.86	7.12	59,499.55	405.02	3,516.35	0.15
High:	233.32	42.41	147,311.78	968.09	4,079.42	**Portfolio**
Low:	125.60	28.17	28,312.67	158.06	(2,953.28)	1.39
	ProfitFactor	**RiskFactor**	**MaxDD**	**PercDD**	**PercTime**	**AvgLength**
Average:	1.49	0.30	31,178.49	21.78	19.14	4.40
St. Dev:	0.39	0.22	19,451.39	19.07	7.19	1.44
High:	1.88	0.51	50,629.89	40.85	26.33	5.84
Low:	1.11	0.08	11,727.10	2.71	11.96	2.96

TABLE 15.3

Short-side Trading Using Original Expert Exits System

	Original system, short only				PercProf: 69.23	
	Trades	**PercWin**	**NetProfit**	**AvgProfit**	**ProfitStD**	**RiskRatio**
Average:	170.88	29.80	18,437.41	123.15		**Market**
St. Dev:	57.00	7.06	64,994.32	457.02	3,399.69	0.03
High:	227.88	36.86	83,431.72	580.17	3,522.84	**Portfolio**
Low:	113.88	22.75	(46,556.91)	(333.88)	(3,276.54)	0.27
	ProfitFactor	**RiskFactor**	**MaxDD**	**PercDD**	**PercTime**	**AvgLength**
Average:	1.12	0.07	48,524.51	41.45	18.25	4.34
St. Dev:	0.33	0.22	31,726.67	32.58	7.96	1.30
High:	1.45	0.29	80,251.18	74.03	26.21	5.63
Low:	0.80	(0.15)	16,797.84	8.87	10.29	3.04

it, but most important numbers are a little on the low side. But is it really worth trading it from both sides for the downside protection in case of prolonged down-trends, given the fact that the short side also decreases the overall and long-term risk–reward relationship? This is a difficult question to answer, and something you have to do for yourself, considering your own preferences. The question you need to ask yourself is, "Am I willing to sacrifice some trading comfort (and profit) during normal circumstances, to be better prepared to make a profit (or at least scrape by) during the downtrends?" If the answer is yes, you should trade the short side as well; if it's no, you should stick to the long side only.

Table 15.4 illustrates the robustness of this system, traded from both sides. For Table 15.4, the random number generator (RNG) was left on and the system tested 10 times each on all markets for a total of 650 test runs. Because the RNG sometimes allows the system to enter into a trade, and at other times it doesn't, each trading sequence is unique and can consist of any and all of the signals generated. As you can see, this resulted in an even higher average profit per trade and higher profit and risk factors than in the original system, tested the normal way. Thus, only trading the first signal in a series of signals isn't the most lucrative thing to do. However, with additional profit potentials comes additional risk. With a risk–reward ratio of 0.92, this version is slightly riskier to trade than the original version. Lower one-standard-deviation boundaries for the profit and risk factors confirm this observation.

One way to alter the original system is to substitute the fixed stop loss with a trailing stop that, for example, exits a long trade if the market falls a certain amount from the most recent highest high or highest close, or from the entry price immediately after the entry. All trades require a certain amount of leeway to be able to

TABLE 15.4

Trading Both Sides Using RNG

	Original system, both sides, random entries				PercProf: 86.92
	Trades	**PercWin**	**NetProfit**	**AvgProfit**	**ProfitStD**	**RiskRatio**
---	---	---	---	---	---	---
Average:	165.06	32.77	52,947.82	375.55		**Market**
St. Dev:	49.54	7.02	57,816.14	409.49	3,469.47	0.09
High:	214.60	39.79	110,763.96	785.04	3,845.01	**Portfolio**
Low:	115.51	25.75	(4,868.31)	(33.94)	(3,093.92)	0.92

	ProfitFactor	**RiskFactor**	**MaxDD**	**PercDD**	**PercTime**	**AvgLength**
Average:	1.31	0.19	34,605.77	26.90	17.52	4.36
St. Dev:	0.34	0.21	22,807.03	22.76	6.70	1.34
High:	1.65	0.40	57,412.80	49.66	24.22	5.70
Low:	0.97	(0.02)	11,798.74	4.15	10.82	3.02

survive the typical amount of noise in a market. Because you have no idea how much leeway each specific trade will need, the best you can do is estimate an average leeway that seems to work best within each trade for a large group of trades.

For example, a trade with a profit target at 5 percent and stop loss at −1 percent (no trailing stop) has an average wiggle room of 6 percent, no matter how long it lasts. If you use the same wiggle room for all trades, the average wiggle room for all trades will also be 6 percent. If you replace the stop loss with a trailing stop, then the wiggle room within an individual trade that shows a profit will become smaller with time. Therefore, to keep the average wiggle room constant, within both an individual winning trade and all trades (both winners and losers), the wiggle room must be slightly larger at the beginning of a trade with a trailing stop than it must be for a trade with only a stop loss.

This creates a twofold problem: Not only will the largest single-trade loss for a trailing stop be a little larger than that for a fixed stop (because the trailing stop's initially greater leeway means larger potential losses), but the best-case scenario—the profit target—will also not be reached as often as before. This is because some profitable trades that would have remained open if a fixed stop were used (and therefore might have ultimately reached the profit target) will instead be stopped out by the trailing stop. Another way to look at it is to understand that, for a profitable trade, the trailing stop will move in the direction of the trade to decrease the chance for a profitable trade to go bad. Because it's closer to the price than where the fixed stop would have been had we used one, it will also be hit more often, which leaves fewer trades to reach the profit target.

Thus, the profit target must be lowered for two reasons. Reason one is to keep the average wiggle room constant, given that the trailing stop will create more wiggle room at the beginning of the trade, but less at the later stages of a winning trade. Reason two is to increase the number of trades that reach the target, to maximize the profit potential when the trailing stop will make it easier for a trade to exit with a less than maximum profit. However, sometimes the profit target will be increased instead of decreased. Still, however, more often than not, despite the increased profit target, the initial risk–reward relationship going into the trade will not be as favorable as with the same system using a stop loss. Most often, the average profit per trade also will be lower when shifting from a stop loss to a trailing stop.

Therefore, to be effective, a trailing stop must increase the number of winning trades so that the resulting system's slightly smaller winning trade size makes up for its slightly greater largest single-trade losses. A system with a trailing stop can also increase profits further because, more often than not, it will shorten the trade length, which results in more trading opportunities with a higher likelihood of success.

Table 15.5 shows the result of a trailing-stop version of the system, with the trailing stop at 1.6 percent away from the most recent highest high (lowest low in a short trade) —which also is the initial worst-case scenario—and the profit target at 4 percent. If you compare Table 15.5 with Table 15.1, you will find that all the anticipated differences between the two versions also held true in the testing. For one thing, the average profit is slightly smaller for the trailing-stop version, but because the percentage winners and the number of trades are slightly higher, and the trade length is a little shorter, the average net profits are almost the same. A marginally higher risk–reward ratio for the trailing-stop version also indicates that

TABLE 15.5

Using Trailing Stops

	Trailing-stop version, both sides				PercProf: 87.69	
	Trades	**PercWin**	**NetProfit**	**AvgProfit**	**ProfitStD**	**RiskRatio**
Average:	316.60	41.24	90,239.93	329.24		**Market**
St. Dev:	92.40	5.68	87,191.48	308.19	3,007.20	0.10
High:	409.00	46.91	177,431.41	637.43	3,336.44	**Portfolio**
Low:	224.20	35.56	3,048.46	21.05	(2,677.96)	1.07
	ProfitFactor	**RiskFactor**	**MaxDD**	**PercDD**	**PercTime**	**AvgLength**
Average:	1.36	0.20	43,673.54	31.76	26.44	3.46
St. Dev:	0.37	0.20	40,969.57	41.42	8.99	1.15
High:	1.74	0.39	84,643.11	73.18	35.43	4.61
Low:	0.99	(0.00)	2,703.96	(9.66)	17.45	2.31

TABLE 15.6

Trading Long-side Using Trailing Stop

	Trailing-stop version, long only				PercProf: 92.31
	Trades	**PercWin**	**NetProfit**	**AvgProfit**	**ProfitStD**	**RiskRatio**
Average:	186.88	34.67	85,459.01	527.49		**Market**
St. Dev:	53.95	6.80	60,187.21	392.24	3,493.48	0.14
High:	240.83	41.47	145,646.22	919.73	4,020.97	**Portfolio**
Low:	132.93	27.87	25,271.81	135.26	(2,965.99)	1.34
	ProfitFactor	**RiskFactor**	**MaxDD**	**PercDD**	**PercTime**	**AvgLength**
Average:	1.45	0.28	32,835.69	22.37	19.21	4.37
St. Dev:	0.35	0.20	20,403.51	20.14	7.12	1.41
High:	1.81	0.48	53,239.20	42.51	26.32	5.77
Low:	1.10	0.07	12,432.19	2.23	12.09	2.96

its trades are more similar looking than those trades generated by the original stop-loss version of the system. Overall, it's a matter of personal taste, given that the average profit per trade needs to be large enough to warrant trading in the first place. Table 15.6 shows the trailing-stop version of the system traded on the long side only.

Table 15.7 shows how the trailing-stop version fared when trading the entry signals at random. Comparing it first to Table 15.4, we can see that it too confirms

TABLE 15.7

Random Entry Signals and Trailing Stops

	Trailing-stop version, both sides, random entries				PercProf: 86.15
	Trades	**PercWin**	**NetProfit**	**AvgProfit**	**ProfitStD**	**RiskRatio**
Average:	171.22	41.28	48,176.37	320.63		**Market**
St. Dev:	52.87	6.32	54,310.50	357.57	3,002.87	0.10
High:	224.09	47.60	102,486.88	678.20	3,323.50	**Portfolio**
Low:	118.35	34.96	(6,134.13)	(36.94)	(2,682.24)	0.90
	ProfitFactor	**RiskFactor**	**MaxDD**	**PercDD**	**PercTime**	**AvgLength**
Average:	1.37	0.20	31,269.73	24.64	14.53	3.49
St. Dev:	0.42	0.22	23,582.58	23.00	5.90	1.19
High:	1.79	0.41	54,852.31	47.64	20.42	4.67
Low:	0.95	(0.02)	7,687.15	1.64	8.63	2.30

our initial assumptions and the findings from Table 15.5. However, as opposed to Table 15.4 in relation to Table 15.1, Table 15.7 shows both a lower average profit per trade and a lower risk–reward relationship than Table 15.5, which suggests that the trailing-stop version should be traded in a normal fashion on the first signal only. One way to do it might be to trade the trailing-stop version as you'd do with any system, and then add a trade every so often, which you monitor according to the stop-loss rules.

TRADESTATION CODE

```
Variables:
{These variables can also be used as inputs for optimization purposes.}
AllowLong(True), AllowShort(True), RandomEntry(False), TrailingStop(False),
BarsInTrade(8), ProfitExit(4.5){4}, LossExit(1){1.6},
{Leave these variables alone.}
RandomTrigger(0), LongStop(0), ShortStop(0), LongTarget(0), ShortTarget(0),
Top(0), Bottom(0);
RandomTrigger = IntPortion(Random(2));
{Code for normalizing the number of contracts traded goes here.}
If BarNumber = 1 Then Begin
   ProfitExit = ProfitExit / 100;
   LossExit = LossExit / 100;
   LongStop = 1 - LossExit;
   LongTarget = 1 + ProfitExit;
   ShortStop = 1 + LossExit;
   ShortTarget = 1 - ProfitExit;
End;
Top = High;
Bottom = Low;
If (RandomEntry = False or RandomTrigger = 1) and MarketPosition = 0 Then
Begin
   If AllowLong = True and High < High[2] and Close < Open and Open Next Bar
   < High Then
      Buy ("L-June 02") NumCont Contracts Next Bar at High Stop;
   If AllowShort = True and Low > Low[2] and Close > Open and Open Next Bar
   > Low Then
      Sell ("S-June 02") NumCont Contracts Next Bar at Low Stop;
End;
```

```
If EntryPrice > 0 Then Begin
    If MarketPosition = 1 Then Begin
        If TrailingStop = True Then Begin
            Top = MaxList(Top, High);
            ExitLong ("L-Trail") Next Bar at Top * LongStop Stop;
        End
        Else
            ExitLong ("L-Stop") Next Bar at EntryPrice * LongStop Stop;
        ExitLong ("L-Trgt") Next Bar at EntryPrice * LongTarget Limit;
    End;
    If MarketPosition = -1 Then Begin
    If TrailingStop = True Then Begin
        Bottom = MinList(Bottom, Low);
        ExitShort ("S-Trail") Next Bar at Bottom * ShortStop Stop;
    End
    Else
    ExitShort ("S-Stop") Next Bar at EntryPrice * ShortStop Stop;
    ExitShort ("S-Trgt") Next Bar at EntryPrice * ShortTarget Limit;
    End;
    If BarsSinceEntry = BarsInTrade + 1 Then Begin
        ExitLong ("L-Time") Next Bar at Market;
        ExitShort ("S-Time") Next Bar at Market;
    End;
End;
{Code for testing stops in Excel goes here (see Part 3 of book), with
Normalize(False). Set SurfaceChartTest(True). Disable original stops in system.}
{Code for initial market export goes here, with Normalize(True). Set
ExportSwitch(True).}
{Code for testing robustness goes here (see Part 3 of book), with Normalize
(True). Set RobustnessSwitch(True).}
{Code for exporting results for money management analysis goes here (see Part 4
of book), with Normalize(False). Set MoneyExport(True).}
```

CHAPTER 16

Evaluating System Performance

Before we move on to Part 3, let's make a few individual observations for all the systems and a few more general observations.

The meander system had not done well after it was first featured in *Active Trader* magazine, but because it was apparent that it still did a good job finding many good trading opportunities, it was possible to put the performance on track again, by letting the system ride the good trades for a little longer. This was possible because the original average trade length was very short in the first place.

Unfortunately, the system did not function that well on the short side when using the same rules as for the long side. There probably are two major reasons for this. First, a down move does not behave the same as an up move, which means the initial risk–reward relationship going into a trade must be different from that for a long trade. Second, the long version of the system operates with limit orders. Because of the inherent upside bias in the stock market, it probably would be better to trade the short side using stop orders.

The expert exits system (Chapter 15) wasn't really featured here to illustrate a specific entry technique, but rather as a way of optimizing the stops and exits over several different market conditions and markets. However, the entry technique is worth studying, because it works really well in its simplicity—at least on the long side. A relatively low percentage of profitable trades can make this system difficult to trade for those of us who demand immediate positive feedback on our trading.

As far as the average trade length goes, it could be argued that perhaps it is a little too short, and perhaps we could make more of the winning trades by allowing them to go on for a little longer. If that were to happen, however, we must do so without letting the total time spent in a trade increase to a point where we limit our diversification possibilities by being fully invested after only a few trades.

Even without the benefit of hindsight and the original trend filter, the volume-weighted average system (Chapter 13) has held up well throughout the long bear market, although a combined analysis of Tables 13.1 and 13.3 indicates that the average profit per trade on the long side has decreased over the last several years while, at the same time, the average trade length has gotten a little shorter. Both these findings suggest that the thrusts to the upside are not as large and forceful in a downtrend as they are in an uptrend.

The different lookback periods for the short and the long sides, given the results in Tables 13.5 and 13.6, confirm that short-term down moves generally are more explosive in nature than short-term up moves. Another, more philosophical way to look at it, is that the shorter lookback period for the down side indicates that a market discounts and then forgets bad news quicker than it does good news.

The RS system No. 1 (Chapter 9) is one of three systems that, later in the book, will be used as a (trend) filter rather than as an outright entry trigger. As such, it needs to have a slightly longer average trade length to open up a window for the other systems to trigger an entry. However, because this normally also means that the time spent in the market will increase, you have to be careful that the system doesn't spend too much time in the market and thereby make itself useless. In this case, the average trade length on the long side comes out to approximately 20 days.

With the time spent in the market at 70 percent, the system will spend an average of about 10 days out of the market for every 30-day period. Putting this in relation to, for example, the meander system, when using RS system No. 1 as a filter for the meander system, the long side of the meander system will decrease its time in the market to approximately 30 percent and its number of trades per market to approximately 130. This still feels like a little too much for optimal diversification, but we will use these numbers to see what we can learn from them.

At first glance, the code for the relative-strength bands system (Chapter 11) looks very complicated, with a lot of calculations and comparisons between markets. However, if you stop and think about it, it really isn't all that difficult. All we're really doing is comparing the trend of several different markets—something we do in our heads all day long anyway, at least if we also tinker around with the more subjective kind of technical analysis. This is only a way to formalize it all, so that we can digest more information from more markets. Nothing more, nothing less.

If for nothing else, one important thing we learned from this system was that testing only on three markets doesn't even come close to producing results that will be reliable and robust in the long run. However, by expanding the research to include several markets, we had enough observations to allow us some room for tinkering with the system. As it turned out, this system was much better off getting rid of several of the original rules and input variables. With fewer variables tested on more markets, the end versions of this system are much more likely to hold up in the future.

In this case, we ended up with both a long and a short version of the system. Both versions were profitable, but unfortunately this profitability also came at the price of very volatile results, as illustrated by the low risk–reward ratios. For the remainder of the book, this system will be used as a (trend) filter for the other entry techniques, which should help bring down the time spent in the market by approximately 50 percent for most of them.

If we thought that the code for the relative-strength bands system was complicated, then what must we think about the code for the rotation system (Chapter 12)? Again, it really isn't that complicated at all. All that we're doing is comparing the strength of the trend between several markets. But this time, instead of looking at the distance between the relative-strength line and its moving average, we're looking at the slope of the moving average. This is very much like having several charts in front of you, comparing them all with each other, trying to come up with the chart that has the most strength and also is likely to continue strong in the future.

Because the original version of the rotation system was tested in a way similar to the relative-strength bands system, we again had to expand the number of markets tested to come up with statistically reliable results. This time, however, the original results had held up much better since the system was originally featured. However, because all markets were selected at random, the chance also exists that the results from both of these relative-strength systems can be either better or worse than a more thorough examination would reveal. The possibility for that is, however, something most statistical examinations have to live with. The best we can do is make the sample large enough to minimize the possibility.

Note also that I decided to change the logic for the short side halfway through the research process—just like that—and without really starting the research anew. Of course, the correct thing to do would have been to back up and step through the entire research process again, but because we're not using the word "research" here in its most scientific form, but rather as a word for describing my thought process, I decided to just move on as if nothing happened. When it comes to the entry techniques, I am not so much interested in coming up with the optimal solution, but rather a solution that makes sense to me. Right or wrong? We can argue about that later.

For the remainder of the book, this system too will be used as a filter for the other entry techniques, which should help bring down the time spent in the market by approximately 50 percent for most of them.

The hybrid system No. 1 (Chapter 8) was one of the systems that held up best over time. But, as was the case with many of the other systems, it did not fare that well on the short side. Interestingly, it turned out that the best way to modify this system was to make it more aggressive than it was originally. More often than not, when testing an old system on new data, the "best" way to improve it, or to curve fit it to the previously unseen data (if we want to be really critical), is to make it more difficult for the system to enter into a trade. The fact that we didn't have to do that this time is a good sign that this very basic entry technique does a good job of identifying high-probability trading opportunities and that it will continue to work in the future as well.

The two major disadvantages of the system, as of now, are that the average trade length is about twice as long as we would want it to be, and the time spent in a trade is way too long. We really need to get the time spent in a trade down by something like 10 to 15 percent.

When revising the research on the Harris 3L-R pattern variation system (Chapter 14), I found it had one major flaw built into it. This had nothing to do with the original logic, created by Michael Harris, but was completely of my own doing when adding the stops and exits to go with the entry technique.

However, when altering the exit rules, it also turned out the system traded a little too infrequently. To come to grips with that, I had to make a few modifications, such as getting rid of trading on the open the day after the signal and not asking for two consecutive lows (highs) before the market turns and breaks higher (lower). Because both modifications not only increase the results, but also relax the criteria for getting into a trade, it is fair to say that this new version of the system actually is less curve fitted than the original one, and therefore also more robust and more likely to hold up in the future.

As a general observation, it is evident that I have not done a particularly good job of making these systems profitable on the short side. However, there are several reasons for that. First, when many of these systems were featured for the first time in *Active Trader* magazine, the bear market wasn't developed enough to test the systems and, in many instances, I decided to make them long only because that is what most of my readers are most familiar with.

In revising the research, I was stuck with the original idea and logic behind the systems and, therefore, had to work with what I had. Maybe, just maybe, I could have done a better job with the short side as well, had I been able to start from scratch. Granted, some of you still might say that I could have done a better job with what I had, but the question is, how far should I have taken the research to do so? Sure, I could have indulged in more testing and optimizations, but I have other topics that I need share with you as well. The purpose behind all this is to give you a glimpse inside my head while I work with different system concepts for *Active Trader* magazine, so that you can go out and do a better job yourself. I can't provide you with the definitive answers, because there are none.

Another important observation is that many of these systems are quite complex in their nature, which contradicts what I wrote in *Trading Systems That Work*, that I like simplicity, and that preferably a system should not have more than three rules or calculations. Clearly, many of these systems have more rules than that. I still stand by that rule of thumb, although I have to admit that I have relaxed it quite a bit at times—obviously. If for nothing else, one simple reason is that it is very hard to come up with system ideas to test every month. I apologize for this, but hope that you will still be able to take the concepts as such, run with them, and perhaps boil them down to something that will fit the three-rules rule as well.

Also, many of the systems seem more complicated than they really are. This is especially true for the relative-strength systems that compare several markets with each other. But all we're really doing is formalizing something most of us are trying to do in our heads all the time anyway.

Finally, I've already mentioned that I really don't regard the exits as part of the systems' rules. In a little while, we will get rid of most of them completely and substitute them for a new set of expert exits, developed individually for each system, just as we did in the experts exits system. Enough said. These are the systems we will work with for the remainder of the book.

PART THREE

Stops, Filters, and Exits

In this part of the book, we will look at various ways of adding stops and exits to our entry techniques. If the preceding chapters were basically a demonstration of how system development is more of an intuitive art form than a science, where you rely more on your own gut feel and mental picture of what you want the system to do, this part will be more scientific in nature. Here we only rely on what the hard cold figures tell us, and we will be as precise as possible, without losing track of the fact that the system needs to work as well in the future as it has in the past.

If you compare the final system with a painting representing reality, in Part 2, we applied the paint in broad strokes and perhaps even in a cubistic fashion, leaving a lot to the interpreter to figure out what we want the system to represent and do. In this part, we use a much smaller brush and try to paint in as much detail as possible and in as realistic a fashion as possible, without forgetting that we can never be 100 percent scientific or precise; we always leave a little piece of artistic freedom in there. Otherwise, the system would work perfectly in the past, but not at all in the future. Although we strive to be as precise as possible, it is that little piece of artistic freedom and how we interpret things that sets us apart from other painters (system builders) and assures our future success.

CHAPTER 17

Distribution of Trades

I don't know how many articles and seminars I have read and listened to that stressed the importance of keeping your losses short. Many of them illustrated with figures like Figures 17.1 and 17.2, which show the distribution of a set of trades before (Figure 17.1) and after (Figure 17.2) a stop loss has been applied to the system. In both figures, each column represents a number of trades ending at a certain profit or loss. For example, the tallest column in both figures tells us that this system had 17 trades that ended with a profit of three units (dollars, cents, apples, whatever—it doesn't matter at this point). Also, note in Figure 17.1 how the distribution of the trades resembles the classic bell-shaped normal distribution.

As you can see, Figures 17.1 and 17.2 are essentially the same. The only difference is that a few trades have been taken away from the losing end in Figure 17.2. In Figure 17.1, the average profit per trade comes out to 2.8 units. In Figure 17.2, the average profit per trade is 3.31 units. Thus, the logic behind many of the articles I've read and seminars I've listened to is that by cutting the losses short, we can increase the profit per trade considerably (in this case by close to 20 percent). Or can we? Before you read any further, look at Figure 17.2 for a while and try to figure out what's wrong with it.

Can you see it? What's wrong is that the largest losing trades are missing completely, as if they were never made in the first place, which they must have been. To get it right, we need to add those large losers from Figure 17.1 to the column representing the number of largest losers in Figure 17.2. If we do that, the result will be as shown in Figure 17.3. If you compare Figures 17.2 and 17.3, you will notice that the leftmost column is taller in Figure 17.3 than it is in Figure 17.2. With these trades prudently added back to the sample of trades, the average prof-

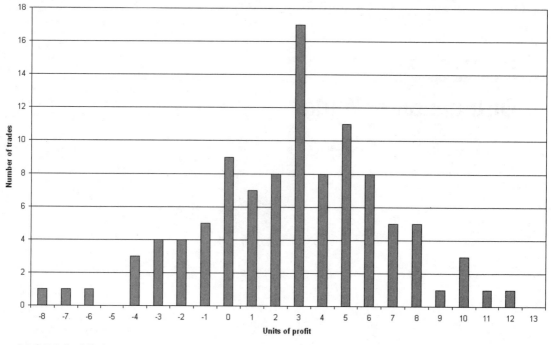

FIGURE 17.1

Distribution of trades before use of stop loss.

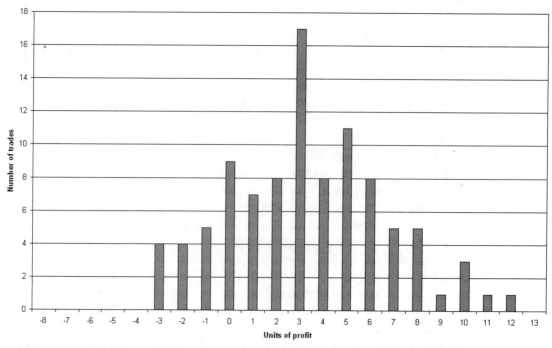

FIGURE 17.2

Distribution of trades after use of stop loss.

it for all trades comes out to 2.94, which is considerably less than the 3.31 units from Figure 17.2, which made it so easy to believe.

But that isn't enough. Plenty of other things are wrong here that we still need to address. Let's take a close look at Figure 17.3 and try to figure out what we need to address next.

Can you see it? What is wrong is that Figures 17.2 and 17.3 look exactly the same with the exception of the leftmost column. This would not be the case in real-life trading. Instead, several of the trades that ended up as winners in the system without a stop loss, would end up as losers. In the system without the stop loss, all trades could fluctuate as they wanted until they got stopped out for reasons other than having reached a certain maximum allowed loss. Several of those winning trades would also have fluctuated, one or several times, around the stop-loss level, which wasn't in effect. But with the stop loss in effect, a trade can only touch this level once and it is stopped out. There would be no second chance for that partic-ular trade to prove itself and turn a profit. Instead, once the stop is hit, that trade is out with a loss, and it is moved from its column in Figure 17.1 to the maximum loss column in Figures 17.2 and 17.3.

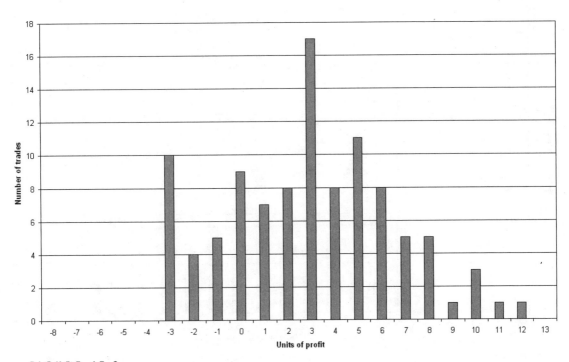

FIGURE 17.3

Adding in the largest losing trades.

For these particular charts, all trades were generated using Excel's random-number generator, and there is no way to tell exactly which and how many trades would have been exited above the stop loss, had it not been in place. Therefore, for demonstration purposes only, I lifted a few trades off the other columns and added them to the maximum loss column. The result can be seen in Figure 17.4. For good measure, I also placed one trade to the left of the maximum loss column, as there always will be a few trades that slip through the safety net (the stop loss), for one reason or another. With the distribution looking like that in Figure 17.4, the average profit per trade now comes out to 1.89 units, which is more than 30 percent less than the original results in Figure 17.1, and more than 40 percent less than in Figure 17.2, where most other writers and seminar speakers would have left you. That is, thanks to the stop loss, we are now making less money per trade than we did originally.

Considering that we are now making less money than originally, if you compare Figures 17.3 and 17.4 would you say that I took away too many profitable trades and added them to the maximum allowed loss column? Well, I don't know what you think, but I believe I most likely didn't. Specifically, I believe I didn't move enough of the largest winners. For a trade to become a large winner, it needs

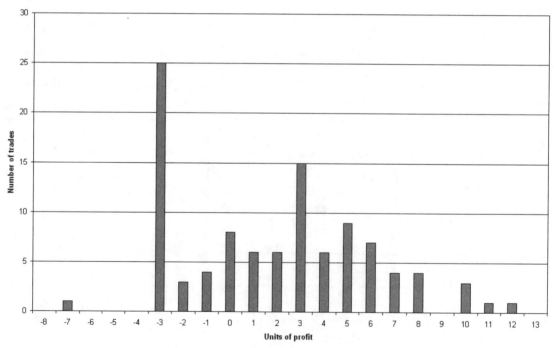

FIGURE 17.4

Adding to the maximum loss column.

volatility. But because volatility works both ways, without the stop loss, some of the large winners actually started out as large losers. Therefore, with the stop loss in place, a few of the would-be large winners would have ended up as small losers.

The same reasoning also holds true if we were to add a profit target. In that case, all trades above a certain profit would have ended up no larger than what the profit target would have allowed. But there also would be a few trades that originally ended up with a profit below the profit target, after they've had an open profit above it, which now will end up at the maximum allowed profit column. This is depicted in Figure 17.5, whose distribution of trades shows an average profit of 1.95 units. This is slightly more than in Figure 17.4, which doesn't always have to be the case.

Note that the numbers here were generated at random and that the actual numbers will, of course, vary with the system, but the general relationships between the different stages of the research process always hold true, no matter what. Also note that just because the average profit per trade decreased by more than 30 percent from Figure 17.1 to Figure 17.4, it doesn't mean that the system behind the results in Figure 17.4 will be less profitable in the end. Quite the contrary. Because the stop loss also narrows down the possible outcomes for the

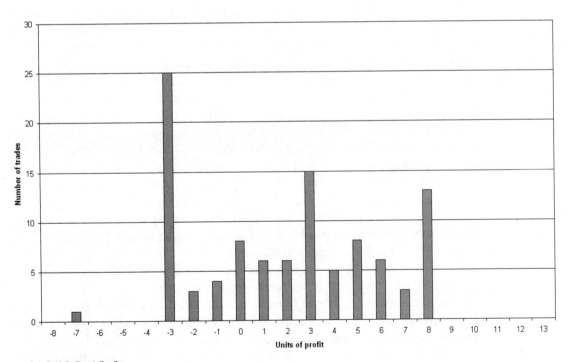

FIGURE 17.5

Maximum allowed profit.

trades, the standard deviation of the returns will also decrease. Thus, the system will be less risky to trade, and consequently you can dare to take a larger position, which in the end might result in a larger profit than what would have been the case with the original system.

Note also that the profit target in Figure 17.5 actually managed to increase the average profit per trade and decrease the standard deviation of the returns at the same time. Although this is not very likely to happen in a real system, it is a possibility that only proper research and trade management will give you. Yet another reason why a system with a stop loss and a profit target might be more profitable than a similar system without those features, and despite a lower average profit per trade, is that the shorter trade lengths will make it possible to trade more often on more markets.

As a final observation, note that we have taken a set of close to normally distributed trades and turned them into a distribution with a few very distinctive outcomes and a few trades scattered in between. That is, adding a set of thoroughly researched exits, such as a stop loss and a profit target, makes it possible to calculate exactly what to expect from each trade in precise quantitative terms, instead of just "knowing" that each trade can either be a winner or a loser ending up somewhere within the normal distribution curve. More important, however, is that the end result of your trading becomes a function of your skills as a trade manager, instead of random market fluctuations. And you don't want your trading results to be a function of randomness, do you? Let's state that a little differently: If the outcome of your trades resembles the bell-shaped normal distribution curve, most likely the outcome of your trading (no matter if you're a winner or a loser) is a function of randomness and can be explained only as good or bad luck, instead of skill.

Now, we could stop here and conclude that it pays off to do the homework and think about a problem all the way to its end. But have we thought about it all the way to the end? No, we haven't. The truth is, we haven't even started. In fact, all we've just learned is wrong for one very specific reason: Every time we make a change to a system, no matter how small it is, we change its characteristics and need to start the research all over. For example, when you add or change your stop losses and profit targets, the trade length of several of the original trades will change as well. Most likely, adding a profit target and a stop loss will shorten the trade length. And shortening the trades means that we free up money and markets that otherwise wouldn't have been available for trading, which will produce a completely new set of trades that needs to be added to the mix.

For example, consider a system without a stop loss and profit target that enters into its first trade, which then lasts for 10 days. Then nothing happens for another five days before the system enters into a new trade that lasts for eight days. Now take the same system, with the same entry rules, but add a stop loss and profit target and do the research again. Now the first trade only lasts for five days before it is stopped out. Then two days of no trading occur before the system enters into a new trade that is still open on the day the second trade started in the original system. Note that the second trade in the latter version of the system is possible because a signal that day went unnoticed by the original system because it was in a trade already. The second trade in the latter version of the system then is stopped out after 10 days, which would have been while the second trade in the original system still remained open.

From this simple example, it is already easy to see that although the original entry and exit rules are the same for the two system versions, the stop loss and the profit target added to the second version make it a completely different system, with a completely different set of trades. Therefore, when experimenting with a system, you always have to do the research from scratch for every little change you make. You still can work according to the general plan outlined by Figures 17.1 to 17.5, but you have to remember that for every little change you do, you might end up with a completely new set of trades, with their own combined characteristics, forming the characteristics of the system.

This also hints at another important consideration: A real-life track record is worth nothing in this case, since you cannot do this research on a set of historical trades that you might have generated in real life. This is because a lot (if not all) of those trades would not have happened in the way suggested by the changes you make during your research. Instead, you only can do this with hypothetically generated make-believe trades, because that's the only way you can track and make the most out of all the changes you make to the system and arrive at the robust solution you're looking for.

To add extra reliability and robustness, you could do your testing according to the principles outlined in Chapter 15, where we looked at a method for testing the signals and the individual trades rather than the system itself. There, each trade was traded at random and completely separated from the other trades generated during the same test run. This can be done without renouncing any of the principles we've learned about in this chapter. We will try to use all that we have learned so far in this chapter when we look for the optimal stop and exit levels for all the systems described earlier. First, however, we need to learn how to examine the data, which we discuss in Chapter 19. But first, let's talk about why and how to exit a trade in the first place.

CHAPTER 18

Exits

Basically, there are four major reasons to exit a trade:

- Limiting a loss
- Taking a profit
- End of event
- Money better used elsewhere

Let's take a brief look at each one of these reasons and when they should be used.

LIMITING A LOSS

I recently participated as a speaker in a seminar, where I asked the other participants which was the most common reason to exit a trade. About two-thirds of them said taking a profit or cashing in on a good trade. Only one-third immediately said that the stop loss probably was the most common reason. From what you know about trading, which one of the two groups do you think is right?

As far as I know, it is group two, which said the stop loss. Just take a look at the systems we worked with in Part 2. None of them has more than 50 percent profitable trades, which means that a majority of the trades are exited with a loss, and logic has it that's the only way it could ever be. Think about it: When you enter a trade, you might have a slightly better than 50 percent chance that the trade will go your way, but because you also need to look for a risk–reward relationship of about 3:1 to make the trade worth the risk you're assuming, there is still a much larger likelihood that the market will move against you by one unit (or 1 percent, or 1 dollar, or whatever) than with you by three units (percent, dollars, etc.). Call me a bad systems developer, but I believe there is no way around this sad fact.

To be fair to the group that first mentioned taking a profit as the most common exit reason, it didn't take them long to change their opinion after they reasoned about it among themselves for a while. It's still scary, though. Taking a profit still was the first thing that came into their minds when asked, and taking a profit probably also is the first thing that comes into their minds when entering a trade in real life. Conditioning yourself to believe most trades will be profitable simply can't be the best way to prepare yourself to take that inevitable loss that will happen more often than you care to think about. (I know, this contradicts what I've said previously: Why enter into a trade in the first place if you don't think it will be a winner? But such is your life as a trader, full of contradictions and "sure things" that don't turn out as they should.)

I also believe that not being prepared to take the loss right away makes us take the loss for the wrong reason once we do take it. How many of us haven't, for example, done a trade like this: You enter the market believing this trade will be a sure winner, only to find it moving against you right off the bat. After a while, it also has passed through the level where you originally had decided to take a loss, but because you were so conditioned to think this trade was going to be a winner, you just can't make yourself take the loss. Not until you have an open loss twice the size that you were originally prepared to accept does the market turn around and start trading your way. But before the trade starts to show a profit, the market stalls and trades sideways. After having watched the market move sideways for quite some time, frustrated, you finally decide to get out of the trade with a small loss.

What happened here? In the end, you did manage to end up with a smaller loss than originally accepted, but was it worth it? For one thing, do you know how many trading opportunities in this or other markets you missed because you had your money and your attention focused on this trade? Probably not. Perhaps you would have been better off taking the loss right away, so that you could have entered this or another market a second time a little later. In that case, the frustrating sideways move might have come in a situation where you actually had a small profit. Then you would have been in a much better position to just wait it out, which you couldn't do this time. And last but not least, didn't you end up exiting a trade with a loss, even though it, in essence, finally went your way? There was a sideways move going on, but hadn't the trend reversed earlier? Yes, it had, and I believe that taking a loss in this way is probably the most common exit there is. It's good to take a loss, but not for all the wrong reasons.

Consequently, the best and most efficient way to end a losing trade is with a stop loss that preferably should be in place the second after you've entered the market. This is also necessary for money management purposes, which we will talk more about in the next chapter. Here, I only state that, if you have a well-working system, money management will make more of your bottom line than the actual entry and exit rules themselves.

TAKING A PROFIT

I don't know about your trading habits, but taking a profit is not the most common reason to exit a trade in any of my systems. I wish it were, but I'm afraid it never will be.

In my opinion, only two ways exist to take a profit. Technique number one is to work with a profit target that lets you exit with a limit order. Technique number two is to work with a trailing stop that moves in the direction of the trade, trailing it at some specified distance. A trailing stop is probably the most common technique to exit a longer term trend-following trade. However, a trailing stop can also result in a loss, depending on how the trailing stop is designed and if it also can operate as a stop loss during the initial stages of a trade.

However, a trailing stop might not be the best way to exit a short-term trade with a trading horizon of around three to ten days. All trades need a little wiggle room, or leeway, to cope with the typical amount of noise in the market: Because you have no idea how much leeway each specific trade will need, the best you can do is estimate an average leeway that seems to work best for a large group of trades and within each trade. We will do this shortly for our systems.

For example, a trade with a profit target at 5 percent and stop loss at -1 percent (no trailing stop) has an average wiggle room of 6 percent no matter how long it lasts. If you use the same wiggle room for all trades, the average wiggle room for all trades is also 6 percent. If you substitute the stop loss with a trailing stop, then the wiggle room within an individual trade that shows a profit will become smaller with time, and sometimes the wiggle room will become too small and have you stopped out of trades just moments before the market is about to take off in your direction. If you work with a profit target, you might also have to place the target closer to the entry price if you work with a trailing stop than you would had you only worked with a stop loss. Because of the large wiggle room, some profitable trades that would have remained open if a fixed stop loss were used—and therefore might have ultimately reached the profit target—will instead be stopped out by the trailing stop. To increase the number of target hits when using a trailing stop, the target needs to be placed closer to the entry. This limits the profit potential even further when compared to the stop-loss version of the system, but increases the profit potential for the trailing-stop version (when examined by itself), because more trades will be exited at a maximum profit instead of a trailing stop.

But that isn't all. To keep the average wiggle room constant over time, both within an individual winning trade and all trades (both winners and losers), the wiggle room also needs to be slightly larger at the beginning of a trade with a trailing stop than it needs to be for a trade with only a stop loss.

To be effective, then, a trailing stop must increase the number of winning trades so that the resulting system's slightly smaller winning trade size makes up for its slightly greater largest single-trade losses. In the best of worlds, a trailing stop can increase profits further because it shortens the trade length, which results in more trading opportunities with a higher likelihood of success. But this will not work at all times, because shortening the average trade length might demand a longer maximum allowed trade length, to keep the average trade length within desirable limits. As you can see, this is a complex matter and, depending on your trading horizon and entry technique, it might be impossible to fit a trailing stop into the equation.

END OF EVENT

Whatever chart pattern or indicators you're using to enter a trade, some sort of news or other fundamental event is usually behind the technical formation that triggers the entry. Whenever we're entering a trade, we need to be aware of this event and ask ourselves at the end of the day exactly what that event was and if it's likely to play a role in the stock's future development over the next several days. Can you remember what type of fundamental news it was that made you buy and sell today? Can you remember what it was yesterday or two days ago? Are those reasons still valid, and is the market still talking about them? You probably can remember these things and the reasons probably are still valid.

But can you remember what drove the market 10 or 15 days ago? Are those factors still making the headlines? They probably aren't, and most likely you can't remember what they were without looking in an old newspaper. Thus, a majority of those reasons to be in a trade are no longer valid. The market has moved on to discount other things, and so should you. In fact, I believe this is one of the most underestimated reasons to exit a trade.

The difficulty with the end-of-event exit, however, is that it is very difficult to measure and research. Most often, you have to implicitly assume the event is over, based on other pieces of evidence the market gives you. For example, if you measure how the market behaves one to several days after an entry signal, you might find that after a certain number of days, the results, or the many different paths the market can take, become more widespread or dispersed. Maybe a majority of your trades still move in the right direction, but those that don't start to stick out more. This is an indication that other pieces of news have hit the market and that the market now prefers to discount that news instead of whatever piece of news was behind your trade.

As we all know by now, the more widespread the outcome, the more volatile the market, and the more volatile the market, the riskier it is. The more widespread the different outcomes, the higher the standard deviation in relation to the esti-mated profit from the trades that are going your way. Sooner or later, there comes a point when the risk outweighs the diminishing reward for being in the trade. That is when you should exit and ready yourself to trade the next event. Most of my research on the NASDAQ stocks indicates an optimal maximum trade length of five to nine days, depending on the entry technique.

Working with end-of-event exits also seems to produce the best results together with breakout-type entries. This is pretty obvious, because breakouts are the type of patterns most likely associated with some type of news fueling the market and creating the swift move needed to create the breakout. Swing trading patterns also can work well with an end-of-event stop. Usually, however, the swing is a pattern that forms in several stages, with the final stage occurring some time after the news first hit the market, which means the trade will usually be triggered one or two bars after the breakout trade. This is not a watertight rule, however, and sometimes the swing will trigger the trade before the breakout does—especially if the market is anticipating something in the works for the stock in question.

Measuring the end of an event in units of time isn't the only way to do it. Another way is to measure how much the market is likely to move after a certain entry is triggered. For this to work, you need to have researched how far the market is likely to move, on average, after an entry signal is hit. With this information at hand, you can place a profit target this distance (and sometimes plus one or two standard deviations) away from the entry. If and when this profit target is hit, you know the market has done a better than average job of discounting the news that fueled the move, and you can exit with a decent profit before the market realizes it has done too good a job and starts to fall back to its starting level. Using this logic, the end-of-event exit also functions as a profit target.

Many might argue that the above scenario is instead a good opportunity to add to the trade. That might be so, and I haven't extensively researched that possibility. The way I see it, however, is that the later in a move you enter into a trade, or if you scale in, the greater the chance that that last entry will result in a loss. Better, I think, to exit with a decent profit and prepare yourself for the next signal with the same odds for success as the first one, in either the same or any other market. Why tie up capital in a trade with ever decreasing odds for a continuous profitable development? This conveniently brings us to the next reason to exit a trade.

MONEY BETTER USED ELSEWHERE

What do we do when nothing happens? We have just entered the market, and the trade is going nowhere. This is an especially important question for those of us whose funds are limited. Maybe our entire capital is tied up in one or more trades like this and, as long as it is, we're really not monitoring the market for other trading opportunities. Thus, even though this specific trade is going nowhere, it is still costing us money because it keeps us from entering into other trades. Where, how, and when do we decide that we should get out and ready ourselves for another trading opportunity?

As is the case with the end-of-event exit, the slow-trade exit also can be based on some intermediate target in time or price. For example, if the trade hasn't moved into positive territory or reached a certain profit after one quarter or one third of its expected life span, it could be cut. Had we kept it open, it might have taken off eventually, but so can any other trade we can enter with the money from this one. And while all other future and so far untaken trades haven't proved themselves in any way, at least this one—the slow one we're just about to exit—has proved itself exactly that: a slow one. Consequently, you probably stand a better chance entering into another market instead, or exiting and waiting for a new entry signal in this market. In a short-term system, you could use the slow-trade exit the same way as the end-of-event exit. If the event behind the move hasn't proved itself within the time frame during which it should have done so, then it's time to exit no matter the outcome.

This is also an important question to ask if you're a more long-term trader having trades lasting longer than a month. Many traders miss the fact that, when they try to get as many profitable trades as possible, many times it is more important to get as many profitable time periods, such as months or quarters, rather than profitable trades. Staying in a trade that is going nowhere or is losing money at a slow but steady rate without hitting the stop loss, might weigh down your results for several months in a row. As in the case of a more short-term trade, it also keeps you from using that money in another trade that might have been more profitable.

Another way to watch for slow trades is to monitor and analyze volume and open interest (in the futures and options markets). Measuring the relative strength between different stocks or markets also could be a good idea. Perhaps you simply are trading the wrong stock in a group of similar stocks? These alternative methods could also be used for the end-of-event exit. For this book, however, I will only look closer into a few time-based techniques.

CHAPTER 19

Placing Stops

Basically, two ways can determine where to place a stop, both in relation to the entry price and in relation to the current price of the market. Furthermore, there also are two very wrong ways of doing this. Unfortunately, these two very wrong ways also are the most commonly used methods. Therefore, let's talk briefly about the very wrong methods before we move on to the two methods we will use for the remainder of this book.

Wrong method No. 1 is to assign an arbitrarily chosen dollar value to stocks trading within a certain price range. For example, I recently was asked to test a system that had assigned a $2 trailing stop to stocks trading within the $5 to $10 price range, a $3 stop for stocks trading between $10 to $20, and so on. For stocks priced over $50, the system called for a 10 percent trailing stop.

Thus, for a stock trading at $5, the system developer thought it was wise for you to risk 40 percent ($2 / 5 = 0.4$) of your invested capital in one trade, but "only" 10 percent for stocks priced above $50. Why? What's the reason for this discrepancy? True, lower-priced stocks at times can be more volatile than higher-priced stocks, but does this justify taking a 300 percent ($40 / 10 - 1 = 3$) larger risk in the low-priced stock? If so, will the profit potential be 300 percent greater as well? Nobody knows, and no matter what, allowing a trade to move against him by 40 percent is not the hallmark of a good trader. Heck, allowing a trade to move against him by 10 percent isn't the hallmark of a good trader, either.

Even within the same stock-price bracket, the difference in risk is as much as 100 percent $[(2 / 5) / (2 / 10) - 1 = 0.4 / 0.2 - 1 = 1 = 100\%]$. And what about those stocks that fluctuate back and forth between two brackets? For a stock fluctuating around $10, for example, the risk could either be 20 percent ($2 / 10 =$

0.2) or 30 percent (3 / 10 = 0.3), which is a difference of 50 percent (20 / 30 − 1 = 0.5). Should you change in the middle of a trade?

Furthermore, assuming there is something to the logic behind this method, still not everything is what it seems to be. Just because a stock seems to have been priced around $5 way back when, that most likely wasn't the case at the time. Take Microsoft, for example. Looking at any chart updated today it seems as if the stock traded at $5 in 1993 to 1994. But the only reason why that seems to be the case is because the stock has been split several times, and the historical price has been adjusted down. In real life, in 1993 to 1994, Microsoft traded around $80. And even though the price has been adjusted down, the behavior is still baked into the historical bars. This reasoning is also closely related to what we said about split-adjusted prices in Chapter 2.

Also, in the case of Microsoft and other highly liquid and highly traded stocks, I doubt the behavior will change that much, no matter the actual price. Consequently, the best you can do when back testing a system is to treat every stock the same all the time and exactly as all other stocks, no matter the price. This method doesn't do that, and even though it might have its merits, it is not the best way to go for back testing robust trading systems.

Wrong method No. 2 takes less explanation to dismiss. This method states that you should never risk more than a specified amount of your trading capital in any trade. For example, in the commodity futures markets, many system vendors recommend that you should not risk more than $2,000 on any trade. What is that all about? While it is prudent not to risk too much, the market doesn't give a hoot if you can't afford to risk more than a specified amount on each trade. Instead, the market will do what the market will do, and if you can't adjust your maximum allowed loss to the conditions that the market gives you, then the prudent thing to do is not to trade. Period.

As already mentioned in Chapter 1, depending on the market value of the market and the long-term trend, the effect of such a stop is that it will have you stopped out time and time again on a high-priced market, but hardly ever on a low-priced market. It will be too tight for the high-priced market, but too wide for the low-priced market, in relation to the respective markets' normal price swings.

Therefore, this system design blunder also can result in two opposite types of drawdowns (or at least unwanted system characteristics), both of them very hard to detect because they're masking each other. In the case of the low-priced market, a larger than necessary drawdown can be a result of a few but larger than necessary losers, while in the case of the high-priced market, a larger than necessary drawdown can be a result of a large amount of unnecessary small losers. Not knowing this, you might only worsen the effects from one type of drawdown while addressing the other. Stick to a strategy like this and you will be broke before you can say honorificabilitudinitatibus (the longest word ever used by Shakespeare).

PERCENT STOPS

The percent stop method is the more straightforward of the two correct methods used in this book. Simply put, it places the stop the same relative distance away from the entry point, no matter the price of the stock. For example, a 10 percent stop should be placed $1 away from the entry price if the entry price is $10, but $10 away from the entry price if the entry price is $100.

To calculate what a percentage-based stop means in dollar terms for a specific stock, simply multiply the price of the stock by the fractional value representing the percentage value. For example, because the fractional value for 5 percent is equal to 0.05, a 5 percent stop on a $60 stock should be placed $3 away from the price of the stock (60 * 0.05 = 3).

To calculate how many percentages a certain dollar-based stop represents on a certain stock, divide the stop distance by the price of the stock, and multiply by 100 to transform the fractional value to a percentage value. For example, if you use a $6 stop on an $80 stock, the stop is 7.5 percent away from the entry price (6 / 80 * 100 = 7.5).

The last example was deliberately chosen so that I can refer back to the Microsoft example. If it just so happened that you used a $6 stop on Microsoft back in 1993, then you need to use a 38 cent stop (5 * 0.075 = 0.375) if you would like to back test the system you used then on the same data as you used then: What once was actually priced at $80 now seems to be priced at $5, and to make your system behave the same, you need to adjust the stop so that it reflects the split-induced changes in the price.

The main advantage of the percentage-based stop is that it works equally as well, on average and over time, over a large number of stocks and different markets, no matter each individual market's price at the time. Another advantage is that it doesn't need any new optimizable variables for its calculations. True, the actual percentage values are optimizable, and the most optimal values will change over time and vary from one stock to the next, but with a large enough sample for testing, you will find the values that work best on average, around which the ever-changing most optimal values will fluctuate.

The main disadvantage of the percentage-based stop is that it's rather static in nature and very seldom will it be the perfect stop for any individual trade. It implicitly assumes constant market volatility, equal to the volatility that works the best with whatever stop settings are in question. But because the volatility never remains the same, and the changes only can be observed in hindsight, the percentage stop will only be almost perfect almost all the time. When it isn't, it's usually because the volatility is too high or too low.

If the volatility is too low, none of the stops and exits will get hit and the trade will linger in no-man's land for as long as the maximum allowed trade length allows it to. This might result in several small losses and profits, with the profits perhaps not even making up for the costs of trading. If the volatility is too high, all stops and exits will be hit too soon, which will result in a higher than normal amount of losing trades, and winning trades that aren't as large as they could have been, given the momentum created by the volatility.

The same two things can go wrong with the fixed-dollar stop just described. The differences lie in the fact that the efficiency of the percentage stop will vary rather quickly over time as the volatility fluctuates, and this error is not dependent on the price or current trendiness of the market, as it is for the dollar-based stop. Thus, in using a dollar-based stop, we're making a systematic error that might compound and worsen over time, which will not be the case for the percentage-based stop. Instead, only the short-term efficiency of the short-term stop will vary, while the long-term efficiency is more likely to remain constant.

VOLATILITY

Unfortunately, while volatility can be observed all the time, it can only be measured in hindsight. But if you're prepared to work under the assumption that the most recent volatility also is a good indication of the volatility in the immediate future, then you can replace the percentage-based stops with a set of more dynamic stops based on the current market volatility.

If you do, you have to remember that the volatility also must be measured so that it becomes universally applicable on all markets. Basically, there are two common ways to do that. The first way is to calculate the moves from one close to the next, measured in percentage terms, and then calculate the standard deviation of the price swings. This method is most commonly used in the academic world and by options traders, who use it as a part of an options-evaluations formula, such as Black–Scholes, to calculate the fair value of an option. (Options traders use a logarithmic scale, but in essence, it's the same thing.)

Using this formula, the larger the swings, the larger the standard deviation and the further away the stops and the exits can be placed from the entry price to avoid being stopped out too early. For example, by placing the stop one standard deviation away from the entry price, only 16 percent of all price moves should reach the stop. If the stop is placed two standard deviations away from the entry price, only 2.5 percent of all price moves should reach the stop. Whatever you decide, the distance between the entry price and the stop will remain constant in standard deviation terms, but vary in percentage terms with the most recent market action. (Note that this is not the same as to say that only 16 or 2.5 percent of your trades will be stopped out. There still is a 50–50 chance for the trade to reach the lower standard-deviation boundary, as compared to its corresponding upper standard-deviation boundary.)

However, for the standard deviation calculation to be statistically reliable, it needs at least 20 to 30 observations (close-to-close moves), which means the lookback period for the calculation will be a little longer than desirable for a short-term system. Remember, we strive to find a maximum trade length of no more than 10 days, because that's how long the market will remember why it took off one way or another, and created our trading opportunity in the first place. By the same token, we shouldn't use any more data than that to calculate our stops and exit points when entering the trade. If we use more data than necessary, that data will be obsolete and only help us arrive at a suboptimal solution. If it's reasonable to believe that the market will only remember what triggered a trade for five to ten days, then it's equally reasonable to assume that the market won't remember the fundamental reasons leading into the trade for more than five to ten days either.

The second way to measure volatility is the *average true range method*, which is very well known in technical analysis circles. To calculate the daily true range, simply take the highest of the previous day's close and today's high, and subtract the lowest of the previous day's close and today's low. Most often the daily true range simply will be the distance between today's high and low, but on days when the market gaps higher or lower, that gap will be accounted for by adding the distance between yesterday's close and whichever of today's extremes is closest to it. To calculate the average true range over a certain number of bars or days, simply sum up all true ranges for all bars in the lookback period and divide by the number of bars.

The calmer the market over the lookback period, the smaller the average true range and the closer the stops and exits will be to the entry price. For example, if the average true range over the lookback period is 4 percent, and you've decided to place a stop two average true ranges away from the entry price, then that stop will be 8 percent away. If the price of the stock is $100, the stop will be placed $8 away, but if the price of the stock is $50, then the stop will be $4 away from the entry price. If, on the other hand, the average true range was only 3 percent, then a stop loss will be placed $6 away from a $100 stock and $3 away from a $50 stock. In this way, the average true range becomes a universal measure that can be applied to all stocks, no matter the price.

The major advantage of the average true range method, compared to the standard deviation method, is that the former doesn't need as much data to make the calculations reliable.

The major disadvantage of the average true range method, compared to the percentage method, is that the former needs a certain amount of historical data for its calculations, which presents yet another optimization problem. To solve this, I have equalized the lookback period for the average true range calculation with the maximum allowed holding period for a trade. For example, if the maximum holding period for a trade is set to six days, then the lookback period for the average true range calculation also will be six days. Likewise, if I test a system using varying holding periods, say from one to ten days, in steps of one day, the lookback period for the average true range calculation will always be the same as the maximum holding period. This makes perfect sense in regard to the memory of the market. We'll take a close look at this second volatility method shortly, but first we need to learn how to analyze the results.

SURFACE CHARTS

When trying to figure out where to place the stops in the system I'm working with, I like to use a *surface chart*, which provides an excellent method for getting a feel for how the output variable (for example, the average profit per trade) reacts to two different input variables (for example, the stop-loss and profit-target distances) and how the inputs are interacting with each other. In the upcoming analysis of our systems, we look at the following output variables and how they change with the addition and changes to the various stops we already have defined:

- The average profit per trade
- The standard deviation of all trades
- The average percentage of winning trades

Of course, one can use other evaluation parameters and output variables as well, such as the final net profit, drawdown, profit factor (gross profit divided by gross loss), average trade lengths, and the average number of trades. But at some point it becomes information overload, and we won't be able to digest it all—not to mention the redundancy of the output variables basically telling us the same thing.

Figures 19.1 and 19.2 show what a couple of typical surface charts look like. In Figure 19.1, the output variable is the average profit per trade. In Figure 19.2, the output variable is the risk–reward ratio (the average profit per trade, divided by the standard deviation of all trades). The different values of the output variable are represented by the different colors. The legend to the right of the chart tells us which specific value each color represents. The values for the input variables are represented by the numbers on the horizontal and vertical axes. The output variables for both figures are the maximum allowed trade length on the horizontal axis, and the stop loss on the vertical axis. The numbers on the axis tell us that this particular system has been tested for maximum trade lengths varying from one to ten days, in steps of one day, and for stop-loss distances away from the entry price varying from 0.2 percent to 2 percent, in increments of 0.2 percent.

The grid inside the charts helps us find the output value that corresponds to a specific combination of the input variables. For example, in Figure 19.1, the little square surrounds the intersection on the grid that represents a system with a four-day maximum allowed trade length and a 1 percent stop loss. Matching the color that covers this area of the chart with the colors in the legend, we see that this version of the system produced an average profit per trade somewhere between 0.4 and 0.5 percent. To be prudent, we will go with the lower value and say that the average profit per trade is 0.4 percent.

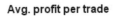

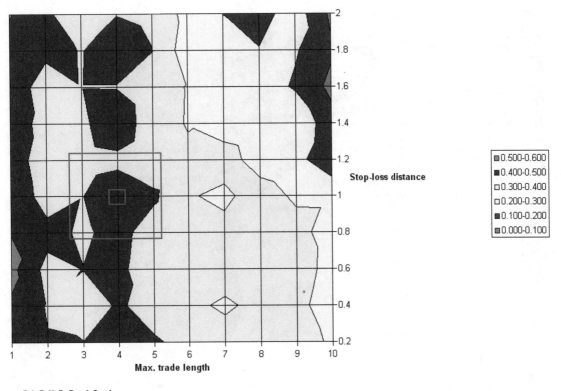

FIGURE 19.1

Surface chart with average profit per trade as output variable.

When reading surface charts, look for as many large, preferably uninterrupted, areas of the same color as possible, which represent values as high as possible, as indicated by the legend. In this way, we'll make sure that the system not only works with that specific variable combination but also with other adjacent combinations, which gives us some room for error and adjustments if market conditions change.

If you look at the color chart as a weather map, with each line separating the different colors representing the air pressure lines on the weather map, the tighter the lines, the more unstable the weather, with really tight lines forming a tornado or hurricane (or at least a very unstable weather situation) that no one wants to be in. Or look at the chart as a topographical map, with the colors representing changes in elevation. With that in mind, it is easy to understand that you'd be standing safer on a large, relatively flat and uninterrupted plateau than on a pointy peak.

Also, when putting together charts like this, it's important to have a feel for what will likely be the best values for the input variables, given the desired char-

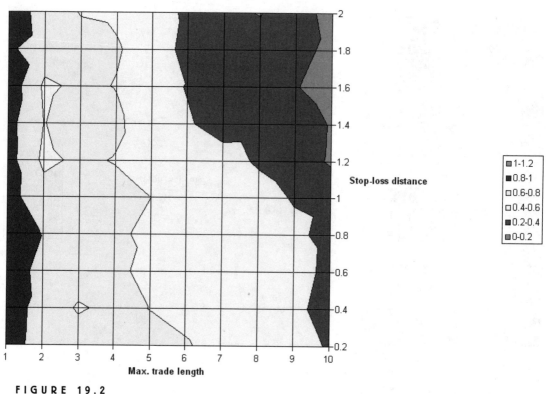

FIGURE 19.2

Surface chart with risk–reward ratio as output variable.

acteristics of the system, so that the very best values don't fall on the very edge of the chart. If they do, there is no way of knowing how the system will perform if the conditions happen to change in the wrong direction and cause the best variable combinations to fall outside of the chart.

The larger square in Figure 19.1 encapsulates an area that is relatively large and flat, which suggests that all trade-length/stop-loss combinations surrounding the four-day/1-percent combination in the little square will produce similar results. Therefore, the best alternative in this chart is the four-day/1-percent combination, and if it just so happens that adjacent combination would have worked better in real-life trading, at least we've gotten close enough to that combination to make a profit, or at least avoid a catastrophe.

However, just looking at one chart like this isn't enough; and that is where Figure 19.2 comes into play. Figure 19.2 shows the risk–reward ratio as the average profit per trade, divided by the standard deviation of all trades. The greater the risk–reward ratio, the greater the profit in relation to the uncertainty of the outcome, and the better off we are. In the case of the four-day/1-percent combination from Figure 19.1, the risk–reward ratio comes out to 0.6. According to Figure 19.2, this is as good as it will get, given the information from this chart.

To put together a surface chart in Excel, the data first need to be organized in a matrix, like the portion of one shown in Figure 19.3, which depicts the data behind the chart in Figure 19.1. Looking at the numbers in Figure 19.1, we can see that the four-day/1-percent combination in fact has an average profit of 0.450 percent per trade, but also that this wasn't the highest value. In fact, a couple of values in the one-day column are much higher, but because they also are surrounded by lower values, they do not represent as robust and stable variable combinations as the four-day/1-percent combination. With the data organized in this way, all you have to do is click the chart wizard button in Excel and follow the instructions. To get the data collected into a matrix is, however, a completely different story. The data are normally organized into columns, as in Figure 19.4, which show a small part of the data behind the matrix in Figure 19.3.

The data sort, row( ), column( ), and index( ) functions in Excel are used to move data from the columns in Figure 19.4 to the matrix in Figure 19.3.

Getting the data into the columns in Figure 19.4 is a whole lot easier, but let's examine the columnar data. In this case, column A holds the ticker symbol for the markets tested; column B holds an index number for the test run (we will talk more about this later); column C holds the values for the stop-loss input variable; column D holds the values for the trade-length input variable: and column E holds the values for the output variable, which in this case is the average profit per trade.

Note that in the case of Figure 19.4, each market has been tested 10 times with the exact same setting for the input variables (columns C and D), but with a

	1	2	3	4	5
0.2	0.489	0.405	0.402	0.453	0.409
0.4	0.485	0.392	0.352	0.411	0.364
0.6	0.528	0.368	0.402	0.424	0.337
0.8	0.497	0.435	0.384	0.434	0.351
1	0.486	0.351	0.398	0.450	0.417
1.2	0.474	0.322	0.366	0.380	0.336
1.4	0.463	0.359	0.382	0.459	0.350
1.6	0.487	0.336	0.397	0.396	0.344
1.8	0.477	0.430	0.396	0.446	0.402
2	0.505	0.416	0.349	0.398	0.379

FIGURE   19.3

Matrix of data for Excel chart.

	A	B	C	D	E
1	MXIM	0	0.2	1	0.81
2	MXIM	1	0.2	1	0.5
3	MXIM	2	0.2	1	0.68
4	MXIM	3	0.2	1	1.01
5	MXIM	4	0.2	1	0.99
6	MXIM	5	0.2	1	0.56
7	MXIM	6	0.2	1	1.1
8	MXIM	7	0.2	1	0.74
9	MXIM	8	0.2	1	0.29
10	MXIM	9	0.2	1	0.95
11	SEBL	0	0.2	1	1.09
12	SEBL	1	0.2	1	1.36
13	SEBL	2	0.2	1	0.82

FIGURE 19.4

Columnar arrangement of data for surface chart.

different value for the output variable for each test run (column E). How can that be? This is because these data are used to develop the system using a random-entry method that allowed us to test all the individual signals the system generated, regardless of whether all signals would have been traded, depending on if we would have been in a trade or not already. The numbers in column B keep track of each test run. For each test run, each time the system encounters a bar in a market with all its regular entry criteria fulfilled, the system will enter the trade at random. In some test runs it will, in others it won't. Thus, although many of the trades will be the same in many of the test runs, each test run will hold a completely unique set of trades, different from all other test runs, which then results in a different average profit per trade.

For the purposes of this book, I did not use the random-testing procedure because it adds to the time it takes to test a system. I will, however, incorporate the possibility for you to do so yourself, in the code I present in an upcoming chapter. Be warned, though, this can be a very time-consuming task.

It also is very difficult to test more than three variables at one time, and you can only examine the variables two at the time. Consider the testing we will walk through: I will test ten values each for three variables at the time for two different exit and stop concepts. For each test run, only one variable will alter its value, while the other variables remain constant. Thus, each test will have to run through each stock 2,000 times (10 * 10 * 10 * 2). Had I added the random-entry feature and asked the system to test each stock an additional 10 times, each stock would have been tested a total of 20,000 times. With the computer I'm using, a dual processor 500 MHz Pentium III, with 256 MB RAM, running one system through one stock takes about 40 minutes. Running one system through all 65 stocks takes about 45 hours. And I had to do 10 tests like this. I dare to say that no one has ever done such a thorough back testing of their systems before they try to sell them to you for prices many times higher than the price of this book.

Also, even if I wanted to test each stock 20,000 times or more, I wouldn't be able to do so in a convenient manner with this many stocks. Excel can only hold a little more than 65,000 rows of data, and with 65 stocks tested at 1,000 times each per exit concept, that's exactly how many rows of data each Excel file will hold. We have simply reached the ceiling for what today's computers and software packages allow us to do.

Before we move on, I also would like to point out that you could use this type of testing procedure to test your entry rules as well. This works especially well if you use indicators and patterns that can vary in length and lookback periods, such as moving averages and crosses above and below the highs and the lows over a certain number of days.

Adding Exits

In Part 2, it became obvious that most systems didn't work all that well when traded from the short side, so from now on we will place most of our focus on the long side. However, when testing the stops, we will test both sides simultaneously and use the settings that work the best, on average, on the long side only. The reason for this is basically the same as for why we want to test a system in as many markets as possible, and why we want every market, profitable or not, to influence the final parameter settings to an equal degree. Namely, we never know when a profitable market will start behaving as a unprofitable market (and vice versa). Therefore, we want to prepare ourselves by letting the unprofitable markets influence the variable settings so that when less-profitable periods come along, at least they won't ruin us completely.

The same reasoning goes for the long and short trades. We never know when the now-profitable long side will start to behave as the less-profitable short side. Therefore, we want to prepare for that by letting the short side influence the variable settings from the very beginning. This will lower the profit potential for all long trades, but also make it more likely that a bad period will only end in a modest drawdown instead of a complete disaster.

Yet another reason for not testing the long and the short sides separately from each other is a more pragmatic one. Namely, it will double the number of test runs necessary, to 4,000 runs per stock, or as many as 40,000 runs per stock, had I included the random-testing procedure as well.

For each system, four stops and exit versions will be examined. Two versions will be based on a regular percentage-stop method, and two versions will be based on the true-range method. One version from each of these two methods will work with a stop loss, profit target, and time-based stop, while the other version will work with a trailing stop, profit target, and time-based stop.

Let's start the testing procedure using the code given in the next section on the first of our systems, Hybrid system No. 1, featured in the September 2000 issue of *Active Trader* magazine. With four stops and exit versions per system, comparing all input variables with each other two at a time, looking at three different output variables, this research will produce a hell of a lot of surface charts. Because of the large number of charts produced for each system, I will describe the complete process only for one of the two most profitable versions of the first system. For other versions and systems, I will only briefly comment on the result and illustrate it with a chart or two and a few summary tables.

The research is only performed on the five short-term systems that don't depend on any intermarket relationships. These five systems are Hybrid system No. 1; Meander system, V.1.0; volume-weighted average; Harris 3L-R pattern variation; and expert exits. The other three systems, RS system No. 1, Relative strength bands, and Rotation, will be filter-tested later.

SURFACE CHART CODE

```
{Export for finding optimal stops with surface charts in Excel.

{1} Set SurfaceChartTest(True)}

Variable: SurfaceChartTest(True);

If SurfaceChartTest = True Then Begin

{2}   Inputs:
      TestRunVar(1), StopTypeVar(1), StopLossVar(1), ProfTargVar(4.5),
      TrailStopVar(0), MaxBarsVar(8);

      Variables:

      SCT.LongLoss(0), SCT.ShortLoss(0), SCT.LongTrailing(0),
      SCT.ShortTrailing(0), SCT.LongTarget(0), SCT.ShortTarget(0),
      SCT.TrueLength(0), EP(0), SCT.TRLoss(0), SCT.TRTarget(0),
      SCT.TRTrailing(0);

      {Code for stop type 1 (percentage stops) goes here, see below. Set
      StopTypeVar(1)}

      {Code for stop type 2 (true-range stops) goes here, see below. Set
      StopTypeVar(2)}

      Variables:

      SCT.TradeType(""), SCT.NameLength(0), SCT.StopType(""),
      AvgTradeVar(0), StDevVar(0), NoTradesVar(0), PercWinVar(0),
      SCT.MarketPos(0), SCT.PosProfit(0), SCT.SetArrayPos(0),
      SCT.SumProfit(0),
```

```
        SCT.ArrayPosition(0), SCT.WinTrades(0), SCT.SumSqProfit(0),
        SCT.TestString(""), SCT.FileString("");
{3}   Arrays:
        SCT.TradeProfit[2000](0);
{4}   If BarNumber = 1 Then Begin
          If AllowLong = True Then
            SCT.TradeType = "Long";
          If AllowShort = True Then
            SCT.TradeType = "Short";
          If AllowLong = True and AllowShort = True Then
            SCT.TradeType = "Both";
          SCT.NameLength = StrLen(GetStrategyName) - 6;
          If StopTypeVar = 1 Then
            SCT.StopType = "Perc-"
          Else If StopTypeVar = 2 Then
            SCT.StopType = "TR-";
          SCT.FileString = "D:\BookFiles\" + SCT.StopType + "Test - " +
          RightStr(GetStrategyName, SCT.NameLength) + " - " +
          RightStr(NumToStr(CurrentDate, 0), 4) + ".csv";
          {SCT.TestString = "Market" + "," + "Direction" + "," + "Test Run" + "," +
          "Stop Loss" + "," + "P-Target" + "," + "Trail Stop" + "," + "Max Bars" +
          "," + "Avg Trade" + "," + "StDev Prof" + "," + "No Trades" + "," + "Perc
          Win" + NewLine;
          FileAppend(SCT.FileString, SCT.TestString);}
        End;
{5}   NoTradesVar = TotalTrades;
        SCT.MarketPos = MarketPosition;
        If NoTradesVar > NoTradesVar[1] Then Begin
          If MarketPosition(1) = 1 Then
            SCT.PosProfit = (ExitPrice(1) - EntryPrice(1)) / EntryPrice(1);
          If MarketPosition(1) = -1 Then
            SCT.PosProfit = (EntryPrice(1) - ExitPrice(1)) / EntryPrice(1);
          SCT.TradeProfit[SCT.SetArrayPos] = SCT.PosProfit;
          SCT.SetArrayPos = SCT.SetArrayPos + 1;
        End;
{6}   If LastBarOnChart Then Begin
          {Alt: If LastCalcDate = Date + 1 Then Begin}
```

```
        For SCT.ArrayPosition = 0 To (NoTradesVar - 1) Begin
            SCT.SumProfit = SCT.SumProfit +
            SCT.TradeProfit[SCT.ArrayPosition];
            If SCT.TradeProfit[SCT.ArrayPosition] > 0 Then
            SCT.WinTrades = SCT.WinTrades + 1;
{7}     End;
        If NoTradesVar <> 0 Then Begin
            AvgTradeVar = SCT.SumProfit / NoTradesVar;
            PercWinVar = SCT.WinTrades * 100 / NoTradesVar;
        End
        Else Begin
            AvgTradeVar = 0;
            PercWinVar = 0;
        End;
{8}     For SCT.ArrayPosition = 0 To (NoTradesVar - 1) Begin
            SCT.SumSqProfit = SCT.SumSqProfit +
            Square(SCT.TradeProfit[SCT.ArrayPosition]);
{9}     End;
        If NoTradesVar <> 0 Then
            StDevVar = SquareRoot((NoTradesVar *
            SCT.SumSqProfit - Square(SCT.SumProfit)) / (NoTradesVar *
            (NoTradesVar - 1)))
        Else
            StDevVar = 0;
{10}    SCT.TestString = LeftStr(GetSymbolName, 5) + "," + SCT.TradeType
        + "," + NumToStr(TestRunVar, 0) + "," + NumToStr(StopLossVar, 2) + ","
        + NumToStr(ProfTargVar, 2) + "," + NumToStr(TrailStopVar, 2) + "," +
        NumToStr(MaxBarsVar, 0) + "," + NumToStr(AvgTradeVar * 100, 2) +
        "," + NumToStr(StDevVar * 100, 2) + "," + NumToStr(NoTradesVar, 0) +
        "," + NumToStr(PercWinVar, 2) + "," + NewLine;
        FileAppend(SCT.FileString, SCT.TestString);
        End;
End;
{11}  Code for stop type 1 (percentage stops).}
If StopTypeVar = 1 Then Begin
    If BarNumber = 1 Then Begin
        SCT.LongLoss = 1 - StopLossVar * 0.01;
```

```
            SCT.ShortLoss = 1 + StopLossVar * 0.01;
            SCT.LongTrailing = 1 - TrailStopVar * 0.01;
            SCT.ShortTrailing = 1 + TrailStopVar * 0.01;
            SCT.LongTarget = 1 + ProfTargVar * 0.01;
            SCT.ShortTarget = 1 - ProfTargVar * 0.01;
        End;
        If EntryPrice > 0 Then Begin
            If MaxBarsVar > 0 and BarsSinceEntry + 1 >= MaxBarsVar Then
                SetExitOnClose;
            If StopLossVar > 0 Then Begin
                ExitLong ("SCT.L-Loss(P)") Next Bar at EntryPrice * SCT.LongLoss
                Stop;
                ExitShort ("SCT.S-Loss(P)") Next Bar at EntryPrice * SCT.ShortLoss
                Stop;
        End;
        If TrailStopVar > 0 Then Begin
            SCT.TrueLength = BarsSinceEntry + 1;
            ExitLong ("SCT.L-Trail(P)") Next Bar at
            Highest(High, SCT.TrueLength) * SCT.LongTrailing Stop;
            ExitShort ("SCT.S-Trail(P)") Next Bar at
            Lowest(Low, SCT.TrueLength) * SCT.ShortTrailing Stop;
        End;
        If ProfTargVar > 0 Then Begin
            ExitLong ("SCT.L-Trgt(P)") Next Bar at EntryPrice * SCT.LongTarget
            Limit;
            ExitShort ("SCT.S-Trgt(P)") Next Bar at EntryPrice * SCT.ShortTarget
            Limit;
            End;
        End;
    End
    {12} Code for stop type 2 (true-range stops).}
    Else If StopTypeVar = 2 Then Begin
            EP = EntryPrice;
            If TrailStopVar <= 0 and EP <> EP[1] and EP > 0 Then Begin
                SCT.TRLoss = AvgTrueRange(MaxBarsVar) * StopLossVar;
                SCT.TRTrailing = AvgTrueRange(MaxBarsVar) * TrailStopVar;
                SCT.TRTarget = AvgTrueRange(MaxBarsVar) * ProfTargVar;
```

```
    End
    Else If TrailStopVar > 0 Then Begin
        SCT.TRLoss = AvgTrueRange(MaxBarsVar) * StopLossVar;
        SCT.TRTrailing = AvgTrueRange(MaxBarsVar) * TrailStopVar;
        SCT.TRTarget = AvgTrueRange(MaxBarsVar) * ProfTargVar;
    End;
    If EntryPrice > 0 Then Begin
        If MaxBarsVar > 0 and BarsSinceEntry + 1 >= MaxBarsVar Then
            SetExitOnClose;
        If StopLossVar > 0 Then Begin
            ExitLong ("SCT.L-Loss(TR)") Next Bar at EntryPrice - SCT.TRLoss
            Stop;
            ExitShort ("SCT.S-Loss(TR)") Next Bar at EntryPrice + SCT.TRLoss
            Stop;
        End;
        If TrailStopVar > 0 Then Begin
            SCT.TrueLength = BarsSinceEntry + 1;
            ExitLong ("SCT.L-Trail(TR)") Next Bar at
            Highest(High, SCT.TrueLength) - SCT.TRTrailing Stop;
            ExitShort ("SCT.S-Trail(TR)") Next Bar at
            Lowest(Low, SCT.TrueLength) + SCT.TRTrailing Stop;
        End;
        If ProfTargVar > 0 Then Begin
            ExitLong ("SCT.L-Trgt(TR)") Next Bar at EntryPrice + SCT.TRTarget
            Limit;
            ExitShort ("SCT.S-Trgt(TR)") Next Bar at EntryPrice - SCT.TRTarget
            Limit;
        End;
    End;
End;
```

COMMENTS ON THE CODE

1. The variable SurfaceChartTest(True) needs to be placed on top of the code or even as an input. The other variables will only become active when SurfaceChartTest is set to True. To speed up the computing time, the program will not run through the rest of the code, as long as SurfaceChartTest is set to False.

2.   The input TestRunVar will not be used here, but is present so that you can run through your own systems using the random-entry feature. The code for the random-entry feature can look something like this:

```
Variable: RandomTrigger(0);
RandomTrigger = IntPortion(Random(2));
If RandomTrigger = 1 and (rest of entry criteria) Then Begin
    Final buy or sell trigger rule
```

An example of how to use the code can be found in Part 2.

3.   We need to create one array to contain the data for our calculations. We could have done without the array and instead run through all the calculations for each bar, but to speed up the computing time, we will do most of the calculations only once, on the very last bar on the chart. The array is now set to hold 2,000 trades. The larger the arrays, the slower the calculations, so you might want to change this number to what makes the most sense for the system you currently are working on.

4.   These calculations and exports only need to be done once, on the very first bar on the chart. By altering the state of the variables AllowLong and AllowShort at the very top of the code (see the code for any of the individual systems), we can test all long and short trades, either separately from each other or together. Then we create the file that we will import into Excel (variable SCT.FileString) and the column headers for the data we need to export later (variable SCT.TestString).

5.   These calculations are done on every bar on the chart. We are now filling the array SCT.TradeProfit with the end result of each trade. An array is a series of values stored in a specific order. In this case, the first position in the array will hold the result of the first trade, and so on.

6.   All remaining calculations will only be executed on the very last bar of the chart. Note: If you plan to use this code and use the criteria Open Next Bar (or Open Tomorrow) for your entries and exits, you must use the alternative function. First, we run a loop (that starts with the word "For") to calculate the total profit (variable SCT.SumProfit) by adding all the values contained in the array SCT.TradeProfit. We also count the number of winning trades in the variable SCT.WinTrades.

7.   Moving out of the first loop, we now calculate the variables AvgTradeVar and PercWinVar, which are self-explanatory.

8.   The second loop (also starting with the word "For") sums up the squared profits from all trades in the SCT.SumSqProfit variable.

9.   Moving out of the second loop, we calculate the standard deviation of all trades (variable StDevVar).

10. Finally, all the necessary data will be stored in the variable SCT.TestString and exported into a file that we can open with Excel, with the help of the

SCT.FileString. The file export takes place in the command FileAppend. The name of the file is specified by the variable SCT.FileString, created in step 4.

11. The code for the stop type 1 (the percentage stop) will test the following four exit techniques: the stop loss, the profit target, the trailing stop, and the time-based stop. In the first round of testing, we will leave out the trailing stop. In the second run of testing, we will leave out the stop loss, letting the trailing stop function as a stop loss as well.

12. The code for the stop type 2 (the true-range stop) will test the following four exit techniques: the stop loss, the profit target, the trailing stop, and the time-based stop. In the first round of testing, we will leave out the trailing stop. In the second run of testing, we will leave out the stop loss, letting the trailing stop function as a stop loss as well. When testing using the stop loss, the true ranges used will be fixed at the day for the entry. When testing with the trailing stop, the true ranges will be recalculated for each bar. In both cases, the lookback period for the average true ranges is set to equal the maximum allowed trade length as defined by the variable MaxBarsVar.

HYBRID SYSTEM NO. 1

In the case of the Hybrid system, it turned out that the true range-based stops produced the best results. Remember, we tested two different concepts of each stop and exit methodology, and two different methods of each concept.

Stop-loss Version

For the true range concept, method one consisted of a stop loss (varying between 0.2 and 2 average true ranges, in steps of 0.2), a profit target (varying between 0.5 and 5 average true ranges, in steps of 0.5), and a maximum trade length (varying between 1 and 10 bars, in steps of 1).

The best way to sift through all the surface charts produced by the code, is to start by looking at the standard deviations of the returns, which should be as low as possible. This will give us a first clue on how to interpret the rest of the data. Figures 20.1 to 20.3 show the standard deviations of the returns for various combinations of the input variables. In Figure 20.1, for example, the input variables are the profit target on the x-axis and the stop loss on the y-axis.

To keep the standard deviations as low as possible, Figures 20.1 to 20.3 indicate that we should strive to come up with a combination of the three input variables that place us as far down and as far to the left as possible in all the other charts. This means that the values for all input variables should be as low as possible. (This will hold true for all other systems as well.)

Figure 20.4 shows the average profit per trade in relation to the profit target and the stop loss. As you can see, a profit target between 1 and 1.5 average true ranges

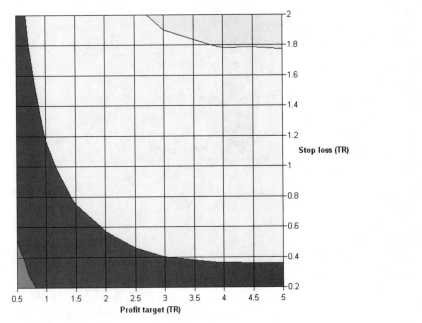

FIGURE 20.1

Standard deviation of returns (1).

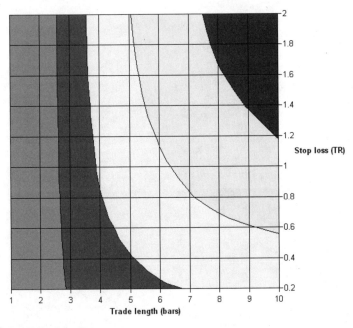

FIGURE 20.2

Standard deviation of returns (2).

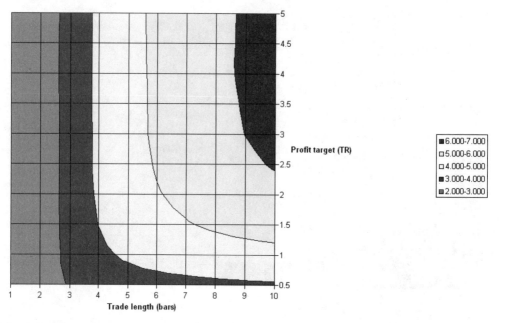

St. devs. of profits

Profit target (TR)

■ 6.000-7.000
□ 5.000-6.000
□ 4.000-5.000
■ 3.000-4.000
■ 2.000-3.000

Trade length (bars)

FIGURE 20.3

Standard deviation of returns (3).

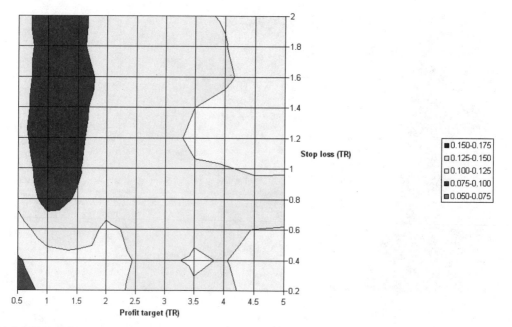

Avg. profit per trade (%)

Stop loss (TR)

■ 0.150-0.175
□ 0.125-0.150
□ 0.100-0.125
■ 0.075-0.100
■ 0.050-0.075

Profit target (TR)

FIGURE 20.4

Average profit per trade versus profit target and stop loss.

(ATR) will produce the highest average profit per trade (as indicated by the legend to the right of the chart), together with any stop loss ranging from 0.8 to 2 ATR. However, because of the information from Figure 20.1, we know that the tighter the stop loss the better off we will be when it comes to the system's risk–reward ratio.

Figure 20.5 shows the average profit per trade in relation to the maximum trade length and the profit target. In this case, it is easy to see that the best choice for the maximum trade length is six days, which works with almost all profit target distances. At this point, we can decide that the maximum trade length should be six days and the profit target should be placed either 1 or 1.5 ATRs away from the entry price. All that is left is to see if we can fit a stop loss into the mix that preferably should be no larger than 1.2 ATRs.

Figure 20.6 confirms that the maximum trade length should be six days. From Figure 20.6 we can see that the best choice for our stop loss is to place it 1 ATR from the entry price, because this stop loss is the tightest stop that is surrounded by two other stops that produce similar results. The 0.8 ATR stop is not a good alternative, because of the lower average profit produced by the 0.6 ATR stop.

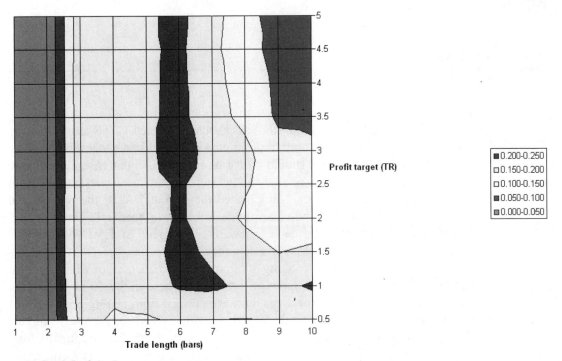

FIGURE 20.5

Average profit per trade versus maximum trade length and profit target.

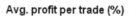

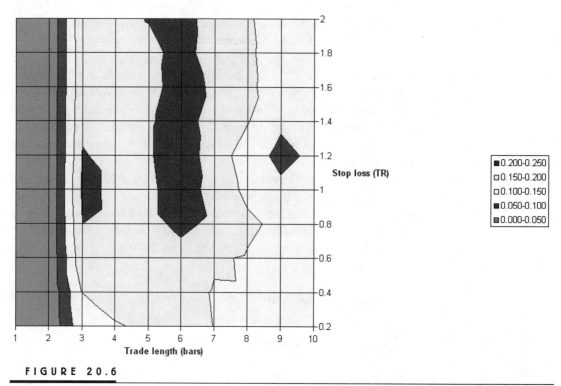

FIGURE 20.6

Maximum trade length of six days.

Now we've decided that the stop loss should be placed 1 ATR away from the entry price and that the maximum trade length should be six days. It remains to be seen whether the profit target should be at 1 or 1.5 ATRs. In this case, I decided to place it at 1.5 ATRs, which is slightly contradictory to what we learned from Figures 20.1 to 20.3. However, had I placed the stop at 1 ATR, the risk–reward relationship going into any individual trade would have been 1:1. Going with a higher profit target for an initial risk–reward relationship of 1.5:1 (or 3:2) will demand a lower percentage of profitable trades.

This makes sense when looking at Figures 20.7 to 20.9, all of which suggest that the number of profitable trades will fall somewhere in the 40 to 50 percent region. Note, however, that these results were derived from testing both sides of the market (both long and short trades). But because we already know from Part 2 that the short side most likely won't perform as well, the results for the long side most likely will be better than indicated by these charts. Hopefully, the results also will be better than where we left off in Part 2 (at this point I honestly don't know).

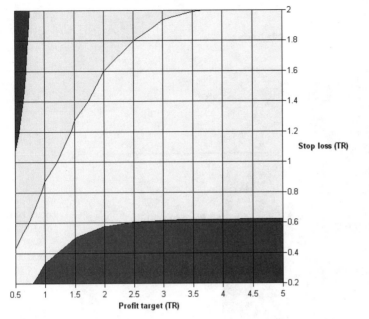

Percent profitable trades

Stop loss (TR)

■ 60.000-70.000
□ 50.000-60.000
□ 40.000-50.000
■ 30.000-40.000
■ 20.000-30.000

Profit target (TR)

FIGURE 20.7

Number of profitable trades, variable 1.

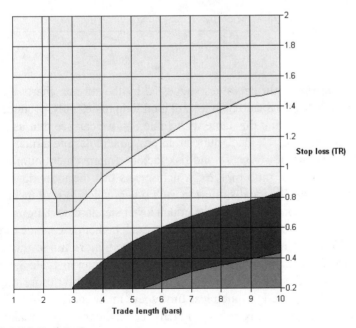

Percent profitable trades

Stop loss (TR)

□ 50.000-60.000
□ 40.000-50.000
■ 30.000-40.000
■ 20.000-30.000

Trade length (bars)

FIGURE 20.8

Number of profitable trades, variable 2.

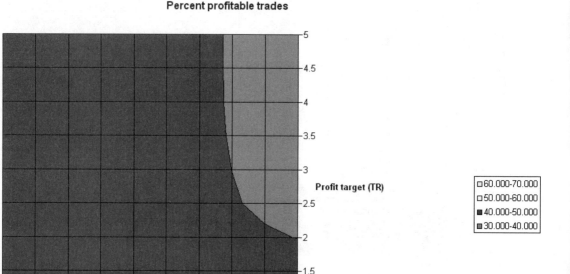

FIGURE 20.9

Number of profitable trades, variable 3.

Plugging these stops with the values suggested by the surface charts into the system as we left it in Chapter 8, and then testing it on long trades only, produced the results in Table 20.1. Comparing this table with Table 8.4, we can see that using the stops and exits from our research made quite an improvement, despite a much lower average profit per trade and lower profit and risk factors. Improvement number one is a much higher risk–reward ratio of 1.26, which means that the individual trades have become more homogenous and similar to each other, which in turn means that the risk is much lower. This is also reflected in much lower standard deviations for the profit and risk factors. The second improvement is a much higher percentage of profitable trades, which, if nothing else, should make the system more fun to trade. The drawdown measured in percentage terms also is a little lower than in Table 8.4.

Last but not least, the average trade length has decreased by more than 60 percent, which also has resulted in much less time spent in the market. At the same time, the average profit per trade is only cut in half. Thus, the trades we make with the optimized stops and exits are much more profitable and efficient per days spent in a trade. Theoretically speaking, spending only one-third of the time in a

TABLE 20.1

Results of Stop-loss Version for Hybrid System

		Long only: 1 ATR stop loss, 1.5 ATR profit target, 6 bars max. trade length				PercProf: 92.31
	Trades	**PercWin**	**NetProfit**	**AvgProfit**	**ProfitStD**	**RiskRatio**
Average:	261.09	50.27	109,684.19	452.49		**Market**
St. Dev:	56.83	3.41	78,567.54	358.72	4,724.28	0.10
High:	317.92	53.68	188,251.72	811.21	5,176.77	**Portfolio**
Low:	204.26	46.87	31,116.65	93.77	(4,271.79)	1.26
	ProfitFactor	**RiskFactor**	**MaxDD**	**PercDD**	**PercTime**	**AvgLength**
Average:	1.29	0.14	57,809.84	30.26	31.18	4.94
St. Dev:	0.23	0.10	32,859.60	18.62	3.84	0.26
High:	1.52	0.24	90,669.44	48.88	35.02	5.20
Low:	1.06	0.04	24,950.25	11.64	27.33	4.68

trade per market means that we could stay fully invested all the time by jumping from trade to trade among three markets. In that case, the net profit from trading all three markets would be three times the average net profit in Table 20.1, which would be far greater than the average profit from Table 8.4.

Also note that the average trade length in Table 20.1 is close to five days. However, as opposed to the maximum trade length behind the surface charts, this number includes weekends and holidays, which means that the effective trade length, measured in number of bars, is slightly shorter. The average trade length also counts the entry and exit bars as full trading days, which means that another full trading day (or bar) can be deducted from that number.

The number of bars spent in a trade also relates to the average percentage of profit per trade of around 0.2 percent per trade, as indicated by the surface charts. Now, 0.2 percent per trade for a trade lasting on average around three days (or around 0.07 percent per day) doesn't sound like much. But we have to remember that this is on the average for all trades: Both the average winning and average losing trades are larger than this. And if we do the math, 0.07 percent per day for a full year isn't bad at all, as it actually comes out to a simple (noncompounded) yearly return of 17.5 percent (0.07 * 250 trading days), or a compounded return of 19 percent (1.0007^{250}), which is well above the long-term buy-and-hold average of 12 percent.

Trailing-stop Version

Staying with the true-range concept but substituting the stop-loss method with a trailing stop method produced another profitable stop and exit combination for this system. First, let's take a look at Figures 20.10 to 20.12, which show the average profit per trade in relation to the three input variables. It is evident that the maximum trade length should be six days. What is not so obvious, however, is what the values for the profit target and trailing stop should be. In situations like this, there is room for some personal interpretations and compromises that make the most sense to you as an analyst.

Looking at Figure 20.11, the 3-ATR profit target seems to be the best profit target to go with a six-day maximum trade length, because it is the lowest value surrounded by equally good values above and below it. The same reasoning applies to Figure 20.12, which suggests the trailing stop should be placed 1.5 ATR away from the highest high price during the life of the trade. However, combining these findings and the data from Figure 20.10 places us on the slope of a not-so-profitable area (remember the analogy to the topographical map, in Chapter 19) with plenty of other low-profit variable combinations surrounding it. It is better to lower the trailing stop to 1.2 ATR, so that we at least end up on top of the most profitable zone.

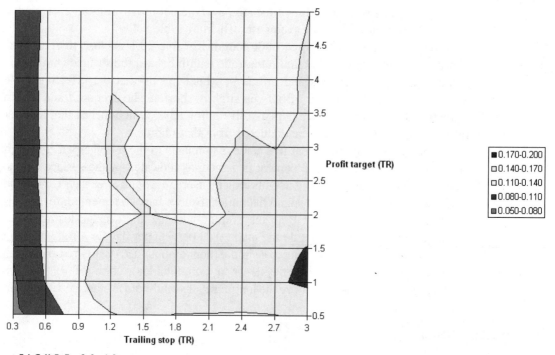

FIGURE 20.10

Average profit per trade for input variable 1.

Avg. profit per trade

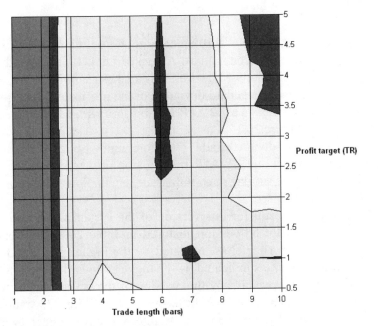

Profit target (TR)

0.200-0.250
0.150-0.200
0.100-0.150
0.050-0.100
0.000-0.050

Trade length (bars)

FIGURE 20.11

Average profit per trade for input variable 2.

Avg. profit per trade

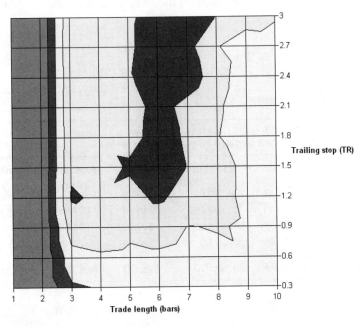

Trailing stop (TR)

0.200-0.250
0.150-0.200
0.100-0.150
0.050-0.100
0.000-0.050

Trade length (bars)

FIGURE 20.12

Average profit per trade for input variable 3.

But even so, Figure 20.10 shows this is not as good a solution as, for example, a 2.4 ATR trailing stop combined with a 1 ATR profit target. The main disadvantage with the latter combination is, however, that it takes us too far to the right in the chart, which increases the standard deviation of the profits. A 1 ATR profit target also doesn't match as well as a 1.2 ATR trailing stop with what we learned to be the best solution in Figure 20.11. Lastly, it also gives us a weird risk–reward relationship going into any individual trade. Therefore, and despite the disadvantages of a 3 ATR profit target and 1.2 ATR trailing stop, it seems to be the best combination together with the six-day maximum trade length. Sometimes you just have to make a few compromises.

Table 20.2 shows the result for this version of the system when tested on our 65 markets. Compared to the version featured in Table 20.1, this version seems to be a little more profitable, as indicated by the higher profit and risk factors, but also a little riskier, as indicated by the higher standard deviations for the same. However, the only reason why this version of the system seems to be a little more profitable is that it trades a little more often, with 278 trades on average per market. Strangely, this happens despite a slightly longer average trade length, which illustrates the fact that there are no sure conclusions to be made when changing the rules for the system, however small these changes might be. Note also that because the average profit per trade is almost unchanged, this version of the system is not as efficient per bars or days in trade as that in Table 20.1. Nonetheless, we will continue to work with both to see how they fare in the competition.

TABLE 20.2

Results of Trailing Stop on Hybrid System

		Long only: 1.2 ATR trailing stop, 3 ATR profit target, 6 bars max. trade length				PercProf: 93.85
	Trades	**PercWin**	**NetProfit**	**AvgProfit**	**ProfitStD**	**RiskRatio**
Average:	278.25	43.94	119,238.87	456.56		**Market**
St. Dev:	62.58	4.43	82,037.26	345.76	4,877.49	0.10
High:	340.82	48.37	201,276.13	802.32	5,334.05	**Portfolio**
Low:	215.67	39.51	37,201.61	110.80	(4,420.93)	1.32
	ProfitFactor	**RiskFactor**	**MaxDD**	**PercDD**	**PercTime**	**AvgLength**
Average:	1.35	0.18	65,289.25	31.68	34.21	5.09
St. Dev:	0.38	0.16	39,924.48	18.60	4.31	0.23
High:	1.73	0.35	105,213.73	50.28	38.52	5.32
Low:	0.97	0.02	25,364.77	13.08	29.91	4.87

MEANDER SYSTEM, V.1.0

The meander system also did best with stops and exits based on the true-range concept. The first of the two versions operates with a stop loss of 1.8 ATR, a profit target of 3 ATR, and a maximum trade length of nine days. Figures 20.13 to 20.15 illustrate how these numbers where derived.

Stop-loss Version

From Figure 20.13 we can see that to get as many profitable trades as possible, the profit target should be as close to the entry as possible. But even with a profit target as far away from the entry as 4.5 ATR, the number of profitable trades still exceeds 50 percent, as long as the stop loss is sufficiently far away from the entry as well. However, what is alarming in Figure 20.13, which also finds confirmation in Figure 20.14, is that the stop loss probably needs to be further away from the entry than the 2 ATR that we've decided to be the maximum. We really should re-

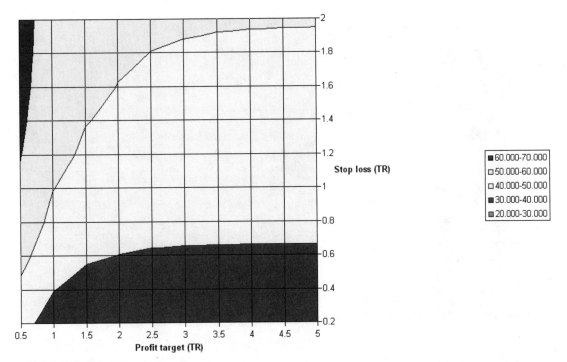

FIGURE 20.13

Profit target versus number of profitable trades.

Avg. profit per trade (%)

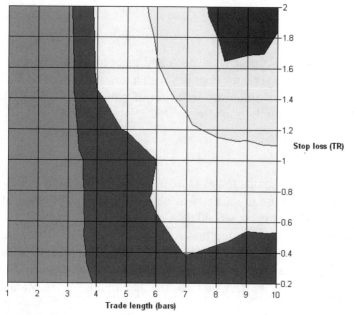

0.480-0.600
0.360-0.480
0.240-0.360
0.120-0.240
0.000-0.120

FIGURE 20.14

A stop loss of 1.8 ATR.

Avg. profit per trade (%)

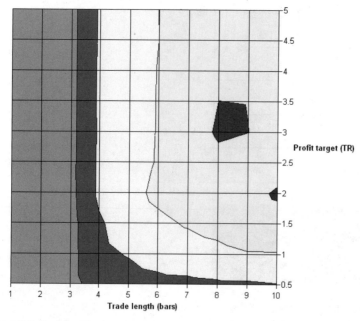

0.400-0.500
0.300-0.400
0.200-0.300
0.100-0.200
0.000-0.100

FIGURE 20.15

Maximum trade length versus number of profitable trades.

run the optimization procedure and allow for even larger stop-loss distances, but for the purposes of this book, these results will have to do.

Moving on, Figure 20.14 tells us we have no other choice than to go with a 1.8 ATR stop loss (never go with the extreme values of the charts, because we have no idea of what's happening with values outside it), combined with a maximum trade length of eight or nine days. By doing so, the legend in Figure 20.14 indicates that the average profit per trade will be at least as high as 0.48 percent per trade, regardless of the number of ATRs we choose for the profit target. The major disadvantage with this setting is, however, that it is in the upper right-hand corner of the chart, which means the standard deviation (and thereby the risk) will be high as well. (To get the best risk–reward relationship, try to keep the input variables as short-term as possible.)

Comparing our findings in Figure 20.14 with the information in Figure 20.15, we can see that we probably are better off with a maximum trade length of eight days. Not only will that take us a little further to the left of the chart, but given that the estimated profits are pretty much the same for the eight- and nine-day settings, an eight-day setting will give us a little more bang for the buck in regard to trading efficiency. Figure 20.15 also indicates that we should go with a profit target of 3 ATR away from the entry price.

Table 20.3 shows the results of plugging these values into the meander system, substituting the original stops and exits, and then testing the system on the same markets as before. Before we compare Table 20.3 with Table 10.5, again note that the average trade lengths in Table 20.3 are longer than the maximum trade lengths specified by the exit rules. This is because the average trade lengths in the

TABLE 20.3

Results of Stop Loss for Meander System

		Long only: 1.8 ATR stop loss, 3 ATR profit target, 8 bars max. trade length				PercProf: 90.77
	Trades	**PercWin**	**NetProfit**	**AvgProfit**	**ProfitStD**	**RiskRatio**
Average:	198.42	53.83	149,951.03	838.77		**Market**
St. Dev:	48.26	4.70	94,746.93	621.34	6,484.33	0.12
High:	246.67	58.54	244,697.96	1,460.11	7,323.11	**Portfolio**
Low:	150.16	49.13	55,204.10	217.43	(5,645.56)	1.35
	ProfitFactor	**RiskFactor**	**MaxDD**	**PercDD**	**PercTime**	**AvgLength**
Average:	1.39	0.17	65,254.96	30.82	39.76	8.32
St. Dev:	0.27	0.11	36,474.46	19.36	6.06	0.40
High:	1.66	0.28	101,729.42	50.18	45.82	8.71
Low:	1.11	0.06	28,780.50	11.46	33.70	7.92

tables also count the weekends and holidays. You can get a better estimate for the effective average trade length by using the following formula:

$$EAL = TAL * (250 / 365) - 1$$

Where:

EAL = Estimated average trade length

TAL = Table average trade length

This gives an effective estimated average trade length of 4.70 days (8.32 * 250 / 365 − 1) for the version of the meander system featured in Table 20.3. You can apply the same formula on all systems to come.

Comparing Table 20.3 with Table 10.5, the first thing to notice is that we actually managed to increase the average profits per trade, from $788 in Table 10.5 to $839 in Table 20.3. Not only did the average profit per trade increase, we also managed to do so while increasing the risk–reward ratio from an already very high 1.21 to 1.35. Additional good news is that the standard deviations for both the profit and risk factors decreased as well.

Trailing-stop Version

Table 20.4 shows the results from another version of this system, made up of a trailing stop of 2.7 ATR, a profit target of 3.5 ATR, and a maximum trade length of nine days. Because the surface charts showed little of interest, I left them out of the analysis for this version of the system.

TABLE 20.4

Results of Trailing Stop for Meander System

		Long only: 2.7 ATR trailing stop, 3.5 ATR profit target, 9 bars max. trade length				PercProf: 93.85
	Trades	**PercWin**	**NetProfit**	**AvgProfit**	**ProfitStD**	**RiskRatio**
Average:	188.14	52.67	156,028.96	916.86		**Market**
St. Dev:	45.16	4.16	98,506.56	674.05	6,968.87	0.13
High:	233.30	56.83	254,535.52	1,590.91	7,885.73	**Portfolio**
Low:	142.98	48.51	57,522.40	242.81	(6,052.01)	1.36
	ProfitFactor	**RiskFactor**	**MaxDD**	**PercDD**	**PercTime**	**AvgLength**
Average:	1.40	0.18	65,561.77	31.53	43.65	9.62
St. Dev:	0.28	0.12	37,024.95	17.47	6.53	0.45
High:	1.68	0.30	102,586.72	49.00	50.18	10.07
Low:	1.12	0.07	28,536.82	14.07	37.12	9.17

The reasoning used in the stop-loss version of the system also holds true for the trailing-stop version, with the addition that the trailing-stop version even is a tad better still.

All in all, we can be very sure that we will be able to repeat these historical and hypothetical results in the future when we trade meander on previously unseen data. The only two negatives are the amount of time spent in the market and the percentage drawdowns, which still are relatively high compared to the version depicted by Table 10.5. Nonetheless, we're looking forward to continuing our work with this system and believe we will be able to address both the time spent in the market and the drawdown shortly, with the help of a few (trend) filters.

VOLUME-WEIGHTED AVERAGE

This system presented us with a couple of interesting choices. When tested using the stop-loss method, the percentage-stop concept indicated the system would work best with a stop loss of 0.4 percent, a profit target of 4.5 percent, and a seven-day maximum trade length. The estimated average profit came out to 0.3 percent, with about 35 percent profitable trades. The ATR concept, on the other hand, indicated the system would work the best with a trailing stop of 1.4 ATRs, a target of 2 ATRs, and a six-day maximum trade length. The estimated average profit per trade came out to 0.4 percent, with about 45 percent profitable trades.

Stop-loss Version

This is a good illustration of how the very same set of entry signals can produce two distinctly different types of systems, even though both versions are fairly short-term, with maximum trade lengths of six and seven days, respectively. Note that for the percentage method, the initial risk–reward relationship going into the trade is more than 12:1 (4.5:0.4). This is not the true and final risk–reward relationship: Given that the stop is fairly tight, while the target is rather generous, it is reasonable to assume that most losing trades will be stopped out at the maximum allowed loss, which explains the relatively high amount of losing trades. Most winners, however, will be stopped out on the seventh day in the trade, before they reach the target. Assuming the average loser also equals 0.4 percent, we can estimate the average winner to be 1.6 percent [(0.3 * 1 + 0.4 * 0.65) / 0.35] for a more accurate risk–reward relationship of 4:1.

We really can't do the same type of calculation for the ATR concept. The most obvious reason for this is that we use different measuring sticks for the input and output variables. Because the inputs are measured in ATRs and the output in percent, we can't combine them into one formula, as we just did for the percentage concept. But even if the inputs and output where the same, the numbers for this system still tell us we cannot use the formula to come up with a more accurate risk–reward relationship.

In the case of the ATR method, the stop loss is relatively far away from the entry price, which means that more trades are likely to get stopped out with a loss because they've reached their maximum allowed trade length. These losses are likely to fall somewhere between the entry price and the stop loss, but because we don't know exactly where, it is impossible—using only the information at hand— to calculate the average loss and the average winner.

Anyhow, an average profit of 0.4 percent per trade with 45 percent profitable trades for the ATR concept is better than 0.3 percent per trade with only 35 percent profitable trade for the percent concept. The ATR concept also allows us to go with two input values (the trade length and the profit target) that are placed closer to the left-hand corner of each chart, which is where we want them to keep the standard deviation of the returns as low as possible. The surface charts were uninformative, so let's move directly to Table 20.5 and compare it to Table 13.5. Unfortunately, this system did not benefit much (if at all) from the stops. First, the average profit per trade is slightly lower in Table 20.5 than in Table 13.5. This negative piece of news is also confirmed by both lower profit and risk factors, and a lower standard deviation of the returns. The latter is also confirmed by a lower number of profitable markets. The only positive is a good increase in the percentage of profitable trades.

Trailing-stop Version

Moving on to the trailing-stop version of the system, Figures 20.16 to 20.18 provide a good illustration on how to use the surface charts when everything lines up

TABLE 20.5

Long Only Trade Length

		Long only: 1.4 ATR stop loss, 2 ATR profit target, 6 bars max. trade length				PercProf: 79.37
	Trades	**PercWin**	**NetProfit**	**AvgProfit**	**ProfitStD**	**RiskRatio**
Average:	108.21	52.28	61,624.43	606.89		**Market**
St. Dev:	28.36	6.21	65,767.56	774.61	5,436.33	0.11
High:	136.57	58.50	127,391.99	1,381.49	6,043.21	**Portfolio**
Low:	79.84	46.07	(4,143.13)	(167.72)	(4,829.44)	0.78
	ProfitFactor	**RiskFactor**	**MaxDD**	**PercDD**	**PercTime**	**AvgLength**
Average:	1.36	0.15	43,035.37	28.14	14.82	5.82
St. Dev:	0.39	0.16	22,579.47	17.31	2.64	0.21
High:	1.76	0.32	65,614.83	45.44	17.46	6.03
Low:	0.97	(0.01)	20,455.90	10.83	12.18	5.61

nicely. Starting with Figure 20.16, we can see that a profit target 2 ATRs away
from the entry price produces the highest profits, together with a trailing stop
between 2.4 and 2.7 ATRs.

With this information at hand, we move to Figure 20.17, which shows that a
profit target of 2 ATRs also should work well with a trade length ranging from four
to nine days. (We're trying to avoid the three- and ten-day setting at the beginning
and end of the range.) In both cases, the average profit comes out to approximately 0.35 percent per trade. So now we know that a profit target of 2 ATRs works
well with several different settings for both the trailing stop and the maximum
allowed trade length. It remains to be seen if we can make the maximum trade
length work equally as well with any of the trailing stop lengths suggested by
Figure 20.16.

And what do you know? Looking at Figure 20.18, we see that a maximum
trade length of six days should work well with both a trailing stop of 2.4 ATR and

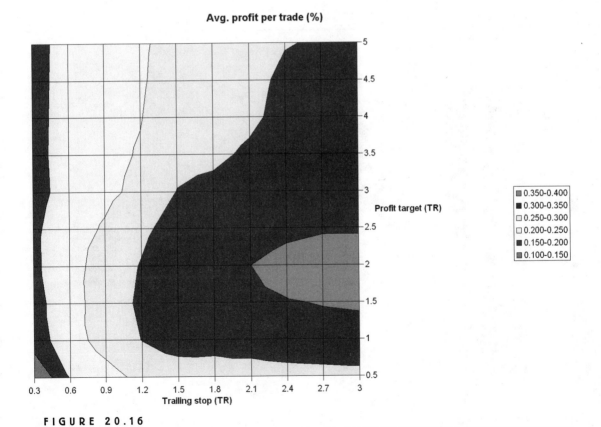

Avg. profit per trade (%)

	0.350-0.400
	0.300-0.350
	0.250-0.300
	0.200-0.250
	0.150-0.200
	0.100-0.150

FIGURE 20.16

Profit target using trailing stop 1.

Avg. profit per trade (%)

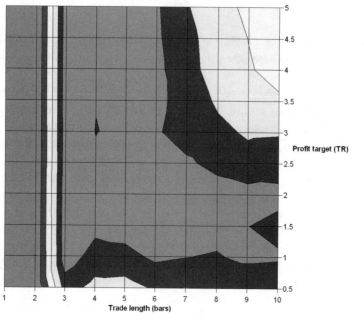

FIGURE 20.17

Profit target using trailing stop 2.

Avg. profit per trade (%)

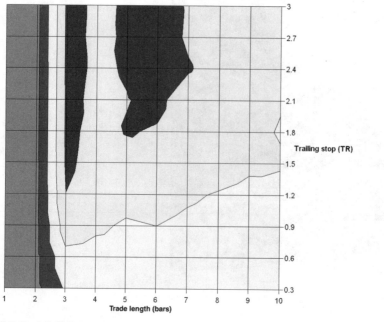

FIGURE 20.18

Profit target using trailing stop 3.

a trailing stop of 2.7 ATR. In this case, we will go with the 2.4-ATR stop because it keeps us closest to the left-hand corner of the chart.

The only not so good thing with the final input values for this system is the fact that the trailing stop initially is further away from the entry price than the profit target, which in this case results in a risk–reward relationship of approximately 0.8:1 going into the trade (2:2.4). This, of course, is not an ideal situation, but sometimes we have to work with what we have, so let's try this system out before we discard it. Table 20.6 shows the combined results for this version of the system.

When this table is compared to Table 13.5, we see that this version of the system generates a slightly higher average profit per trade, but that it also comes with a slightly higher risk, as illustrated by a slightly lower risk–reward ratio of 0.83 compared to 0.95 in Table 13.5. The risk and profit factors also are slightly lower than for the original system. All in all, this indicates that the system is doing very well on some of the markets, but not so well on others. However, the markets that are producing a profit also do so with a large percentage of profitable trades, which results in a total of 54 percent profitable trades for all markets, including the not-so-profitable ones, a very good number indeed.

HARRIS 3L-R PATTERN VARIATION

This was the only system that did not produce profitable results across all variable combinations. More specifically, the system did not work well with the ATR concept that has worked so well with the previous three systems.

TABLE 20.6

Results of Trailing Stop on Value-weighted Averages System

Long only: 2.4 ATR trailing stop, 2 ATR profit target, 6 bars max. trade length					PercProf: 84.13
	Trades	**PercWin**	**NetProfit**	**AvgProfit**	**ProfitStD**	**RiskRatio**
Average:	105.89	54.10	66,831.69	667.86		**Market**
St. Dev:	27.38	6.23	68,883.10	804.79	5,576.14	0.12
High:	133.27	60.33	135,714.78	1,472.65	6,244.00	**Portfolio**
Low:	78.51	47.87	(2,051.41)	(136.93)	(4,908.29)	0.83
	ProfitFactor	**RiskFactor**	**MaxDD**	**PercDD**	**PercTime**	**AvgLength**
Average:	1.40	0.16	43,617.24	28.18	15.38	6.17
St. Dev:	0.43	0.17	22,329.77	17.05	2.73	0.21
High:	1.84	0.33	65,947.01	45.23	18.10	6.38
Low:	0.97	(0.01)	21,287.48	11.14	12.65	5.95

Stop-loss Version

As it turned out, the best version of this system, using the percentage concept, only managed to produce an average profit per trade of 0.12 percent. However, one major reason for this is the much shorter average trade length, when compared to the other three systems tested so far. The best version of the system incorporates a stop loss of 0.4 percent, a profit target of 3 percent, and a maximum trade length of four days. Figure 20.19 and Table 20.7 show the results for this version, to be compared to Table 14.6.

Table 20.7 shows that this latest version of the system has a slightly lower average profit per trade than its predecessor. That the risk–reward ratio also is slightly lower than previously also adds to the not-so-good news. However, the situation isn't as bad as it might seem at first glance, because both the profit and risk factors are slightly higher, albeit with a higher standard deviation as well. Another piece of good news comes with this latest version of the system: If you divide the

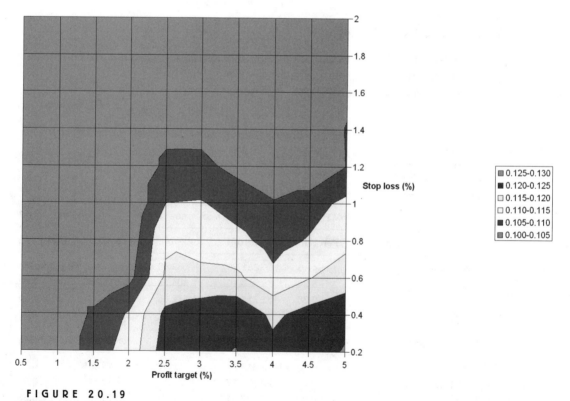

FIGURE 20.19

Results of stop loss on Harris 3L-R pattern variation.

TABLE 20.7

Results of Stop-loss on Harris 3L-R Pattern Variation

		Long only: 0.4% stop loss, 3% profit target, 4 bars max. trade length			PercProf: 83.08	
	Trades	**PercWin**	**NetProfit**	**AvgProfit**	**ProfitStD**	**RiskRatio**
Average:	157.95	37.78	45,342.07	296.69		**Market**
St. Dev:	40.00	7.68	47,437.17	324.30	2,915.76	0.10
High:	197.95	45.45	92,779.24	620.99	3,212.45	**Portfolio**
Low:	117.95	30.10	(2,095.09)	(27.61)	(2,619.07)	0.91
	ProfitFactor	**RiskFactor**	**MaxDD**	**PercDD**	**PercTime**	**AvgLength**
Average:	1.38	0.21	29,338.37	21.44	10.20	2.74
St. Dev:	0.47	0.25	16,921.27	15.53	1.91	0.21
High:	1.84	0.46	46,259.64	36.97	12.11	2.94
Low:	0.91	(0.05)	12,417.10	5.91	8.29	2.53

average profit per trade by the average number of days in a trade, you will find that it is slightly higher for this version than the previous one. In fact, the good news is that this value stays above $100 per bar, which means that the average profit per bar in a trade will be 0.1 percent, given that we invest $100,000 per trade (100 / 100,000 * 100).

If we can be in a trade every trading day of the year, making 0.1 percent per day, the noncompounded return will be 25 percent per year (0.1 * 250), given an initial investment of $100,000, which is way more than the long-term average for the market as a whole. Remember, however, these numbers do not include slippage and commission. But this is counterweighted by the possibility of compounding the returns when trading several markets within one portfolio. More about this in Part 4.

Another piece of good news is that the time spent in the market is much lower for this version of the system. This increases the possibility of compounding the returns when trading several markets and systems at once. The less time spent in the market for any specific system–market combination, the more room we have to diversify. The more systems and markets we can trade, the faster we can compound our returns.

Trailing-stop Version

Basically, what could be said about the stop-loss method of this system also can be said about the trailing-stop method, except the results for the trailing-stop version are a tad lower, which Table 20.8 illustrates. Note especially that, despite a higher

TABLE 20.8

Results of Trailing Stop on Harris 3L-R Pattern Variation

	Long only: 2.7% trailing stop, 4.5% profit target, 5 bars max. trade length					PercProf: 83.08
	Trades	**PercWin**	**NetProfit**	**AvgProfit**	**ProfitStD**	**RiskRatio**
Average:	154.55	44.29	47,503.23	316.53		**Market**
St. Dev:	37.97	5.83	49,797.29	362.77	3,359.87	0.09
High:	192.52	50.12	97,300.52	679.31	3,676.40	**Portfolio**
Low:	116.58	38.45	(2,294.06)	(46.24)	(3,043.34)	0.87
	ProfitFactor	**RiskFactor**	**MaxDD**	**PercDD**	**PercTime**	**AvgLength**
Average:	1.30	0.15	33,669.37	24.18	13.11	3.57
St. Dev:	0.33	0.16	17,285.23	16.13	3.51	0.65
High:	1.63	0.32	50,954.59	40.31	16.62	4.22
Low:	0.97	(0.01)	16,384.14	8.05	9.61	2.92

average profit per trade, this version of the system calls for a longer maximum trade length, which will lower the average profit made per bars in trade. The only positive is that the number of profitable trades is slightly higher, at 44 percent.

EXPERT EXITS

Like the Harris system, the expert exits system also worked best using the percentage concept. It would be interesting to examine the differences between those two systems that worked best using the percentage concept, when compared to those three systems that worked best using the true-range concept. A few observations can be made right away that could serve as a starting hypothesis for your own research into this.

One observation is that the systems that worked best with the percentage concept also are the latest two systems tested, and did best on the short side. It could be that we are better off using the percentage concept if we would like to work with identical stop and exit settings for both long and short trades. These two systems may have worked the best in the bear market simply because there were plenty of bear markets to test them on.

Another reason why the latest two systems worked best using the percentage concept could be because they are by far the simplest and most short-term in their construction, relying on only a few comparisons between the very last bars leading up to the trade. This also results in the shortest average trade lengths. The exact reason for this, however, I will leave for you to research. You know almost as much about these systems now as I do.

Stop-loss Version

Using the stop-loss method, the best version of this system incorporated a stop loss of 0.6 percent, a profit target of 3.5 percent, and a maximum trade length of three days, which resulted in a very profitable system, indeed. Table 20.9 shows that this version of the system makes an average profit of $532, with a risk–reward ratio of 1.46. These good numbers are also confirmed by very high profit and risk factors and very low standard deviations. Note also that the average trade length is less than three days, including the weekends and holidays, which means that this system will make $200 a day, on average, when in a trade. The percent time spent in the market also looks low enough to make it possible to combine it with other systems for a well-diversified portfolio.

Trailing-stop Version

Table 20.10 shows that the trailing-stop version of this system is not quite as profitable as the stop-loss version, but it isn't far from it. Note that this version has a much wider stop loss combined with only a slightly longer average trade length. Thus, most losses for this version of the system may come because of the trade-length stop. Nonetheless, both versions of the system are definitely among the best versions tested. It only goes to show what one can do with a very basic entry technique, as long as you keep track of where and when to exit.

TABLE 20.9

Results of Stop Loss on Expert Exits System

		Long only: 0.6% stop loss, 3.5% profit target, 3 bars max. trade length				PercProf: 96.92
	Trades	**PercWin**	**NetProfit**	**AvgProfit**	**ProfitStD**	**RiskRatio**
Average:	195.74	41.19	89,268.37	532.72		**Market**
St. Dev:	59.54	6.89	55,718.56	365.61	2,957.72	0.17
High:	255.28	48.08	144,986.93	898.33	3,490.44	**Portfolio**
Low:	136.20	34.30	33,549.81	167.11	(2,424.99)	1.46
	ProfitFactor	**RiskFactor**	**MaxDD**	**PercDD**	**PercTime**	**AvgLength**
Average:	1.60	0.33	26,910.20	17.66	13.11	2.83
St. Dev:	0.43	0.22	19,000.36	18.08	3.44	0.23
High:	2.03	0.55	45,910.56	35.74	16.55	3.06
Low:	1.17	0.11	7,909.84	(0.41)	9.67	2.60

TABLE 20.10

Results of Trailing Stop on Expert Exits System

		Long only: 2.7% trailing stop, 4.5% profit target, 4 bars max. trade length				PercProf: 90.77
	Trades	**PercWin**	**NetProfit**	**AvgProfit**	**ProfitStD**	**RiskRatio**
Average:	192.15	46.25	87,226.75	529.15		**Market**
St. Dev:	56.68	5.37	62,318.27	388.33	3,321.90	0.15
High:	248.84	51.62	149,545.02	917.48	3,851.05	**Portfolio**
Low:	135.47	40.88	24,908.47	140.82	(2,792.75)	1.36
	ProfitFactor	**RiskFactor**	**MaxDD**	**PercDD**	**PercTime**	**AvgLength**
Average:	1.51	0.26	31,946.18	20.77	16.40	3.58
St. Dev:	0.38	0.19	21,181.11	20.01	5.30	0.65
High:	1.89	0.44	53,127.29	40.78	21.70	4.23
Low:	1.13	0.07	10,765.07	0.76	11.10	2.93

UNCOMMENTED BONUS STOPS

Because I had to keep the stops fairly basic for the research in this book, here are a bunch of more complex bonus stops you can experiment with yourself:

```
{***** Percentage-based Stops *****}
Variables:
StopLoss(4), TrailingStop(2), ProfitStop(25), TargetStop(8), SlowBar(3),
MinBarMove(0.25), MaxLength(10), LongLoss(0), ShortLoss(0), LongTrailing(0),
ShortTrailing(0), TrueLength(0), TrueProfitStop(0), LongProfit(0), ShortProfit(0),
TrueMinBarMove(0), LongTarget(0), ShortTarget(0), TrueSlowBar(0),
TrueNextBar(0), TrueMaxLength(0);
If BarNumber = 1 Then Begin
    LongLoss = 1 - StopLoss * 0.01;
    ShortLoss = 1 + StopLoss * 0.01;
    LongTrailing = 1 - TrailingStop * 0.01;
    ShortTrailing = 1 + TrailingStop * 0.01;
    TrueProfitStop = 1 - ProfitStop * 0.01;
    LongTarget = 1 + TargetStop * 0.01;
    ShortTarget = 1 - TargetStop * 0.01;
    TrueSlowBar = SlowBar - 1;
    TrueMinBarMove = MinBarMove * 0.01;
    TrueMaxLength = MaxLength - 1;
```

```
End;
If StopLoss > 0 Then Begin
    If Close < EntryPrice * LongLoss Then
        ExitLong ("L.C-Loss") on Close;
    If Close > EntryPrice * ShortLoss Then
        ExitShort ("S.C-Loss") on Close;
End;
If EntryPrice > 0 Then Begin
    {***** The Stop Loss *****}
    If StopLoss > 0 Then Begin
        ExitLong ("L-Loss") Next Bar at EntryPrice * LongLoss Stop;
        ExitShort ("S-Loss") Next Bar at EntryPrice * ShortLoss Stop;
    End;
    {***** The Trailing Stop *****}
    If TrailingStop > 0 Then Begin
        ExitLong ("L-Trail") Next Bar at  Close * LongTrailing Stop;
        ExitShort ("S-Trail") Next Bar at Close * ShortTrailing Stop;
    End;
    {***** The Profit Protector *****}
    If ProfitStop > 0 Then Begin
        TrueLength = BarsSinceEntry + 1;
LongProfit = (Highest(Close, TrueLength) - EntryPrice) * TrueProfitStop;
ShortProfit = (EntryPrice - Lowest(Close, TrueLength)) * TrueProfitStop;
ExitLong ("L-Prft") Next Bar at EntryPrice + LongProfit Stop;
        ExitShort ("S-Prft") Next Bar at EntryPrice - ShortProfit Stop;
    End;
    {***** The Profit Target *****}
    If TargetStop > 0 Then Begin
        ExitLong ("L-Trgt") Next Bar at EntryPrice * LongTarget Limit;
        ExitShort ("S-Trgt") Next Bar at EntryPrice * ShortTarget Limit;
    End;
    If BarsSinceEntry >= TrueSlowBar Then Begin
        {***** The Slow-trade Stop *****}
        If TrueSlowBar > 0 and OpenPositionProfit < 0 Then Begin
            ExitLong ("L-Slow") on Close;
            ExitShort ("S-Slow") on Close;
```

```
      End;
      {***** The Min-move Stop *****}
      If TrueMinBarMove > 0 Then Begin
         TrueNextBar = BarsSinceEntry + 2;
         ExitLong ("L-Min") Next Bar at EntryPrice *
         (1 + (TrueMinBarMove * TrueNextBar)) Stop;
         ExitShort ("S-Min") Next Bar at EntryPrice *
         (1 - (TrueMinBarMove * TrueNextBar)) Stop;
      End;
   End;
   {***** The Max-length Stop *****}
   If MaxLength > 0 and BarsSinceEntry >= TrueMaxLength Then Begin
      ExitLong ("L-Time") on Close;
      ExitShort ("S-Time") on Close;
   End;
End;
{***** True-range Stops *****}
Variables:
StopLoss(2), TrailingStop(1), ProfitStop(25), TargetStop(4), SlowBar(3),
MinBarMove(0.25), MaxLength(10), RangePeriod(20), OneRange(0),
StopRange(0), TrailRange(0), TrueLength(0), TrueProfitStop(0), LongProfit(0),
ShortProfit(0), MinTradeMove(0), TargetRange(0), TrueSlowBar(0),
TrueNextBar(0), TrueMaxLength(0);
If BarNumber = 1 Then Begin
   TrueProfitStop = 1 - ProfitStop * 0.01;
   TrueSlowBar = SlowBar - 1;
   TrueMaxLength = MaxLength - 1;
End;
OneRange = AvgTrueRange(RangePeriod);
If EntryPrice > 0 Then Begin
   {***** The Stop Loss *****}
   If StopLoss > 0 Then Begin
      StopRange = StopLoss * OneRange;
      ExitLong ("L-Loss") Next Bar at EntryPrice - StopRange Stop;
      ExitShort ("S-Loss") Next Bar at EntryPrice + StopRange Stop;
   End;
   {***** The Trailing Stop *****}
```

```
If TrailingStop > 0 Then Begin
    TrailRange = TrailingStop * OneRange;
    ExitLong ("L-Trail") Next Bar at  Close - TrailRange Stop;
    ExitShort ("S-Trail") Next Bar at Close + TrailRange Stop;
End;
{***** The Profit Protector *****}
If ProfitStop > 0 Then Begin
    TrueLength = BarsSinceEntry + 1;
LongProfit = (Highest(Close, TrueLength) - EntryPrice) * TrueProfitStop;
ShortProfit = (EntryPrice - Lowest(Close, TrueLength)) * TrueProfitStop;
ExitLong ("L-Prft") Next Bar at EntryPrice + LongProfit Stop;
ExitShort ("S-Prft") Next Bar at EntryPrice - ShortProfit Stop;
End;
{***** The Profit Target *****}
If TargetStop > 0 Then Begin
TargetRange = TargetStop * OneRange;
    ExitLong ("L-Trgt") Next Bar at EntryPrice + TargetRange Limit;
    ExitShort ("S-Trgt") Next Bar at EntryPrice - TargetRange Limit;
End;
If BarsSinceEntry >= TrueSlowBar Then Begin
    {***** The Slow-trade Stop *****}
    If TrueSlowBar > 0 and OpenPositionProfit < 0 Then Begin
        ExitLong ("L-Slow") on Close;
        ExitShort ("S-Slow") on Close;
    End;
    {***** The Min-move Stop *****}
    If MinBarMove > 0 Then Begin
        TrueNextBar = BarsSinceEntry + 2;
        MinTradeMove = MinBarMove * OneRange * TrueNextBar;
        ExitLong ("L-Min") Next Bar at EntryPrice +
MinTradeMove Stop;
        ExitShort ("S-Min") Next Bar at EntryPrice −
MinTradeMove Stop;
    End;
End;
{***** The Max-length Stop *****}
```

```
    If MaxLength > 0 and BarsSinceEntry >= TrueMaxLength Then Begin
        ExitLong ("L-Time") on Close;
        ExitShort ("S-Time") on Close;
    End;
End;
```

CHAPTER 21

Systems as Filters

You can determine the long-term trend several ways. The most straightforward way is simply to use your own fundamental and discretionary judgment about where the economy in general and your stocks in particular are heading, and then stick to that prognosis over a prolonged period of time. Other ways could be to trade only in the same direction of a long-term moving average, or some other indicator suitable for more long-term analysis.

Over the years I proved that this works, in several articles for *Futures* and *Active Trader* magazines, and also in my first book, *Trading Systems That Work*. For example, in *Trading Systems That Work*, I examined 16 different futures markets over the period January 1980 to October 1999. First, I tested all markets 12 times each with a system that entered the market randomly in either direction, and stayed in the trade for five days. Then I added a 200-day moving average and altered the rules for the system so that it was allowed to enter randomly only in the same direction as the long-term trend.

Without the trend filter, only seven markets had an average profit factor above one, but for none of them could we say with 68 percent certainty that the true profit factor also would be above one. For all markets combined, trading without a trend filter, the true profit factor was, with 68 percent certainty, likely to be found somewhere within the interval 0.88 to 1.12. With the trend filter, however, all markets but one had an average profit factor above one, and for a total of nine we also could say that we could be 68 percent sure that the true profit factor, trading with the trend filter, also would be above one. For all markets combined, the true profit factor could with 68 percent certainty be found in the interval 1.03 to 1.29.

In the April 2000 issue of *Active Trader* magazine, I illustrated the importance of only trading with the long-term trend on the stock market ("Short-term Strategy," "Long-term Perspective"). This time, I tested the thirty stocks in the Dow Jones Index, over the period January 1990 to October 1999. The rules for trading with and without the trend filter were the same as for the test on the futures markets, except that those stocks I "only" tested 10 times each. Tables 21.1 and 21.2 show the results of these tests.

TABLE 21.1

Testing without Trend Filter

Company	PF	St. dev.	% win	St. dev.
3M	1.05	0.15	52.52	2.66
Alcoa	0.99	0.07	52.69	**2.27**
American Express	1.05	0.14	51.28	2.76
AT&T	0.96	0.22	49.85	4.71
Boeing	1.08	0.11	51.88	**1.42**
Caterpillar	1.06	0.11	52.84	**2.26**
Citigroup	0.99	0.12	51.02	2.82
Coca-Cola	1.08	0.18	51.97	3.32
Disney	0.96	0.18	50.73	2.41
DuPont	1.05	0.21	50.56	2.67
Exxon	0.92	0.12	50.33	2.57
General Electric	0.95	0.11	50.10	1.86
General Motors	1.03	0.12	51.17	2.79
Home Depot	0.94	0.18	50.37	2.10
Honeywell	1.09	0.22	52.53	3.62
Hewlett-Packard	1.00	0.18	50.53	1.53
IBM	1.00	0.27	50.73	3.16
International Paper	1.01	0.18	51.89	3.14
Intel	1.01	0.11	50.15	2.38
Johnson & Johnson	1.02	0.19	51.16	1.61
JP Morgan	1.07	0.23	51.69	3.67
Kodak	0.99	0.18	51.43	2.61
McDonalds	0.89	0.12	49.85	3.15
Merck	1.08	0.20	51.58	2.19
Microsoft	0.92	0.13	50.96	2.85
Procter & Gamble	1.02	0.23	50.83	2.39
Philip Morris	1.12	0.20	53.42	2.09
SBC Communications	0.98	0.15	50.07	3.41
United Technologies	1.04	0.29	52.34	2.53
Wal-Mart	1.11	0.28	51.40	3.14

TABLE 21.2

Testing with Trend Filter (200-day Moving Average)

Company	PF	St. dev.	% win	St. dev.
3M	0.85	0.12	48.14	2.48
Alcoa	1.00	0.13	48.10	2.12
American Express	1.14	0.16	53.59	2.66
AT&T	1.11	0.26	51.70	2.69
Boeing	0.91	0.12	52.19	2.54
Caterpillar	0.94	0.22	50.62	2.56
Citigroup	1.29	0.22	57.01	3.85
Coca-Cola	1.01	0.19	52.96	2.68
Disney	0.97	0.20	52.22	3.62
DuPont	0.93	0.15	48.39	3.07
Exxon	0.91	0.15	50.73	1.22
General Electric	1.37	0.25	55.10	2.48
General Motors	0.96	0.11	49.61	2.25
Home Depot	1.29	0.16	54.86	3.05
Honeywell	1.11	0.10	54.90	1.73
Hewlett-Packard	1.07	0.14	50.96	1.43
IBM	1.22	0.22	58.36	1.75
International Paper	0.78	0.14	48.42	2.86
Intel	1.26	0.20	52.39	2.50
Johnson & Johnson	1.17	0.17	54.03	2.84
JP Morgan	1.06	0.14	51.68	2.57
Kodak	0.96	0.16	50.70	3.38
McDonalds	1.01	0.19	51.98	1.91
Merck	1.07	0.16	57.32	3.08
Microsoft	1.49	0.41	56.52	2.61
Procter & Gamble	1.06	0.18	49.58	2.45
Philip Morris	1.26	0.17	55.33	2.05
SBC Communications	1.01	0.20	51.24	2.44
United Technologies	1.26	0.19	55.51	2.87
Wal-Mart	1.42	0.24	58.61	3.58

Figure 21.1 shows that without the trend filter, 18 markets had an average profit factor above one. However, we cannot say that the true profit factor is above one for any of them, because the one standard deviation will bring the one-standard-deviation boundary below one, when deducted from the profit factor. Also, 28 markets had more than 50-percent profitable trades, but only three of them were sufficiently above the 50-percent mark, for us to say that we can be 68 percent sure that the true percentage profitable trades also should be above 50 percent. For all stocks combined, the true profit factor will, with 68 percent

certainty, fall somewhere in the interval 0.83 to 1.19, while the true percentage of profitable trades will, with 68 percent certainty, fall somewhere in the interval 48.48 to 54.05.

In Table 21.2, 21 markets have a profit factor above one, and 19 markets have a higher profit factor than in Table 21.1. Of all 30 markets, we also now can say that 11 of them also have a high enough profit factor so that we can be 68 percent sure that their true profit factors will be above one. Using the trend filter, 21 markets also had a higher percentage of profitable trades, as compared to without the filter. Of these 21 markets, for 14 of them, we also can say that we can be 68 percent certain that the true percentage of profitable trades is over 50 percent. For all stocks combined, the true profit factor will, with 68 percent certainty, fall somewhere in the interval 0.85 to 1.35, while the true percentage of profitable trades will, with 68 percent certainty, fall somewhere in the interval 48.77 to 56.69.

Although the test shows that we still can't be sure that the average profit factor for all stocks will be above one, it still shows that most stocks will benefit from a trend filter, even as rudimentary and arbitrarily chosen as this one. We still can't say with 68 percent certainty that the profit factor for all stocks will be above one because a few stocks didn't like this trend filter at all and therefore contributed to increase the standard deviation of the results.

In the same article, another test showed that it was possible to increase the performance of a short-term system traded on the S&P 500 futures market, by only taking the trades in the direction indicated by a 200-day on-balance-volume indicator. In short, this test lowered the number of trades from 332 to 177, while at the same time it increased the profit factor from 1.21 to 1.56 and the number of profitable trades from 53.31 percent to 58.19 percent.

While the on-balance-volume indicator is one of my favorite trend indicators, because it incorporates all the concepts of technical analysis (price and volume) into one simple-to-understand number, the lookback period for this indicator too was arbitrarily chosen. Plenty of other tests in *Trading Systems That Work*, on other futures markets, using other systems and filtering techniques, confirm the importance of always trading with the trend.

That said, this isn't exactly what this chapter will be about. Yes, we will apply three different filters to the five short-term systems we have worked with in this section, the three filters being the more long-term relative strength systems we introduced in Part 2. However, the major difference between the testing we will do here and the tests just mentioned is that, for the tests to come, we are not all that interested in the actual long-term trend of the markets, but rather if the market we intend to trade shows a greater potential for moving the way we want it to, as compared to one or several other markets. As a consequence of that, we might or might not trade with the direction of the long-term trend, and at this point I have no idea what the results will be.

As it turned out, this was a very interesting piece of research where very few of the ten different versions of the five systems—to which we just applied the stops and exits—did better with the intermediate-term filters. Looking through the results, there are several possible reasons for this.

Reason number one is that none of the filters is an actual trend filter, but rather a relative strength filter, which means that we will filter away plenty of good trading opportunities in good trends, only because the stock in question wasn't among the very strongest ones at that particular point in time, despite the fact that it too was in a good trend. This actually means that we will filter away more good trades than bad trades. Because during times when the trend goes completely against the anticipated direction of the trade, the trend filter will still allow a trade to take place, as long as the stock in question is among the strongest ones, no matter the actual direction of the trend.

Reason number two is that, while each filter might do a good job isolating the intermediate-term relative strength between the stocks in question, it seems it isn't necessarily a good idea to trade the strongest of these stocks in the short term. In fact, reversing the logic for a few of the filters before trading with a few of the short-term systems reveals that it actually could be a better idea to trade the weakest stock in a group of stocks, as long as it trends in the right direction. The logic is as follows: If the trend for all stocks is up, those that seem the most likely to explode to the upside in the short term are those that have lagged behind in the intermediate term.

Reason number three is that, the more rules we stack on top of each other within one single strategy, the fewer the markets that will be able to produce a profit, simply because the added rules mean curve fitting to more specific market conditions, which fewer and fewer markets will be able to meet. During the testing, this can show up in a higher average profit factor for the filtered version of the system because it is doing extremely well on a few markets, which even can boost the average profit factor for all markets—especially if the winning markets also trade relatively infrequently, so that the gross profits and losses are relatively small. At the same time, though, the average profit and number of profitable markets will decrease, because the added rules make an increasing number of markets unprofitable.

For example, if one market produces a gross profit of $20 and a gross loss of $10, its profit factor will be 2 (20 / 10), and its total profit and average profit per trade will both be positive. At the same time, another market produces a gross profit of $980 and gross loss of $1,020, which results in a profit factor of 0.96 (980 / 1020), and its total profit and average profit will be negative. Looking at the two markets combined, we see that the average profit factor will be 1.48 [(2 + 0.96) / 2], suggesting that both markets will trade profitably together. However, that this will not be the case is revealed by the combined total and average profits, which will be negative.

Reason number four is the order of the systems in the first place. In this case, we started by adding the stops to all systems and markets, traded in any market condition. We did so because we wanted the systems to work on average equally well all the time. However, we could have defined the market condition under which we want the system to operate first, and then optimized the stops for that condition only. As it is now, the settings for the stop and exit lengths and times also are influenced by conditions under which we wouldn't have traded anyway, given the filters we just added.

From a practical point of view, this means that most stops, exits, and time frames probably are a little too tight to be optimal, given the market conditions under which they are supposed to operate. During the bad periods, the systems try to make a buck as quickly as possible or stop out a loser as soon as possible. During good periods, on the other hand (those supposedly identified by the filters), the systems really should make the profits run a little longer and keep the stops a little further away from the entry price, to give the systems a better chance to make use of the favorable conditions. They apparently don't manage to do this as things are right now.

Aside from these reasons, adding a filter will almost always also reduce the risk–reward ratio, simply because the filter also reduces the number of trades that go into the calculation for this system measure. There isn't much we can do about that. To achieve smoother returns through diversification, we have to make room for several systems and markets to be traded simultaneously. To do so we need to trade each system–market combination less frequently by somehow filtering out some of the trades. The fewer trades produced by a specific system–market combination, the less we can say about its outcome in the future.

Let's look through the results for the select system and filter combinations that we will take with us to the money management analysis in Part 4. Remember that all systems are long only.

RS SYSTEM NO. 1 AS THE FILTER

Table 21.3 shows that the stop-loss version of the meander system, together with RS system No. 1 as the filter, didn't do much worse than the filterless version, depicted in Table 20.3. In fact, given the anticipated decrease in performance in general and in the risk–reward ratio in particular, the only true negative is that the percent of time spent in the market didn't decrease as much as desired. The meander system definitely has some serious potential.

The same holds true for the trailing-stop versions of the volume-weighted average system (Table 21.4) and the Harris 3L-R pattern variation (Table 21.5). The only true negative here is their relatively low risk–reward ratios, compared to the original versions in Tables 20.6 and 20.8, respectively. One good thing with these systems, as with the stop-loss version of the expert exits system (Table 21.6),

TABLE 21.3

Meander System Using RS System No. 1 as Filter

	Meander system, V.1.0: 1.8 ATR stop loss, 3 ATR profit target, 8 bars max. trade length				PercProf: 86.67	
	Trades	**PercWin**	**NetProfit**	**AvgProfit**	**ProfitStD**	**RiskRatio**
Average:	144.58	52.97	99,512.31	756.36		**Market**
St. Dev:	34.32	4.41	76,271.48	623.94	6,790.48	0.11
High:	178.90	57.38	175,783.79	1,380.30	7,546.84	**Portfolio**
Low:	110.26	48.56	23,240.82	132.41	(6,034.13)	1.21
	ProfitFactor	**RiskFactor**	**MaxDD**	**PercDD**	**PercTime**	**AvgLength**
Average:	1.32	0.14	64,199.52	32.83	28.47	8.34
St. Dev:	0.25	0.11	35,052.61	19.02	4.14	0.25
High:	1.57	0.25	99,252.12	51.85	32.61	8.58
Low:	1.08	0.04	29,146.91	13.80	24.33	8.09

is the relatively little time they spend in the market, which makes plenty of room for diversification with other systems and markets. Note also that both the meander system and the expert exits systems still have risk–reward ratios well above one, which means that at least 84 percent of all trading sequences will produce a profit, statistically speaking.

TABLE 21.4

Volume-weighted System Using RS System No. 1 as Filter

	Volume-weighted average: 2.4 ATR trailing stop, 2 ATR profit target, 6 bars max. trade length				PercProf: 80.00	
	Trades	**PercWin**	**NetProfit**	**AvgProfit**	**ProfitStD**	**RiskRatio**
Average:	61.78	52.85	33,372.20	565.68		**Market**
St. Dev:	19.62	8.02	49,494.94	1,143.89	5,677.57	0.10
High:	81.41	60.87	82,867.14	1,709.57	6,243.25	**Portfolio**
Low:	42.16	44.83	(16,122.75)	(578.21)	(5,111.89)	0.49
	ProfitFactor	**RiskFactor**	**MaxDD**	**PercDD**	**PercTime**	**AvgLength**
Average:	1.39	0.15	39,605.78	29.51	8.90	6.13
St. Dev:	0.57	0.24	22,762.27	19.87	2.16	0.23
High:	1.96	0.39	62,368.06	49.38	11.06	6.36
Low:	0.83	(0.09)	16,843.51	9.65	6.74	5.90

TABLE 21.5

Harris 3L-R Path Variant Using RS System No. 1 as Filter

Harris 3L-R pattern variation: 2.7% trailing stop, 4.5% profit target, 5 bars max. trade length					**PercProf: 75.00**	
	Trades	**PercWin**	**NetProfit**	**AvgProfit**	**ProfitStD**	**RiskRatio**
Average:	108.78	42.60	29,297.27	277.68		**Market**
St. Dev:	28.71	5.16	38,649.73	472.58	3,530.43	0.07
High:	137.50	47.77	67,947.01	750.27	3,808.11	**Portfolio**
Low:	80.07	37.44	(9,352.46)	(194.90)	(3,252.75)	0.59
	ProfitFactor	**RiskFactor**	**MaxDD**	**PercDD**	**PercTime**	**AvgLength**
Average:	1.25	0.13	30,240.42	23.10	9.03	3.49
St. Dev:	0.32	0.19	14,074.59	13.47	2.36	0.57
High:	1.57	0.32	44,315.01	36.57	11.39	4.06
Low:	0.93	(0.06)	16,165.83	9.64	6.68	2.93

RELATIVE-STRENGTH BANDS AS THE FILTER

The hybrid system No. 1 probably least liked the filters, no matter which filter it was teamed up with (Table 21.7). In fact, the only good news is that the percentage of time spent in the market also decreased by approximately 50 percent, to a tolerable 15 percent (compare with Table 20.1). Other than that, the stop-loss ver-

TABLE 21.6

Expert Exits System Using RS System No. 1 as Filter

Expert exits: 0.6 % stop loss, 3.5% profit target, 3 bars max. trade length					**PercProf: 96.67**	
	Trades	**PercWin**	**NetProfit**	**AvgProfit**	**ProfitStD**	**RiskRatio**
Average:	127.75	43.99	49,501.30	442.65		**Market**
St. Dev:	39.57	4.83	32,839.33	362.72	2,950.79	0.15
High:	167.32	48.82	82,340.64	805.37	3,393.44	**Portfolio**
Low:	88.18	39.16	16,661.97	79.93	(2,508.14)	1.22
	ProfitFactor	**RiskFactor**	**MaxDD**	**PercDD**	**PercTime**	**AvgLength**
Average:	1.52	0.28	22,920.70	15.94	7.34	2.44
St. Dev:	0.40	0.19	13,920.08	9.66	1.83	0.08
High:	1.92	0.47	36,840.78	25.60	9.17	2.52
Low:	1.11	0.08	9,000.62	6.28	5.51	2.36

TABLE 21.7

Hybrid System Using Relative-strength Bands as Filter

	Hybrid system No. 1: 1 ATR stop loss, 1.5 ATR profit target, 6 bars max. trade length				PercProf: 72.00
	Trades	**PercWin**	**NetProfit**	**AvgProfit**	**ProfitStD**	**RiskRatio**
Average:	97.00	48.31	28,607.08	295.41		**Market**
St. Dev:	35.80	7.09	53,259.36	707.02	4,275.30	0.07
High:	132.80	55.39	81,866.44	1,002.42	4,570.71	**Portfolio**
Low:	61.20	41.22	(24,652.28)	(411.61)	(3,979.90)	0.42
	ProfitFactor	**RiskFactor**	**MaxDD**	**PercDD**	**PercTime**	**AvgLength**
Average:	1.24	0.10	34,905.87	26.43	15.02	4.87
St. Dev:	0.39	0.18	25,342.23	16.00	3.91	0.33
High:	1.62	0.28	60,248.10	42.42	18.93	5.20
Low:	0.85	(0.08)	9,563.64	10.43	11.12	4.54

sion of this system lost as much as one-third of its average profit per trade and two-thirds of its risk–reward ratio. The number of profitable markets also decreased from over 90 percent to a more modest 72 percent.

However, reversing the rules for many of the filters before applying them to this system improved the performance for many of the new system–filter versions considerably. This is not shown, but you can try it yourself on a system that actually does best when trading the weakest stock in a group of stocks (according to our second reason why an intermediate-term relative-strength filter might not always function as anticipated).

The stop-loss version of the meander system continued to do fairly well with the relative-strength bands as filters. If you compare this version of the system, in Table 21.8, with the ones in Tables 20.3 and 21.3, you will find that this version of the system actually had both the highest average profit per trade and the least time spent in the market of all three versions. A much lower risk–reward ratio of 0.76 is, however, an indication that we cannot be as sure about this version's future performance as we can of the others. The time spent in the market is also a little too high for optimal diversification possibilities.

The trailing-stop version of the volume-weighted average system also holds up well together with the relative-strength bands as a filter. Comparing Table 21.9 with Tables 20.6 and 21.4, we can see that this version doesn't fall too far behind the original version in Table 20.6, having an average profit per trade only some 5 percent lower and a much higher risk–reward ratio than the version in Table 21.4.

The stop-loss version of the Harris 3L-R pattern variation, in Table 21.10, is a good example of a system–filter combination that boosts the profit factor despite a

TABLE 21.8

TABLE 21.8

Meander System Using Relative-strength Bands as Filter

	Meander system, V.1.0: 1.8 ATR stop loss, 3 ATR profit target, 8 bars max. trade length				PercProf: 76.00	
	Trades	**PercWin**	**NetProfit**	**AvgProfit**	**ProfitStD**	**RiskRatio**
Average:	94.20	52.95	61,158.69	848.19		**Market**
St. Dev:	36.77	6.27	66,828.26	1,112.10	6,144.18	0.11
High:	130.97	59.22	127,986.95	1,960.29	6,992.38	**Portfolio**
Low:	57.43	46.67	(5,669.58)	(263.90)	(5,295.99)	0.76
	ProfitFactor	**RiskFactor**	**MaxDD**	**PercDD**	**PercTime**	**AvgLength**
Average:	1.39	0.16	39,925.46	29.14	24.06	8.23
St. Dev:	0.44	0.18	18,362.82	16.54	4.66	0.53
High:	1.83	0.35	58,288.28	45.68	28.71	8.76
Low:	0.95	(0.02)	21,562.64	12.59	19.40	7.70

general decrease of performance, compared to trading without the filter. In this case, the profit factor comes out to 1.52, compared to 1.38 in Table 20.7, while, for example, the risk–reward ratio is more than cut in half. The same goes for the trailing-stop version of the same system, in Table 21.11. Although, in this case, given that a small deterioration of performance because of the filter was expected, it's almost fair to say that the filter version of this system is doing better than its predecessor, in Table 20.8.

TABLE 21.9

Volume-weighted System Using Relative-strength Bands as Filter

	Volume-weighted average: 2.4 ATR trailing stop, 2 ATR profit target, 6 bars max. trade length				PercProf: 69.57	
	Trades	**PercWin**	**NetProfit**	**AvgProfit**	**ProfitStD**	**RiskRatio**
Average:	37.52	56.17	14,106.93	639.20		**Market**
St. Dev:	19.00	9.81	24,036.62	1,009.94	5,309.69	0.09
High:	56.52	65.97	38,143.55	1,649.15	5,948.89	**Portfolio**
Low:	18.52	46.36	(9,929.70)	(370.74)	(4,670.48)	0.63
	ProfitFactor	**RiskFactor**	**MaxDD**	**PercDD**	**PercTime**	**AvgLength**
Average:	1.36	0.12	25,606.39	20.93	7.49	6.18
St. Dev:	0.55	0.20	12,433.08	11.55	2.89	0.34
High:	1.91	0.32	38,039.47	32.48	10.38	6.53
Low:	0.80	(0.08)	13,173.31	9.38	4.60	5.84

TABLE 21.10

Harris 3L-R Pattern Variation Using Relative-strength Bands as Filter

	Harris 3L-R pattern variation: 0.4% stop loss, 3% profit target, 4 bars max. trade length				PercProf: 68.00	
	Trades	**PercWin**	**NetProfit**	**AvgProfit**	**ProfitStD**	**RiskRatio**
Average:	65.32	37.32	17,490.02	250.19		**Market**
St. Dev:	28.55	10.77	31,467.95	563.44	2,603.15	0.09
High:	93.87	48.09	48,957.97	813.63	2,853.34	**Portfolio**
Low:	36.77	26.54	(13,977.94)	(313.25)	(2,352.96)	0.44
	ProfitFactor	**RiskFactor**	**MaxDD**	**PercDD**	**PercTime**	**AvgLength**
Average:	1.52	0.25	17,136.27	14.77	5.86	2.78
St. Dev:	0.85	0.47	11,128.15	10.49	1.35	0.30
High:	2.37	0.72	28,264.42	25.27	7.20	3.09
Low:	0.67	(0.21)	6,008.13	4.28	4.51	2.48

The stop-loss version of the expert exits system using the relative-strength bands as a filter, in Table 21.12, also is a good example of a system–filter combination that increases performance enough on a few markets to increase the combined profit factor, but not enough to increase the average profit per trade to compensate for a decreased performance in many of the other markets. If we compare this version of the system to those in Table 20.9 and 21.6, we can see that

TABLE 21.11

Harris 3L-R Pattern with Trailing Stop Using Relative-strength Bands as Filter

	Harris 3L-R pattern variation: 2.7% trailing stop, 4.5% profit target, 5 bars max. trade length				PercProf: 64.00	
	Trades	**PercWin**	**NetProfit**	**AvgProfit**	**ProfitStD**	**RiskRatio**
Average:	63.40	46.02	19,020.12	307.22		**Market**
St. Dev:	26.95	8.53	34,674.05	570.95	3,096.72	0.10
High:	90.35	54.55	53,694.17	878.17	3,403.94	**Portfolio**
Low:	36.45	37.48	(15,653.93)	(263.73)	(2,789.50)	0.54
	ProfitFactor	**RiskFactor**	**MaxDD**	**PercDD**	**PercTime**	**AvgLength**
Average:	1.39	0.17	18,830.92	16.03	7.51	3.68
St. Dev:	0.63	0.29	10,629.65	10.14	2.14	0.83
High:	2.03	0.46	29,460.57	26.16	9.65	4.51
Low:	0.76	(0.11)	8,201.27	5.89	5.37	2.85

TABLE 21.12

Expert Exits System Using Relative-strength Bands as Filter

		Expert exits: 0.6% stop loss, 3.5% profit target, 3 bars max. trade length				PercProf: 88.00
	Trades	**PercWin**	**NetProfit**	**AvgProfit**	**ProfitStD**	**RiskRatio**
Average:	82.60	44.77	30,342.81	363.19		**Market**
St. Dev:	33.57	11.55	32,531.17	447.60	2,634.63	0.15
High:	116.17	56.33	62,873.98	810.79	2,997.82	**Portfolio**
Low:	49.03	33.22	(2,188.35)	(84.42)	(2,271.44)	0.81
	ProfitFactor	**RiskFactor**	**MaxDD**	**PercDD**	**PercTime**	**AvgLength**
Average:	1.66	0.29	16,355.26	14.12	6.71	2.47
St. Dev:	0.77	0.33	12,780.59	12.57	1.97	0.09
High:	2.43	0.62	29,135.84	26.69	8.69	2.56
Low:	0.88	(0.05)	3,574.67	1.56	4.74	2.37

despite the fact that this version has the highest profit factor, it still has the lowest average profit per trade and risk–reward ratio. A lower percentage of profitable markets traded also is an indication of the same problem: Namely, that it works very well on a few markets, but not so well in others, thus causing an overall deterioration of the performance.

ROTATION AS THE FILTER

Tables 21.13 and 21.14 (to be compared to Tables 20.2 and 20.4, respectively) show the trailing-stop versions of the hybrid and meander systems, respectively, using the rotation system as a filter. In both instances, these versions of the systems don't do as well as the originals, although the meander system isn't doing too badly, given the fact a slight depreciation of performance was to be expected. Again, the largest negative for the meander system is that it spends a little too much time in the market for optimal diversification possibilities. For the hybrid system, however, the situation looks less tantalizing. Just as the version of this system depicted in Table 21.7, this version, too, has lost approximately one-third of the value of its average trade and about two-thirds of its risk–reward ratio.

The performance summary for the trailing-stop version of the volume-weighted average system in Table 21.15 gives rise to another interesting observation: The same short-term system can behave very differently, only because the logic behind the stops and exits changes. If you look at Tables 21.4 and 21.9, they too represent the trailing-stop version of the system. The filter is the only difference among these three tables. What is interesting, however, is what is not shown

TABLE 21.13

Hybrid System Using Rotation as Filter

	Hybrid system No. 1: 1.2 ATR trailing stop, 3 ATR profit target, 6 bars max. trade length					PercProf: 66.67
	Trades	**PercWin**	**NetProfit**	**AvgProfit**	**ProfitStD**	**RiskRatio**
Average:	89.46	42.95	26,583.22	285.47		**Market**
St. Dev:	41.84	6.64	46,784.46	695.78	4,273.36	0.08
High:	131.30	49.59	73,367.68	981.25	4,558.83	**Portfolio**
Low:	47.62	36.31	(20,201.24)	(410.31)	(3,987.90)	0.41
	ProfitFactor	**RiskFactor**	**MaxDD**	**PercDD**	**PercTime**	**AvgLength**
Average:	1.34	0.16	30,883.59	24.18	13.78	4.98
St. Dev:	0.55	0.27	19,786.34	17.34	4.29	0.27
High:	1.89	0.43	50,669.94	41.53	18.07	5.25
Low:	0.79	(0.10)	11,097.25	6.84	9.49	4.71

in these tables: Namely, the terrible results produced by the stop-loss version of this system, no matter which filtering technique it was teamed up with.

For example, Table 21.15 shows that this version of the system has an average profit of close to $500 and a risk–reward ratio of 0.5. The stop-loss version, on the other hand (not shown), ended up with an average profit per trade of $176, even though it too had an average trade length of about six days and a risk–reward ratio as low as 0.18, which was the lowest one in the entire test.

TABLE 21.14

Meander System Using Rotation as Filter

	Meander system, V.1.0: 2.7 ATR trailing stop, 3.5 ATR profit target, 9 bars max. trade length					PercProf: 80.00
	Trades	**PercWin**	**NetProfit**	**AvgProfit**	**ProfitStD**	**RiskRatio**
Average:	71.36	51.78	39,375.24	707.74		**Market**
St. Dev:	37.07	6.15	48,763.34	1,048.08	6,188.83	0.09
High:	108.43	57.93	88,138.58	1,755.82	6,896.57	**Portfolio**
Low:	34.29	45.64	(9,388.10)	(340.33)	(5,481.08)	0.68
	ProfitFactor	**RiskFactor**	**MaxDD**	**PercDD**	**PercTime**	**AvgLength**
Average:	1.32	0.14	37,021.84	24.83	20.42	9.55
St. Dev:	0.45	0.17	16,271.10	11.64	6.79	0.68
High:	1.78	0.31	53,292.94	36.47	27.21	10.23
Low:	0.87	(0.04)	20,750.73	13.18	13.63	8.87

TABLE 21.15

Volume-weighted Averages System Using Rotation as Filter

Volume-weighted average: 2.4 ATR trailing stop, 2 ATR profit target, 6 bars max. trade length					PercProf: 65.22
	Trades	PercWin	NetProfit	AvgProfit	ProfitStD	RiskRatio
Average:	32.09	54.44	11,369.15	491.88		**Market**
St. Dev:	17.49	10.08	26,040.11	979.71	4,787.07	0.08
High:	49.58	64.52	37,409.26	1,471.59	5,278.95	**Portfolio**
Low:	14.59	44.37	(14,670.95)	(487.82)	(4,295.19)	0.50
	ProfitFactor	RiskFactor	MaxDD	PercDD	PercTime	AvgLength
Average:	1.43	0.15	20,580.19	17.79	6.45	6.24
St. Dev:	0.80	0.30	12,290.52	11.35	3.26	0.36
High:	2.23	0.45	32,870.71	29.13	9.71	6.60
Low:	0.62	(0.15)	8,289.68	6.44	3.19	5.88

The average profit per trade for the stop-loss version of the Harris 3L-R pattern variation isn't much to brag about either. The difference is, however, that this system spends less than three days in the market per trade, which makes its daily return much higher than for a system with the same average profit but more days in a trade. But even so, comparing Table 21.16 with Tables 20.7 and 21.10, it's easy to see that pairing the system with rotation as the filter has deteriorated

TABLE 21.16

Harris 3L-R Pattern Variation Using Rotation as Filter

Harris 3L-R pattern variation: 0.4% stop loss, 3% profit target, 4 bars max. trade length					PercProf: 68.00
	Trades	PercWin	NetProfit	AvgProfit	ProfitStD	RiskRatio
Average:	53.48	35.50	9,741.54	166.28		**Market**
St. Dev:	27.30	10.26	24,440.34	471.66	2,499.11	0.07
High:	80.78	45.77	34,181.88	637.93	2,665.39	**Portfolio**
Low:	26.18	25.24	(14,698.81)	(305.38)	(2,332.83)	0.35
	ProfitFactor	RiskFactor	MaxDD	PercDD	PercTime	AvgLength
Average:	1.39	0.19	15,278.38	13.86	4.66	2.77
St. Dev:	0.73	0.42	10,931.42	11.05	1.58	0.28
High:	2.12	0.61	26,209.79	24.92	6.24	3.05
Low:	0.66	(0.23)	4,346.96	2.81	3.08	2.49

performance quite a bit. Again, the risk–reward ratio is almost one-third the size of the original system, and the average profit per trade is cut in half. And by now, perhaps, the time spent in the market is a little too low to make the results reliable for real-life trading on unseen data.

Let's round off by looking at two more versions of the expert exits system. Table 21.17 shows the results for the stop-loss version of the system, to be compared with Tables 20.9, 21.6, and 21.12. This system has a very high profit factor, which means that it probably trades really well on a few markets. Unfortunately, the high profit factor also is accompanied by the lowest average profit per trade and risk–reward ratio for all stop-loss versions looked at in this test, although they're not as low as for the trailing-stop version in Table 21.18 (to be compared with Table 20.10). In both cases, however, the average profit per trade is still very good, given the short average trade length of these systems.

CHAPTER 22

Variables

Most of the time, when building a system, we talk about making the system robust, meaning it should be as little curve fitted as possible to increase its chances of holding up in the future as well as it has in the past or when developed. However, just using one word for this important consideration—the word *robust*— is not enough if we want to get a firm grip on how to go about increasing our chances for future success. If you ask me, I think there are at least three things we need to consider, all of which fit within the term robust, as we have used it so far. Instead of just talking about robustness, I would like to propose that we talk about robustness, stability, and consistency. Let's start with the term stability, which is a concept we've stressed throughout Part 3.

Stability means that the system should work equally as well, on average and over time, using several different variable settings. For example, if you use a nine-day moving average for a system, there is no way for you to find out in advance if you might have been better off with a 10-day average over a certain time period. If that would have been the case, your nine-day setting should not have worked that much worse, and definitely not have produced catastrophic results, whereas the 10-day setting would have shown a profit. In the long run and over several subperiods, it should not have mattered that much which of the two settings you would have gone with.

Another example is when the best variable setting, in hindsight, turned out to be way off from the one you used. In that case, the best setting might have resulted in a decent profit, but you suffered a rather severe drawdown. That drawdown should not, however, have been of such magnitude that it forced you out of the game. The best way to assure stability, as I have defined it here, is to make the system as broad in scope as possible, work with as few optimizable variables as possible (preferably more than three), and avoid aiming for the stars when it comes to the performance of the system. A small but steady average profit per trade, resulting in modest profit and risk factors and high risk–reward ratios, is the way to go.

All the analysis we did when looking for the optimal and on average best-working stops really was to assure stability. We did this using several surface charts, which helped us compare several input combinations with each other and find a combination that was surrounded by other combinations, that produced similar results, or at least not results that were catastrophically different.

A robust system is a system that works equally as well, on average and over time, on several different markets and market conditions. For example, if you use a nine-day moving average on Microsoft, you should be able to use a nine-day moving average on General Electric as well without running the risk of being ruined. Maybe a nine-day setting has worked much better on Microsoft historically, but you must test the system in such a way so that you can trust it on General Electric as well. At the very least, you should feel confident that if and when Microsoft starts to behave as General Electric has in the past, you should still be left with plenty of time to observe and correct.

The two markets might not always be profitable with this setting and General Electric might only be so under very special conditions (such as a prolonged bear market). But when these conditions do occur, you want to be prepared. The price you pay for being this prepared is to allow yourself to lose a little trading General Electric during normal conditions, and perhaps not make as much on Microsoft as you could have using the optimal setting for Microsoft, because the nine-day setting you're working with is the one that works best on average over several markets. The robustness of each system has been examined using the performance-summary tables throughout the book, especially when we also compared the average profit per trade with the risk–reward ratio.

But it's also fair to say that we looked at each system's *consistency*, or how well the system is likely to perform in several continuous and well-defined time periods, such as quarterly or yearly. It all depends on how you look at it. If you look at each series of trades on a specific market as only that, then you are evaluating robustness. But if you look at each series of trades without taking into consideration where and when they were produced, then you evaluate the system's consistency.

There also is another way to research and analyze consistency. Once you've decided on your basic entry and exit rules, and tested the system over several markets to make sure it works equally as well, on average, over several types of market conditions (uptrends, downtrends, low–high volatility periods, etc.), there is one more thing you can do to make sure the results aren't just a fluke. So far, a trading sequence has contained trades only from one market. In real life, however, a trading sequence over a certain period of time can hold trades from several markets. There is also no saying in what order these trades will occur.

Even if we assume that one or several trading sequences on different markets give an accurate picture of how the trades will be distributed in the future, in regard to the relative amount of winners and losers and all the shapes and forms they can take, there is still no saying that a certain-sized winner will be followed by a certain-sized loser, or that there won't be more than a certain number of losers in a row. In real-life trading on unknown data, anything can happen by pure chance.

To prepare for that, you need to take all the generated trades and scramble them around, then pick one trade at a time, at random, to create one or several new trading sequences, based on the original trades from one or several markets or systems. The reasoning behind this analysis is that if the system is robust and stable, it will continue to produce trades similar to those already generated, with the only significant difference being the sequence of these trades and how they are positioned in relation to each other.

To collect all your trades in one bag, so to speak, you can use the following piece of TradeStation code, which simply exports the end result of each trade into a text file, where all trades will be stored in one column.

```
{Robustness export, with Normalize(True). Set RobustnessSwitch(True).}
Variable: RobustnessSwitch(True);
If RobustnessSwitch = True Then Begin
    Variables: RobNameLength(0), RobFileString(""), ResultString(""),
    EndTrade(0);
    If BarNumber = 1 Then Begin
        RobNameLength = StrLen(GetStrategyName) - 6;
        RobFileString = "D:\BookFiles\RobustTest-" + RightStr(GetStrategyName,
        RobNameLength) + "-" + RightStr(NumToStr(CurrentDate, 0), 4) + ".csv";
    End;
    EndTrade = TotalTrades;
    If EndTrade > EndTrade[1] Then Begin
        ResultString = NumToStr(PositionProfit(1), 2) + NewLine;
        FileAppend(RobFileString, ResultString);
    End;
End;
```

Once the trades are collected, they can be pasted into an Excel spreadsheet, which has been prepared for the scrambling and the random picking of all trades, to form as many new and randomly created trading sequences as you wish. Figures 22.1 to 22.3 show what parts of such a spreadsheet could look like. Let's look at Figure 22.1, which shows a small part of a subsheet named "Data." The trades used here have nothing to do with the systems tested in this book, and for this analysis

	A	B	C	D	E	F
3	-185.57		(185.57)		0	-795.29
4	-242.4		(242.40)		-2840.88	-4928.28
5	7.2		7.20		-4822.4	46583.49516
6	-859.2		(859.20)		-3082.82	8010.2
7	57.36		57.36		-1227.93	1267.84
8	432.59		432.59		-7536.1	19792.2
9	3586.66		3,586.66		-6336.07	-505.7
10	2436.28		2,436.28		4795.02	-11604.5

FIGURE 22.1

Excel spreadsheet showing randomly selected trades (data subsheet).

	A	B	C	D	E	F
1						
2		Number of trades:		1,998		1373.33039
3		St.devs winners:		2		22605.0824
4		St.devs losers:		4		46,583.50
5						(89,047.00)
6						

FIGURE 22.2

Excel spreadsheet showing randomly selected trades (tables subsheet).

	D	E	F	G	H
201					
202		1440.283352	-61.6869242	726.9829758	1488.548329
203		9065.038866	7486.97808	7141.925933	9728.677457
204		0.158883307	-0.008239229	0.101790887	0.153006237
205					
206		608554.6403	398902.2352	478001.5252	636332.3158
207		-320497.97	-411239.62	-332604.93	-338622.65
208		1.898778455	0.969999523	1.437145039	1.879178241
209					
210		81	85	83	88
211		40.5	42.5	41.5	44
212		113	110	112	111
213		0.507809827	-0.016500262	0.244801222	0.487943924
214					

FIGURE 22.3

Excel spreadsheet showing randomly selected trades (equations).

I will not go through all the systems tested, but simply describe the process so that you can do it yourself on your own systems, later on.

Column A, in Figure 22.1, contains all the historical and hypothetical trades, copied and pasted from the comma-separated text file they were exported to with the help of the *export* function. (Before you copy the trades into column A, remember to erase any old data you might have saved in column A from the last time you used the spreadsheet.)

Column C holds an adjusted value for each trade. Depending on whether the individual trade is a winner or loser, its outcome can be adjusted downwards or upwards, respectively, to minimize the effect of winners or losers that are deemed too large. This is a useful feature if you'd like to make sure the results aren't too dependent on any exceptionally large winners or losers (especially the winners). The specified levels can be set in cells D3 and D4 in the subsheet "Tables" (see Figure 22.2). If the system still produces profitable random trading sequences with the value in cell D3, in subsheet "Tables" set to one or two standard deviations, it's even more likely it will continue to work in the future, and perhaps even be better than expected, because the exceptionally large winners now come as happy surprises instead of necessary life savers.

The formula in cell C3 in Figure 22.1 looks like this:

$$=IF(A3>0,MIN(A3,Tables!F\$4),MAX(A3,Tables!F\$5))$$

Copy the formula in cell C3 all the way down to the last row containing a trade in column A.

Columns E to X hold randomly picked trades from column C.

The formula in cell E3 looks like this:

$$=INDEX(\$C:\$C,RANDBETWEEN(1,Tables!\$D\$2))$$

Copy it 20 columns to the right and 200 rows down, to create 20 random trading sequences with 200 trades each (or 200 random trading sequences with 20 trades each; you can look at it both ways) The formula will pick a trade at random from column C.

In Figure 22.2, the subsheet "Tables" contains a few basic values and formulas. The number of trades in columns A and C in subsheet "Data" is typed into cell D2. The number of standard deviations that should not be surpassed by the winners and losers are typed into cells D3 and D4. The average profit per trade, based on the data in column A, subsheet "Data," is calculated in cell F2 [formula: =AVERAGE(Data!A:A)]. The standard deviation of the data in column A, subsheet "Data," is calculated in cell F3 [formula: =STDEV(Data!A:A)]. The actual values not to be surpassed by the data in column C, subsheet "Data," are calculated in cells F4 and F5 [formulas: =F2+D3*F3 and =F2−D4*F3]. Note that these cell references go into cell C3 in subsheet "Data."

Figure 22.3 shows some of the equations needed to calculate most of the statistics that can be derived from this analysis. In this case, the data are calculated for 200 trades in 20 sequences. A similar set of calculations is done to calculate the statistics for 20 trades in 200 sequences. All the calculations in cells E202 to E213 are copied 20 cells to the right, to cells X202 to X213.

Cell E202 calculates the average profit per trade according to the formula =AVERAGE(E1:E200).

Cell E203 calculates the standard deviations of profits according to the formula =STDEV(E1:E200).

Cell E204 calculates the risk-adjusted return according to the formula =E202/E203.

Cell E206 calculates the gross profit according to the formula =SUMIF(E1:E200,">0",E1:E200).

Cell E207 calculates the gross loss according to the formula =SUMIF(E1:E200,"<0",E1:E200).

Cell E208 calculates the profit factor according to the formula =E206/ABS(E207).

Cell E210 calculates the number of winning trades according to the formula =COUNTIF(E1:E200,">0").

Cell E211 calculates the percentage of winning trades according to the formula =E210/200*100.

Cell E212 calculates the number of losing trades according to the formula =COUNTIF(E1:E200,"<0").

Cell E213 calculates the risk factor according to the formula =(E206+E207)/ABS(E207/E212*200).

With all the calculations in place we can set up a couple of tables resembling those we used during the initial system testing, based on the data derived by the *large export function*, described in Part 2. Table 22.1 shows that of all 200 trading sequences holding 20 trades each, used for this example, 75 percent tested profitably. The average profit per trade came out to 448.21, and the profit factor came out to 2.30.

Table 22.2, on the other hand, shows that of all 20 trading sequences, holding 200 trades each, 95 percent came out profitable. The average profit per trade came out to 448.21, and the profit factor came out to 1.77. Note that the average profit per trade is exactly the same in both tables, because we're using exactly the same randomly deducted trades. But even if we're using the exact same trades, a higher percentage of profitable sequences occurs in Table 22.2 than in Table 22.1. The standard deviations for the average profit per trade, and the profit and risk factors also are much lower in Table 22.2. How can this be? The answer lies in the

TABLE 22.1

All 200 Trading Sequences Holding 20 Trades Each

| | 20 trades, 200 sequences | | | PercProf: 75.00 |
	Trades	**NetProfit**	**AvgProfit**	**ProfitStD**	**RiskRatio**
Average:	20.00	8,964.21	448.21		**Market**
St. Dev:		12,829.55	641.48	2,734.62	0.14
High:		21,793.76	1,089.69	3,182.83	**Portfolio**
Low:		(3,865.35)	(193.27)	(2,286.41)	0.70
	PercWin	**ProfitFactor**	**RiskFactor**	**MaxDD**	**FlatTime**
Average:	50.38	2.30	0.50	7,284.10	10.31
St. Dev:	11.91	1.97	0.72	4,359.14	5.36
High:	62.29	4.26	1.22	11,643.24	15.66
Low:	38.46	0.33	(0.22)	2,924.96	4.95

number of trades in each sequence. The more trades used for the calculations, the more sure we can be that the calculated averages are close and accurate estimates of the true averages, and the more trades used, the closer each trading sequence will be to the averages for that amount of trades.

Figure 22.4 shows how the equity can vary over 20 randomly picked trades for 200 different trading sequences. Basically, the end result can be all over the place, and although the expected net profit over one sequence is $8,964, it can eas-

TABLE 22.2

All 20 Trading Sequences Holding 200 Trades Each

| | 200 trades, 20 sequences | | | PercProf: 95.00 |
	Trades	**NetProfit**	**AvgProfit**	**ProfitStD**	**RiskRatio**
Average:	200.00	89,642.05	448.21		**Market**
St. Dev:		44,490.38	222.45	2,906.93	0.15
High:		134,132.44	670.66	3,355.14	**Portfolio**
Low:		45,151.67	225.76	(2,458.72)	2.01
	PercWin	**ProfitFactor**	**RiskFactor**	**MaxDD**	**FlatTime**
Average:	50.38	1.77	0.37	22,625.23	60.70
St. Dev:	4.54	0.45	0.20	8,068.98	29.93
High:	54.92	2.22	0.57	30,694.20	90.63
Low:	45.83	1.32	0.17	14,556.25	30.77

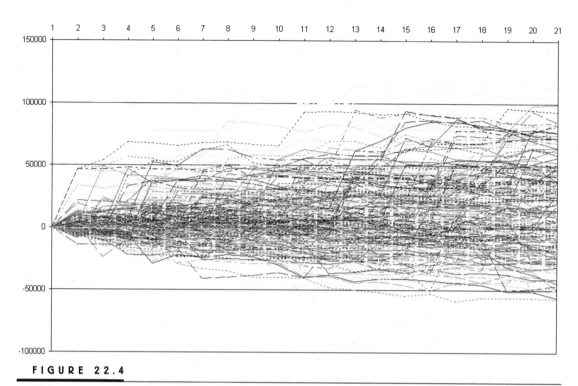

FIGURE 22.4

Equity variation over the randomly picked trades.

ily vary between a profit of $100,000 and a loss of $50,000. Most likely, however, you will end up somewhere in the interval plus/minus one standard deviation away from the mean, which should hold approximately 68 percent of all outcomes. But what happens if one trading sequence ends up with a loss of close to $50,000? Is that an indication that the loss will be $100,000 after two trading sequences?

No, it is not. It can happen, but it is unlikely that we will lose as much a second time. To understand why this is, we need to remember that two trading sequences of 20 trades each also equal one trading sequence of forty trades, and that the more trades in a sequence, the closer its average profit per trade will be to the true average profit for the system over an infinite number of trades. Of course, there are no guarantees and a system can simply cease to work at any time, but as long as the system delivers results within its statistical confines, no such conclusions can be made.

Figure 22.5 shows one trading sequence that shows a loss of close to $75,000 after about 40 trades. However, even this initially really bad sequence eventually turned around to end up with a final profit very close to the estimated average. Note that if you start to trade this system today, you can expect to make approximately $175,000 over 200 trades. But if after 200 trades your net profit is only

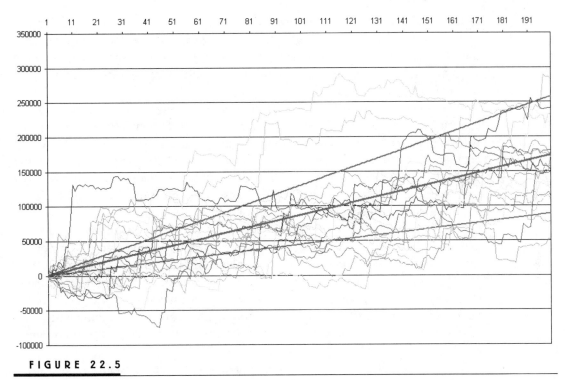

FIGURE 22.5

Loss of close to $75,000.

$100,000, which is just above the lower one-standard-deviation boundary, there is nothing wrong with the system. It just so happened that you caught a sequence of trades with a lower average profit per trade than could have been expected from the historical estimate, based on 20 such sequences.

In fact, more than every third trading sequence will produce a profit between the average expected profit and its lower one-standard-deviation boundary, and about every fifth trading sequence will produce a profit that is lower still. And every so often (perhaps every 50th sequence or so) there will even be a loss. Also, the fewer the trades used to calculate the average profit per trade, the more likely it is that that average is negative. Figure 22.5 shows that still plenty of trading sequences are left in negative territory after 50 trades or so, and that it takes some 120 trades before the last sequence turns positive. The longer the sequence, however, the closer each sequence will be to the estimated average profit.

Similarly, a system that produces better than expected results (as indicated by the estimated average profit per trade) still works as it should: you just happened to luck out with a couple of extraordinarily good trades over a period. The most dangerous thing you could do at this point is to increase your positions in the belief that the system has become more robust and reliable. Look at the two sequences in Figure 22.5 that have the best results after some 110 trades. They both start to move downward from there to get closer to the estimated average profit over 200 trades. What if you had decided to double your positions for these trading sequences after 110 trades? The drawdowns would have been twice as steep as they now appear in Figure 22.5.

So the question still remains: If the final outcome for one trading sequence can vary this much with the system still working as it should, how do we decide when a system's inherent characteristics change to the better or worse? (A system changing to the better, or seemingly better, without us knowing is not a good thing either. The very same reasons that now make us richer than trolls could be what ruin us in the end, because we haven't adjusted the position size of the trades to accommodate for the new circumstances.)

This is a very difficult question to answer, and I feel I really don't have the experience to do it. Nonetheless, I would say that if a system performs way out of what could be expected (say more than two standard deviations away from the estimated mean) over at least two reasonable, long sequences of trades, it's reasonable to assume that something has changed so that the estimated statistics can no longer be trusted. It may be that you did something wrong from the beginning when constructing the system, or the assumptions on which the system is based no longer are valid.

Unfortunately, however, I have a gut feeling that most systems get discarded way before this happens and while the system is still working as it should, simply because the trader had no idea that the system could produce the type of drawdown numbers it eventually did. Hence, he starts trading it way undercapitalized. Analyzing the systems for consistency could help you get a better feel for what types of drawdowns your systems are most likely to generate, given the statistical distribution of the trades. With this information at hand, you should not have to be forced out of the game, despite a good system but because of lack of capital.

CHAPTER 23

Evaluating Stops and Exits

Part 3 started with a discussion of the distribution of the trades and how it changes with alterations to the stop and exit levels of the system. Altering the stops and exits ever so slightly can alter the characteristics and results of a system very drastically. Therefore, to be prudent, one should really start the entire research process anew for every little change made to the system. Also, because even the smallest of changes will add or wash away trades, alter flat times, and move drawdown periods around, one cannot use historical real-life trades and performance summaries as a base for this type of analysis.

Ideally, a trade should only have two possible outcomes: A loser of a specific size or a winner of a specific size. This is almost never the case, and the number of possible outcomes still is infinite, which produces the money management consequences we deal with in Part 4. Nonetheless, making a serious effort to keep the number of possible outcomes as low as possible is one of the hallmarks of a good trader. In fact, this analysis showed that a normal distribution of the trades is a sign of sloppy trading, in which we let the trades behave as they wish once we have entered the market. It is not the distribution of the individual trades that should be normal, it is the monthly results, or the results over several similar time frames, that should be normal.

We also learned that the most important thing isn't to increase the value of the average trade all by itself, but rather to increase it in relation to the standard deviation of all trades. As long as the average profit per trade remains large enough to make trading worthwhile, it could be a good thing to lower the average profit per trade as long as the insecurity of the outcome is lowered to a larger degree. If we manage to do this, we can increase the dollar returns simply by putting on larger positions, possible thanks to the increased security of the outcome.

To limit the possible outcomes for a trade, we need to think about the reasons to exit the trade. Basically, there are four different reasons why we should no longer stay in a trade. Of the four reasons to exit, two reasons are price-based and two are time-based. Many times the reasons and methods intertwine, which makes it all the more important to know what you're doing.

The most obvious reason to exit is to limit a loss in a trade that goes against us. For most traders this is easier said than done, and many times when we are limiting a loss, we are doing so at the least opportune moment. It is important that the loss is taken immediately and where it's supposed to be taken according to the strategy rules, so that we can free up the money quickly, put it to use elsewhere, and leave all bad trades behind us as quickly as possible. Remember that the most important thing isn't to have as many winning trades as possible, but rather as many winning time periods as possible. The best way to achieve that is to cut the losers as soon as possible, so that we are left with as much time and money as possible to achieve that goal for each time period.

The second reason to exit is to make the most out of a favorable move and take a profit. Basically, there are two ways to lock in a profit. The most straightforward method is to take the profit with a limit order as soon as it reaches a predefined level. This is a good way to keep the standard deviations of the outcomes to a minimum. If, in hindsight, it turned out you exited the market prematurely, you are always free to enter again in this or any other market. The second way to lock in a profit is to apply a trailing stop slightly below the current price (above for a short trade). In this way you give back some of the open profit, but you also give the trade a chance to capture that part of the move a profit target might have kept you out of.

The third reason to exit is after it is fair to assume the market has discounted the reason that triggered the trade in the first place. To measure this, we need to get a feel for both the time horizon and magnitude of the moves the system is most suited to capture. To calculate an exact number of bars to stay in a trade can be very difficult, and it will alter depending on what type of system you have. However, a rule of thumb is that a short-term system should not stay in a trade any longer than the amount of historical data going into the system calculations to trigger the move.

For example, if your system makes use of five days of historical data to calculate the pattern or indicator that triggers the entry, in essence what you have told yourself is that, in this particular case, the market has a memory of five days—looking further back in time won't improve the results for this entry technique. Therefore, if the market has a five-day memory going into the trade, it only makes sense it should have a five-day memory leading out of the trade, on average and over a large number of trades.

A profit target also could be used as an end-of-event exit. This happens when the anticipated magnitude of the move is reached before the maximum allowed trade length. In that case, it is not unlikely that the market has overextended itself in the short run, and it could be a good idea to take a profit with a limit order, and then enter anew after the market has retraced parts of that move.

The fourth reason is that the money invested in the trade could be put to better use elsewhere, no matter the performance of this trade. Obviously this is the case with a trade that goes against us, but this also could be a good reason to exit a winner, if you also monitor and trade several other markets and systems. If you're in a slow winner, this could be a difficult exit to execute, but remember that your research has told you what to expect from a trade. While there is no way to know how a future trade will develop, at least you have a clear picture of what you want out of it, and while a future trade still has to prove itself, a slow trade already has proved itself to be just that—a slow trade.

The most straightforward way to calculate where to place your stops and exits is to calculate the most opportune percentage distances from the entry price. The major advantage with this method is that it doesn't add any new optimizeable variables that complicate the rulings for the system and detract from the robustness and reliability when traded on future data.

The major disadvantage is that it is rather static, which will alter its performance with the volatility of the market. If the volatility is higher than average, the system will have you stopped out with a loss more often than necessary, while at the same time taking profits too soon, given the potential of the move as induced by the increased volatility. If the volatility is lower than average, the profits will be smaller than normal and more trades will be stopped out by the time-based stops.

To come to grips with the volatility changes over time, another way to calculate where to place the stops and exits is to use the average true range method. Using this method, you always let the trade move with or against you with a pre-specified number of true ranges. Because the true ranges will vary in size with the volatility of the market, so will the distance between the entry price and the exit points.

The major disadvantage with this method is that it needs historical data for the true-range calculations, which complicates the system and makes it less robust. You can work around this by setting the lookback period for the true range equal to either the lookback period for the rest of the indicator or pattern, or to the maximum allowed trade length. Personally, I prefer to go with the maximum allowed trade length, and then test the trade length and the lookback period for the true range simultaneously. As already mentioned, the maximum allowed trade length shouldn't differ that much from the lookback period for the indicator or pattern, anyway.

The best way to find the most optimal input-variable combinations is to analyze them using a surface chart, in which the color of the chart indicates the value of the output. Once you've learned to interpret the information in a surface chart, it becomes a breeze to find the values for the input variables that suit you and the system best. Usually I test the system for three input variables at a time.

For example, for this book I tested the stop-loss and profit target distances together with the maximum allowed trade length. I then compared the variables two at a time, disregarding the third variable for the moment. In this way, I got 10 different test runs per variable combination and market tested. When looking at the surface chart, I always try to come up with the variable combination that seems to work best on average, over all test runs and markets tested.

An alternative way is to test for only two variables at a time and substitute for the third variable a random-number generator that will produce a unique sequence of trades each time you run the system through the market. The expert exits system was developed this way for the June 2002 issue of *Active Trader* magazine. Be forewarned, however, that this method is very time consuming.

Using surface charts to examine several different stop and exit levels for five of our systems, it turned out that the average true range concept worked best for most systems. Interestingly, however, the percentage concept, which worked best for the most short-term systems, also happened to work the best on both sides of the market (both long and short trades).

The testing was done on both sides of the market for all systems tested, although in the end we would only apply it to the long side. Similarly, the exits were applied to all systems before the relative strength filters were added. We did this because I believe that the more market conditions and circumstances that are allowed to influence the final parameter setting, the more robust and reliable the system will be when traded on future data.

Another way might have been first to apply the filters and then test only the side of the markets that would be traded. This would probably have boosted the profits considerably on the historical data, as the system would have been more curve fitted to those exact conditions. The drawback would have been that the system would have been less robust and reliable for real-life trading in the future, where everything still can happen.

While testing the stops and exits, we found several examples of how changing from a stop loss to a profit target resulted in completely different characteristics for a system. This is because a system often produces a series of entry signals that might or might not result in a trade, depending on if we're in a trade already or not. Altering the way we exit the market also alters which signals will be available to enter on, which in turn will alter the most optimal exit levels and trade lengths, and so on. These differences were further exaggerated when adding the three systems saved for filtering, in Chapter 21.

The research in Chapter 21 also revealed that using a relative-strength filter doesn't necessarily add to the bottom line and the robustness of the combined strategy. We identified several reasons. One of these reasons was that trading the stock that seems to be the strongest both in the intermediate-term and short-term isn't necessarily a good idea. Instead, it could be a better idea to trade the weakest stock in a group of stocks as long as the general trend is in the direction of the anticipated trade. The reason behind this logic is that the weakest stock is more prone to an explosive move in the direction of the anticipated trade, to catch up with the others.

We ended Part 3 by discussing an additional research method to gain further confidence in the system. This method took all the trades produced by a system and scrambled them around, before it put together several random trading sequences, with new trading sequences made up of the historical trades. Using this method, we examined a system for its consistency and likelihood for producing profitable trading sequences in the future, given that the profits and losses remain within the statistical confines identified by the historical testing, but with the actual order between the trades unknown.

PART FOUR

Money Management

Ironically, chances are that the less sure a trader is that the next trade will be a winner, the better the trading strategy or the system. It sounds strange, but there are two ways to think about this paradox so that it makes sense.

One way is to assume that the markets are as close to random as they possibly can be. Therefore, a strategy that works in a close-to-random environment needs to be robust enough to maximize the potential of any nonrandom market behavior when it appears, while still keeping you in the game when the market is random. In other words, the best you can hope for is a strategy that can turn a profit under the worst of long-term circumstances (randomness).

Hence, most trades signaled by a system, whether they turn out to be winners or losers, are because of random market moves; only a few trades, scattered among all the signaled trades, are actually because of the type of nonrandomness the system tries to catch. The trick is to make the most of the latter category of trades while breaking even or just barely producing a profit on all others. Unfortunately, however, there is no way to distinguish one type of trade from the other beforehand.

The second way is to look at the system as a tool with which we can soak up and make use of the information the market gives us. If we were only trading on random noise, the trades and the result would be random. If we were trading on sure deterministic facts, the outcome of all trades would be certain. When we make use of the information the market gives us, we're taking the information from the market and planting it into the system or trading model. The more information we take from the market, the less information is left to make use of, up until the point there is only random market noise left. The more random noise is left in relation to unused information, the closer to random the strategy will behave, which ties back to our first way of thinking.

Traders instinctively want to avoid randomness, but this should not be the case. Say you have discovered that your trading system, on average, produces two winners for every three trades. This may be good news, but it does not mean the strategy will always produce two winners followed by one loser, followed by two winners, and so on.

To think that the strategy will follow a distinct pattern of wins and losses is dangerous, because this assumption may cause you to risk too much on a losing trade and not enough on a winning trade, when the pattern that you thought existed breaks down. Therefore, the more difficult it is to predict the outcomes of two or more consecutive trades, the better the system will perform, because it will not be based on potentially erroneous assumptions about the outcomes of any particular trades.

Following these lines of thinking, you can decrease your dependence on luck by not only making sure your strategy is highly likely to produce winners (i.e., do a good job of profiting from those rare nonrandom market moves and situations that the system is designed to catch), but also, strange as it might sound, by making sure you still can't predict the outcome of the next trade.

When it comes to the reliance on luck, both profitable and unprofitable traders can be divided into smaller subgroups: those who are skilled and those who are just plain lucky. If you truly care about your trading results, you need to know how much of your profits depend on pure luck. Certainly, every active trader is lucky to a certain extent, because the truth is there's always a chance—however slim—that the market will blow you out completely.

The trick is to make the likelihood for this as small as possible by keeping your skill–luck ratio as large as possible. If you've managed to make a good living from trading, how do you know you couldn't have done even better with a little more knowledge or skill? Or, if you currently are in a losing streak, is it your high skill level that keeps you from losing even bigger during this dry spell, or just dumb luck that is keeping you down?

CHAPTER 24

The Kelly Formula

Adhering to your stops and exit signals is of paramount importance in becoming a skillful trader. If for nothing else, even though you can't make sure of the outcome of the next trade, you can decide what the maximum loss will be if it turns out to be a loser by always risking the same relative amount on each trade. The word *relative* is used to indicate that the amount risked should be constant, relative to the available capital, so that when your account grows, you will risk more in dollar terms to keep a constant risk per trade in percentage terms.

The amount risked should stay constant because if there is no way of knowing the outcome of the next trade, the best we can do is risk the same amount all the time, on all the trades. To state that another way, if an obvious relationship existed between the outcomes of all trades, you should vary the bet size based on whether the next trade would likely be a winner or a loser. However, because we already know that there is no such relationship between trades for a good system, the best we can do is risk the same amount all the time.

Also, even if there were such an historical relationship in the past, you are probably still better off risking the same amount for all trades, as this relationship may or may not continue to exist in the future. If it doesn't, you again run the risk of risking too much at some times and too little at others, which not only will result in a slower than optimal equity growth but also an increased likelihood of going broke.

Therefore, much of the balance between skill and luck is captured in how you determine the size of each trade. One way to enhance your performance in this area is to use the Kelly formula, which calculates how much capital should be risked on each trade. However, the Kelly formula is only applicable to strategies where every winner is the same size and every loser is the same size—hardly the case in actual trading. Therefore, it should only be used as an approximate value that should not be exceeded in trading. The Kelly formula looks like this:

$$K = W - (1 - W) / R$$

Where:

K = Kelly value
W = Historical winning percentage
R = Historical average win–loss ratio

To begin using the formula, we need to collect some information. Suppose your five most recent trades ended with a win of 5 percent, a loss of 2, a win of 3, a win of 1, and a loss of 6, then:

The average value of your winning trades is 3 percent [(5 + 3 + 1) / 3].
The average value of your losing trades is 4 percent [(2 + 6) /2].
The average win–loss ratio is 0.75 (3 / 4).
The likelihood for a winning trade is 0.6 (3 / 5).
The likelihood for a losing trade is 0.4 (1 − 0.6).

With W equal to 0.6 and R equal to 0.75 (3 / 4), K equals 0.067 [0.6 − (1 − 0.6) / 0.75]. Thus, to make the most of your ability to pick good entry and exit points, in this particular case no more than 6.7 percent of your trading capital should be risked on each trade.

Once you know how much of your total equity to risk, you also can calculate how many shares or contracts to buy to take on that risk and how much of your available equity you should put toward a particular trade. To do this, you will need a predetermined stop loss per share or contract. For example, say you're considering a stock that currently trades at $50, and its chart shows $46 to be a good stop-loss point. If you currently have $100,000 of trading capital, here's how to figure how much you can trade:

Calculate the amount to risk as the Kelly value times the account size (0.067 * 100,000 = $6,700). With a stop loss of 4 points, determine how many shares you can buy as the amount to risk divided by the stop-loss distance (6,700 / 4 = 1,675). Calculate the amount of your capital that needs to go towards this trade as the stock price times the number of shares to buy (50 * 1,675 = $83,759).

The larger K is, the more money you can put into one trade; the smaller K is, the less money you should put into one trade. Also, the tighter the stop loss, the more of your capital you need to put into one trade; the wider the stop loss, the less capital you need to put into one trade. For example, if the stop loss were only two points away from the entry, then the Kelly formula suggests you should buy 3,350 (6,700 / 3) shares for a total value of $167,500 (3,350 * 50), which you cannot do because you only have a $100,000. Or, if the K value equals 0.03, the amount to risk should be $3,000 (0.03 * 100,000), and the number of shares to buy would be 750 (3,000 / 4), for a total value of $37,500 (750 * 50).

Therefore, the larger K is, the looser the stop loss should be, so that the suggested amount to trade won't exceed the available capital, or your maximum allotted (relative) amount for one trade. The looser the stop loss, the larger K can be without making you exceed your available capital. Again, the word *relative* is within parentheses to indicate that the maximum allotted amount can vary with the total equity. Another hallmark of a skillful trader is the ability to find the right balance between these two variables, so that he can be in the desired number of positions simultaneously.

In the first example, we can only be in one trade at a time, given the amount of money we have at hand [Integer(100,000 / 83,759) = 1]. In the second example, we can't trade at all [Integer(100,000 / 167,500) = 0]. In the third example, we can be in two trades at a time [Integer(100,000 / 37,500) = 2]. Obviously, as short-term system traders, we would like to be in at least 10 to 20 trades simultaneously. Thus, the distance between the stop loss and the entry price must be very large, and the more positions we want to be in simultaneously, or the less we want to risk per trade, the larger this distance should be. We will learn how to deal with this in a little while, given that we already have decided on where to place our stops in Part 3.

However, even armed with the knowledge of the system's K value, there is no guarantee that we won't be extremely unlucky in the future. Figure 24.1 shows the results from 100 trade simulations using the winning and losing percentages and average trade values we have worked with so far. The y-axis represents the profit or loss (the starting balance was set to 100). A large number of these simulations end up as losing propositions, even though we're risking 6.7 percent of available equity with a 60 percent chance of success. However, where and when these winning and losing trades happen, which is determined randomly, still can determine the overall profitability.

In the case of Figure 24.1, the best run produces an average profit per trade of $426, while the worst run produces an average loss of 96 cents per trade, with 25 percent of all test runs ending up in negative territory. The risk–reward ratio, calculated as the average profit per trade produced by all 100 test runs divided by the standard deviation of all average profits, comes out to 0.41 (28.6 / 69.8), which is not particularly good. (As already discussed earlier, preferably this value should be above one.)

Obviously, a strategy needs to be better than this to keep the bad-luck consequences to a minimum. Let's see what happens if we increase the win–loss ratio in Figure 24.1 from 0.75 to 0.8 (for example, by trading a strategy with an average winner of 4 points and an average loser of 5 points), which also increases the K value to 0.1. Figure 24.2 shows the outcome of 100 such simulations.

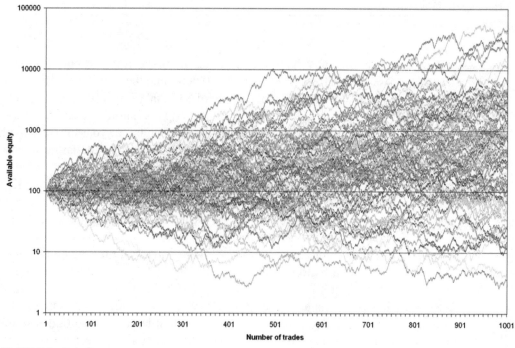

FIGURE 24.1

Kelly formula applied to 100 trades.

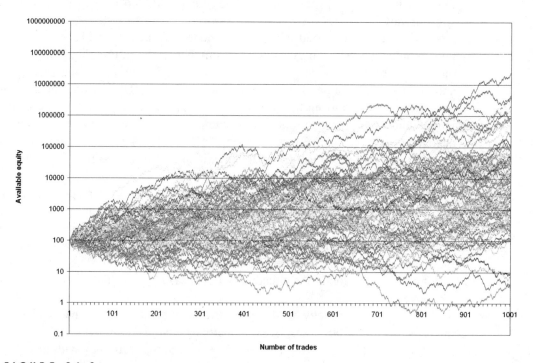

FIGURE 24.2

Kelly formula using increased win-loss ratio.

B	C	D	E	F	G	H	I	J	K	L	M
		Win / loss	Perc. win	K value		Max	Min	Average	stdev	Ratio	above 0
0.067		0.75	0.60	0.067		1,099.95	(0.90)	39.38	148.84	0.26	90.00
100	100	100	100	100	100	100	100	100	100	100	100
93.3	93.3	105.025	105.025	93.3	93.3	105.025	105.025	93.3	105.025	105.025	93.3
97.98833	97.98833	97.98833	110.3025	97.98833	97.98833	110.3025	110.3025	87.0489	110.3025	97.98833	97.98833
102.9122	91.42311	102.9122	115.8452	102.9122	91.42311	102.9122	115.8452	91.42311	115.8452	102.9122	91.42311
108.0836	96.01712	96.01712	108.0836	108.0836	96.01712	108.0836	108.0836	85.29776	108.0836	108.0836	96.01712
113.5148	89.58397	100.842	113.5148	100.842	100.842	100.842	100.842	79.58281	113.5148	113.5148	89.58397
105.9093	94.08557	94.08557	105.9093	94.08557	105.9093	105.9093	94.08557	83.58185	119.2189	119.2189	94.08557

FIGURE 24.3

Spreadsheet data for Kelly formula in Figures 24.1 and 24.2.

These results look much better, with the best run producing an average profit per trade of $1,064,251, while the worst run produces an average loss of 97 cents per trade. Even in this case, however, a slight (4 percent) chance exists that the strategy will end up in negative territory. The charts in Figures 24.1 and 24.2 were produced with a simple spreadsheet, of which you can see a small part in Figure 24.3.

To recreate the spreadsheet in Figure 24.3, type in the following formulas and values:

In cell D3: Type in the ratio between the average winner and average loser.

In cell E3: Type in the percentage of winning trades.

In cell F3: Type in the formula $=E3-(1-E3)/D3$.

In cells B6 to CW6: Type in the value 100.

In cell B7: Type in the formula $=IF(RAND()<=\$E\$3,1+\$B\$3*\$D\$3,1-\$B\$3)*B6$, and drag and fill it into all cells down to CW1006.

In cell B1008: Type in the formula $=(B1006-100)/100$, and drag and fill it into all cells to CW1008.

In cell H3: Type in the formula $=MAX(B1008:CW1008)$.

In cell I3: Type in the formula $=MIN(B1008:CW1008)$.

In cell J3: Type in the formula $=AVERAGE(B1008:CW1008)$.

In cell K3: Type in the formula $=STDEV(B1008:CW1008)$.

In cell L3: Type in the formula $=J3/K3$.

In cell M3: Type in the formula $=COUNTIF(B1008:CW1008,">0")$.

In cell B3: Type in the value in cell F3.

Ideally, the better a strategy is at picking tops and bottoms, the more you should risk per trade. However, the more you risk per trade, the more you stand to lose when that inevitable series of bad trades strikes. And the higher the K, the shorter that series of bad trades needs to be to wipe you out.

The previous examples also assume that what held true in the past also will hold true in the future. Most likely, though, that will not be the case. Extrapolating a little from Murphy's Law, a strategy will most likely not work as well in the future as it has in the past or during testing. Therefore, one should always trade at a K value considerably lower than what is calculated as ideal to maximize the equity. Although this might mean a less-than-optimal equity growth, it also means a higher likelihood of not being thrown out of the game. In other words, you're decreasing the role of luck—good and bad—in your trading.

For example, with the help of the spreadsheet you can try different K values higher or lower than the one calculated. If you do, you will find that trading at a K value higher than the calculated K might result in a few test runs producing higher returns, but also that more test runs will end up with a loss. Similarly, trading at a K value lower than the calculated K will result in a slower equity growth for most test runs, but also in more runs that are profitable.

In the extreme example, if you risk everything you have on each trade, it will only take one loser to wipe you out completely. Even if you don't risk everything on each trade, a series of bad trades, where you've risked too much, can still force you out of the game. On the other hand, being too conservative won't make the most out of a good trading strategy. Generally speaking, the relationships are as follows:

Risking too little on each trade results in small losses and shallow drawdowns, but the equally small profits will keep you in the drawdowns for a long time and the overall equity growth will be slow. When risking too much on each trade, the losses will be large and the drawdowns deep, but the large winners will help you get out of them rather quickly and the overall equity growth will be fast. The paradox is that the larger the drawdowns you allow, the faster the equity growth. But the larger the drawdowns allowed, the larger the likelihood to go bust. Also, the larger the drawdowns, the more erratic your equity curve, the riskier the trading in general terms, as measured by the risk–reward ratio. Thus, we need to balance the steepness of the equity curve with its smoothness so that the steeper the better and the smoother the better. We do this by finding the proper amount to risk, which will govern the size (both in magnitude and time) of the drawdowns. One way to do this is to use the Kelly formula, and not trade past the calculated K value.

As already mentioned, the major flaw of the Kelly formula is that it assumes two outcomes only—a winner of a certain magnitude and a loser of a certain magnitude. Trading, with its virtually infinite number of potential outcomes per trade, is not such a simple game, however. The Kelly formula should, therefore, be used only for initial research and experimentation. For a better approximation of the optimal trade size, one should determine what is popularly known as the optimal *f*, which requires a slightly more complex calculation.

CHAPTER 25

Fixed Fractional Trading

Because winners and losers obviously aren't always the same size, we need to find a formula that can account for varied trade outcomes. One such formula is the formula for optimal f, which was popularized by Ralph Vince in his book *Portfolio Management Formulas: Mathematical Trading Methods for the Futures, Options, and Stock Markets* (John Wiley & Sons, 1990). This formula is designed to maximize equity growth by making the outcome of each trade dependent on the amount you are willing to risk in relation to the risk per share traded and the worst historical losing trade.

The formula works with compounded returns and the fixed fraction of your capital to risk per trade that produces the highest compounded return, which Ralph Vince named terminal wealth relative (TWR) or optimal f. Because the returns are compounded, TWR is calculated by multiplying the percentage returns from each individual trade, so that:

$$TWR = HPR1 * HPR2 * HPR3 * \ldots * HPRi$$

Where:

TWR = Terminal wealth relative, expressed as the percentage compounded return over a trading sequence.

HPR_n = The holding period return for trade n, expressed as a percentage of your total equity going into the trade.

That is, the HPR_n is the percentage profit for trade n, for a given fraction (f) risked per trade, with the same fraction for all trades within the same test run or sequence of trades. Altering the fraction to risk of the available equity will produce different HPRs and consequently different TWRs for different test runs or trading sequences. To calculate the HPR_n, Ralph Vince suggested the following formula:

$$HPR_n = 1 + f * (Profit_n / WCS)$$

Where:

f = the fixed fraction of your capital to risk in all trades.

$Profit_n$ = The profit or loss from trade n in dollars on a constant-shares-invested basis.

WCS = The historical worst-case scenario in dollars on a constant-shares-invested basis (expressed as a positive number).

According to the terminology used by Ralph Vince, the value of f that produces the highest TWR is the called the optimal f. The best way to find optimal f is to build a spreadsheet in which the results are dependent on f. In other words, the spreadsheet should be designed so that typing in a new value for f changes the values in all other cells. This is how a recommended risk level is determined for the Trading Systems Lab in *Active Trader* magazine.

Figure 25.1 shows a small part of such a spreadsheet that allows you to test either a random or an actual trading sequence of 100 trades. The result from each trade is typed or imported into cells B13 to B112. If you use a random series just

	A	B	C	D	E	F	G	H	I	J	K	L	M
1													
2					Stop loss (%)		2.00						
3					Largest winner (%)		6.00						
4					Percent winners		32.00						
5													
6					Max TWR		1.65	Total return (%)		64.66			
7					Optimal f (%)		10.50						
8					GM		1.0050	Average trade (%)		0.50			
9													
10													
11				f (%)	0.0	0.5	1.0	1.5	2.0	2.5	3.0	3.5	4.0
12			0		1	1	1	1	1	1	1	1	1
13		(0.81)	1		1.0000	0.9980	0.9959	0.9939	0.9919	0.9898	0.9878	0.9857	0.9837
14		(0.25)	2		1.0000	0.9973	0.9947	0.9920	0.9894	0.9868	0.9841	0.9815	0.9788
15		(1.79)	3		1.0000	0.9929	0.9858	0.9787	0.9717	0.9647	0.9577	0.9508	0.9438
16		(1.61)	4		1.0000	0.9889	0.9779	0.9669	0.9561	0.9453	0.9346	0.9240	0.9135
17		(0.04)	5		1.0000	0.9888	0.9777	0.9667	0.9557	0.9448	0.9341	0.9234	0.9128
18		(0.15)	6		1.0000	0.9884	0.9769	0.9656	0.9543	0.9431	0.9319	0.9209	0.9100
19		(0.91)	7		1.0000	0.9862	0.9725	0.9590	0.9456	0.9323	0.9192	0.9063	0.8935
20		(1.28)	8		1.0000	0.9830	0.9663	0.9498	0.9335	0.9174	0.9016	0.8860	0.8706
21		(0.14)	9		1.0000	0.9827	0.9656	0.9488	0.9322	0.9158	0.8997	0.8838	0.8681

FIGURE 25.1

Spreadsheet data used to calculate optimal f.

to get a feel for how it works, you can change the largest winning and losing trades allowed and the desired percentage of profitable trades, in cells G2 to G4. To create a similar spreadsheet for yourself, type in the following formulas:

In cell G2: Type in the value of your largest loser in percent (in this case "2").

In cell G3: Type in the value of your largest winner in percent (in this case "6").

In cell G2: Type in the desired percentage of winning trades (in this case "32").

In cells E11 to GW11: Type in the value for f in percent, in steps of 0.5 percents, starting with zero in cell E11, ending with 100 in cell GW11.

In cells E12: Type in the value "1," and drag and fill it all the way to cell GW12.

In cell C12 to C112: Type in a number series, in steps of one, starting with zero in cell C12, ending with 100 in cell C112.

In cell B13: Type in the formula
=IF(RANDBETWEEN(1,100)<=G$4,RAND()*G$3,−RAND()*G$2), and drag and fill it into all cells down to B112. (This formula can be replaced by typed-in or imported results from real trades.)

In cell E13: Type in the formula =(1+($B13/$G$2)*(E$11/100))*E12, and drag and fill it into all cells to GW112.

In cell E113: Type in the formula =IF(E112=$G6,E11,0), and drag and fill it all the way to cell GW113.

In cell G6: Type in the formula =MAX(E112:GW112).

In cell G7: Type in the formula =SUM(E113:GW113).

In cell G8: Type in the formula =G6^(1/100).

In cell J6: Type in the formula =(G6-1)*100.

In cell J8: Type in the formula =(G8-1)*100.

Once this setup is created, you can recalculate the spreadsheet using random numbers by pressing the F9 button, or calculate the TWRs corresponding to each f, for a real or back-tested trading sequence. Figure 25.2 shows a chart for how TWR relates to f for such a random run, with the maximum allowed largest winner and loser and percent profitable trades according to the values in Figure 25.1. As you can see from Figures 25.1 and 25.2, the optimal f for this random series equals 10.5 percent, which means that to achieve the highest possible TWR, we should risk exactly 10.5 percent of our available equity in each trade. If we risk less than that, we won't optimize our profit potential, as will a risk of more than 10.5 percent. And if we risk as much as 25 percent of our available capital per trade, we won't make any money at all, but start losing it instead.

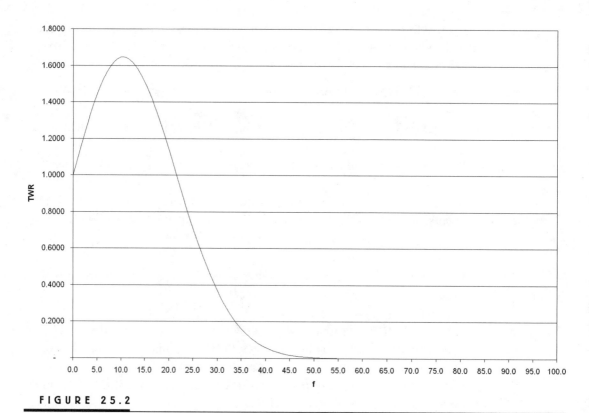

FIGURE 25.2

TWR relative to f in a random trading run.

Furthermore, even though we might not risk as much as 25 percent per trade, which assures that we will go broke eventually, we still run a larger risk of going broke if we risk slightly more than the optimal f, compared to risking slightly less than the optimal f. The more we risk, the larger the price swings—both good and bad—and the larger the swings, the greater the risk that one of the swings to come will be too large to handle. Figure 25.3 shows how the equity varies with different fs. As you can see, the lower the f, the smoother the equity curve and the smaller the drawdowns, but also the slower the equity growth. On the other hand, the larger the f, the faster the equity growth—up to a point—but also the deeper the drawdowns and the corresponding time it will take to recover from them.

A simple example can further explain the formulas for TWR and HPR. Assume that we already found optimal f to be 0.05, which means that we should risk 5 percent of our equity per trade. Suppose also that our worst historical loser was $10,000 and that we have two trades that each produced a profit of $5,000 on a constant-shares basis. In that case, each HPR comes out to 1.025 [1 + 0.05 * (5,000 / 10,000)] and the TWR comes out to 1.0506, which equals a total return of 5.06 percent on total equity going into the trading sequence.

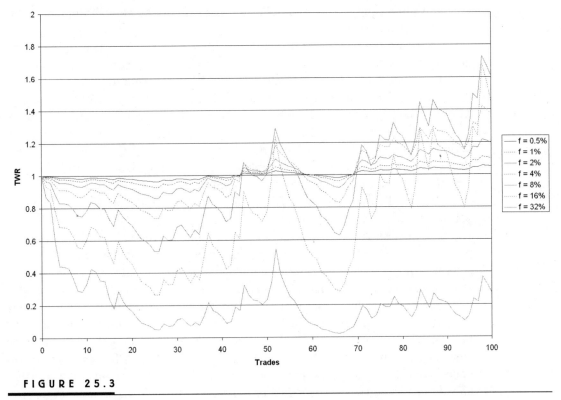

FIGURE 25.3

Equity versus optimal f.

Applying this kind of money management means we always make use of our winnings from the previous trade, which is why all HPRs are multiplied with each other when calculating the TWR and why two trades that produce a profit of 2.5 percent each produce a total profit of slightly more than 5 percent.

For example, if your initial capital is $100,000 and you make 2.5 percent per trade on two consecutive trades, your total profit will be $5,063. The $2,500 profit on the first trade would be added to your capital, and you'd make $2,563 on the second trade (102,500 * 0.025).

Two main points of criticism of this version of the optimal f formula arise. First, the better the underlying buy and sell decisions, the higher the optimal f. The higher the optimal f, the more you stand to lose in a losing trade, simply because the formula tells you to risk more. Some would say that this makes fixed fractional trading too risky for any practical purposes.

Second, to keep the fractional risk amount constant, the dollar amount risked will vary with the account size. For large accounts, this can translate into enormous and very uncomfortable amounts of dollars risked. For small accounts, the relatively slow equity growth in dollar terms might not be enough to increase the number of shares traded.

However, the way I see it, the critics overlook two important points. First, nothing forces anyone to trade the exact optimal f. The important thing is to not take any unnecessary risk by trading above it. Also, never forget that the optimal f value is based on historical or back-tested trades. As already stated, chances are Murphy's Law will make sure that the system will not work as well in the future as it has in the past—at least not initially—which means that the true f for that period of trading will be lower than the historical f. Therefore, it's better to be safe than sorry and trade at an f considerably lower than the optimal f derived from historical data. To do that, you need to know where f is in the first place.

To trade below the historical optimal f, you need to decide how much below you must go to achieve a suitable risk–reward relationship. Remember, the less you risk, the less you will lose and the smaller the drawdowns will be. For example, it is fully possible to calculate an f that aims to find an equity curve that is as smooth as possible in relation to the equity growth, or one that simply aims to minimize drawdowns and/or flat times, or....

Second, in Ralph Vince's original version of the formula, f depends on the worst historical loser. We use the largest historical loser in the formula for the HPR because we implicitly assume that one reason why we're trading this system in the first place is that its largest historical loser is within the limits for what we can tolerate given the system's overall profit potential, but also because the loss has already happened (whether for real or during testing), which, because of its size, makes it less likely to happen again.

Note, however, that the "better" the system, the higher the optimal f will be, because the better the system, the more we should be able to risk per trade to make the most out of the system by maximizing its profit-generating potentials. However, if we ever were to encounter a loss of the same size as the worst historical loser, so that $Profit_n$ equals WCS, then the HPR for that trade also will equal f, according to the formula $HPR_n = 1 + f$. Thus, the better the system, or the higher its profit-generating potential, and the higher the f, the more you stand to lose on one single trade, should the system once again experience a loser of the same magnitude as the worst historical loser.

I know of traders who claim to have systems good enough that they trade them with an f of 0.20, meaning they're risking 20 percent of their capital in any one trade. Is this a wise thing to do, no matter how good the system is? No, of course not. Risking as much as 20 percent per trade means that it will only take three losing trades in a row to deplete the trading capital by close to 50 percent. That is, after three trades, losing 20 percent of your capital in each trade, you'd be in a 50 percent drawdown. To get back to where you started you would need to increase your current capital by 100 percent, for which you'd need at least four 20 percent winners in a row—how likely is that?

No serious trader should ever risk more than a few percent of his total capital per trade. Trading with such a high f as 20 percent will severely reduce your staying power when you hit a streak of bad trades (and in this case you only need three to reach a drawdown of 50 percent), which will unarguably happen at some point.

There also are plenty of other ways to calculate an f that is not based on the worst historical loser. Personally, I prefer to substitute for the worst historical loser whatever I am prepared to lose per share for that particular trade. This is easily done by substituting the WCS with the stop-loss level for that particular trade and for all trades and do all the calculations on a one-share basis. In this case, the worst-case scenario will be based on what you're willing to tolerate for this very trade, instead of what you were willing to tolerate in the past while hoping that experience won't repeat itself.

For example, assume again we already found the optimal f to be 2 percent. Suppose also that we are willing to risk $2 per share on a $100 stock and that the trade ended with a profit per share of $5. Then, the HPR for that trade will be 1.05 $[1 + 0.02 * (5/2)]$, or 5 percent of available equity going into the trade. Now, suppose a second trade on a different stock, priced at $50 and with a stop loss of $1.25, ends up with a profit of $2. Then the HPR for that trade will be 1.032 $[1 + 0.02 * (2/1.25)]$, or 3.2 percent of available equity going into the trade. The TWR for these two trades will be 1.0836 (1.05 * 1.032), or 8.36 percent of the available equity going into the trades.

It is also a good thing to substitute for the WCS an individual stop loss for each trade because the stop loss is not a once-in-a-lifetime (hopefully) terrifying experience, but a rather reasonable amount that you are prepared to encounter frequently. This is good news, because if you take a look at the formula for the HPR again, you will see that the smaller the WCS, the larger the factor Profit_n / WCS. Thus, the f can be lowered to produce the same HPR. In other words, the less we are willing to risk per share traded, by lowering the value for the WCS to an amount more suitable to each specific trade, the less we need to risk of account equity to achieve the same HPR and, ultimately, TWR.

Using a variable stop loss while risking the same relative amount of your capital for each trade, it still is simple to calculate the number of shares to trade and the exact amount of capital needed for each trade. First, after figuring out the percentage of capital you're willing to risk, determine the stop loss for your next trade. For example, if you go long at 100 and your stop loss is placed at 96, you are willing to lose four points per share. Next, multiply your account balance entering the trade with the f value you have decided on. For example, if your account balance is $100,000 and your f is 0.02 (2 percent), you're willing to lose $2,000 per trade (100,000 * 0.02).

Then divide the total amount you're willing to risk per trade by the amount you are willing to risk per share to arrive at how many shares you need to buy. In this case, you're willing to risk $2,000, and your risk per share is four points, so you need to buy 500 shares to take on a total risk of $2,000 (2,000 / 4). Finally, if the stock is priced at $100, the entire trade will tie up $50,000 of your capital (100 * 500). These calculations are essentially the same as those we just did in Chapter 24, when discussing the Kelly formula. More formally, the formulas can be stated as follows:

$$ST = (AC * f) / SL$$

and

$$MT = ST * EP$$

Where:

ST = Shares to trade

AC = Available capital

f = Fraction of capital to risk

SL = Stop loss, distance transformed to points from percentages between the entry price and stop-loss level

MT = Money tied up in trade

EP = Entry price of stock

I'm being redundant here, but I want you to get a firm understanding of this, and as the saying goes, repetition is the mother of all knowledge. On that note, I once again would like to point out that the more you are willing to risk per share and the lower the f, the less money you tie up in the trade. The trick, then, is to balance the f and the SL so that you can be in as many positions as you desire at the same time. In the previous example, with the account balance at $100,000 and with the trade tying up $50,000, you can only be in two similar positions at the same time [Integer(100,000 / 50,000)].

However, if you lower the f to 1 percent and increase the SL to six points, a single position will tie up $16,600 [100,000 * 0.01 / 6 * 100], and you can be in six similar positions at the same time [Integer(100,000 / 16,600)]. The chore is to find a trading strategy that makes it possible to be in the desired number of positions given your account equity. The difficulty is, however, that to increase the number of possible positions to be in at any one time, the stop loss needs to be placed further away from the entry price than what might make sense for a short-term strategy.

In the last example, the stop loss was placed 6 percent away from the entry. For a decent risk–reward relationship going into the trade, the profit potential, therefore, needs to be at least 12 percent, for an initial risk–reward relationship of 2:1. This isn't all that realistic for a short-term trading strategy. We will learn how to work around this dilemma soon, but first we need to back up to the formula for calculating the TWR, to gain a little better understanding of how the entire process works.

Just as one can calculate an arithmetic average for any data series, so too can we calculate an average value representing all the HPRs making up the TWR. Because we are working with multiplication and compounded returns, however, this average must be a *geometric average*. For example, to calculate the average arithmetic return from three profitable trades of 3, 5, and 7 percent, respectively, simply add them up and divide by the number of trades. In this case, the arithmetic average equals 5 percent [(3 + 5 + 7) / 3]. Without compounding the returns, the total return can be calculated either as (3 + 5 + 7 = 15), or as (3 * 5 = 15). With an initial account equity of, for example, $100,000, the resulting balance is $115,000 [100,000 * (1 + 15 / 100)].

Using compounding, we need to use multiplication instead of addition. Therefore, the three different returns need to be expressed as 1.03 (1 + 3 / 100), 1.05, and 1.07. Had one of the returns been negative because of a losing trade, the plus sign would have been replaced by a minus sign, so that, for example a 3 percent losing trade would have been stated as 0.97 (1 − 3 / 100). Multiplying these values would result in a compounded return of 1.1572 (1.03 * 1.05 * 1.07), which would result in a compounded resulting balance over the three trades of $115,720 (100,000 * 1.1572). Now, to calculate the average return over the three trades, we need to calculate the *geometric mean* (GM), which, because we're dealing with multiplications will be 1.0499 (1.1572(1/3)), or 4.99 percent [(1.0499 − 1) / 100]. A more general relationship between TWR, HPR, and GM can be expressed as:

$$TWR = GMN = HPR1 * HPR2 * HPR3 * \ldots * HPRi$$

So that:

$$GM = (HPR1 * HPR2 * HPR3 * \ldots * HPRi)^{(1/N)} = TWR^{(1/N)}$$

Where:

GM = The geometric mean

N = Number of trades

The formulas might look a little advanced, but don't forget that the entire process is akin to calculating the regular arithmetic average profit per trade, expressed in percentages. Now, the next step also might look a little advanced, but it really isn't. Let's just settle for the fact that there is an alternative way to calculate GM that incorporates the arithmetic average profit, which we calculated at 5 percent in the previous example. This formula looks like this:

$$GM = (APM^2 - SD^2)(1/2)$$

Where:

APM = The average profit multiplier, calculated as the average percentage profit per trade divided by 100, plus one, which, using the numbers from the example above, comes out to 1.05 (1 + 5 / 100).

SD = Standard deviation of all trades, measured in percentage terms, so that for a standard deviation of 25 percent, SD equals 0.25 (25 / 100).

Given these formulas, the TWR also can be expressed as:

$$TWR = GMN = (APM^2 - SD^2)^{(1/2)N} = (APM^2 - SD^2)^{(N/2)}$$

This formula also might seem a little complicated at first glance, but the interpretation is quite simple. To end up with a positive TWR, all we need to do is keep APM larger than SD. This should explain all the hard work we went through earlier to lead to this part on money management. This is why we want the system to operate with specific stop loss, profit target levels, and trade lengths, and also to work on as many markets or market situations as possible. Because when it does, we know we've done everything we can, not only to make sure that APM is as large as possible in relation to SD, but also to make sure that this relationship will hold up in the future.

If we can achieve this, the end result for TWR will only be a function of f (the fraction of available equity to risk) and N (the total number of trades). The more trades, the greater TWR will be. This also explains our obsession with testing the system on as many markets as possible and making the trades as short term and similar as possible, because to maximize TWR we need plenty of trades, and to maximize N we need markets to trade. With a large number of markets to trade, producing a large number of trades, we can tailor TWR to our needs and expectations, by experimenting with different fs, according to the formula for HPR.

CHAPTER 26

Dynamic Ratio Money Management

Tailoring optimal f, TWR, and HPR to our goals brings us back to the importance of finding the right balance between f and the amount to risk per share, so that we can make as many trades as possible, in as many markets as possible, wasting as little time as possible. Frequent short-term trading usually means a rather low average profit per trade and the use of tight stop losses that make sense in relation to the estimated and desired average trade length. The drawback is that the shorter-term the system, the tighter the stops on a one-share basis need to be, and the tighter the stops, the fewer trades we can be in simultaneously for any given f. The less we risk per share, the more shares we need to buy to reach f, and the more shares we need to buy, the more money we need to tie up in the trade.

For example, say that our system calls for a stop loss that is placed only 2 percent away from the entry point, on average. For a $100 stock, this means two points (100 * 0.02). Further, assume that we don't want to risk more than 1 percent of our available capital per trade. With $100,000 in available capital, we therefore should buy 500 shares of the $100 stock [(100,000 * 0.01) / 2], which will tie up $50,000 of our capital (500 * 100). As a consequence, we can only be in two similar trades simultaneously [Integer(100,000 / 50,000)].

Note that it doesn't matter how much money we have or how much the stock costs. Given a 2 percent stop loss and an f of 1 percent, we can only be in two trades simultaneously, no matter the values of the other variables. For example, if we substitute a $10 stock for a $100 stock and increase the available capital to $1,000,000, at first glance it seems as if we should be able to be in plenty more positions at one time. But because the stop loss will be only 20 cents away from the entry price (10 * 0.02), and the number of shares we need to buy will be 50,000

[(1,000,000 * 0.01) / 0.2], for a total amount of $500,000 (50,000 * 10), once again this only allows for two positions [Integer(1,000,000 / 500,000)].

To work around this, separate the stop loss (SL) from what I call the money management point (MMP). So far, we've assumed SL to be equal to MMP, which implicitly has resulted in the following formula:

$$ST = (AC * f) / SL = (AC * f) / MMP$$

Where:

MMP = Money management point in distance from the entry price, to calculate the number of shares to trade

However, by separating the two and placing MMP further away from the entry price, we can lower ST and also MT, which makes it possible to be in more positions at the same time. As a consequence of this, the f used in the formula ST = (AC * f) / MMP won't represent the true fraction risked of the available equity, but rather just a fictive fraction used to calculate ST and MT. Therefore, from now on, let's call the f in the formula ST = (AC * f) / MMP for f_{fict}, so that the formula instead reads:

$$ST = (AC * f_{fict}) / MMP$$

Where:

f_{fict} = Fictive fraction of capital to risk to calculate the number of shares to trade

Because the account equity and the price of the stocks have nothing to do with how many positions we can be in using a DRMM regimen, the formulas for the average number of simultaneously open positions and the average percentage amount of equity tied up in one position can be simplified to the following two formulas, respectively:

$$MMP / f_{fict}$$

and

$$f_{fict} / MMP$$

Figures 26.1 and 26.2 show how these formulas can be used to put together tables that will help us get a feel for how to balance MMP and f_{fict} against each other, so that we can trade as many positions simultaneously as we desire. For example, for an f_{fict} of 2 percent, Figure 26.1 shows that we need the MMP to be at least 20 percent away from the entry price so that we can be in 10 positions simultaneously. Figure 26.2, in turn, shows that we then will tie up 10 percent of our equity in each position, on average. To create the tables, simply type in the values for MMP and f_{fict} manually in column C and row 4, respectively, then:

Average number of positions open at one time

Maximum fictiv loss for portfolio, fictive f (%)

MMP, percent away from entry price

	0.25	0.50	0.75	1.00	1.25	1.50	1.75	2.00	2.25	2.50	2.75	3.00	3.25	3.50	3.75	4.00
1	4	2	1	1	-	-	-	-	-	-	-	-	-	-	-	-
2	8	4	2	2	1	1	1	1	-	-	-	-	-	-	-	-
3	12	6	4	3	2	2	1	1	1	1	1	1	-	-	-	-
4	16	8	5	4	3	2	2	2	1	1	1	1	1	1	1	1
5	20	10	6	5	4	3	2	2	2	2	1	1	1	1	1	1
6	24	12	8	6	4	4	3	3	2	2	2	2	1	1	1	1
7	28	14	9	7	5	4	4	3	3	2	2	2	2	2	1	1
8	32	16	10	8	6	5	4	4	3	3	2	2	2	2	2	2
9	36	18	12	9	7	6	5	4	4	3	3	3	2	2	2	2
10	40	20	13	10	8	6	5	5	4	4	3	3	3	2	2	2
11	44	22	14	11	8	7	6	5	4	4	4	3	3	3	2	2
12	48	24	16	12	9	8	6	6	5	4	4	4	3	3	3	3
13	52	26	17	13	10	8	7	6	5	5	4	4	4	3	3	3
14	56	28	18	14	11	9	8	7	6	5	5	4	4	4	3	3
15	60	30	20	15	12	10	8	7	6	6	5	5	4	4	4	3
16	64	32	21	16	12	10	9	8	7	6	5	5	4	4	4	4
17	68	34	22	17	13	11	9	8	7	6	6	5	5	4	4	4
18	72	36	24	18	14	12	10	9	8	7	6	6	5	5	4	4
19	76	38	25	19	15	12	10	9	8	7	6	6	5	5	5	4
20	80	40	26	20	16	13	11	10	8	8	7	6	6	5	5	5
21	84	42	28	21	16	14	12	10	9	8	7	7	6	6	5	5
22	88	44	29	22	17	14	12	11	9	8	8	7	6	6	5	5
23	92	46	30	23	18	15	13	11	10	9	8	7	7	6	6	5
24	96	48	32	24	19	16	13	12	10	9	8	8	7	6	6	6
25	100	50	33	25	20	16	14	12	11	10	9	8	7	7	6	6

FIGURE 26.1

The equation MMP/f_{fict}.

Average amount of equity committed to one position (%)

Maximum fictiv loss for portfolio, fictive f (%)

MMP, percent away from entry price

	0.25	0.50	0.75	1.00	1.25	1.50	1.75	2.00	2.25	2.50	2.75	3.00	3.25	3.50	3.75	4.00
1	25	50	100	100	-	-	-	-	-	-	-	-	-	-	-	-
2	13	25	50	50	100	100	100	100	-	-	-	-	-	-	-	-
3	8	17	25	33	50	50	100	100	100	100	100	100	-	-	-	-
4	6	13	20	25	33	50	50	50	100	100	100	100	100	100	100	100
5	5	10	17	20	25	33	50	50	50	50	100	100	100	100	100	100
6	4	8	13	17	25	25	33	33	50	50	50	50	100	100	100	100
7	4	7	11	14	20	25	25	33	33	50	50	50	50	50	100	100
8	3	6	10	13	17	20	25	25	33	33	50	50	50	50	50	50
9	3	6	8	11	14	17	20	25	25	33	33	33	50	50	50	50
10	3	5	8	10	13	17	20	20	25	25	33	33	33	50	50	50
11	2	5	7	9	13	14	17	20	25	25	25	33	33	33	50	50
12	2	4	6	8	11	13	17	17	20	25	25	25	33	33	33	33
13	2	4	6	8	10	13	14	17	20	20	25	25	25	33	33	33
14	2	4	6	7	9	11	13	14	17	20	20	25	25	25	33	33
15	2	3	5	7	8	10	13	14	17	17	20	20	25	25	25	33
16	2	3	5	6	8	10	11	13	14	17	20	20	25	25	25	25
17	1	3	5	6	8	9	11	13	14	17	17	20	20	25	25	25
18	1	3	4	6	7	8	10	11	13	14	17	17	20	20	25	25
19	1	3	4	5	7	8	10	11	13	14	17	17	20	20	20	25
20	1	3	4	5	6	8	9	10	13	13	14	17	17	20	20	20
21	1	2	4	5	6	7	8	10	11	13	14	14	17	17	20	20
22	1	2	3	5	6	7	8	9	11	13	13	14	17	17	20	20
23	1	2	3	4	6	7	8	9	10	11	13	14	14	17	17	20
24	1	2	3	4	5	6	8	8	10	11	13	13	14	17	17	17
25	1	2	3	4	5	6	7	8	9	10	11	13	14	14	17	17

FIGURE 26.2

The equation f_{fict}/MMP.

In cell D5: Type in the formula =INT($C5/D$4), and drag and fill it into all cells to S29.

In cell D34: Type in the formula =IF(D5>0,1/D5,0)*100, and drag and fill it into all cells to S58.

Note that the term "on average" is used, because just as the stop loss can fluctuate with the average true range, so can the MMP. The next trick, then, is to figure out approximately how far it is to a certain percentage distance, on average and over the long term. First, we need to figure out what our true f will be, given a f_{fict}, a MMP, and a SL. If f_{fict} and f are expressed as fractions (i.e., the percentage value divided by 100), the formula is:

$$f = f_{fict} * (SL / MMP)$$

For example, if the MMP is placed 10 percent away from the entry price, and we calculate the number of shares and the amount of money to tie up in the trade according to an f_{fict} of 4 percent, then, if the trade hits the stop loss at, say 3 percent away from the entry price, the true f of the available equity risked and lost on the trade will be 1.2 percent [(4 / 100) * (3 / 10) * 100]. However, just as the losses actually will be smaller than the fictive risk we take, so will the profits. From the formula above, we can see that the larger the difference between SL and MMP, the smaller the true profits and losses will be for any given f_{fict}. This is also something we need to balance to find the desired smoothness and growth rate of the equity curve.

The questions that now remain to be answered are how many positions, on average, do we want to be in simultaneously, and how many markets do we need to track for trading opportunities to make that possible? The first question you must answer subjectively, with the answer based on your trading experience and desire for action, but let's say that we would like to be in 10 positions simultaneously, on average.

Having decided on an average of 10 positions, we can go back to the table in Figure 26.1, where we can see that if we place the MMP 10 percent away from the entry price, on average, then we should set f_{fict} to no higher than 1 percent. Likewise, if we set f_{fict} to 2 percent, then we can place the MMP 20 percent away from the entry price, on average. Because we know from experience that we most likely won't set f_{fict} any higher than 2 percent or any lower than 1 percent, let's try to set MMP approximately 15 percent away from the entry price, so that the desired amount of open positions corresponds to a f_{fict} of 1.5 percent. Many times, we might be in fewer positions and at times we might be in a few more. It all depends on the volatility of the market, which will alter the magnitude of the true range. On average, however, we will be in 10 positions simultaneously.

With this decision made, we need to go back to the normalized performance summary for the system, which we made extensive use of in Parts 2 and 3, and figure out how much time each stock spends in a trade. For example, if each stock examined spends an average of 25 percent of its time in a trade, theoretically we then could spend 100 percent of the time in the market, in one stock or another, by moving in and out of four stocks, if we always could exit one trade and immediately enter into a new trade.

But because no four stocks will move in perfect synchronization like this, we might need to track another one or two stocks, to always be prepared to take a trade. In doing so, however, there also might be situations when we can't take a trade because we might be fully invested already. Better to miss a trade because we're fully invested than to miss a profit opportunity because we're not tracking enough stocks.

Likewise, if the average time spent in the market for a specific stock is 15 percent, then we need six to seven perfectly synchronized stocks to be in the market 100 percent of the time. Adding one or two stocks for a little overlap, we might need to track seven to eight stocks, so that we can have at least one open position at any time.

Given that most (short-term) strategies spend around 15 to 20 percent in the market per stock traded, and given that we will try to be in no more than 10 stocks, on average, simultaneously, this means that we need to track 60 to 70 stocks. The more systems we trade, the fewer the markets we need to track, because each system adds to the time spent in the market for any individual stock. (This gives rise to two interesting questions we will leave unanswered in this book, but that are nonetheless important to contemplate: First, are we better off diversifying via the number of markets monitored or the number of systems traded? Second, should the systems themselves be looked upon as separate asset classes?)

One question we will answer is how wide, in percentage terms, is one average true range? Knowing this, we will know how many average true ranges away from the entry price we should place the MMP, so that it will be 15 percent on average. The answer is that, at the time of writing, one average true range is approximately 4 percent wide in relation to the close of the same bar. This number is calculated over the last 2,500 days on the 58 stocks used to research this book. To place the MMP 15 percent away from the entry price, on average, we therefore need approximately four true ranges, rounded to the nearest whole numbers.

Incidentally, all this makes perfect sense from a risk management point of view. The logic is as follows: The lower the volatility, the closer SL and MMP will be to the entry price, and the more shares and money we dare tie up in any individual trade, because the volatility and risk is low. Also, because the risk is low, we don't need to diversify as much, which we can't do anyway because each trade ties up more money than normal. On the other hand, if the volatility and the risk is higher than normal, the further away SL and MMP are from the entry price. Thus, we avoid getting stopped out too frequently, while at the same time the fewer shares and less money we dare tie up in any one position. Also, because the risk is higher, we would like to diversify more, which we can do because of the smaller amount of money tied up in each position.

Note that using DRMM does not mean that we let the volatility of the market alter the amount risked. Instead, it means that we let it alter the *way* we risk it, by altering the ratio between the total amount risked and the risk per share—by altering the ratio between the stop loss and money management point and the entry price. In the end, this also alters the ratio between the number of possible open positions and the number of stocks tracked. Because these ratios constantly change with the volatility of all markets tracked and the *f* we have decided to use, to achieve our desired risk–reward ratio when it comes to the equity growth, I have dubbed this money management method dynamic ratio money management, or DRMM, for short.

BUILDING A SAMPLE SPREADSHEET

We now know how to set a stop loss and a money management point, calculate the number of shares to trade and the total amount committed, and how much we stand to win or lose on the trade, all depending on the fictional *f* we decide to apply to the system. But how to decide on the fictional *f*? And how to do that for all open trades on several different markets, traded with several different systems, running simultaneously? Let's take this process step-by-step and at the same time construct an Excel spreadsheet that will do the work for us:

The first step is to type down the development of each trade, on a one-share basis, as in Figure 26.3. Figure 26.3 shows a few trades for Market 2, recorded in columns L to P. In this case, the spreadsheet is for three markets, with the same data for Markets 1 and 3 recorded in columns B to F and V to Z, respectively. Figure 26.3 shows that the first trade for this market started on row 11 and ended on row 14. Each row represents one day of trading. The actual dates for this trade aren't shown, but are recorded in the A column (hidden from view in Figure 26.3).

Figure 26.3 shows that the entry price for the first trade was $32 (column L) and, at the time for the entry, the MMP was set to 2 points (columns M) and the stop loss to 0.75 points (column N). These values remain the same for as long as the trade remains open at the end of that day's trading, going into the next day. Consequently, as long as the trade remains open at the end of the day, the open profit and loss is recorded in column O. At the end of the last day of the trade (row 14), only the closed-out profit or loss is recorded (column P).

This particular trade lasts for two full days, plus one day when the entry took place (which could have happened anytime during the day), plus one day when the exit took place (which also could have happened anytime during the day). Here it lasted four days, but different software calculates the number of days differently. TradeStation, for example, doesn't count the day of the entry as a day in a trade.

	L	M	N	O	P
8	Market 2				
9	EP	MMP	SL	Open	Close
10					
11	32.00	2.00	0.75	2.00	
12	32.00	2.00	0.75	4.00	
13	32.00	2.00	0.75	6.00	
14					8.00
15					
16					
17					
18					
19					
20	42.00	5.00	2.00	1.00	
21	42.00	5.00	2.00	2.00	
22	42.00	5.00	2.00	3.00	
23	42.00	5.00	2.00	4.00	
24	42.00	5.00	2.00	5.00	
25	42.00	5.00	2.00	6.00	
26	42.00	5.00	2.00	7.00	
27	42.00	5.00	2.00	8.00	
28					6.00
29					
30					
31					
32					
33					
34					
35	50.00	5.00	2.50	(2.00)	
36	50.00	5.00	2.50	(2.00)	
37					(2.50)
38					
39					

FIGURE 26.3

Trades to be tracked for the Excel spreadsheet.

Figure 26.4 shows the input variables we can alter to alter the calculated results in Figure 26.5. By altering the fictive risk in cell C3, all the values in Figure 26.5 will change as a result of all the changes that will take place for each day or row, for all markets and trades recorded in the spreadsheet. More specifically, by altering the value for the fictive risk in cell C3, we alter the amount of money allowed to be risked in each trade, given the total amount of money available as a result of all the days of trading leading up to each new trading day.

Thus, although the data recorded on a one-share basis always will look the same, the actual result of that trade will change with the value in cell C3, and how that value not only changes the amount of capital allotted to a specific trade, but to all other trades as well.

AP58	▾	=	
	A	B	C	D
1				
2		Init. bal.	$ 100,000	
3		Fict. risk	2.00%	
4		Costs	$ 20	
5				
6				

FIGURE 26.4

Input variables to be altered.

AP58	▾	=			
	F	G	H	I	J	K
1						
2		End. eq.	$ 127,830	Max DD	5.30%	
3		Tot. ret.	27.83%	Max FT	22	
4		Tot. tr.	31	R-R ratio	0.2592	
5		Win %	41.94%	P. factor	2.73	
6						

FIGURE 26.5

Results of varied input variables.

The trick is to test your system with several different fictive risk levels and decide on one that makes sense to you. As already mentioned, the optimal f, as defined by Ralph Vince, only looks at the fastest historical equity growth, which could make the system very risky to trade on future unseen data. Other ways to select f could be to go for the f generating the highest profit factor, the highest risk–reward ratio, the smallest average drawdown, the shortest flat time, the most profitable time periods (such as weeks or months), or the best compromise based on all this information. Remember never to trade a system on its historical optimal f for the fastest equity growth, as that most likely will be too risky.

Figure 26.5 shows the evaluation variables we will learn to calculate with this spreadsheet. These are far from all the variables needed, but it would be impossible for me to describe them all. Figures 27.2 and 27.3 show you a more professional set of evaluation variables, which are derived with the help of the spreadsheet I use to build the systems for *Active Trader* magazine. But for now, let's stick to Figure 26.5 and describe each evaluation variable one at a time.

The ending equity in cell H2 is the value of our portfolio at the end of the testing period, including the value of any open positions, based on the price of the stock, the number of shares purchased, and the profit or loss of the open position.

The total return in cell H3 is the percentage difference between the starting balance in cell C2 and the ending equity in cell H2. In this case, we only examine

AT77	▾		=	
Q	**R**	**S**	**T**	**U**
8 Market 2				
9 **Shares**	**Tied**	**Risk**	**Open**	**Close**
10				
11 1,000	$ 32,000	$ 750	$ 1,980	$ -
12 1,000	$ 32,000	$ 750	$ 3,980	$ -
13 1,000	$ 32,000	$ 750	$ 5,980	$ -
14 -	$ -	$ -	$ -	$ 7,980
15 -	$ -	$ -	$ -	$ -
16 -	$ -	$ -	$ -	$ -
17 -	$ -	$ -	$ -	$ -
18 -	$ -	$ -	$ -	$ -
19 -	$ -	$ -	$ -	$ -
20 440	$ 18,480	$ 880	$ 420	$ -
21 440	$ 18,480	$ 880	$ 860	$ -
22 440	$ 18,480	$ 880	$ 1,300	$ -
23 440	$ 18,480	$ 880	$ 1,740	$ -
24 440	$ 18,480	$ 880	$ 2,180	$ -
25 440	$ 18,480	$ 880	$ 2,620	$ -
26 440	$ 18,480	$ 880	$ 3,060	$ -
27 440	$ 18,480	$ 880	$ 3,500	$ -
28 -	$ -	$ -	$ -	$ 2,620
29 -	$ -	$ -	$ -	$ -
30 -	$ -	$ -	$ -	$ -
31 -	$ -	$ -	$ -	$ -
32 -	$ -	$ -	$ -	$ -
33 -	$ -	$ -	$ -	$ -
34 -	$ -	$ -	$ -	$ -
35 439	$ 21,950	$ 1,098	$ (898)	$ -
36 439	$ 21,950	$ 1,098	$ (898)	$ -
37 -	$ -	$ -	$ -	$ (1,118)
38 -	$ -	$ -	$ -	$ -
39 -	$ -	$ -	$ -	$ -

FIGURE 26.6

Total number of shares, amount risked, and profits for each trade.

short period of trades. If the testing period stretches out for several years, you could also calculate the average return for various time periods, such as years, months, and quarters.

The value in cell H4 shows the total number of trades taken during the test period. Note that this number can alter depending on the value in cell C3. The more we risk per trade, the more we also need to tie up in that trade, and if we tie up too much, there won't be any money left for any succeeding trades as long as the current trades remain open. Thus, the percentage of winning trades in cell H5 can also change because of the same reason.

The value for the maximum drawdown in cell J2 will most likely increase the higher the value in cell C3. Note, however, that where and when the maximum

AT77	▾	=				

	AF	AG	AH	AI	AJ	AK	AL
8			Portfolio				
9	New	Equity	Avail	Top	DD	FT	Daily
10		$ 100,000	$ 100,000	$ 100,000	0.00%	0	
11	2	$ 101,794	$ 48,020	$ 101,794	0.00%	0	1.79%
12	-	$ 103,627	$ 48,020	$ 103,627	0.00%	0	1.80%
13	-	$ 106,460	$ 48,020	$ 106,460	0.00%	0	2.73%
14	-	$ 107,627	$ 88,000	$ 107,627	0.00%	0	1.10%
15	-	$ 107,794	$ 88,000	$ 107,794	0.00%	0	0.15%
16	1	$ 109,501	$ 64,975	$ 109,501	0.00%	0	1.58%
17	-	$ 109,808	$ 89,515	$ 109,808	0.00%	0	0.28%
18	-	$ 109,975	$ 89,515	$ 109,975	0.00%	0	0.15%
19	-	$ 110,141	$ 89,515	$ 110,141	0.00%	0	0.15%
20	1	$ 110,728	$ 71,035	$ 110,728	0.00%	0	0.53%
21	-	$ 111,334	$ 71,035	$ 111,334	0.00%	0	0.55%
22	-	$ 112,107	$ 92,327	$ 112,107	0.00%	0	0.69%
23	1	$ 113,025	$ 71,909	$ 113,025	0.00%	0	0.82%
24	-	$ 113,714	$ 71,909	$ 113,714	0.00%	0	0.61%
25	1	$ 113,113	$ 50,201	$ 113,714	-0.53%	1	-0.53%
26	-	$ 113,229	$ 70,917	$ 113,714	-0.43%	2	0.10%
27	-	$ 113,793	$ 70,917	$ 113,793	0.00%	0	0.50%
28	-	$ 112,664	$ 92,017	$ 113,793	-0.99%	1	-0.99%
29	-	$ 110,423	$ 110,423	$ 113,793	-2.96%	2	-1.99%
30	1	$ 110,183	$ 83,081	$ 113,793	-3.17%	3	-0.22%
31	-	$ 109,962	$ 83,081	$ 113,793	-3.37%	4	-0.20%
32	-	$ 109,631	$ 83,081	$ 113,793	-3.66%	5	-0.30%
33	-	$ 109,962	$ 83,081	$ 113,793	-3.37%	6	0.30%
34	-	$ 109,962	$ 83,081	$ 113,793	-3.37%	7	0.00%
35	2	$ 109,632	$ 42,672	$ 113,793	-3.66%	8	-0.30%
36	-	$ 109,632	$ 42,672	$ 113,793	-3.66%	9	0.00%
37	-	$ 108,825	$ 63,505	$ 113,793	-4.37%	10	-0.74%
38	-	$ 109,119	$ 63,505	$ 113,793	-4.11%	11	0.27%
39	-	$ 108,604	$ 90,165	$ 113,793	-4.56%	12	-0.47%

FIGURE 26.7

A running total portfolio summary.

drawdown took place doesn't have to remain the same, but can change with the fictive f. In Figure 27.2, I also calculate the average drawdown, which can function as an input to the drawdown freak-occurrence calculation we learned about in Part 1. Remember, the drawdown is not a core system characteristic, but a function of other system characteristics, and a large drawdown isn't necessarily a bad thing.

There is no saying how the maximum flat time will change with changes in the fictive f. Sometimes a large f creates deep drawdowns that take a long time and many trades to get out of; at other times a large f increases the value of the winning trades leading out of a drawdown, thus shortening the time it takes to get out. As with the drawdown, the time covering the longest flat time also can change with the f.

For this spreadsheet, the risk–reward ratio is calculated as the average daily equity growth in percent, divided by the standard deviations of the daily percentage returns. These numbers are calculated for the total value of the portfolio, incorporating the returns for both open and closed out trades. In Figure 27.2, this value is referred to as the *Sharpe ratio*. In a more professional spreadsheet, this value can be calculated on the monthly and yearly period returns, which also takes other income streams, such as the interest earned on the money in the account, into consideration. The higher this number, the faster the equity growth in relation to the fluctuations in the returns.

The profit factor is the gross profit divided by the gross loss from all trades actually executed. This number will change with f for two reasons. First, the size of a specific profit or a loss will depend on the amount invested in that trade, which depends on the outcome of all trades preceding it. Second, as already mentioned, if the f is too high, some trades might be skipped completely.

The formulas for this specific spreadsheet and Figure 26.5 read as follows:

To calculate the ending equity, in cell H2 type: =AG128, where cell AG128 denotes the ending equity for this trading sequence. Remember to change row references with the length of the test period and the column reference with the number of markets.

To calculate the total return, in cell H3 type: =(H2−C2)/C2, where cell C2 denotes the initial balance (see Figure 26.4).

To calculate the number of trades, in cell H4 type:
=COUNTIF(K11:K128,"<>0")+COUNTIF(U11:U128,"<>0")
+COUNTIF(AE11:AE128,"<>0"), where columns K, U, and AE denote the results from each trade in Markets 1, 2, and 3, respectively. (See sample trades for Market 2 in Figure 26.6, other markets not shown.)

To calculate the percentage of winning trades, in cell H5 type:
=(COUNTIF(K11:K128,">0")+COUNTIF(U11:U128,">0")
+COUNTIF(AE11:AE128,">0"))/H4

To calculate the largest drawdown, in cell J2 type: =−MIN(AJ10:AJ128), where column AJ denotes the daily drawdown number for the portfolio (see Figure 26.7).

To calculate the longest flat time, in cell J3 type: =MAX(AK10:AK128), where column AK denotes the number of days since the last equity high (see Figure 26.7).

To calculate the risk–reward ratio based on the daily fluctuations in the equity, in cell J4 type: =AVERAGE(AL11:AL128)/STDEV(AL11:AL128), where columns AL denotes the daily equity fluctuations (see Figure 26.7).

To calculate the profit factor, in cell J5 type:
=(SUMIF(K11:K128,">0")+SUMIF(U11:U128,">0")+

SUMIF(AE11:AE128,">0"))/−(SUMIF(K11:K128,"<0")+SUMIF(U11:U12
8,"<0")+
SUMIF(AE11:AE128,"<0"))

Before we can calculate the evaluation variables in Figure 26.5, we need to know what a specific f will mean for each trade in the spreadsheet. Figure 26.6 shows what an f of 2 percent will do for the trades recorded in Figure 26.3. In this case, a starting balance of $100,000 and an f of 2 percent means that we should buy 1,000 shares for a total value of $32,000, and that the actual amount we're risking to lose is $750. As the trade develops over the next several days, we go from an open profit of $1,980 to a closed-out profit of $7,980, with the costs for the trade also taken into consideration, as specified in cell C4 in Figure 26.4.

Note that the total risk for this trade is $750, which corresponds to only 0.75 percent of the total amount going into the trade. This is because the stop loss is closer to the entry price than the money management point, which is a necessity for a short-term system to be able to trade as many markets as possible.

The formulas for this specific spreadsheet and Figure 26.6 read as follows:

To calculate the number of shares, in cell Q11 type:
=IF(AND(L11<>L10,L11>0), MIN(INT($AG10*$C$3/M11),
$AH10/$AF11/L11),IF(L11=0,0,Q10)), where column L denotes the entry price, column AG denotes the total equity for the portfolio, cell C3 denotes the fictive percentage risk per trade, column M denotes the MMP, column AH denotes the available equity, and column AF denotes the number of entry signals that day. (See Figure 26.3 for columns L and M, Figure 26.4 for cell C3, and Figure 26.7 for columns AG, AH, and AF.)

To calculate the amount tied up in the trade, in cell R11 type:=L11*Q11

To calculate the actual amount risked in the trade, in cell S11 type:
=N11*Q11, where column N denotes the stop loss.

To calculate the open profit or loss of the trade, in cell T11 type:
=IF(Q11>0,O11*Q11−$C$4,0), where column O denotes the open profit or loss for one share, and cell C4 denotes the costs (see Figure 26.3).

To calculate the closed-out profit or loss of the trade, in cell U11 type:
=IF(AND(Q11=0,Q10>0),P11*Q10-$C$4,0), where column P denotes the closed-out profit or loss for one share (see Figure 26.3).

Highlight the cells in row 11 and drag down to fill the cells below with the formulas in row 11, for as many cells as necessary to accommodate all trades in all markets. Do the same for all other markets. In this case, the spreadsheet is prepared for three markets, with the data for Market 1 in columns B to F, the calculations for Market 1 in columns G to K, the data for Market 3 in columns V to Z, and the calculations for Market 3 in columns AA to AE.

Three items of importance to note about the formulas for Figure 26.6 are that even though a trade is signaled on a one-share basis in columns L to P, in Figure 26.3, a trade still might not take place if all the money already is tied up in other trades. Second, if the f is so high that the amount of capital needed to buy the shares specified by f isn't available, we will buy as many shares as possible, given the money at hand, not already tied up in other positions.

Third, because all signals and trades are recorded at the end of a trading day, there is no way to tell the true intra-day order of the trades in case the system gave several signals in several markets during the same day. Therefore, the best com- promise for our analysis is to split the money between these signals.

For example, if, at the end of one day, we have $30,000 available on the account (not already tied up in any trades), but also three new signals, each one asking for $20,000 from the available money, we will give each new signal $10,000. After this, the available money will be zero, unless we have no closed- out trades, which will transfer to the account the exit price of that market, multi- plied by the number of shares in the closed-out trade.

Last, we need to calculate the combined result from all trades, open and closed, on a daily basis, to find out how that will affect our portfolio as a whole. This is done in columns AF to AL in Figure 26.7. First, we need to calculate the number of new signals we have each day, so that we know how to divide the money among them, according to the rules just described (column AF). Once that is done, the account equity for each day is calculated as the previous day's equity, plus the change from one day to the next in the open profit or loss for all open trades, plus the closed-out profit or loss from all trades closed out that day (column AG).

The available equity, in column AH, is calculated as the total equity, in col- umn AG, minus the open profit or loss (column T, for Market 2), minus the initial amount tied up in all open trades (column R, for Market 2). The daily percentage fluctuations in the total equity are calculated in column AL. To calculate the draw- downs (in column AJ) and flat times (in column AK), we first need to calculate the latest equity top in column AI.

The formulas for this specific spreadsheet and Figure 26.7 read as follows:

To calculate the number of new entry signals, in cell AF11 type:
=IF(AND(B11<>B10,B11>0),1,0)+IF(AND(L11<>L10,L11>0),1,0)+IF(AND(V11<>V10,V11>0),1,0), where columns B and V denote the entry price for Markets 1 and 3, respectively. (Markets 1 and 3 not shown.)

To start the portfolio equity calculation, in cell AG10 type: =C2.

To calculate the portfolio equity, in cell AG11 type:
=AG10+SUM(J11−J10,T11−T10,AD11−AD10)+SUM(K11,U11,AE11), where columns J and AD denote the open profit or loss for markets 1 and 3, respectively, and columns K and AE denote the closed-out profit or loss for markets 1 and 3, respectively.

To start the available equity calculation, in cell AH10 type: =AG10.

To calculate the available equity, in cell AH11 type:
AG11−SUM(J11,T11,AD11)−SUM(H11,R11,AB11), where columns H and AB denote the tied up capital in trades in markets 1 and 3, respectively.

To start the equity top calculation, in cell AI10 type: =AG10.

To calculate the equity top, in cell AI11 type: =MAX(AG$10:AG11).

To calculate the drawdown, in cell AJ10 type: =−(AI10–AG10)/AI10.

To calculate the flat time, in cell AK10 type: =IF(AJ10<0,AK9+1,0).

To calculate the daily return, in cell AL11 type: =(AG11−AG10)/AG10.

Highlight the cells in row 11 and drag down to fill the cells below with the formulas in row 11, for as many cells as necessary to accommodate all trades in all markets. Note that new columns must be added in case you add more markets to the calculations, and that the column references for the portfolio calculations will change depending on the number of markets used.

To get a more visual feel for the system, we can make a chart of the equity curve, as in Figure 26.8, and a chart of the drawdowns as in Figure 26.9. All the

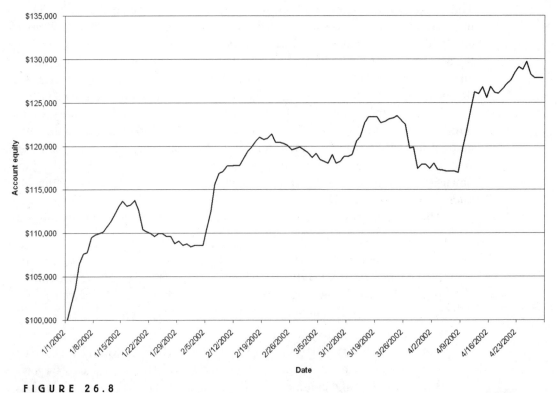

FIGURE 26.8

Equity curve chart.

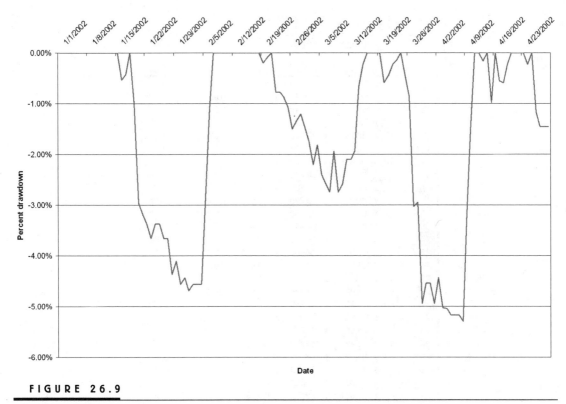

FIGURE 26.9

Drawdown underwater chart.

dips below the zero line in the drawdown chart correspond to the downturns in the equity chart. Note in Figure 26.9 how the largest drawdown is only a tad larger than the second largest drawdown, and how the system manages to trade itself out of it and set another new equity high before the end of the testing period.

A few of these numbers change when we change the fictive f from 2 to 4 percent. First, note in Figure 26.10 how the available equity in row 11 goes down to $10,040, as compared to $48,020 in Figure 26.7. This is because the amount tied up in the two positions that day increased with the amount risked. In fact, in the case of market 2, the suggested amount tied up, based on the total equity, increased to an amount surpassing the amount available in Figure 26.10. Therefore, the amount tied up in Figure 26.11 reaches its maximum of $50,000, which is calculated as the amount available from the end of the previous day (cell AH10, in Figure 26.10), divided by the number of new signals that day (cell AF11, in Figure 26.10).

A few rows in Figure 26.10 also indicate that no equity is available at the end of that day, going into the next day's trading (rows 25, 35, and 36). Had there been any trades signaled for rows 26, 36, and 37, we would not have been able to take those trades, simply because all our money would have been tied up in other trades already.

	AF	AG	AH	AI	AJ	AK	AL
	BD73	▾		=			
8				Portfolio			
9	New	Equity	Avail	Top	DD	FT	Daily
10		$ 100,000	$ 100,000	$ 100,000	0.00%	0	
11	2	$ 102,752	$ 10,040	$ 102,752	0.00%	0	2.75%
12	-	$ 105,544	$ 10,040	$ 105,544	0.00%	0	2.72%
13	-	$ 110,334	$ 10,040	$ 110,334	0.00%	0	4.54%
14	-	$ 111,794	$ 72,520	$ 111,794	0.00%	0	1.32%
15	-	$ 112,127	$ 72,520	$ 112,127	0.00%	0	0.30%
16	1	$ 115,666	$ 24,520	$ 115,666	0.00%	0	3.16%
17	-	$ 116,306	$ 75,700	$ 116,306	0.00%	0	0.55%
18	-	$ 116,639	$ 75,700	$ 116,639	0.00%	0	0.29%
19	-	$ 116,972	$ 75,700	$ 116,972	0.00%	0	0.29%
20	1	$ 118,220	$ 36,430	$ 118,220	0.00%	0	1.07%
21	-	$ 119,488	$ 36,430	$ 119,488	0.00%	0	1.07%
22	-	$ 121,089	$ 79,034	$ 121,089	0.00%	0	1.34%
23	1	$ 123,080	$ 34,918	$ 123,080	0.00%	0	1.64%
24	-	$ 124,553	$ 34,918	$ 124,553	0.00%	0	1.20%
25	1	$ 123,619	$ -	$ 124,553	-0.75%	1	-0.75%
26	-	$ 124,033	$ 33,335	$ 124,553	-0.42%	2	0.33%
27	-	$ 125,237	$ 33,335	$ 125,237	0.00%	0	0.97%
28	-	$ 122,829	$ 78,195	$ 125,237	-1.92%	1	-1.92%
29	-	$ 117,987	$ 117,987	$ 125,237	-5.79%	2	-3.94%
30	1	$ 117,495	$ 59,521	$ 125,237	-6.18%	3	-0.42%
31	-	$ 117,024	$ 59,521	$ 125,237	-6.56%	4	-0.40%
32	-	$ 116,316	$ 59,521	$ 125,237	-7.12%	5	-0.60%
33	-	$ 117,024	$ 59,521	$ 125,237	-6.56%	6	0.61%
34	-	$ 117,024	$ 59,521	$ 125,237	-6.56%	7	0.00%
35	2	$ 116,972	$ -	$ 125,237	-6.60%	8	-0.04%
36	-	$ 116,972	$ -	$ 125,237	-6.60%	9	0.00%
37	-	$ 115,495	$ 28,252	$ 125,237	-7.78%	10	-1.26%
38	-	$ 116,202	$ 28,252	$ 125,237	-7.21%	11	0.61%
39	-	$ 115,024	$ 85,284	$ 125,237	-8.15%	12	-1.01%

FIGURE 26.10

Changing f from 2 to 4 percent.

In Figure 26.11, note how the values of both the two winning trades and the losing trades are larger than for the same trades in Figure 26.6. This is not always a given, just because we're risking more in the trades in Figure 26.11. Many times, risking more might mean a faster equity growth and higher equity in the end, but it also might mean a more volatile development, which means situations where the equity may have dipped to such low levels that the dollar values of the positions are lower, despite a higher risk per trade. A limited amount of capital available for new positions also might limit the amount invested (and consequently also won or lost), on those days where the system signals several new positions simultaneously.

Figure 26.12 shows the end result from trading these three markets with a fictive f of 4 percent. As you can see, the total return is higher, but there defi-

	Q	R	S	T	U
	AR82	▾		=	
	Q	R	S	T	U
8	Market 2				
9	**Shares**	**Tied**	**Risk**	**Open**	**Close**
10					
11	1,563	$ 50,000	$ 1,172	$ 3,105	$ -
12	1,563	$ 50,000	$ 1,172	$ 6,230	$ -
13	1,563	$ 50,000	$ 1,172	$ 9,355	$ -
14	-	$ -	$ -	$ -	$ 12,480
15	-	$ -	$ -	$ -	$ -
16	-	$ -	$ -	$ -	$ -
17	-	$ -	$ -	$ -	$ -
18	-	$ -	$ -	$ -	$ -
19	-	$ -	$ -	$ -	$ -
20	935	$ 39,270	$ 1,870	$ 915	$ -
21	935	$ 39,270	$ 1,870	$ 1,850	$ -
22	935	$ 39,270	$ 1,870	$ 2,785	$ -
23	935	$ 39,270	$ 1,870	$ 3,720	$ -
24	935	$ 39,270	$ 1,870	$ 4,655	$ -
25	935	$ 39,270	$ 1,870	$ 5,590	$ -
26	935	$ 39,270	$ 1,870	$ 6,525	$ -
27	935	$ 39,270	$ 1,870	$ 7,460	$ -
28	-	$ -	$ -	$ -	$ 5,590
29	-	$ -	$ -	$ -	$ -
30	-	$ -	$ -	$ -	$ -
31	-	$ -	$ -	$ -	$ -
32	-	$ -	$ -	$ -	$ -
33	-	$ -	$ -	$ -	$ -
34	-	$ -	$ -	$ -	$ -
35	595	$ 29,760	$ 1,488	$ (1,210)	$ -
36	595	$ 29,760	$ 1,488	$ (1,210)	$ -
37	-	$ -	$ -	$ -	$ (1,508)
38	-	$ -	$ -	$ -	$ -
39	-	$ -	$ -	$ -	$ -

FIGURE 26.11

Changing f from 2 to 4 percent.

nitely was a price to pay for the higher return as compared to the return from risking only 2 percent per trade in Figure 26.5. The first thing we notice is that the largest drawdown is almost twice as deep in Figure 26.12 as in Figure 26.5. The longest flat time also is six days longer. These changes can also be seen in Figures 26.13 and 26.14. In Figure 26.14, the largest drawdown goes on for another several days as compared to the largest drawdown in Figure 26.9. This shows up on Figure 26.13 in the form of a more flattened out equity curve than that in Figure 26.8.

The larger swings in the equity curve also show up as a lower risk–reward ratio in Figure 26.12. That the larger price swings are mostly connected to the losing trades is evident from the lower profit factor, which, despite the higher profit,

AD74	▼		≡	=IF(AA74>0,Y74*AA74-
	F	G	H	I	J	K
1						
2		End. eq.	$ 144,246	Max DD	9.93%	
3		Tot. ret.	44.25%	Max FT	28	
4		Tot. tr.	31	R-R ratio	0.2363	
5		Win %	41.94%	P. factor	2.41	
6						

FIGURE 26.12

End result of f–4 percent on three markets.

indicates that we now are losing proportionally more money in the losing trades. The cost for making a profit has increased with the increased risk per trade.

However, this is not to say that the 2 percent risk per trade is the preferred alternative. That is completely up to you to decide, after having tested the system for different risk levels and comparing all the results in a way that feels most comfortable to you.

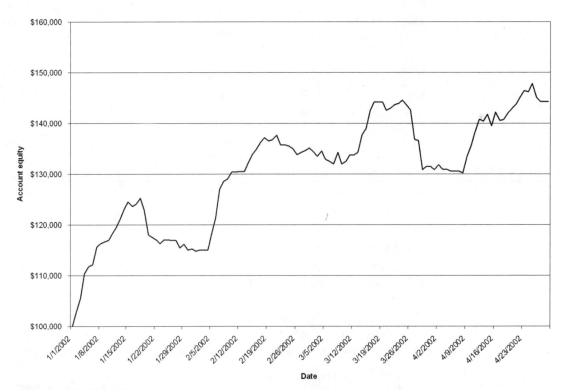

FIGURE 26.13

Flattened equity curve.

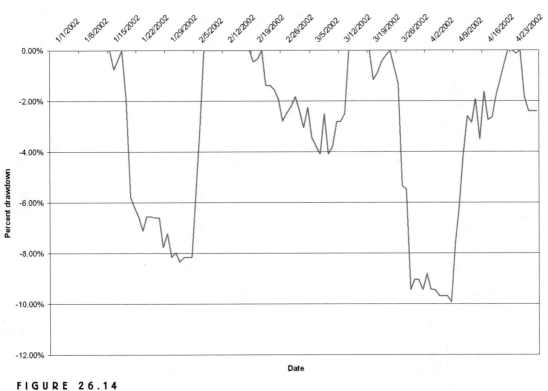

FIGURE 26.14

Increased drawdown time.

CHAPTER 27

Spreadsheet Development

Now that we have learned how to build a simple spreadsheet to calculate *f*, let's look at a more professional version and what we can analyze with it. This spreadsheet is the one that I use to calculate the result for the systems in *Active Trader* magazine. All the initial performance summaries in Part 2 were, for example, put together with this spreadsheet. I wish I could show you how to put together a spreadsheet like this, but there is simply too much going on here to make that possible. This spreadsheet can calculate the combined results from 2,500 days of trading (approximately 10 years) on 60 markets simultaneously.

Figure 27.1 shows the initial parameter setting that you can experiment with. The initial equity, risk-per-trade multiple, and average commissions are the same as those in Figure 26.3. To this, I have added the possibility to adjust for dividends and for an interest rate earned on the money left on the account.

The max margin-to-equity ratio keeps the system from entering into any new positions if this number is surpassed, to avoid having all money tied up in open positions, if the unthinkable happens and everything starts to move against you. The max drawdown and max monthly drawdown values let you stop trading mid-month if the drawdown reaches intolerable levels. In both cases, the trading resumes at the beginning of the next month, but will only be allowed to continue as long as the trading goes your way. The mean accepted return is used to calculate the *Sortino ratio* in Figure 27.2.

For the strategy summary and rolling time window return analysis I strived to gather as much information as possible, similar to the Institutional Advisory Services Group (IASG) Web site. Figures 27.4 to 27.7 show the Web site.

L33	▼	=	
	B	C	D
9			
10	**Initial settings**		
11	**Initial equity**		$1,000,000
12	**Risk/trade (multiple)**		2.00%
13	**Average commissions**		$25
14	**Margin***		100%
15	**Dividends****		-1.00%
16	**Interest rate**		
17	**Min accepted return****		10.00%
18	**Max margin to equity**		100%
19	**Max drawdown**		100%
20	**Max monthly DD**		100%

FIGURE 27.1

Initial parameter settings.

In Figure 27.2, the ending equity and the total return are the same as those in Figure 26.3. The average annual return is the compounded (or geometric) return, which means the calculation makes use of the profits from previous years going into each new year. The gain-to-loss ratio is similar to the profit factor, but instead of dividing the gross profit by the gross loss, the gain-to-loss ratio divides the average gain over a specific length (a month) of winning periods, with the average loss over the same-length losing periods.

The winning months show the percentage of all months that end up with a profit. Remember, often it is more important to have a high percentage of winning months, rather than a high percentage of winning markets or trades.

The maximum drawdown and flat times are the same as in Figure 26.5, except the flat time is expressed in months instead of days. The average drawdown sums all the deepest points (one per drawdown) in all drawdowns and divides by the number of drawdowns.

The Sharpe ratio is the average growth rate in the equity per month, minus the risk-free interest rate (as defined in Figure 27.1), divided by the standard deviation of the monthly returns. The Sortino ratio is another risk–return ratio that compares the monthly returns above a certain threshold level (see Figure 27.1) with those below the same level.

N33		=							
E F	G	H	I	J	K	L	M	

Strategy summary

Profitability			Drawdown & risk			
Ending equity ($):		2,067,431	DD max / average (%):		30.39	4.75
Total return (%):		107	Flat max / average (m):		44.60	2.26
Average annual return (%):		7.87	Sharpe ratio monthly / yearly:		0.11	0.52
Gain to loss ratio:		1.54	Sortino ratio monthly / yearly:		(0.00)	(0.20)
Profit to loss ratio ($):		1.44	Margin req. max / avg (%):		24.14	3.45
Winning months (%):		48.28	Time in market (%):		70.28	28.15

Trade statistics				Trade frequency			
Average contract / trade ($):		57.08	848.51	Contracts / Trades per million:		12,193	820
Average win / loss ($):		15,165.84	(7,893.72)	Average days in trade:			3.38
Largest win / loss ($):		105,730.00	(57,372.50)	Trades total / month:		1,258	10.94
Win. markets / trades (%):		66.67	36.27	Trades / (system/market) / year:			21.88

Distribution analysis					
Skewness:		0.83	Kurtosis:		1.62

Miscellaneous					
System/market combinations:		6	Total commissions ($):		467,500
Years tested:		9.58	Accrued dividends ($):		-
Start / End dates:	01/01/93	08/01/02	Accrued interest ($):		-

FIGURE 27.2

The strategy summary for the professional spreadsheet.

The maximum and average margin requirements show how much of the total equity is tied up in one or several positions, as the highest value over the whole testing period or as an average for all days tested, including those days when we have no open positions at all. The time in market shows how much time the entire strategy, made up of all systems and markets tested and the average of all system-market combinations, spent in a trade.

Of the numbers mentioned, those to take most notice of are the average annual return in relation to the Sharpe ratio, the maximum drawdown and flat time in relation to the average drawdown, the gain-to-loss ratio, and the percentage of winning months. The rest of the numbers grouped under Trade statistics, Trade frequency, Distribution analysis, and Miscellaneous are less important, simply because it's too much to keep track of, rank against everything else, and compromise between.

For example, if a strategy has a skewness and kurtosis I am not all that happy with, but otherwise shows a good profit potential and a low risk, I am not about to

N59	=								
B C	D E	F	G	H	I	J	K	L	M

Rolling time window return analysis								
Cumulative	1 month	3 months	6 months	12 months	24 months	36 months	48 months	60 months
Most recent:	2.38%	-2.77%	-11.54%	-8.30%	20.77%	26.18%	75.15%	89.69%
Average:	0.78%	2.10%	4.31%	9.10%	19.44%	31.22%	43.14%	55.41%
Average win:	5.10%	8.16%	10.45%	17.13%	30.69%	47.58%	61.05%	58.81%
Average loss:	-3.30%	-5.38%	-7.97%	-8.42%	-11.18%	-10.04%	-7.58%	-4.71%
Best:	22.04%	28.96%	29.86%	52.95%	86.74%	101.76%	135.61%	147.21%
Worst:	-13.53%	-19.43%	-18.26%	-15.56%	-22.47%	-25.96%	-17.60%	-6.38%
Standard deviation:	5.64%	8.68%	11.20%	15.03%	26.07%	37.05%	44.71%	46.18%
Gain standard deviation:	4.69%	6.35%	8.03%	10.62%	21.03%	30.73%	38.18%	45.11%
Loss standard deviation:	2.69%	4.11%	4.46%	4.72%	5.89%	7.78%	4.75%	1.50%
Downside deviation:	3.49%	5.90%	7.95%	10.85%	18.37%	25.66%	31.93%	34.08%
Annualized	1 month	3 months	6 months	12 months	24 months	36 months	48 months	60 months
Most recent:	32.54%	-10.64%	-21.75%	-8.30%	9.90%	8.06%	15.04%	13.66%
Average:	9.78%	8.68%	8.80%	9.10%	9.29%	9.48%	9.38%	9.22%
Average win:	81.60%	36.84%	21.99%	17.13%	14.32%	13.85%	12.65%	9.69%
Average loss:	-33.18%	-19.83%	-15.31%	-8.42%	-5.75%	-3.46%	-1.95%	-0.96%
Best:	991.36%	176.57%	68.64%	52.95%	36.65%	26.36%	23.89%	19.84%
Worst:	-82.54%	-57.86%	-33.19%	-15.56%	-11.95%	-9.53%	-4.72%	-1.31%
Standard deviation:	93.14%	39.48%	23.65%	15.03%	12.28%	11.08%	9.68%	7.89%
Gain standard deviation:	73.32%	27.90%	16.70%	10.62%	10.01%	9.34%	8.42%	7.73%
Loss standard deviation:	37.44%	17.49%	9.12%	4.72%	2.90%	2.53%	1.17%	0.30%
Downside deviation:	50.92%	25.75%	16.53%	10.85%	8.80%	7.91%	7.17%	6.04%

FIGURE 27.3

Rolling time window analysis for the professional spreadsheet.

start tweaking that system any further to come to grips with the skew and kurtosis. I'd rather start working on a new system to see if I can combine new systems and markets to come up with a new strategy that also has good skew and kurtosis figures. If that doesn't work either, so be it. I think you already have discovered that to build and research a system, combine several systems and markets into a whole strategy, and incorporate fixed fractional money management rules can be as complex and time consuming as you want it to be.

Just to show you the complexity of the formulas going into this spreadsheet, this formula calculates the amount risked in a trade for one market at a specific point in time:

=IF(AND(INDEX(NewSignals,ThisRow)>0,INDEX(EntryM4,ThisRow)<>
INDEX(EntryM4,ThisRow−1),INDEX(EntryM4,ThisRow)>0),
MIN(INT(INDEX(TradeableEquity,ThisRow–1)*WeightM4*PercentRisk2/
(INDEX(RiskM4,ThisRow)*PointValM4))*IF(MarginReqM4=0,
INDEX(EntryM4,ThisRow),MarginReqM4),IF(MarginReqM4=0,INDEX(Trade
ableEquity,ThisRow−1)*(1/INDEX(NewSignals,ThisRow)),

INT(INDEX(TradeableEquity,ThisRow−1)*(1/INDEX(NewSignals,ThisRow))/

MarginReqM4)*MarginReqM4)),IF(INDEX(ProfitM4,ThisRow)=0,

INDEX(CommM4,ThisRow–1),0))

This formula calculates the accrued interest:

=INDEX(AvailableEquity,ThisRow)*((1+InterestRate2)^(1/365)−1)

This formula calculates the bottom of a drawdown:

=IF(INDEX(FlatTime,ThisRow)>INDEX(FlatTime,ThisRow+1),

MIN(INDEX(Drawdown,ThisRow−INDEX(FlatTime,ThisRow)+1):

INDEX(Drawdown,ThisRow)),"")

Note that none of the formulas makes use of any normal cell references, such as "B14," referring to the cell in column B, row 14. To speed up the computing time and to simplify error checking, I have given all the input and output variables specific names, just as one would do to program the entire analysis spreadsheet in a regular programming language, such as Visual Basic or Delphi.

Figures 27.4 to 27.7 are taken from the IASG Web site (www.iasg.com) and are provided just to give you something to compare with. IASG is a Chicago-based brokerage company that also tracks and publishes the results of many commodity trading advisors and fund managers. The IASG Web site also has a comprehensive help page that describes and shows the calculations behind many of the evaluation variables used.

Other companies that also track many CTAs and fund managers include The Barclays Group (www.barclaygrp.com), Van Hedge Fund Advisors (www.hedgefund.com), Hedgefund.net (www.hedgefund.net), Hedgefund247 (www.hedgefund247.com), International Traders Research (www.managedfutures .com), and Risk & Portfolio Management (www.rpm.se) in Sweden.

The numbers in Figures 27.4 to 27.7 are all real performance numbers from real fund managers and CTAs. Note that several performance numbers in these figures can't be found in my spreadsheet in Figures 27.2 and 27.3, such as the monthly performance summary in Figure 27.2 and several of the different ratios in Figure 27.3. The time-window analysis in Figure 27.6 is basically the same as that in Figure 27.3, except Figure 27.3 also holds the annualized numbers. Some of the information in Figures 27.4 to 27.7 also is redundant, such as the monthly numbers in Figure 27.4 and the chart of the monthly ROR at the bottom left in Figure 27.7.

Figure 27.7 shows a few charts that also can be found on the IASG Web site. The top left chart shows the equity growth of a specific advisor, while the bottom right chart shows the drawdowns. These are essentially the same charts as those we put together in Figures 26.8 and 26.9, and 26.13 and 26.14. They are also essen-

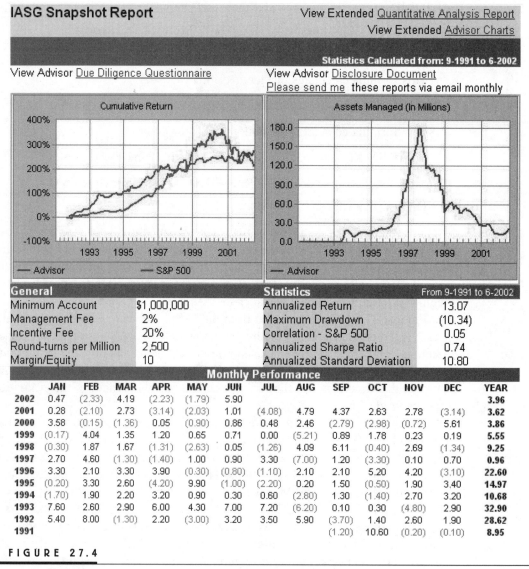

IASG Snapshot Report

View Extended Quantitative Analysis Report
View Extended Advisor Charts

Statistics Calculated from: 9-1991 to 6-2002

View Advisor Due Diligence Questionnaire

View Advisor Disclosure Document
Please send me these reports via email monthly

General		Statistics	From 9-1991 to 6-2002
Minimum Account	$1,000,000	Annualized Return	13.07
Management Fee	2%	Maximum Drawdown	(10.34)
Incentive Fee	20%	Correlation - S&P 500	0.05
Round-turns per Million	2,500	Annualized Sharpe Ratio	0.74
Margin/Equity	10	Annualized Standard Deviation	10.80

Monthly Performance

	JAN	FEB	MAR	APR	MAY	JUN	JUL	AUG	SEP	OCT	NOV	DEC	YEAR
2002	0.47	(2.33)	4.19	(2.23)	(1.79)	5.90							**3.96**
2001	0.28	(2.10)	2.73	(3.14)	(2.03)	1.01	(4.08)	4.79	4.37	2.63	2.78	(3.14)	**3.62**
2000	3.58	(0.15)	(1.36)	0.05	(0.90)	0.86	0.48	2.46	(2.79)	(2.98)	(0.72)	5.61	**3.86**
1999	(0.17)	4.04	1.35	1.20	0.65	0.71	0.00	(5.21)	0.89	1.78	0.23	0.19	**5.55**
1998	(0.30)	1.87	1.67	(1.31)	(2.63)	0.05	(1.26)	4.09	6.11	(0.40)	2.69	(1.34)	**9.25**
1997	2.70	4.60	(1.30)	(1.40)	1.00	0.90	3.30	(7.00)	1.20	(3.30)	0.10	0.70	**0.96**
1996	3.30	2.10	3.30	3.90	(0.30)	(0.80)	(1.10)	2.10	2.10	5.20	4.20	(3.10)	**22.60**
1995	(0.20)	3.30	2.60	(4.20)	9.90	(1.00)	(2.20)	0.20	1.50	(0.50)	1.90	3.40	**14.97**
1994	(1.70)	1.90	2.20	3.20	0.90	0.30	0.60	(2.80)	1.30	(1.40)	2.70	3.20	**10.68**
1993	7.60	2.60	2.90	6.00	4.30	7.00	7.20	(6.20)	0.10	0.30	(4.80)	2.90	**32.90**
1992	5.40	8.00	(1.30)	2.20	(3.00)	3.20	3.50	5.90	(3.70)	1.40	2.60	1.90	**28.62**
1991									(1.20)	10.60	(0.20)	(0.10)	**8.95**

FIGURE 27.4

The IASG Web site.

tially the same as those in Figures 27.8 and 27.9, which are made with the help of my own professional spreadsheet.

The monthly distributions in the top right chart in Figure 27.7 illustrate the same thing as Figure 27.10 from my professional spreadsheet. Note especially in Figure 27.7 how close to a normal distribution the monthly returns are, and remember what we learned in Part 3—the returns over specific periods of time should be normally distributed around an average profit per

IASG Quantitative Analysis Report	View IASG Snapshot Report
Benchmark Analysis	View Extended Advisor Charts

Statistics Calculated from: 9-1991 to 6-2002

View Advisor Due Diligence Questionnaire   View Advisor Disclosure Document
                                              Please send me these reports via email monthly

RECENT RETURNS	BENCHMARK ANALYSIS	TIME WINDOWS ANALYSIS	DRAWDOWN ANALYSIS

vs. S&P 500

	Monthly		Quarterly		Annualized	
	Manager	**Benchmark**	**Manager**	**Benchmark**	**Manager**	**Benchmark**
Compound Return	1.03%	0.88%	3.12%	2.66%	13.07%	11.09%
Arithmetic Mean	1.08%	0.97%	3.15%	3.08%	N/A	N/A
Standard Deviation	3.12%	4.16%	5.55%	6.68%	10.80%	14.41%
Sharpe Ratio	0.21	0.13	0.35	0.28	0.74	0.47
Gain Deviation	2.28%	2.42%	4.25%	4.58%	7.89%	8.40%
Loss Deviation	1.63%	2.74%	1.44%	4.21%	5.65%	9.49%
Downside Deviation MAR	1.97%	3.00%	3.22%	4.45%	6.81%	10.39%
Downside Deviation RF	1.76%	2.80%	2.55%	3.90%	6.10%	9.71%
Downside Deviation 0%	1.56%	2.61%	1.90%	3.38%	5.41%	9.03%
Sortino Ratio MAR	0.12	0.03	0.22	0.06	0.41	0.10
Sortino Ratio RF	0.35	0.17	0.74	0.37	1.22	0.58
Sortino Ratio 0%	0.66	0.34	1.64	0.79	2.28	1.17
Skewness	0.26	-0.46	0.32	-0.04	N/A	N/A
Kurtosis	0.46	0.82	-0.80	1.39	N/A	N/A
Sterling Ratio	0.20	-0.35	N/A	N/A	N/A	N/A
Calmar Ratio	0.36	-0.28	N/A	N/A	N/A	N/A
Losing Streak	0.00%	-33.18%	N/A	N/A	N/A	N/A

Regression Analysis	Monthly	Quarterly	Performance Ratios	Monthly	Quarterly
Annualized Alpha	13.22%	9.87%	Outperform Up Markets	26.83%	28.13%
Beta	0.04	0.25	Outperform Down Markets	77.08%	90.91%
Correlation	0.05	0.30	Outperform All Markets	45.38%	44.19%
R-Squared	0.00	0.09	Up Capture Ratio	15.13%	38.31%
Tracking Error	0.18	0.25	Down Capture Ratio	(18.35)%	(41.57)%
Information Ratio	0.11	0.02	% Up in Up Markets	71.95%	65.63%
Treynor Ratio	2.13	0.30	% Down in Down Markets	47.92%	18.18%
Jensen Alpha	0.65%	2.08%	Periods Profitable Ratio	102.44%	93.75%
Active Premium	1.98%	0.63%			

FIGURE 27.5

The IASG Web site.

month, not the trades themselves, which should have a set of few very specific outcomes.

Finally, we've already looked at the monthly return chart at the bottom left corner in Figure 27.7. The professional spreadsheet's version of the same chart can be seen in Figure 27.12, which also holds the same information as the monthly performance numbers in Figure 27.4 and similar type of information as the time-window numbers in Figures 27.3 and 27.6. Aside from all the charts mentioned,

IASG Quantitative Analysis Report
Time Windows Analysis

View **IASG Snapshot Report**
View **Extended** Advisor Charts

Statistics Calculated from: 9-1991 to 6-2002

View Advisor Due Diligence Questionnaire   View Advisor Disclosure Document
Please send me these reports via email monthly

RECENT RETURNS	BENCHMARK ANALYSIS			TIME WINDOWS ANALYSIS			DRAWDOWN ANALYSIS		
Time Windows Analysis	1 Month	3 Month	6 Month	12 Month	18 Month	2 Year	3 Year	4 Year	5 Year
Number of Periods	130	128	125	119	113	107	95	83	71
Percent Profitable	64.62%	74.22%	77.60%	84.03%	92.92%	97.20%	100.00%	100.00%	100.00%
Average Period Return	1.08%	3.16%	6.39%	12.86%	19.70%	25.76%	39.52%	56.84%	75.46%
Average Gain	2.80%	5.37%	9.07%	15.83%	21.44%	26.60%	39.52%	56.84%	75.46%
Average Loss	(2.07%)	(3.19%)	(2.91%)	(2.76%)	(3.19%)	(3.29%)			
Best Period	10.60%	19.64%	34.38%	55.75%	75.80%	91.84%	99.63%	128.77%	176.83%
Worst Period	(7.00%)	(8.99%)	(9.31%)	(10.07%)	(7.02%)	(5.86%)	4.00%	1.88%	14.45%
Standard Deviation	3.12%	5.35%	8.14%	12.86%	17.95%	20.33%	24.69%	34.53%	45.59%
Gain Standard Deviation	2.28%	4.31%	7.17%	11.84%	17.42%	20.00%	24.69%	34.53%	45.59%
Loss Standard Deviation	1.63%	1.76%	2.47%	2.57%	1.92%	2.23%			
Sharpe Ratio (5.0%)	0.21	0.36	0.48	0.61	0.67	0.76	0.96	1.02	1.05
Average Gain/Average Loss	1.35	1.69	3.12	5.73	6.71	8.08			
Profit/Loss Ratio	2.47	4.85	10.82	30.15	88.13	280.22			
Downside Deviation (10.0%)	1.97%	3.05%	4.12%	6.12%	7.76%	8.97%	11.82%	15.45%	18.28%
Downside Deviation (5.0%)	1.76%	2.42%	2.84%	3.44%	3.57%	3.15%	2.36%	3.67%	2.62%
Downside Deviation (0%)	1.56%	1.84%	1.79%	1.49%	0.98%	0.63%			
Sortino Ratio (10.0%)	0.14	0.25	0.37	0.47	0.56	0.53	0.54	0.68	0.79
Sortino Ratio (5.0%)	0.38	0.80	1.38	2.28	3.39	4.93	10.06	9.62	18.28
Sortino Ratio (0%)	0.69	1.72	3.57	8.64	20.20	40.90			

FIGURE 27.6

The IASG Web site.

my professional spreadsheet also has a chart over the drawdown distribution, as shown in Figure 27.11, which holds parts of the information that the IASG drawdown analysis holds (not shown).

Aside from the portfolio analysis, the spreadsheet also can look at the individual markets to help you get a feel for how they interact with each other and the portfolio as a whole. The most interesting numbers here are the percentage contribution and the percentage correlation, in Figure 27.14. The percentage contribution number shows how large the profit or loss is in an individual market in relation to the total profit or loss of the portfolio. The percentage correlation number shows how much the equity curve of the individual market correlates with the total equity.

However, because all markets are dependent on each other, the relationships between the results for the individual markets and the portfolio as a whole are not

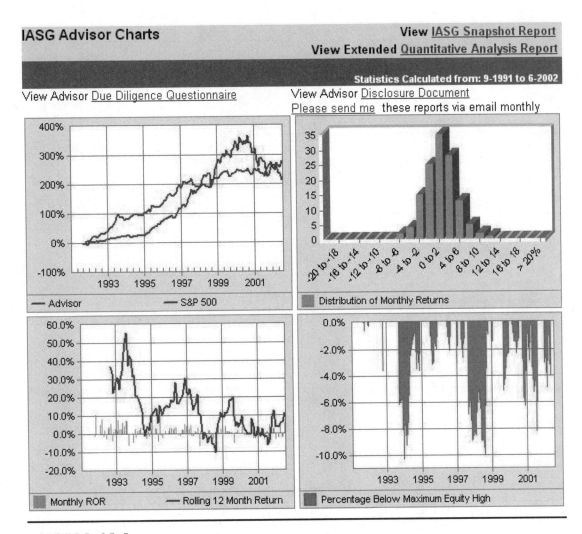

FIGURE 27.7

The IASG Web site.

linear, so that, for example, a positive equity for one market will not always mean a positive contribution to the portfolio equity. Instead, it all depends on where and when all the contributions, in the form of winning and losing trades, happen in relation to each other.

For example, a market with a negative contribution and a negative correlation still might add positively to the overall result, because of its tendency to be profitable when all other markets are not. This helps keep up the portfolio equity and allows for larger positions in the other markets, once they start to function again.

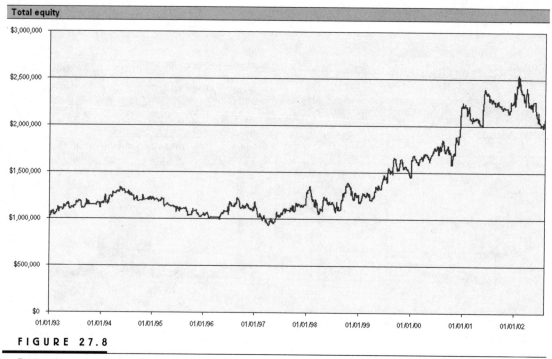

FIGURE 27.8

Total equity curve from spreadsheet.

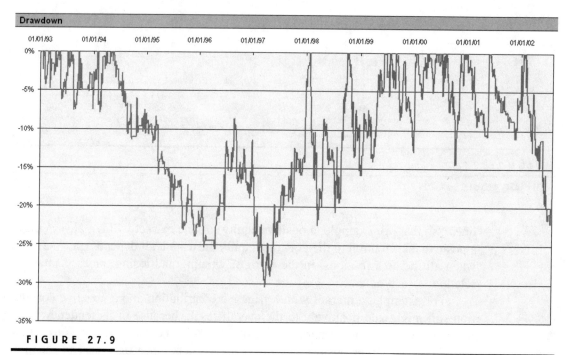

FIGURE 27.9

Drawdown curve from spreadsheet.

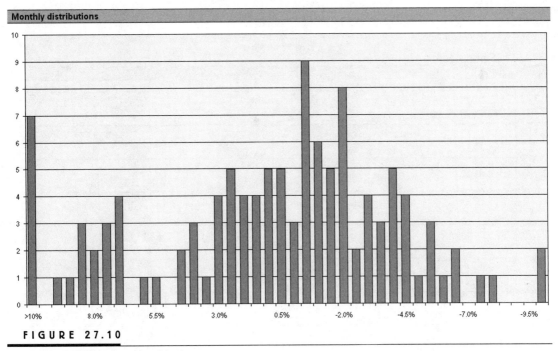

FIGURE 27.10

Monthly distributions from spreadsheet.

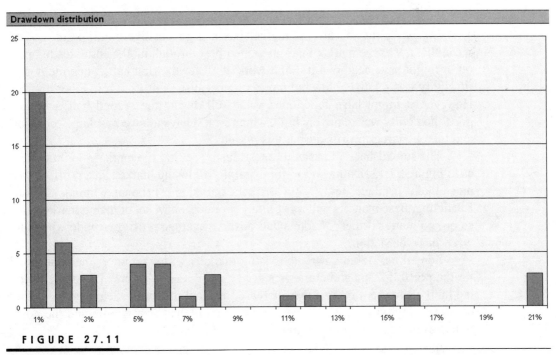

FIGURE 27.11

Distribution of drawdowns from spreadsheet.

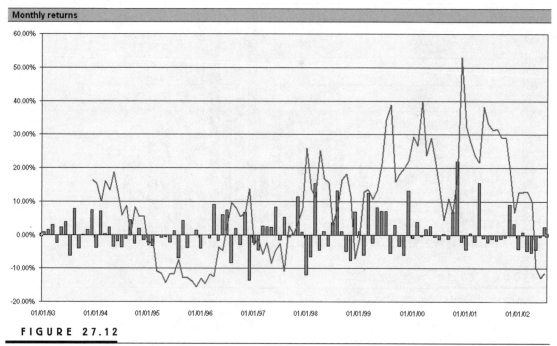

Monthly returns

FIGURE 27.12

Cumulative monthly returns from spreadsheet.

Likewise, just because a market has a high positive contribution doesn't mean that it was the market that functioned best throughout the entire testing period. It might have been that it didn't work at all for the first half, when the portfolio equity was relatively low but increasing because of profits from other markets. However, it might have functioned very well during the second half, when the portfolio equity was relatively high, which would have allowed for larger positions and thereby larger profits during this period.

The spreadsheet allows you to test this by setting the market weight to zero, as in Figure 27.13. Doing so for, for example, all losing markets in a portfolio will most likely produce new losing markets out of the original winning markets. Excluding these markets will most likely produce a new set of losing markets, and so on, no matter if these markets had positive average profit per trade when analyzed in TradeStation.

Sometimes, taking away the losing markets will even lower the final profit for the portfolio, and sometimes it's even a good idea to throw in a couple of losing markets to the mix, to either increase the final profit for the portfolio or even out the equity growth, which would result in a higher Sharpe ratio and the possibility for more aggressive trading.

In short, because all markets are dependent on one another, there are no sure winners or losers. It all depends on where and when all individual markets' prof-

FIGURE 27.13

First part of individual market summary.

Chart Area											
B	C	D	E F	G	H	I	J	K	L	M	
190											
191	**Individual markets summary**										
192	**Markets**	**Weight**	**Point val.**	**No. trades**	**Perc. win.**	**Avg. trade**	**Avg. win**	**Avg. loss**	**Lrg. win**	**Lrg. loss**	
193	DJ0_I0B	1.0	$10.0	140	31.43%	$880.90	$14,960.88	($5,664.30)	$46,119	($13,537)	
194	ND0_I0B	1.0	$20.0	240	25.83%	($349.52)	$10,323.57	($4,067.11)	$24,018	($10,395)	
195	S)0_I0B	1.0	$50.0	234	33.33%	$501.41	$13,715.82	($6,151.76)	$59,535	($29,270)	
196	DJ0_I0B	2.0	$10.0	151	43.71%	$2,055.34	$18,616.13	($11,011.16)	$81,940	($44,828)	
197	ND0_I0B	2.0	$20.0	252	37.70%	($178.27)	$12,915.97	($8,101.53)	$66,906	($31,123)	
198	S)0_I0B	2.0	$50.0	241	45.64%	$2,677.29	$20,462.65	($12,366.45)	$105,730	($57,373)	
199		-									

FIGURE 27.14

Second part of individual market summary.

Chart Area											
B	C	D	E F	G	H	I	J	K	L	M	
255											
256	**Individual markets summary** (cont.)										
257	**Markets**	**Margin**	**Pr. fact.**	**Gr. profit**	**Gr. loss**	**End. eq.**	**TIM (%)**	**Avg. DIT**	**Cont. (%)**	**Corr. (%)**	
258	DJ0_I0B	$4,000	1.21	$658,279	($543,773)	$123,326	22%	3.98	5.97%	95.46	
259	ND0_I0B	$4,500	0.88	$640,061	($723,945)	($83,884)	21%	2.16	-4.06%	-59.55	
260	S)0_I0B	$3,000	1.11	$1,069,834	($959,675)	$117,329	48%	5.13	5.68%	74.31	
261	DJ0_I0B	$4,000	1.31	$1,228,664	($935,949)	$310,356	16%	2.66	15.01%	93.27	
262	ND0_I0B	$4,500	0.96	$1,227,017	($1,271,940)	($44,923)	16%	1.63	-2.17%	-41.74	
263	S)0_I0B	$3,000	1.39	$2,250,892	($1,620,004)	$645,227	45%	4.69	31.21%	98.41	
264											

its and losses came in relation to the equity of the portfolio. Altering the fractional amount risked per trade also might change things around.

MONEY MANAGEMENT EXPORT CODE

Figure 27.15 shows what the raw data look like for one market on a one-share basis. Figure 27.15 is similar to Figure 26.3, except that the stop loss and money management point (MMP) distances are excluded and replaced by the risk column (column L). In this case, the risk column holds the distance between the entry price (column K) and the MMP. Columns M and N hold the open and closed-out profits at the end of the day. In this case, the stop-loss distance isn't necessary for the calculations, but when it is, it will be the same as the MMP distance and show up in the risk column. The data in Figure 27.15 can either be entered manually one day at a time for one market at a time (there is room for 60 system–market combinations), or imported from TradeStation with the help of a special export function created in TradeStation's EasyLanguage, which can look as follows:

AD72	▼	=		

	B	K	L	M	N
1					
2				**Market 3**	
3	Date	S)0_I0B	Risk ($)	Open ($)	Close ($)
4	01/01/93				
5	01/04/93	754.7000	15.8000	5.3500	
6	01/05/93	754.7000	15.8000	6.2500	
7	01/06/93				6.3500
8	01/07/93				
9	01/08/93				
10	01/11/93	743.2000	10.2000	1.6500	
11	01/12/93	743.2000	10.2000	2.1000	
12	01/13/93	743.2000	10.2000	4.0000	
13	01/14/93	743.2000	10.2000	6.9500	
14	01/15/93	743.2000	10.2000	7.1000	
15	01/18/93	743.2000	10.2000	7.9500	
16	01/19/93	743.2000	10.2000	6.2000	
17	01/20/93	743.2000	10.2000	3.8000	
18	01/21/93	743.2000	10.2000	6.9500	
19	01/22/93	743.2000	10.2000	7.3000	
20	01/25/93				6.8500
21	01/26/93	755.4500	15.6001	1.8000	
22	01/27/93	755.4500	15.6001	3.5000	
23	01/28/93	755.4500	15.6001	2.8000	
24	01/29/93	755.4500	15.6001	3.3500	
25	02/01/93	755.4500	15.6001	-0.9000	
26	02/02/93	755.4500	15.6001	-1.4500	
27	02/03/93	755.4500	15.6001	-6.3000	
28	02/04/93				-7.5550
29	02/05/93	762.8000	12.7998	-0.4000	
30	02/08/93	762.8000	12.7998	0.5000	
31	02/09/93	762.8000	12.7998	2.8500	
32	02/10/93	762.8000	12.7998	1.8500	
33	02/11/93	762.8000	12.7998	0.9000	
34	02/12/93	762.8000	12.7998	4.2500	
35	02/15/93	762.8000	12.7998	4.2500	
36	02/16/93	762.8000	12.7998	15.1500	
37	02/17/93	762.8000	12.7998	15.2500	
38	02/18/93	762.8000	12.7998	16.6000	
39	02/19/93	762.8000	12.7998	13.8500	

FIGURE 27.15

Raw data for one market, one-share basis.

{The RiskCalc variable is necessary for the Money Export function, and should be placed adjacent to the stops and exits.}

{1} Variable:

RiskCalc(0);

RiskCalc = TrueRange * 4;

{Money management export, with Normalize(False). SetMoneExport(True).}

Variables:

{2} MoneyExport(True);

If MoneyExport = True Then Begin

Variables: MP(0), TT(0), FileName(""), TradeString(""), OldString(""),
FirstExpDate(0), Missing(0), FillDate(0), SteppinIn(0), PosProfit(0),
ClosedProfit(0), StopLoss(0), RiskValue(0), ExcelMonth(0), ExcelDay(0),
ExcelYear(0), ExcelDate("");

{3}   If BarNumber = 1 Then Begin

      FileName = "D:\Temp\Optisize-" +

      RightStr(NumToStr(CurrentDate, 0), 4) + "-" +

      LeftStr(GetSymbolName, 4) + ".csv";

      FileDelete(FileName);

      TradeString = "Date" + "," + LeftStr(GetSymbolName, 8) + "," +

      "Risk ($)" + "," + "Open ($)" + "," + "Close ($)" + NewLine;

      FileAppend(FileName, TradeString);

      FirstExpDate = DateToJulian(LastCalcDate) - 2500 * 1.4;

      If DateToJulian(Date) >= FirstExpDate Then Begin

         For Missing = FirstExpDate To (DateToJulian(Date) - 1) Begin

            FillDate = JulianToDate(Missing);

            If DayOfWeek(FillDate) > 0 and

            DayOfWeek(FillDate) < 6 Then Begin

{4}   ExcelMonth = Month(FillDate);

               ExcelDay = DayOfMonth(FillDate);

               ExcelYear = Year(FillDate);

                 If ExcelYear >= 100 Then

                   ExcelYear = 2000 + (ExcelYear - 100);

                 ExcelDate = NumToStr(ExcelMonth, 0) + "/" +

                 NumToStr(ExcelDay, 0) + "/" + NumToStr(ExcelYear, 0);

                 TradeString = ExcelDate + "," + "0" + "," +

                 "0" + "," + "0" + "," + "0" + NewLine;

                 If TradeString <> OldString Then

                   FileAppend(FileName, TradeString);

                 OldString = TradeString;

              End;

           End;

         End;

      End;

```
{5}   If DateToJulian(Date) >= FirstExpDate Then Begin
           If DateToJulian(Date) - DateToJulian(Date[1]) > 1 Then Begin;
                For Missing = (DateToJulian(Date[1]) + 1) To (DateToJulian(Date) - 1)
                Begin
                     FillDate = JulianToDate(Missing);
                     If DayOfWeek(FillDate) > 0 and
                     DayOfWeek(FillDate) < 6 Then Begin
                        ExcelMonth = Month(FillDate);
                        ExcelDay = DayOfMonth(FillDate);
                        ExcelYear = Year(FillDate);
                        If ExcelYear >= 100 Then
                           ExcelYear = 2000 + (ExcelYear - 100);
                        ExcelDate = NumToStr(ExcelMonth, 0) + "/" +
                           NumToStr(ExcelDay, 0) + "/" + NumToStr(ExcelYear, 0);
                        TradeString = ExcelDate + "," + NumToStr(SteppinIn[1], 4) +
                        "," +
                        NumToStr(RiskValue[1], 4) + "," + NumToStr(PosProfit[1],
                        4) + "," +
                        "0" + NewLine;
                        If TradeString <> OldString Then
                           FileAppend(FileName, TradeString);
                        OldString = TradeString;
                     End;
                End;
           End;
{6}   ClosedProfit = 0;
      If MarketPosition = 0 Then Begin
         SteppinIn = 0;
         RiskValue = 0;
         PosProfit = 0;
      End;
      If MarketPosition <> 0 Then Begin
         SteppinIn = EntryPrice;
         RiskValue = RiskValue[1];
         If MarketPosition = 1 Then
            PosProfit = Close - EntryPrice;
         If MarketPosition = -1 Then
```

```
            PosProfit = EntryPrice - Close;
        End;
        MP = MarketPosition;
        TT = TotalTrades;
        If TT > TT[1] and MP <> MP[1] Then Begin
            If MP[1] = 1 Then
                ClosedProfit = ExitPrice(1) - EntryPrice(1);
            If MP[1] = -1 Then
                ClosedProfit = EntryPrice(1) - ExitPrice(1);
        End;
        If SteppinIn <> SteppinIn[1] and SteppinIn > 0 Then
            RiskValue = RiskCalc;
{7}     ExcelMonth = Month(Date);
        ExcelDay = DayOfMonth(Date);
        ExcelYear = Year(Date);
        If ExcelYear >= 100 Then
            ExcelYear = 2000 + (ExcelYear - 100);
        ExcelDate = NumToStr(ExcelMonth, 0) + "/" + NumToStr(ExcelDay, 0) +
        "/" + NumToStr(ExcelYear, 0);
        TradeString = ExcelDate + "," + NumToStr(SteppinIn, 4) + "," +
        NumToStr(RiskValue, 4) + "," + NumToStr(PosProfit, 4) + "," +
        NumToStr(ClosedProfit, 4) + NewLine;
        If TradeString <> OldString Then
            FileAppend(FileName, TradeString);
            OldString = TradeString;
        End;   ·
    End;
```

COMMENTS ON THE CODE

Because we already have stepped through a few pieces of code, I will keep the comments brief.

1. The RiskCalc variable must be added to the system code (preferably adjacent to the stops and exits) to calculate the MMP.
2. The variable MoneyExport(True) must be placed on top of the code or even as an input. The other variables will only become active when MoneyExport is set to True. To speed up the computing time, the program will not run through the rest of the code as long as MoneyExport is set to False.

3. The first part of the code only needs to be done once, on the very first bar on the chart. Within that part of the code, we make sure that the first day to be exported is 2,500 days prior to the last day of the chart.

4. This code also transforms the TradeStation data format to Excel date format.

5. The first piece of code that needs to be repeated for every bar makes sure that all data from all markets are synchronized and will fill in all missing days, such as holidays, with yesterday's data. It too transforms the TradeStation data format to Excel date format.

6. The code now starts to look for position changes and alters the values of the variables to be exported, depending on how the position changes from day to day.

7. The final daily export starts with another transformation of TradeStation dates to Excel dates.

CHAPTER 28

Combined Money Market Strategies

With all the bits and pieces in place, let's bring things to a conclusion by looking at a few combinations of our short-term systems and long-term filters, when tested using dynamic ratio money management. In doing so, we will try to optisize most of them in relation to the Sharpe ratio. That is, we will try to come up with the fictive *f* to risk per trade in relation to the distance between the money management point and the entry price for each market in each trade, which gives us the highest possible return in relation to the standard deviations of the returns.

Remember that the money management point will be placed four true ranges away from the entry price only so that we can calculate the number of shares to buy and the amount of the available capital to tie up in the trade. The actual risk (*f*) per trade will be less and vary with the behavior of the market, in accordance with the stop and exit rules for each version of the systems.

To do this, I have used the same type of tables and charts that are featured in the systems lab pages in every issue of *Active Trader* magazine. Unfortunately, the Sharpe ratios are not shown in any of them, but will be mentioned in the text after they have been derived from each strategy's summary table, similar to that depicted in Figure 27.2. In those cases where I haven't optisized in accordance with the Sharpe ratio, it still will be mentioned for comparison purposes.

Also, remember that we don't have to optisize in relation to the Sharpe ratio, but could just as well have decided to focus on any of the other performance parameters in Figure 27.2, such as the total return, the profit factor, the drawdown or the flat time, or any combination or compromise between two or several of these and other variables.

When looking at these strategies, this is also the first time we will take a closer look at the drawdown and use it as an input in our evaluation process. We have not done so before because the drawdown is not a core system characteristic. It still isn't, and we are not optisizing any of the strategies in accordance with it, but because the latest bear market has made all the strategies lose money over the last several months, we will discuss briefly how any eventual changes to either the systems or the strategies could lower the short-term drawdowns without also decreasing the speed of the long-term equity growth.

One important distinction I try to make when tying everything together is to look at the complete picture as a *strategy* as opposed to a *system*. Therefore, when I talk about the strategy, I mean the entire trading machine, including the system with its entry and exit rules, the (trend) filter, the markets traded, and the money management. When I talk about the systems, I mean only the entry and exit rules, and sometimes only the entry rules.

The stocks used for this testing are the same as those used throughout the rest of the book—the 30 Dow stocks and 30 of the most liquid NASDAQ stocks. However, because Intel and Microsoft belong to both these groups, I group these two stocks with the NASDAQ stocks only, so that the group of Dow stocks consists of only 28 stocks. I also won't test any of the strategies on any of the indexes.

In total, I will test 12 different strategies that can be subdivided into four different groups based on the long-term filters. The first six strategies will use the RS system No. 1, with the number of system–market combinations (symacs) varying between 56 and 60 (except for Strategy 4, which has 30), depending on whether the testing uses all stocks from both groups or uses two different systems on the same group of stocks.

Group number two is made up of two strategies tested on 60 symacs each, using the relative-strength bands as the filter. The next two strategies use the rotation as the filter and have also been tested on 60 symacs each. So have the last two strategies that use both the relative-strength bands and the rotation as filters, working independently of each other.

To avoid becoming too redundant, I have tried to spread out the learning experience over all the strategies, so that I won't talk about every single aspect of the evaluation of the results for each and every strategy. For example, we really won't take a closer look at the time-window return analysis until the very last strategy. Hopefully, this also will entice you to jump back and forth between the different strategies to get better practice in how to compare them with each other. For a few of the strategies, I also decided to leave out some of the charts and tables.

When looking at several different strategies or fund managers, it is a good idea to compare them not only with one another but also with a few benchmark indexes. Table 28.1 gives you the most important and basic information for the three most commonly used stock market indexes, over the same time period as we tested our strategies. Our goal for all our strategies is to at least do better than the closest comparable index on every one of these evaluation parameters.

TABLE 28.1

Benchmark Comparisons, January 1993–July 2002

Index	Dow Jones	S&P 500	NASDAQ 100
Annual comp. return	9.68%	7.09%	9.50%
Sharpe yearly	0.65	0.40	0.22
Max drawdown	36%	50%	82%
Longest flat time	30 months	27 months	27 months
Profitable months	63%	61%	56%

Before we comment on the results of the strategies, a few things must be noted. First, note in Table 28.2 that the number of trades with the money management added is slightly less than the amount that could have been expected from Table 21.3, which comes out to 8,352 (144 * 58), because a few trades signaled before we attached the money management and could not be taken because of the financial constraints we applied to the strategy. The signals are still there, but because we were already fully invested, we couldn't take the trades.

Second, the trades missing, combined with a few missing markets (the indexes), also lower the number of profitable trades. Another reason for a lower percentage of profitable trades is that we have added a cost of $20 per trade, which we need to make up for before any individual trade can show a profit.

Third, the profit factor is now at 1.23, which is lower than the 1.32 in Table 21.3. This, too, is a consequence of a lower percentage of profitable trades and the added costs. But even more so, it is a direct consequence of the money management. By altering the amount risked per trade, we also alter the relative size of the winners and losers, which in turn alters the profit factor.

The average trade length and total time spent in a trade also are much shorter in Table 28.2 than in Table 21.3. As mentioned in Part 3, this is because, in Table 21.3 we also count holidays and weekends, which are excluded in Table 28.2.

STRATEGY 1

- Long-term filter: RS system No. 1
- Short-term systems: The stop-loss version of the Meander system v. 1.0
- Markets: 28 Dow stocks, 30 NASDAQ stocks, for a total of 58 system-market combinations (symacs)

Tables 28.2 and 28.3, and Figures 28.1 and 28.2 show the results for this strategy traded on the 58 stocks used for the research. (For the initial research, we used 30 stocks each from the Dow Jones Index and NASDAQ 100 index, with Intel and Microsoft in both groups.) To give you a feel for how this strategy has

TABLE 28.2

Strategy Summary

Profitability		Trade statistics		
End. equity ($):	8,446,897	No. trades:		7,029
Total return (%):	745	Avg. trade ($):		1,059
Avg. annual ret. (%):	24.94	Avg. DIT:		5.8
Profit factor:	1.23	Avg. win/loss ($):	11,003	(9,945)
Avg. tied cap (%):	73	Lrg. win/loss ($):	148,187	(118,190)
Win. months (%):	66	Win. trades (%):		50.8
Drawdown		TIM (%):	100	27.9
Max DD (%):	21.8	Tr./Mark./Year:		12.2
Longest flat (M):	15.5	Tr./Month:		61.1

evolved over the course of the book, you can compare these results with those in Tables 10.5, 20.3, and 21.3.

As with most strategies featured here, this one is optisized to maximize the Sharpe ratio, which in this case comes out to 1.31, with the fictive f set to 3 percent per trade.

With an average annual return of close to 25 percent and a maximum drawdown of 22 percent, this strategy seems to function really well. The percentage of winning months is at a decent 66 percent, which is considerably higher than the percentage of winning trades. This means that the system is doing a good job of

TABLE 28.3

Rolling Time-window Return Analysis

Cumulative	12 months	24 months	36 months	48 months	60 months
Most recent:	−5.22%	−15.84%	34.89%	102.16%	139.34%
Average:	28.51%	70.85%	128.87%	203.80%	300.38%
Best:	60.28%	140.21%	218.43%	316.52%	425.26%
Worst:	−14.19%	−15.84%	34.89%	89.03%	138.81%
St. dev:	18.98%	31.32%	37.85%	48.38%	72.51%
Annualized	**12 months**	**24 months**	**36 months**	**48 months**	**60 months**
Most recent:	−5.22%	−8.26%	10.49%	19.24%	19.07%
Average:	28.51%	30.71%	31.78%	32.02%	31.98%
Best:	60.28%	54.99%	47.12%	42.86%	39.34%
Worst:	−14.19%	−8.26%	10.49%	17.26%	19.02%
St. dev:	18.98%	14.59%	11.29%	10.37%	11.52%

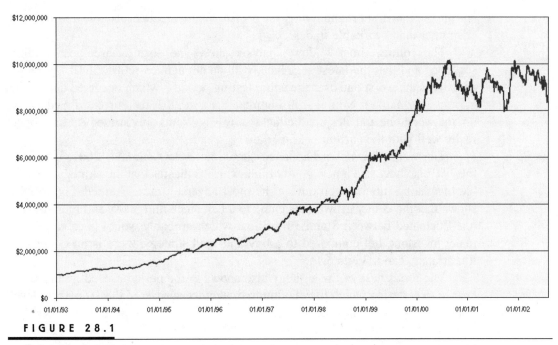

FIGURE 28.1

Strategy 1 equity curve.

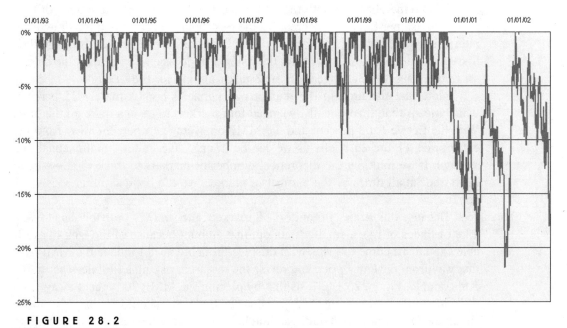

FIGURE 28.2

Strategy 1 drawdown curve.

cutting the losses short and letting the profits run, to create profitable trading periods rather than profitable trades.

The rolling time-window analysis shows no losing three-year trading sequence and that the latest sequence, with an annualized return of 10.5 percent, actually is the worst one over the entire testing period—which occurred during the current bear market. Note that in Figures 28.1 and 28.2, the current drawdown is not the worst one and, despite the fact that this is a long-only strategy, it has coped really well with the current bear market.

The worst drawdown happened sometime in late summer 2001, but since then we also have had a new equity high, which indicates that the strategy is capable of making money even during the most adverse times. Granted, Figure 28.1 shows that the equity growth has come to a halt since mid 2000, and more or less just fluctuated between 8 and 10 million, which probably would have scared off many investors, but compared to a buy-and-hold strategy, there is no doubt that this strategy can hold its own.

The robustness of the strategy also shows in the period preceding the latest bear market during which the maximum drawdown surpassed the 10-percent level only twice. I would most definitely trust this strategy in the future, but probably modify it so that it would trade the short side as well, or combine it with a strategy that does. This would most likely decrease the average annual return in a bull market, but because it also would increase it in a bear market, it is likely that the overall return over a longer period of time remain approximately the same.

Also remember that both the return and the drawdown are functions of how much we risk per trade. By decreasing the risk, both the return and the drawdown numbers will be lower. Therefore, it also is fully possible to first analyze and then trade the strategy so that you lower the risk per trade when it is evident the behavior of the market has changed into unfamiliar ground for the strategy.

Note that the time in the market per symac is approximately 25 percent, which means that, theoretically, we need four markets to be in a trade all the time. With the fictive f at 3 percent and the MMP on average 15 percent away from the entry price, Figure 26.1 tells us we can be in only five trades simultaneously on average. If we multiply the theoretical number of markets to track to allow us to be in trade at all times by the number of markets we can be in simultaneously, we get 20.

Because this strategy monitors 58 markets, the strategy probably has to skip a lot of trades or risk a smaller than optimal amount because of the lack of available capital. To come to grips with this, we probably need to place the MMP further way from the entry price and revise the research, risking a little less per trade. For example, Figure 26.1 tells us that by placing the MMP 20 percent away from the entry price and risking 2.25 percent per trade, we should be in eight trades simultaneously. The added trades should help us increase the return and the Sharpe ratio even further. I leave this to you to research on your own.

STRATEGY 2

- Long-term filter: RS system No. 1
- Short-term systems: Both stop-loss and trailing-stop versions of the Meander system v. 1.0
- Markets: 28 Dow stocks, for a total of 56 symacs

Tables 28.4 and 28.5, and Figures 28.3 and 28.4 show the result from trading both the stop-loss version and the trailing-stop version of the Meander system on the Dow Jones stocks. In this case, we take the initial $1,000,000 to $2.9 million, for an average annual return of 11.72 percent over the 10-year testing period. The Sharpe ratio came out to 1.42.

TABLE 28.4

Strategy 2 Results

Profitability		Trade statistics		
End. equity ($):	2,892,596	No. trades:		7,176
Total return (%):	189	Avg. trade ($):		264
Avg. annual ret. (%):	11.72	Avg. DIT:		6.0
Profit factor:	1.26	Avg. win/loss ($):	2,310	(1,950)
Avg. tied cap (%):	53	Lrg. win/loss ($):	29,226	(17,471)
Win. months (%):	69	Win. trades (%):		48.2
Drawdown		TIM (%):	100	30.6
Max DD (%):	10.8	Tr./Mark./Year:		12.5
Longest flat (M):	9.9	Tr./Month:		62.4

TABLE 28.5

Strategy 2 Time-window Analysis

Cumulative	12 months	24 months	36 months	48 months	60 months
Most recent:	−4.28%	−0.54%	16.20%	29.06%	48.57%
Average:	13.24%	30.73%	51.44%	74.58%	101.28%
Best:	34.89%	54.36%	82.71%	110.11%	132.33%
Worst:	−4.69%	−0.54%	16.20%	24.47%	46.36%
St. dev:	8.26%	12.03%	16.60%	21.44%	22.14%
Annualized	**12 months**	**24 months**	**36 months**	**48 months**	**60 months**
Most recent:	−4.28%	−0.27%	5.13%	6.59%	8.24%
Average:	13.24%	14.34%	14.84%	14.95%	15.02%
Best:	34.89%	24.24%	22.25%	20.40%	18.36%
Worst:	−4.69%	−0.27%	5.13%	5.63%	7.92%
St. dev:	8.26%	5.85%	5.25%	4.98%	4.08%

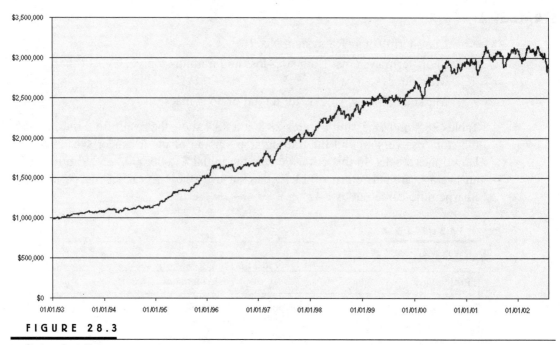

FIGURE 28.3

Strategy 2 equity curve.

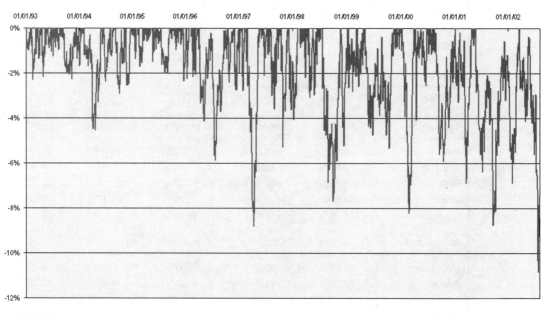

FIGURE 28.4

Strategy 2 drawdown curve.

The strategy was tested with a 1.5 percent risk per trade: when any of the exits for the trailing-stop version of the system were hit, two-thirds of the position were exited, corresponding to 1 percent of the original risk. When any of the stop-loss exits were hit, the position was decreased by what corresponded to 0.5 percent risked of the original position. Using both versions of the system with asymmetric exit rules helps us make the most out of each trade. In this case, we can take a profit as soon as one of the stops or one of the profit targets is hit. Thus, we can remain in the trade with a small position and wait for the market to make the most out of the entry signal we trust.

Compared to the version in Tables 28.2 and 28.3, this version of the system does an even better job of cutting losses and letting profits run, which shows in a lower number of profitable trades (48 percent), but at the same time an even higher number of profitable months (69 percent).

The maximum drawdown is also very low, at a modest 10.8 percent, which is also the drawdown we currently happen to be in. Aside from this drawdown, the maximum drawdown has rarely surpassed 8 percent. However, despite the fact that we happen to be in the maximum drawdown, judging from the slope of the equity curve in Figure 28.3, it doesn't look like the equity growth has stalled the same as it has in Figure 28.1, although it is obvious the strategy did slightly better prior to the current bear market.

The fact that the system currently is in its worst drawdown also indicates that it is the markets not traded that did the best lately. That is, despite the recent free-fall in the NASDAQ stocks, it is largely due to the NASDAQ stocks that the strategy managed to produce the recent equity high in Figure 28.1 and avoid falling into a new maximum drawdown afterwards. This further confirms the strategy's ability to find good, or at least decent, trading opportunities in the most adverse environments, thus helping us to stay afloat while waiting for better times.

Note that the time in the market per symac is approximately 30 percent, which means that theoretically we need three symacs to be in a trade all the time. With the fictive f at 1.5 percent and the MMP on average 15 percent away from the entry price, we can be in 10 trades simultaneously on average. If we multiply the theoretical number of symacs to track to be in a trade at all times by the number of symacs we can be in simultaneously, the answer is 30. (I decided to place the MMP 15 percent away from the entry price based on the assumption that each symac should spend about 20 percent in the market.)

In this case, we are tracking 56 symacs. Normally, this means that we should increase the distance between the MMP and the entry price to allow for more open trades at any one time, but because this strategy consists of two systems with identical entry rules, we are doing fine. The strategy is doing a good job of balancing the trade size with the number of markets tracked and the possibility to trade at any one time.

STRATEGY 3

- Long-term filter: RS system No. 1
- Short-term systems: The trailing-stop version of the volume-weighted average system
- Markets: 28 Dow stocks, 30 NASDAQ stocks for a total of 58 symacs

This strategy has been tested on all 58 stocks, with a fictive risk of 2 percent for the Dow stocks and 6 percent for the NASDAQ stocks. The asymmetrical risk between the two groups of stocks is another way of making the most out of the system and the markets it is applied to. The Sharpe ratio for this strategy comes out

TABLE 28.6

Strategy 3 Results

Profitability		Trade statistics		
End. equity ($):	2,767,231	No. trades:		2,904
Total return (%):	177	Avg. trade ($):		609
Avg. annual ret. (%):	11.21	Avg. DIT:		4.6
Profit factor:	1.14	Avg. win/loss ($):	9,504	(9,715)
Avg. tied cap (%):	55	Lrg. win/loss ($):	144,675	(124,133)
Win. months (%):	61	Win. trades (%):		51.5
Drawdown		TIM (%):	99	9.2
Max DD (%):	28.9	Tr./Mark./Year:		5.1
Longest flat (M):	23.0	Tr./Month:		25.3

TABLE 28.7

Strategy 3 Time-window Analysis

Cumulative	12 months	24 months	36 months	48 months	60 months
Most recent:	−14.33%	−27.86%	1.71%	33.63%	46.37%
Average:	14.58%	34.74%	59.26%	87.46%	120.36%
Best:	42.05%	85.23%	112.12%	156.93%	171.25%
Worst:	−18.50%	−27.86%	1.71%	28.95%	46.37%
St. dev:	13.78%	19.82%	21.09%	27.03%	27.51%
Annualized	**12 months**	**24 months**	**36 months**	**48 months**	**60 months**
Most recent:	−14.33%	−15.06%	0.57%	7.52%	7.92%
Average:	14.58%	16.08%	16.78%	17.01%	17.12%
Best:	42.05%	36.10%	28.49%	26.61%	22.09%
Worst:	−18.50%	−15.06%	0.57%	6.56%	7.92%
St. dev:	13.78%	9.46%	6.59%	6.16%	4.98%

FIGURE 28.5

The equity curve for Strategy 3.

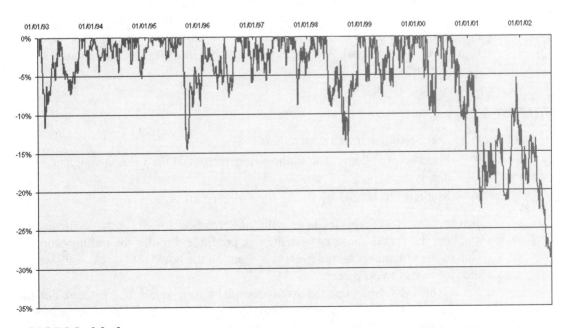

FIGURE 28.6

The drawdown curve for Strategy 3.

to 0.81. Tables 28.6 and 28.7 can be compared to Tables 13.5, 19.1, and 20.5, which show the result during the development of the system.

Comparing the numbers in Tables 28.6 and 28.7 and Figures 28.5 and 28.6 with the numbers for the strategies we've already looked at, it's apparent that this strategy is not as good as the previous two. For one thing, both the average annual return and the profit factor are the lowest, while the maximum drawdown is the highest so far. To achieve these numbers, we also have to risk more, especially in the NASDAQ stocks. Together with the lower Sharpe ratio, this indicates that we're not getting as much bang for the buck as with the other strategies.

However, the fact that we can risk more on the NASDAQ stocks to maximize the Sharpe ratio also indicates that the system is relatively safe to trade on these markets. Remember that the optimal f, when optimizing the equity growth, is an indication of how large we can allow our largest loser to be while still ending up at the highest possible equity level.

Nonetheless, the strategy has not coped well with the latest bear market and is currently in its worst drawdown, at close to 30 percent. This fact, combined with a longest flat time of 23 months, is bad enough to discourage many professional traders and money managers to trade this strategy as is. Thus, it doesn't matter that the strategy has done much better than a buy-and-hold strategy on any of the market indexes. (Don't forget to compare the strategy results for all strategies with the numbers in Table 28.1.)

To trade this strategy, we need to either come up with a way to trade it on the short side as well, or combine it with another short-selling strategy. This new strategy should then be able to deliver a higher risk-adjusted return (the Sharpe ratio) to a lower risk per trade, to make trading it worthwhile when compared to the Meander strategies.

STRATEGY 4

- Long-term filter: RS system No. 1
- Short-term systems: The trailing-stop version of the volume-weighted average system
- Markets: 30 NASDAQ stocks for a total of 30 symacs

Just to show you what you can do with the spreadsheet used for these calculations and how the results can vary with the risk per trade, I traded the trailing-stop version of the volume-weighted average system on the NASDAQ stocks only, setting the fictive risk to 50 percent.

Table 28.8 shows that the average annual return equals 32.5 percent, but also that the largest drawdown, which actually happened in early 2000, surpasses 40 percent (see also Figure 28.7). Interestingly, despite the high risk per trade, the Sharpe ratio still comes out to 0.76, which isn't too bad. Another indication that

TABLE 28.8

Strategy 4 Results

Profitability		Trade statistics		
End. equity ($):	14,900,205	No. trades:		692
Total return (%):	1,390	Avg. trade ($):		20,087
Avg. annual ret. (%):	32.56	Avg. DIT:		4.7
Profit factor:	1.21	Avg. win/loss ($):	230,028	(227,551)
Avg. tied cap (%):	61	Lrg. win/loss ($):	2,194,892	(2,437,892)
Win. months (%):	55	Win. trades (%):		53.8
Drawdown		TIM (%):	73	4.4
Max DD (%):	42.3	Tr./Mark./Year:		2.4
Longest flat (M):	13.3	Tr./Month:		6.0

the strategy is holding up really well in the current market is the fact that it has managed to set two new equity highs since the worst drawdown, with another drawdown of close to 40 percent in between. The drawdown chart (not shown) also shows that the current drawdown is only the fourth worst drawdown since the start of the testing period, surpassed also by the drawdown in 1999, prior to the sharp run up in equity due to the bull market in late 1999 and early 2000.

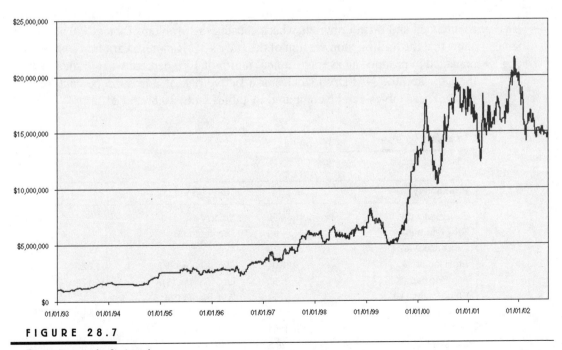

FIGURE 28.7

The equity curve for Strategy 4.

Naturally, had I risked less, the drawdowns would have been smaller, but so would the ending equity and possibly the Sharpe ratio also. Only the most risk-seeking trader would trade this strategy as it stands here and now; for the rest of us, it only serves as a good illustration of how risk and return go hand in hand.

Note also in Table 28.8 that the total number of trades comes out to 692, which translates to only 23 trades per market tested over the entire testing period. However, looking at Table 21.4, we can see that the system itself produces as many as 62 signals per market over the same period. This means that only every third signal will actually end up as a trade because of equity constraints.

Decreasing the fictive f will allow for more trades and a higher Sharpe ratio and possibly also a higher return. Thus, even though we're making some 32 percent per year, in this case we might be able to make more while risking less. This is yet another little thread I leave for you to look into.

STRATEGY 5

- Long-term filter: RS system No. 1
- Short-term systems: The trailing-stop version of the Harris 3L-R pattern variation
- Markets: 28 Dow stocks, 30 NASDAQ stocks for a total of 58 symacs

This and the next strategy are two good examples of when things don't work out as intended and it isn't obvious what's causing the problem. Tables 28.9 and 28.10 show that the trailing-stop version of the Harris 3L-R pattern variation system only managed to produce an average annual return of 1.79 percent when traded on both the Dow and the NASDAQ stocks, at a fictive risk of 2 and 0.5 percent, respectively. These tables can be compared to Tables 14.6, 20.8, and 21.5.

TABLE 28.9

Strategy 5 Results

Profitability		Trade statistics		
End. Equity ($):	1,185,639	No. trades:		5,215
Total return (%):	19	Avg. trade ($):		36
Avg. annual ret. (%):	1.79	Avg. DIT:		2.9
Profit factor:	1.04	Avg. win/loss ($):	1,820	(1,361)
Avg. tied cap (%):	35	Lrg. win/loss ($):	24,178	(16,016)
Win. Months (%):	51	Win. trades (%):		41.6
Drawdown		TIM (%):	99	10.1
Max DD (%):	24.1	Tr./Mark./Year:		9.1
Longest flat (M):	28.3	Tr./Month:		45.3

TABLE 28.10

Strategy 5 Time-window Analysis

Cumulative	12 months	24 months	36 months	48 months	60 months
Most recent:	−8.00%	−20.61%	−16.37%	−4.10%	−1.72%
Average:	2.97%	8.06%	15.50%	22.43%	28.89%
Best:	15.58%	24.08%	32.20%	44.00%	57.38%
Worst:	−16.34%	−21.97%	−16.37%	−5.05%	−4.73%
St. dev:	7.83%	11.95%	11.82%	13.00%	15.46%
Annualized	**12 months**	**24 months**	**36 months**	**48 months**	**60 months**
Most recent:	−8.00%	−10.90%	−5.79%	−1.04%	−0.35%
Average:	2.97%	3.95%	4.92%	5.19%	5.21%
Best:	15.58%	11.39%	9.75%	9.55%	9.49%
Worst:	−16.34%	−11.66%	−5.79%	−1.29%	−0.96%
St. dev:	7.83%	5.81%	3.79%	3.10%	2.92%

When looking at the equity and drawdown charts, some interesting observations can be made. It's obvious that the strategy has not coped well at all with the current bear market. However, the entire testing period leading up to the current downturn has a very smooth and steady equity growth, with only a handful of drawdowns surpassing 5 percent. (The equity and drawdown charts are not shown for this strategy, but they are very similar in look and feel to those for Strategy 6.)

One reason for the poor result could be that the strategy is functioning so badly in the current bear market that it forces us to keep the risk per trade down. Had it functioned a little better in the bear market, it is possible that we could have traded it a bit more aggressively and thereby also increased the profit potential during the bull market of the 1990s. The low drawdown numbers for this period indicate that we could take on plenty more risk per trade without taking the drawdowns to such high levels as 15 to 20 percent. This is probably especially true for the NASDAQ stocks, which we are trading very conservatively using the current settings.

Another reason for the poor results could be that we are not in as many positions as we should be, given our assumptions about the relationships between the stop-loss distance, the average trade length, and the money management point. We aimed at being in approximately 10 open positions at any one time; with 45 trades per month, and the average trade length being close to three days, the strategy is seldom in more than six positions at the same time.

To come to grips with this, we need to either place all the stops and exits further away from the entry, both in terms of price and time, so that we spend more time in a trade, or place the money management point closer to the entry so that we increase the profit potential of each trade using the current stop and exit settings. The closer the MMP, the larger the position must be in terms of number of shares traded, and the more shares traded, the larger the profit and loss potential in any individual trade.

Most likely, we need to look into a combination of the two solutions. With the trades being too short, the profit potential for any individual trade might be too small to make up for the costs of trading to make any of these strategies worthwhile.

STRATEGY 6

- Long-term filter: RS system No. 1
- Short-term systems: The stop-loss version of the expert exits system
- Markets: 28 Dow stocks, 30 NASDAQ stocks for a total of 58 symacs

The conclusions we came to for Strategy 5 also can be made for Strategy 6, except the results are a tad better for this strategy, with an average annual return of 4.86 percent, a maximum drawdown of 17.5 percent, and a Sharpe ratio of 0.53 (0.23 for Strategy 5). In this case, the fictive risk is set to 1 percent per trade, which results in a maximum equity of close to $1.9 million (see Figure 28.8) and only one drawdown surpassing 3 percent (see Figure 28.9) before the bear market sets in.

The important lesson to be learned from these two strategies is that there is no guarantee that the system will work as intended, even after we have gone

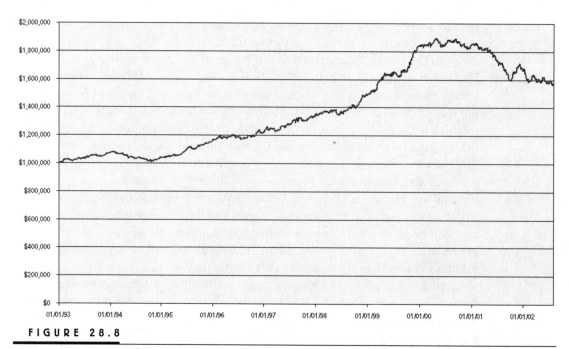

FIGURE 28.8

The equity curve for Strategy 6.

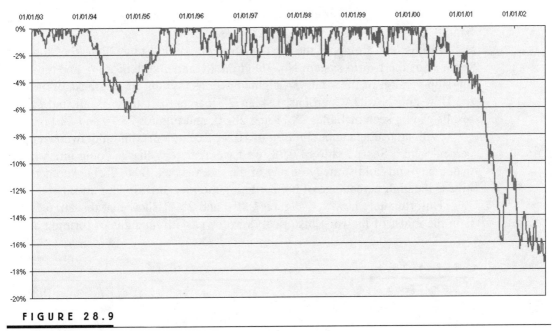

FIGURE 28.9

The drawdown curve for Strategy 6.

through all the elaborate steps of testing and analysis. I know it can be tempting to go ahead and trade them anyway, as a sort of reward for all the hard work, but if they don't work, they don't work and should be scrapped—or at least taken apart, so that their parts can be reused in other systems and strategies. As we will soon see, sometimes when reusing parts from old systems, we strike gold that makes all the hard work worthwhile.

STRATEGY 7

- Long-term filter: Relative-strength bands
- Short-term systems: The stop-loss versions of the hybrid system No. 1 and Meander system, v.1.0, and the trailing-stop version of the volume-weighted average system
- · Markets: 10 Dow stocks, 10 NASDAQ stocks for a total of 60 symacs

With the relative-strength bands and the rotation as the filters, we were only testing 10 markets from each index category per system. Thus, because these filters were true relative-strength filters, we were comparing the stock we intend to trade directly with a set of other stocks instead of a comparable index; this made the testing procedure rather cumbersome and time consuming. So, for each filter and with 20 stocks to test, we can apply three systems to each market, for a total of 60 symacs, which is the maximum our spreadsheet can handle.

In this test, we apply the relative-strength bands as the filter, the stop-loss versions of the hybrid system No. 1 and the Meander system v.1.0, and the trailing-stop version of the volume-weighted average system to 10 stocks each from the Dow and NASDAQ groups, risking 2.5 percent per trade in all trades. The results can be seen in Tables 28.11 and 28.12, and Figures 28.10 and 28.11.

With an average annual return of 10.8 percent, a maximum drawdown of 25 percent, and a Sharpe ratio of 0.73, we have a strategy that is doing much better than a buy-and-hold strategy on any of the indexes (see Table 28.1). Another positive is the high percentage of both winning months and winning trades.

Unfortunately however, Figures 28.10 and 28.11 show that this strategy too is in the midst of its worst historical drawdown, with no signs of forming a bot-

TABLE 28.11

Strategy 7 Results

Profitability		Trade statistics		
End. Equity ($):	2,673,676	No. trades:		3,703
Total return (%):	167	Avg. trade ($):		452
Avg. annual ret. (%):	10.81	Avg. DIT:		4.7
Profit factor:	1.15	Avg. win/loss ($):	6,625	(6,398)
Avg. tied cap (%):	62	Lrg. win/loss ($):	59,944	(54,385)
Win. Months (%):	64	Win. trades (%):		52.6
Drawdown		TIM (%):	99	11.7
Max DD (%):	25.3	Tr./Mark./Year:		6.4
Longest flat (M):	13.0	Tr./Month:		32.2

TABLE 28.12

Strategy 7 Time-window Analysis

Profitability		Trade statistics		
End. Equity ($):	2,084,306	No. trades:		4,535
Total return (%):	108	Avg. trade ($):		239
Avg. annual ret. (%):	7.96	Avg. DIT:		3.4
Profit factor:	1.12	Avg. win/loss ($):	4,388	(3,836)
Avg. tied cap (%):	59	Lrg. win/loss ($):	56,176	(42,637)
Win. Months (%):	59	Win. trades (%):		46.5
Drawdown		TIM (%):	100	10.3
Max DD (%):	20.9	Tr./Mark./Year:		7.9
Longest flat (M):	19.2	Tr./Month:		39.4

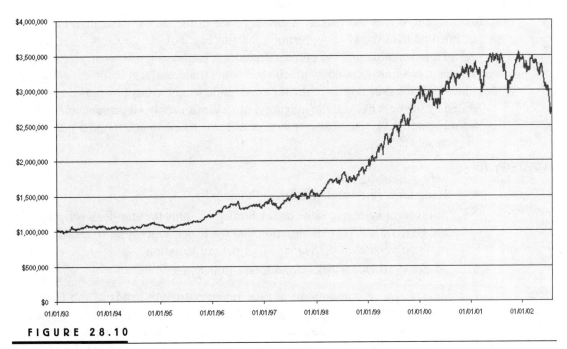

FIGURE 28.10

Strategy 7 equity curve.

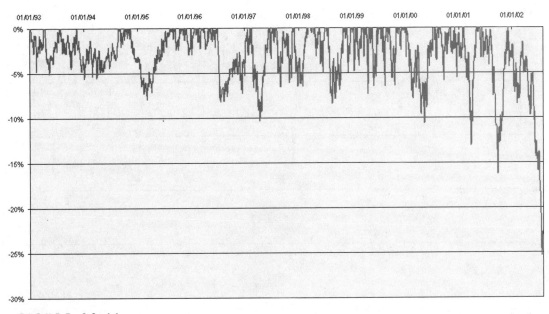

FIGURE 28.11

Strategy 7 drawdown curve.

tom. Again, this is most likely a consequence of the current bear market and the fact that none of the systems forming the strategy looks to go short.

However, although the current drawdown is quite significant in size, remember that it is a function of how much we risk per trade, and that it doesn't come anywhere near the drawdowns of the indexes. Aside from the last few drawdowns generated by the bear market, the maximum drawdown is only 10 percent, and judging from Figure 28.11, the most common drawdown seems to be around 5 percent.

STRATEGY 8

- Long-term filter: Relative-strength bands
- Short-term systems: Same as for Strategy 7, plus the stop-loss versions of the Harris 3L-R pattern variation and the expert exits system, and the trailing-stop version of the Harris 3L-R pattern variation
- Markets: 10 Dow stocks, for a total of 60 symacs

For this strategy, we continue to use the relative-strength bands as the filter, but substitute the three systems trading the NASDAQ stocks with three more systems trading the Dow stocks. Thus, we are now trading the same 10 Dow stocks with six different versions of the systems we have worked with throughout the book. To the systems used in the previous strategy, we have added the stop-loss versions of

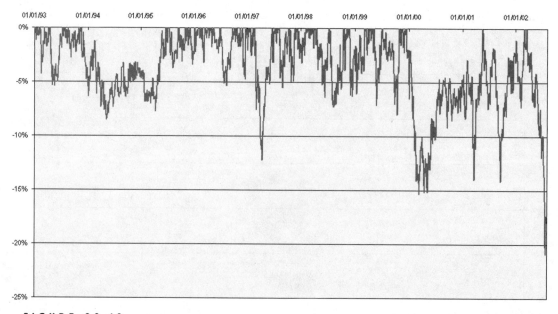

FIGURE 28.12

The drawdown curve for Strategy 8.

both the Harris 3L-R pattern variation and the expert exits system, and the trailing-stop version of the Harris 3L-R pattern variation.

With a fictive risk of 3 percent per trade for all system–market combinations, the average annual return comes out to close to 8 percent, with a maximum drawdown of 21 percent. The Sharpe ratio comes out to 0.81. Although the average annual return is slightly lower than that for a buy-and-hold strategy on the Dow Jones index, a higher Sharpe ratio and a lower maximum drawdown make this strategy a comparable alternative to the buy-and-hold (although it wouldn't have hurt if both the percentage of winning months and winning trades had been a tad higher).

One way to increase the return—or at least the Sharpe ratio (in the form of lower drawdowns)—would be to not trade the same 10 stocks with all systems. Making sure all groups hold a different set of stocks would increase the diversification further and thereby also decrease the risk. Decreasing the risk would in turn allow us to trade the system more aggressively, which would further increase the returns. This would also increase the historical drawdowns somewhat, but judging by Figure 28.12, the drawdowns leading up to the current bear market are very modest. If we can keep the current drawdown under control, increasing the average drawdown wouldn't do that much as long as we also can increase the return and the Sharpe ratio.

STRATEGY 9

- Long-term filter: Rotation
- Short-term systems: The trailing-stop versions of the hybrid system No. 1, Meander system v.1.0, and the volume-weighted average system
- Markets: 10 Dow stocks, 10 NASDAQ stocks, for a total of 60 symacs

TABLE 28.13

Strategy 9 Results

Profitability		Trade statistics		
End. Equity ($):	2,706,109	No. trades:		2,860
Total return (%):	171	Avg. trade ($):		597
Avg. annual ret. (%):	10.95	Avg. DIT:		5.2
Profit factor:	1.12	Avg. win/loss ($):	11,542	(10,471)
Avg. tied cap (%):	68	Lrg. win/loss ($):	201,288	(129,841)
Win. Months (%):	58	Win. trades (%):		49.9
Drawdown		TIM (%):	99	9.6
Max DD (%):	40.9	Tr./Mark./Year:		5.0
Longest flat (M):	20.8	Tr./Month:		24.9

Moving on to the last of our filters, the rotation, we start by testing it on both groups of stocks, together with the trailing-stop versions of hybrid system No. 1, Meander system v.1.0, and the volume-weighted average system, with the fictive risk set to 5 percent for all trades.

Although the average annual return is a tad higher for this strategy than for the previous one, if you only have these two strategies to choose from, this is not the preferred alternative—at least not as it stands right now, without any short-selling possibilities or other markets complementing it on the short side.

This is evident when looking at the Sharpe ratio, which equals 0.5, and a maximum drawdown in the current bear market of 41 percent. Again, both the percentage of winning months and winning trades could have been higher, although there is nothing wrong with 58 percent winning months and close to 50 percent winning trades.

Aside from the actual size of the current drawdown, the way this strategy has handled the bear market also leaves a lot to wish for, when compared to many of the other strategies. The fact that it hasn't managed to set a new equity high over the last several months indicates that it is much more dependent on the long-term underlying trend than many of the other strategies.

However, as long as the trend is right, this strategy works very well, reaching a maximum equity peak of more than $4.5 million, with only one drawdown

FIGURE 28.13

The equity curve for Strategy 9.

surpassing 15 percent on the way. But as soon as the bear market grabs hold of it, the results are less tantalizing. Maybe the thing to do with this strategy would be to put it aside for now and then use it as a complement to other strategies once the long-term trend shows signs of having reversed itself?

STRATEGY 10

- Long-term filter: Rotation
- Short-term systems: Same as for Strategy 9, plus the stop-loss versions of the Harris 3L-R pattern variation and the expert exits system, and the trailing-stop version of the expert exits system
- Markets: 10 NASDAQ stocks, for a total of 60 symacs

Here's another example of a very aggressively traded strategy. In this case, I substituted the systems trading Dow stocks with three more systems trading the NASDAQ stocks. The systems added are the stop-loss versions of the Harris 3L-R pattern variation and expert exits systems, and the trailing-stop version of the expert exits system. All systems and markets were tested with the fictive risk set to 25 percent.

This time the percentage of winning months, at 49 percent, is definitely too low. But looking at the equity curve, we can see that the reason is the long periods of complete inactivity early on in the testing period. This occurs because a few of the 10 stocks used in the testing weren't trading at the time, which also explains the exceptionally long flat period and slow equity growth over the first half of the period. (I picked the stocks at random, so I had no way of controlling this.)

Excluding this period from the testing, the average annual return, which now comes out to 16.6 percent, most likely would have been at least twice as high.

TABLE 28.14

Strategy 10 Results

Profitability		Trade statistics		
End. equity ($):	4,372,678	No. trades:		1,377
Total return (%):	337	Avg. trade ($):		2,449
Avg. annual ret. (%):	16.64	Avg. DIT:		3.2
Profit factor:	1.15	Avg. win/loss ($):	36,194	(30,097)
Avg. tied cap (%):	70	Lrg. win/loss ($):	727,346	(452,035)
Win. Months (%):	49	Win. trades (%):		47.2
Drawdown		TIM (%):	66	3.1
Max DD (%):	40.9	Tr./Mark./Year:		2.4
Longest flat (M):	32.0	Tr./Month:		12.0

FIGURE 28.14

The equity curve for Strategy 10.

(Because of the compounding effect, making the same money over half the time requires an average annual return for the shorter time period that is more than double the return of the longer period.)

Had it just so happened that the stocks used in the test were available for trading from the very beginning, most likely the results would have been much better with both a higher average annual return and Sharpe ratio, which now comes out to 0.36. I doubt, however, that we could have done that much about the latest 41 percent drawdown in the current bear market. Perhaps it wouldn't have been quite as severe, but judging from all the other strategies that use the NASDAQ stocks, we still would have been in a deep drawdown, no matter which and how many NASDAQ stocks we traded. If anything, perhaps one or two more equity highs would have broken apart the current flat period into several shorter periods.

STRATEGY 11

- Long-term filters: Either the relative-strength bands or the rotation, working independently from one another
- Short-term systems: Both versions of hybrid system No. 1, Meander system v.1.0, and the volume-weighted average system
- Markets: 10 Dow stocks, for a total of 60 symacs

For the last two strategies I used two filters working parallel to each other, so that either one of them can open up a trading opportunity for any of the short-term systems. The first strategy trades 10 Dow stocks for a total of 60 system–market combinations, all traded with a fictive risk of 3 percent.

Tables 28.15 and 28.16 show the result for this strategy. With an average annual return of 7.42 percent, a Sharpe ratio of 0.59, a maximum drawdown of 34 percent, and a longest flat time of 20 months, these numbers come very close to those of a buy-and-hold strategy on the Dow. However, one major difference between a trading strategy like this and a buy-and-hold strategy is that in a buy-and-hold strategy you need to be in all the stocks all the time, tying up 100 per-

TABLE 28.15

Strategy 11 Results

Profitability		Trade statistics		
End. equity ($):	1,985,057	No. trades:		4,184
Total return (%):	99	Avg. trade ($):		235
Avg. annual ret. (%):	7.42	Avg. DIT:		5.1
Profit factor:	1.10	Avg. win/loss ($):	4,730	(4,487)
Avg. tied cap (%):	67	Lrg. win/loss ($):	78,548	(36,127)
Win. Months (%):	62	Win. trades (%):		49.9
Drawdown		TIM (%):	100	13.8
Max DD (%):	34.2	Tr./Mark./Year:		7.3
Longest flat (M):	20.0	Tr./Month:		36.4

TABLE 28.16

Strategy 11 Results

Cumulative	12 months	24 months	36 months	48 months	60 months
Most recent:	−19.86%	−25.77%	−21.25%	0.37%	19.36%
Average:	10.22%	25.88%	45.88%	67.86%	92.96%
Best:	40.68%	59.65%	84.98%	112.35%	151.78%
Worst:	−24.93%	−25.77%	−21.25%	−3.97%	11.21%
St. dev:	12.67%	18.45%	23.36%	28.82%	30.64%
Annualized	**12 months**	**24 months**	**36 months**	**48 months**	**60 months**
Most recent:	−19.86%	−13.85%	−7.65%	0.09%	3.60%
Average:	10.22%	12.20%	13.41%	13.83%	14.05%
Best:	40.68%	26.35%	22.76%	20.72%	20.28%
Worst:	−24.93%	−13.85%	−7.65%	−1.01%	2.15%
St. dev:	12.67%	8.84%	7.25%	6.54%	5.49%

cent of your equity at all times. The more money you need to tie up to reach a certain return, the riskier the strategy, because the more you stand to lose if things go
severely against you.

For this strategy, you only need to tie up 67 percent of your capital on average, and only be in each stock 13 percent of the time. Thus, you will have plenty of
available capital left for other investment or trading endeavors, which will increase
your total return even further, while you also achieve additional diversification.

Also, if the strategy is any good, the time spent in the market for any individual stock should be high-quality time, meaning you should only be in a trade when
you have the highest likelihood for success, or at least the lowest likelihood for failure. This too, makes a mechanical trading strategy less risky than staying in a buy-
and-hold, where you have to stay in the market, come hell or high water. This should
show up in the number of profitable months, which should be higher for the mechanical strategy than for the buy-and-hold strategy and preferably also closer to 70 than
60 percent—although this is not the case this time (compare with Table 28.1).

As for the drawdowns, Figures 28.15 and 28.16 once again tell us that the
strategy worked very well up until the latest bear market, at which time it started
to give back previously made profits. To come to grips with this, complement this
strategy with one for the short side and possibly also decrease the amount risked
per trade when all signs indicate we're in a bear market.

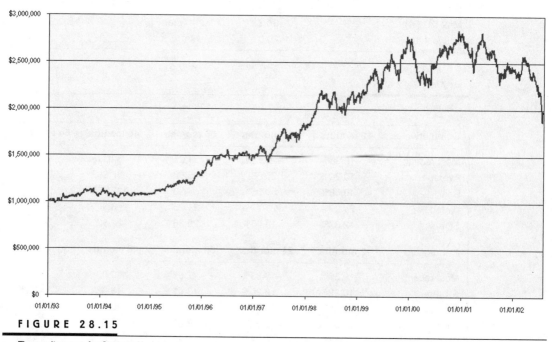

FIGURE 28.15

The equity curve for Strategy 11.

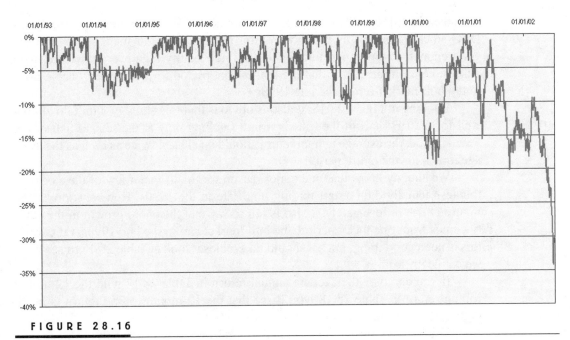

FIGURE 28.16

The drawdown curve for Strategy 11.

STRATEGY 12

- Long-term filters: Either the relative-strength bands or the rotation, working independently of one another
- Short-term systems: Both versions of hybrid system No. 1, Meander system v.1.0, and the volume-weighted average system
- Markets: 10 NASDAQ stocks, for a total of 60 symacs

The very last strategy is the same as the previous one, except 10 Dow stocks are replaced by 10 NASDAQ stocks. In this case, the average annual return comes out to 12.24 percent, the Sharpe ratio to 0.34, the maximum drawdown to 36 percent, and the longest flat time to 21.5 months.

Comparing these numbers to the buy-and-hold stats for the NASDAQ 100 in Table 28.1, we can see that this strategy is doing much better, not only on an absolute return basis, but also on a relative basis, than the previous strategy did when compared to the buy-and-hold stats for the Dow. In this case, the only number that does not hold up is the percentage of profitable months, which, at a mere 53 percent, is not only lower than the 56 percent for the buy-and-hold strategy, but also much lower than we would like it to be.

Two good things are that the drawdown is much lower and the flat time is much shorter than for the buy-and-hold strategy. Although the latest bear market has taken its toll on all the systems, as with all the strategies tested on the NAS-DAQ stocks, it seems as if the volatility of the stocks still manages to produce good-enough trading opportunities to set a new equity high every now and then. Also, note in Figure 28.17 that the longest flat period for this strategy came prior to the bull-market run in the late 1990s.

Looking at Figure 28.18, it also is obvious that this strategy didn't do all that well for the first half of the tested period. Looking only at the second half of the tested period, the average annual return should be at least twice as high as the average return for the entire period.

We already know that one major reason for this is that a few of the stocks in this test actually didn't start trading until late in the 1990s. However, looking at Figure 28.18, unfortunately, it also is fair to say that the entire growth in the equity comes from one lucky period, the bull market run in the late 1990s. Of course, this is not a good thing, but we should take a closer look at Table 28.18 to see what we can learn from it.

If you compare the average annual return in Table 28.17 with the 12-month rolling return in Table 28.18, you'll see that the 12-month rolling return is much higher. How can this be?

The result from one exceptionally good period will not only influence the result for the year it happened, but also for the 12 rolling periods following it. To take it from the beginning:

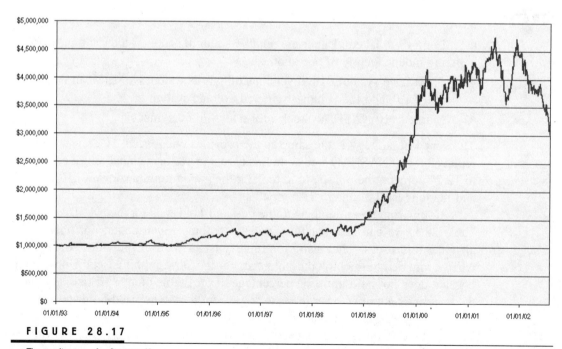

FIGURE 28.17

The equity curve for Strategy 12.

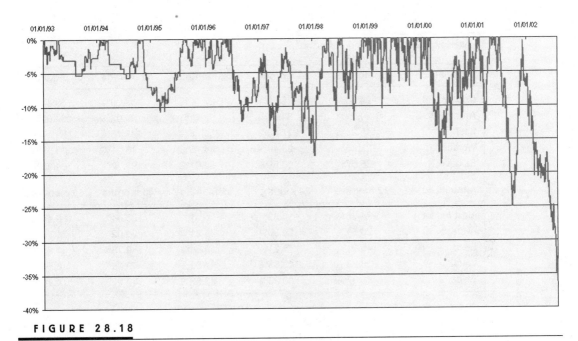

FIGURE 28.18

The drawdown curve for Strategy 12.

To take $1,000,000 to $3,024,987 over 9.58 years, which is the exact length of the testing period, we need a constant compounded equity growth of 0.9588 percent per month. But as soon as we have both winning and losing periods, after a losing month, it takes a relatively larger winning month just to break even. This means that the average arithmetic return needs to be slightly larger that the constant compounded return. In this case, it comes out to 1.0878 percent per month.

TABLE 28.17

Strategy 12 Results

Profitability		Trade statistics		
End. Equity ($):	3,024,987	No. trades:		2,314
Total return (%):	202	Avg. trade ($):		875
Avg. annual ret. (%):	12.24	Avg. DIT:		4.8
Profit factor:	1.17	Avg. win/loss ($):	11,908	(11,461)
Avg. tied cap (%):	56	Lrg. win/loss ($):	94,233	(76,148)
Win. Months (%):	53	Win. trades (%):		52.2
Drawdown		TIM (%):	84	7.5
Max DD (%):	36.2	Tr./Mark./Year:		4.0
Longest flat (M):	21.5	Tr./Month:		20.1

TABLE 28.18

Strategy 12 Rolling Time-window Analysis

Cumulative	12 months	24 months	36 months	48 months	60 months
Most recent:	−24.38%	−25.40%	27.05%	132.20%	153.45%
Average:	20.51%	54.51%	96.31%	129.07%	167.01%
Best:	145.21%	217.60%	255.75%	281.16%	289.60%
Worst:	−28.25%	−25.40%	4.76%	13.21%	19.19%
St. dev:	35.57%	69.90%	89.81%	95.42%	94.23%
Annualized	**12 months**	**24 months**	**36 months**	**48 months**	**60 months**
Most recent:	−24.38%	−13.63%	8.31%	23.44%	20.44%
Average:	20.51%	24.30%	25.21%	23.02%	21.70%
Best:	145.21%	78.21%	52.66%	39.73%	31.26%
Worst:	−28.25%	−13.63%	1.56%	3.15%	3.57%
St. dev:	35.57%	30.35%	23.82%	18.23%	14.20%

For example, if you lose 10 percent of your capital one period, you will need to make 11.1 percent the next just to break even, which would make the constant period return zero, but the average period return to 0.55 percent [(−10 + 11.1) / 2]. The larger the price swings, the greater the differences between the constant period return and the average period return. For example, if you first lose 50 percent one period and gain 100 percent the next, to get back to the break-even point, the constant period return will still be zero, but the average period return will be 25 percent [(-50 + 100) / 2].

Furthermore, a constant monthly growth rate of 0.9588 percent would result in a 12.13 percent growth rate for any 12-month period. But with a varying period return, a large return one month will influence the rolling 12-month return for the next 12 rolling periods, which in turn will make the average 12-month rolling return look higher than the average compounded yearly return. The larger, faster, and more frequent the swings in the equity, the larger the average 12-month rolling return will be, compared to the average compounded yearly return.

In this case, we have one exceptionally fast period of equity growth during 1999, one steep drawdown in 2001, followed by another fast run up (not ending in a new equity high), and yet another fast decline. Consequently, a 12-month rolling return much larger than the average annual return is a good indication that there have been large swings in the equity curve and that the final result might be the result of one large swing in the equity, which is more or less the result of this strategy. Knowing this, you can use this information when comparing several strategies or fund managers with each other and avoid those that simply seemed to luck out over a short period of time.

Other than that, rolling time-window analysis can come in handy when comparing the performance of different strategies over several overlapping periods. It also helps us keep things in perspective during exceptionally good or bad times. For example, despite the fact that we currently are in a 36 percent drawdown and have lost more than 24 percent of our equity over the last 12 months, over the last five years (60 months) we're still up 153 percent, which translates to a growth rate of 20.44 percent per year. This isn't bad at all by any standard and much better than the 3.6 percent yearly produced by the same strategy applied to the Dow stocks.

Also, note that this version of the strategy has no losing 36-month period, which is reassuring to know during the bad times. That is, even during the slowest and dullest times, the NASDAQ version of the strategy has managed to produce a new equity high at least every 36 months, which is not the case with the Dow version. Naturally, the shorter the necessary time window to produce a profit, the better off you are.

To be fair, however, no losing period longer than 36 months isn't all that good either. Ideally, there should be no losing periods longer than 24 months. The closest we get to that in this book are with strategies 1 and 2. Table 28.5 shows that Strategy 2 only loses (at most) 0.54 percent over two years. Table 28.3 shows that Strategy 1 loses (at most) 15.84 percent over two years, but to compensate, it also has made at least 10.40 percent a year for any rolling three-year period.

However, when looking at these numbers, we must keep in mind that we're looking at historical or back-tested results. To get a better feel for what we can expect in the future, we must look at the standard deviations and compare them to the average period return. For example, Table 28.18 tells us that the average 12-month rolling return is 20.51 percent and the standard deviation is 35.57 percent. Thus, 68 percent of all 12-month returns should fall somewhere in the interval -15.05 to 56.08 percent (20.51 ± 35.57), which means that only 16 percent of all rolling returns should come in below -15.05 percent [$(1 - 0.68) / 2$]. Because this is the case with the most recent return of -24.38, we have reason to believe that this is not a typical result for this strategy and that we therefore should do better in the upcoming periods.

For Strategy 11, we have reason to be even more optimistic about the future. Because Table 28.16 tells us that the average period return is 10.22 and the standard deviation is 12.67, we can estimate that 95 percent of all period returns will fall somewhere in the interval -15.12 to 35.56 percent ($10.22 \pm 12.67 * 2$). Because the most recent return falls outside this interval, it is even less likely to be a good estimate of what is to come. In this case, the most recent return belongs to a group of only 2.5 percent [$(1 - 0.95) / 2$] of all returns that are as bad as this one. However, there are no guarantees. The next period return can still be all over the place, with a very high likelihood of being negative.

Looking at the rolling time-window analysis helps us get a feel for how reliable and stable the strategy or the fund manager is and how likely it is that either one will continue to produce the same results in the future as it has in the past.

THE COUNTERPUNCH STOCK SYSTEM

It's important to remember that just because you have taken a system through all the elaborate steps of testing, you don't have to trade it—although it might be tempting to do so just to make all the hard work worthwhile. If a system isn't good enough to be traded, it isn't good enough to be traded, and not all ideas will turn out to be profitable enough in the end, no matter how clever they seemed when conceived.

However, just because you shouldn't trade a system or strategy as it stands here and now, doesn't mean that all its parts are useless. Sometimes it may be a good idea to combine various sets of old entry and exit techniques, with or without filters, and test them as new strategies. After you have tested and developed a few systems and strategies according to these guidelines, you probably will have a basket of unused strategy combinations to choose from.

As a bonus for ending this book, and just to show you that there never is such a thing as a bad idea and all ideas are worth saving, let me show you the results for the last system I developed for *Active Trader*.

The entry idea is from a system I created for *Trading Systems That Work* to be traded on the S&P 500 futures market, but without its original filter. The exit rules are from a series of articles I wrote for *Active Trader* and published over the period March through June 2002. Neither the entry nor the exits have ever been applied to these stocks before.

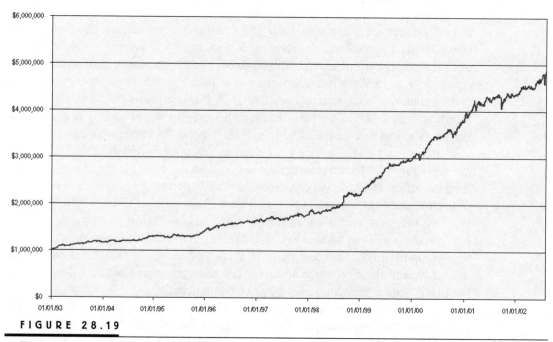

FIGURE   28.19

The equity curve for the counterpunch strategy.

TABLE 28.19

The Results for the Counterpunch Strategy

Profitability		Trade statistics		
End. equity ($):	4,868,697	No. trades:		18,893
Total return (%):	387	Avg. trade ($):		205
Avg. annual ret. (%):	17.96	Avg. DIT:		2.3
Profit factor:	1.24	Avg. win/loss ($):	2,870	(1,343)
Avg. tied cap (%):	57	Lrg. win/loss ($):	26,242	(22,755)
Win. months (%):	72	Win. trades (%):		38.4
Drawdown		TIM (%):	100	28.0
Max DD (%):	7.3	Tr./Mark./Year:		32.9
Longest flat (M):	6.1	Tr./Month:		164.3

TABLE 28.20

The Rolling Time-window Analysis for the Counterpunch Strategy

Cumulative	12 months	24 months	36 months	48 months	60 months
Most recent:	11.45%	37.60%	69.74%	144.87%	180.09%
Average:	17.80%	41.09%	69.79%	102.36%	137.81%
Best:	47.83%	82.37%	128.21%	153.66%	183.47%
Worst:	4.23%	10.48%	34.46%	47.01%	63.91%
St. dev:	10.14%	19.19%	28.64%	37.53%	39.14%
Annualized	**12 months**	**24 months**	**36 months**	**48 months**	**60 months**
Most recent:	11.45%	17.30%	19.29%	25.09%	22.87%
Average:	17.80%	18.78%	19.30%	19.27%	18.92%
Best:	47.83%	35.04%	31.66%	26.20%	23.17%
Worst:	4.23%	5.11%	10.37%	10.11%	10.39%
St. dev:	10.14%	9.17%	8.76%	8.29%	6.83%

Originally featured in November 2002, this countertrend system looks for long positions when everyone else is selling short and vice versa. It is based on the premise that no trend lasts forever, and the longer one lasts, the more likely a short-term reversal will occur.

The system will take a position against the prevailing intermediate-term trend if a price has moved in the same direction for two weeks in a row and for two days in a row in the most recent week. The reversal that follows won't necessarily be of the same magnitude as the trend preceding it, but many times it will be large enough to generate a steady profit for the system.

This system trades both sides of the market the same way, thus short trades made during a prolonged uptrend will probably not fare as well as those made from the long side. However, the counter to this is that when the long-term trend is down, as it has been the last couple of years, the system is well prepared to profit from the short side.

SUGGESTED MARKETS

Stocks, stock-index futures, and stock-index shares.

RULES

Go long tomorrow on the open if a) today's close is below both yesterday's close and the close of the previous week, b) yesterday's close is below the previous day's close and, c) the close of the previous week is below the close of the week before that.

Exit first half of position with a loss if the trade goes against you by 1 percent.
Exit first half of position with a profit if the trade goes your way by 4 percent.
Exit second half with a profit or loss if the trade moves 1.6 percent away from your maximum open profit (i.e., trail a stop 1.6 percent below the high of the trade).
Exit second half with a profit if the trade goes your way by 4.5 percent.
Exit the entire position after eight days in the trade.
Reverse the rules for short trades.

MONEY MANAGEMENT

Risk 2.5 percent of available equity per stock. The number of shares to trade (ST) is determined by the following formula:

$$ST = AC * PR / TR$$

Where:

AC = Available capital
PR = Percent risked (= fictive f in the rest of the book)
TR = Four times the true range for the day preceding the entry

TEST PERIOD

January 1993 to July 2002.

TEST DATA

Daily prices for the 30 stocks making up the Dow Jones Industrial Average. A total of $10 slippage and commission deducted per trade.

STARTING EQUITY

$1 million (nominal).

SYSTEM ANALYSIS

The results of this system are amazing by any standard. The average annual return is almost 18 percent, which is close to twice the buy-and-hold return on the Dow Jones over the same period. The largest drawdown is 7.3 percent, while the longest flat time is six months. For a buy-and-hold strategy on the DJIA, which performed far better than the S&P 500 and NASDAQ indices, those numbers were 36 percent and 30 months, respectively. Also, this system is completely unoptimized, which proves two things:

First, a system doesn't have to be complicated to be profitable. Second, the fewer the rules and the easier the system is to understand, the more likely it will continue to hold up in the future. Because the stock market does not behave the same in a downtrend as it does in an uptrend, to improve this system, the long and short trades could be separated and the entry and exit rules tailored to each.

By either removing a few long-entry rules or adding a few short-entry rules, the system's performance would likely improve and make it relatively easier to enter on the long side.

Likewise, it would probably help to make it relatively easier to exit the short trades by tightening the short-trade exits or loosening the long-trade exits.

However, why tinker? This system is already delivering a risk-adjusted return well above that of the buy-and-hold strategy.

CHAPTER 29

Consistent Strategies

The fourth and final part of the book started by discussing the paradox between a near-random market and a profitable but seemingly random system. With the markets being as close to random as they are, a good trading system must make the most out of the nonrandom periods, while keeping you in the game during the random periods. The more nonrandom information we make use of, the less useful information is left, up to the point where only random market noise is left. The more random noise is left in relation to unused information, the closer to randomly our system will behave.

Therefore, as long as the system has a decent mathematical expectancy, the more nonrandom information the system makes use of, the more difficult it will be to predict the outcome of any of its trades. However, not knowing if the outcome of the next trade will be a winner or a loser makes it all the more important to adhere to your stops and exit signals to keep all the trades as similar to each other as possible. If you follow a consistent trading approach, the more trades that conform to a certain profit–loss size and trade length, the more you can chalk up your success to skill instead of luck.

Furthermore, although you can't be sure of the outcome of the next trade, by adhering to your stops and exits, you can decide what the maximum loss will be by always risking the same relative amount in relation to the available capital on each trade. One way to calculate the proper amount to risk is to use the Kelly formula. Once the Kelly value (K) is determined, you can determine how many shares to buy and how much capital must go towards this trade. The larger the K, the more money you can put into one trade; the smaller the K, the less money you should put into one trade. Also, the tighter the stop loss, the more of your capital you need to put into one trade; the wider the stop loss, the less capital you need to put into one trade.

A good trader also tries to balance the steepness of the equity curve with its smoothness, so that the steeper the better and the smoother the better. The more you risk, the more erratic the equity curve and the riskier the trading in general terms.

The major flaw with the Kelly formula is that it assumes two outcomes only—a winner of a certain magnitude and a loser of a certain magnitude. Therefore, it is better to use the formula for optimal f, as popularized by Ralph Vince.

In Ralph Vince's original version of the formula, f depends on the worst historical loser, because we're implicitly assuming that one reason to trade this system is that its largest historical loser is within the limits for what we can tolerate, given the profit potential of the system.

To make a long story short, calculating the ending equity, which Ralph Vince dubbed terminal wealth relative (TWR), is done using the following formula:

$$\text{TWR} = \text{GMN} = \text{HPR1} * \text{HPR2} * \text{HPR3} * \ldots * \text{HPRi}$$

Where:

$\text{GM} = (\text{APM}^2 - \text{SD}^2)^{(N/2)}$

$\text{HPRn} = 1 + f * (\text{Profit}_n / \text{WCS})$

TWR = Terminal wealth relative, expressed as the percentage compounded return over a trading sequence

GM = The geometric mean

N = Number of trades

APM = The average profit multiplier, calculated as the average percentage profit per trade divided by 100, plus one

SD = Standard deviation of all trades, measured in percentage terms

HPR_n = The holding period return for trade n, expressed as a percentage of your total equity going into the trade

f = The fixed fraction of your capital to risk in all trades

Profit_n = The profit or loss from trade n in dollars on a constant-shares invested basis

WCS = The historical worst-case scenario in dollars on a constant-shares invested basis (expressed as a positive number)

Thus, given the largest historical loser, by altering f we can alter the size of the profit or loss of any individual trade (HPR_n) and consequently alter the TWR. However, from the formula it also follows that TWR depends on how large the average trade is in relation to the outcome of all trades (the larger the better) and the number of trades (the more trades the better).

To end up with a positive TWR, we must make sure APM is larger than SD. If we can achieve this, the end result for TWR will only be a function of f (the fraction of available equity to risk) and N (the total number of trades).

However, if we ever were to encounter a loss of the same size as the worst historical loser, the loss for that trade also will equal f. Thus, the higher the systems profit-generating potential, and the higher the f, the more you stand to lose in one single trade. Therefore, it's better to replace the worst historical loser with the stop-loss level for each individual trade for all trades. By doing so, the worst-case scenario will be based on a reasonable amount that you're willing to risk for each trade, instead of a terrifying amount that you were willing to tolerate in the past, but would rather not encounter again.

However, the dilemma for the short-term trader is that short-term trading usually means a low average profit per trade and the use of tight stop losses that makes sense in relation to the estimated and desired average trade length. But the tighter the stops on a one-share basis, the fewer trades he can be in simultaneously for any given f.

To work around this, separate the stop loss (SL) from the money management point (MMP). Originally, we assumed SL to be equal to MMP, but by separating the two and placing MMP further away from the entry price, we can lower the number of shares to buy and the amount of our capital tied up in each trade. As a consequence of this, the f used to calculate the number of shares to buy won't represent the true fraction risked of the available equity, but rather just a fictive fraction to feed the formula:

$$ST = (AC * f_{fict}) / MMP$$

Where:

ST = Shares to trade

AC = Available capital

MMP = Money management point in distance from the entry price, to calculate the number of shares to trade

f_{fict} = Fictive fraction of capital to risk to calculate the number of shares to trade

To calculate the actual amount risked in each trade, we can use the following formula:

$$f = f_{fict} * (SL / MMP)$$

Where:

SL = Stop loss in distance from entry price

To figure out how many positions we can be in simultaneously, we only need to divide MMP by f_{fict}, or, if we already know how many positions we would like to be in, we can calculate how far away from the entry price we need to place MMP to make that possible by dividing the desired number of positions by f_{fict}. This will place MMP a fixed distance away from the entry price, but by letting the distance for MMP vary around a desired average distance, we can vary the number of maximum positions with the behavior of the markets.

For example, if the volatility is high, we can place MMP further away from the entry price than the desired average distance and thereby make each position smaller. This makes room for more open positions and better diversification during times of turmoil, and vice versa. At the same time, a dynamic stop loss will keep us from getting stopped out too frequently during times of turmoil, while it will stick closer to the price of the stock in calmer times, when our positions are larger.

CONCLUSION

Once we understood the process behind the DRMM, we were able to build a basic spreadsheet for all the necessary calculations. With the help of this spreadsheet, you can test a few system–market combinations traded within one portfolio using the same account equity. We also took a closer look at a more professional spreadsheet and how it compared to a Web-based evaluation of the real-time trading records of professional fund managers and CTAs.

With the help of the professional spreadsheet, we ended our research by taking a look at a few combinations of the systems and filters we worked with throughout the book. By adding the money management and trading all the system–market combinations using a shared account equity, we shifted the focus from the individual system to the complete strategy.

For most of the strategies, we tried to find the fictive f to risk per trade that gave us an equity curve that was as smooth as possible in relation to the growth rate. It's important to note that nothing forces you to trade the exact optimal f for the highest growth rate. Many times this may still be perceived as too risky. The important thing is to not take any unnecessary risk by trading above the optimal f, when the goal is to decrease the risk by optisizing on any other variable.

The first two strategies produced very good and low-risk results, although the current bear market lowered the performance somewhat over the last several months. The conclusion is that the meander indicator does a very good job in finding high-probability trading opportunities with high profit potentials.

Comparing Strategies 3 and 1, it's easy to see that Strategy 3 didn't come anywhere close to the performance of Strategy 1. Even so, it still outperforms a benchmark buy-and-hold strategy and could probably be trusted for real-time trading if combined with a system for trading the short side. Strategy 4 was optisized on the maximum equity growth, rather than the Sharpe ratio and the smoothness of the equity curve, which resulted in an average annual return of 32.5 percent.

Strategies 5 and 6 used the trailing-stop version of the Harris 3L-R pattern variation and the stop-loss version of the expert exits systems. The results from these two strategies were not satisfactory, probably because the systems turned out to be too short term for our purposes. When a system is "too" short-term, with a low risk–reward relationship, the profits won't make up for the costs of trading with slippage and commission included in the calculations. In this case, we probably also need to rebalance the distance between the entry price and the money management point, and the distance between the entry price and the stop loss, to optimize the number of positions we can be in simultaneously.

Strategy 7 produced satisfactory results, although the current bear market once again forced the strategy into a new maximum drawdown. For Strategy 8, the results could not be considered satisfactory. It is apparent that the shorter-term systems—the Harris 3L-R pattern variation and the expert exits system—do not work as intended.

Strategy 9 produced satisfactory results, despite a rather steep recent drawdown. Substituting the 10 Dow stocks in Strategy 9 with the same short-term systems as in Strategy 8 resulted in very choppy results for Strategy 10. Although the profit potential is there, it is doubtful a strategy like this should be trusted for real-time trading—at least not when traded on only a handful of markets.

The last two strategies used a combination of the relative-strength bands and the rotation filters. For Strategy 11, this resulted in a smooth and steady initial equity growth that again was weighted down by a larger than tolerable drawdown over the last few years. For Strategy 12, the results were too choppy and the profits too dependent on the bull-market run of the late 1990s. As was the case for Strategy 10, it is doubtful a strategy like this should be trusted for real-time trading.

Looking through the overall results, three things come to mind. Number one is that the shorter-term systems, the Harris 3L-R pattern variation and the expert exits, did not work as intended, probably for two reasons: Reason one is that their short trading horizons limit the profit potential. Reason two is that the money management point probably is too close to the entry price, given the average stop-loss distance, to allow us to be in an optimal number of positions at one time. Reason two can be dealt with simply by shifting the MMP further away from the entry price; reason one probably calls for a revision of the research surrounding the stops and exits.

The second thing that comes to mind is that the relative-strength bands and the rotation filters allowed us to test only 20 stocks, which limited our diversification possibilities. It is likely the risk-adjusted returns would have been higher for Strategies 7 to 12 had we been able to test them on more stocks. Talking about the filters, it's also worth mentioning that several of the systems might have functioned better without them. I leave that for you to decide.

Last, but not least, most strategies probably should have done much better trading the short side as well, despite the fact that it would have resulted in a slight deterioration of performance over the bull market in the 1990s. Most likely this would have been counterweighted by a better performance over the last few years and perhaps also a smoother equity growth over the entire period. This would have meant that we could have increased the performance even further by daring to risk a bit more in each trade.

However, to be able to identify and do something about any of these reasons for system failure, we need to do the research the right way from the very beginning. In Part 3, we learned how to come up with a set of stops and exits that should work, on average equally as well on all markets.

Although we didn't do it in this book, analyzing two variables at a time using a surface chart also can be used for the entries. Here we instead used a set of entries developed earlier for the Trading Systems lab pages for *Active Trader* magazine. In Part 2, we took the liberty to tinker around with them a bit, analyzing the results from the changes using normalized results.

To work with normalized results, we must make sure that the data are correct, which testing variables are the most important to look at, and what type of results to look for. Without knowing this, there is no way we can isolate any type of problem or error, no matter where it occurs during the testing process. These concepts were covered in Part 1, and thus we have come full circle.

Note: Boldface numbers indicate illustrations.

Thomas Stridsman is a systems researcher and designer for Rotella Capital Management, a Chicago-based commodity trading advisor with approximately $1 billion under management. A popular speaker at industry-related conferences and seminars, Stridsman is the author of *Trading Systems That Work* and a longtime contributor to both *Futures* and *Active Trader*. He is a native of Sweden, where he operated a Web-based financial newsletter and trading advisory service in Stockholm and was chair of the Swedish Technical Analyst Federation.